Down South

A Falklands War Diary

CHRIS PARRY

PENGUIN BOOKS

PENGUIN BOOKS

Published by the Penguin Group
Penguin Books Ltd, 80 Strand, London WC2R ORL, England
Penguin Group (USA) Inc., 375 Hudson Street, New York, New York 10014, USA
Penguin Group (Canada), 90 Eglinton Avenue East, Suite 700, Toronto, Ontario, Canada M4P 2Y3
(a division of Pearson Penguin Canada Inc.)
Penguin Ireland, 25 St Stephen's Green, Dublin 2, Ireland (a division of Penguin Books Ltd)
Penguin Group (Australia), 707 Collins Street, Melbourne, Victoria 3008, Australia
(a division of Pearson Australia Group Pty Ltd)
Penguin Books India Pvt Ltd, 11 Community Centre, Panchsheel Park, New Delhi – 110 017, India
Penguin Group (NZ), 67 Apollo Drive, Rosedale, Auckland 0632, New Zealand
(a division of Pearson New Zealand Ltd)
Penguin Books (South Africa) (Pty) Ltd, Block D, Rosebank Office Park,
 181 Jan Smuts Avenue, Parktown North, Gauteng 2193, South Africa

Penguin Books Ltd, Registered Offices: 80 Strand, London WC2R ORL, England

www.penguin.com

First published by Viking 2012
Published in Penguin Books 2013
001

Copyright © Chris Parry, 2012
All rights reserved

The moral right of the author has been asserted

The following images are © Kevin P. White: 9–11, 15, 17, 19–20, 22–3, 33–35, 38–40, 42, 44, 47–9, 52 and 54–6.
The publishers and author are grateful to Mr White for his permission to use the photographs

Other images: 12–14, 60 © Stewart Cooper; 21 © Richard Hurley; 25 © Chris Sherman; 26 © Crown
copyright. IWM (FKD 60); 27 © Angus Sandford; 28, 31 © Alasdair Maclean; 29 © Declan Ward;
30, 61 © Chris Parry; 32 © Carlos Edwards and Declan Ward; and 36–7 and 46 © Jeremy Lindsay

Every effort has been made to trace the copyright holders. We apologize for any unintentional omission
and would be pleased to insert the appropriate acknowledgement in any subsequent edition

Printed in Great Britain by Clays Ltd, St Ives plc

ISBN: 978-0-241-95962-6

www.greenpenguin.co.uk

MIX
Paper from
responsible sources
FSC
www.fsc.org   FSC® C018179

Penguin Books is committed to a sustainable
future for our business, our readers and our planet.
This book is made from Forest Stewardship
Council™ certified paper.

ALWAYS LEARNING   PEARSON

For the Love in my life

Contents

Acknowledgements

I would like to extend my considerable thanks and appreciation to the band of brother officers, shipmates and colleagues with whom I shared and hazarded my life in 1982. We were 'warriors for the working day' together, and I remember them with affection and pride. Indeed, the best part of publishing this book has been the opportunity to renew old friendships, recall shared experiences and enjoy each other's company again.

Among my fellow officers, I would particularly like to express my gratitude to Angus Sandford, Mike Morgan, Graham Hockley, Richard Hurley, Alasdair Maclean and Kevin White, who all provided me with material and memories that enabled me to validate and decipher various parts of my diary, not least the precise dates on which certain events happened. Nick Bracegirdle, Neil Britten, John Saunders and Declan Ward all cheerfully chipped in with confirming recollections. Photographs were kindly supplied by Kevin White, Richard Hurley, Stewart Cooper, John Saunders and Alasdair Maclean.

Jock Gardner, at the Royal Naval Historical Branch, was extremely generous with his scarce time and shrewd advice, while affording me privileged access to various documents and logs from 1982. The team at the Fleet Air Arm Museum at Yeovilton also took time to locate some photographs.

I was extremely fortunate that two people at Viking Penguin, Tony Lacey and Venetia Butterfield, took me under their wings and chaperoned me during the process of submission and production. In particular, I very much admired Tony's uncommon skill and judgement as an editor, just as I have enjoyed his good company and conversation.

Robert Dudley, my agent, smoothed the path of publication at every stage, with his distinctive style and sympathetic approach. David Leppan, the founder of World Check, has been characteristically generous with his active support and friendship, while it was another friend, Niall Ferguson, who originally and decisively convinced me that the diary might be worthy of wider readership.

Finally, I owe a special thank you to my wife, Jackie, who encouraged, helped and sustained me during the production of this book. She has been an inspirational, steadfast and devoted companion throughout our life together and an unfailing source of loving support and assurance throughout my naval and subsequent career.

Preface

This diary was written during the Falklands crisis of 1982, on a virtually daily basis, on assorted scraps of paper and in an old government-issue exercise book. It was never intended for publication and, hurriedly and carelessly stored away in a trunk almost as soon as the conflict ended, was thought to have been lost in the wake of the break-up of my first marriage in 1986.

The trunk, along with other containers, subsequently followed my naval career, every couple of years. It was never opened during the hectic course of my days and, as I am an incorrigible hoarder of documents and knick-knacks, particularly when things have a sentimental attraction, it simply disappeared amid the accumulated flotsam and jetsam of life. As a result, the trunk sat in successive garages, attics and storerooms and the diary lay undisturbed and unread.

However, when I retired from the Royal Navy in 2007, the clock began ticking on my heap of boxes and stored papers, which now took up considerable space in our home. I held out, with various prevarications and evasions, until early 2010, when I was forced to start the process of reviewing and culling the contents. When I opened my old naval steel trunk, the papers containing this diary started to emerge, in haphazard fashion, and some time elapsed before I could establish that the diary was complete, not least because I began to read individual sheets as they appeared.

I would like to stress that this diary is not a comprehensive, detailed account of the Falklands crisis. It is a contemporaneous record, from the perspective of a 28-year-old Lieutenant serving in a British destroyer, who never expected at the start of 1982 to be involved in a war. As such, I made a heap of all that I observed and, at the time, thought interesting, amusing or memorable.

I was aware from my time at university of Sir Ian Hamilton's perceptive comment: 'On the actual day of battle, naked truths may be had for the asking; by the following morning, they have already begun to get into their uniforms.'* Therefore, I usually wrote up the events and thoughts of the day last thing at night, before I turned in to my bunk, as we say in the Royal Navy. On busy days, I sometimes noted events and details on various scraps of paper as they were happening, but occasionally allowed myself a little more time – a day or so – when the pressure of my normal duties prevented me from writing, but these days were exceptional. I remember that I wanted to leave an account of my unvarnished thoughts and emotions as they occurred at the time, before the mice of hindsight, rationalization and discretion had had a chance to gnaw away at them.

In the interests of maintaining its integrity and context, the diary appears in print as it was written, apart from one or two sentences that I judged would give unnecessary offence and distress to people not involved in the conflict. I have consciously avoided the temptation to correct any errors of perception or observation committed by me at the time. However, I have taken care to ensure that, where contemporary records have survived, the correct spelling and terminology have been checked and used.

By now, I would expect the reader to be thinking that I had plenty of time on my hands to write this diary. The fact is that, when I was not worrying about winning the war or actually taking part, I often filled in odd moments by writing down what was happening and what I was thinking. Why? The answer lies in a combination of motives, both conscious and unconscious. Firstly, as a history graduate, I thought that I had an obligation to record what I thought might be a significant period of my life for its own sake. Secondly, I suppose that I wanted to leave some sort of narrative for my loved ones in case I did not come back from a sortie.

On reflection, I also believe that, as time went by, I became almost superstitious about writing up the events as they happened, as if nothing could happen to the thread of life as long as the narrative was set to continue. Finally, by accident, but not by design, the diary served to anaesthetize me in the face of unusual, unpleasant and unfamiliar experiences. Happily, I believe that I have never suffered from any form of post-traumatic stress since the conflict and it seems to me that the ability to 'out' one's chaotic, potentially traumatic and inexplicable experi-

* Ian Hamilton, *A Staff Officer's Scrap-Book during the Russo-Japanese War* (1906).

ences in as coherent and lucid a way as possible plays no small part in preventing the onset of that particular condition. Cold, sober reflection and the mere act of writing seem to convert the extraordinary into the ordinary. I suppose that in that sense the diary was therapeutic.

The motivation for publishing this diary was the approach of the thirtieth anniversary of the Falklands conflict in 2012. Since 1982, I have seen a great many books published on the subject and I have approached each one in the same way: I read the sections that cover events in which I was involved and, if they were accurate, I read the rest of the book. On those occasions when my experience was at variance with the text, I seldom had the patience and tolerance to continue. Moreover, I have read many inaccurate versions of the events in which I was involved, as well as numerous imperfect rationalizations in secondary accounts. For these reasons, I thought it worthwhile and necessary to publish a bald, contemporary account of what I witnessed at the time.

If there are misperceptions and unkind remarks about individuals in the diary, I must ask unreservedly for the forbearance and tolerance of those who might feel disappointed by what I thought at the time. The chains of cause and effect are not always visible to men engaged in the most intense experience of their lives and, in any case, even a 28-year-old does not know everything. Experience and maturity tend to encourage kinder and more objective assessments in equal measure, but I have not sought to apply the wisdom of hindsight or to revise the text, even to spare people's – or my own – blushes.

After almost thirty years, it is a rare privilege to be able to reconnect with the people we once were and to revive memories of events, emotions and people which had been carelessly and involuntarily, amid the pace of life, cast aside and consigned to oblivion. It also enables anyone with a trace of sentiment to reflect on the person one has become, as a result of – and in spite of – the experiences and personalities one has encountered at a particular stage in one's life.

It is fair to say that my experiences in the Falklands shaped my future attitudes to life in a fighting service and the lessons that I gained there have guided my steps ever since. When I commanded my own ships, my officers used to ask me how they would thrive under my command. I told them simply that, if I would want to have them near me in war or in crisis, if I could introduce them to the Queen without embarrass-ment and if I could survive more than thirty minutes on a run-ashore with them, I would be happy. Officers exist to make a decisive difference, in dealing with situations and in leading their people, but, in a fighting service, their willingness to go in harm's way and competence in war must be the ultimate litmus tests of their suitability for employment and advancement.

I do not believe that any sane person would wish himself in a war, but, unfashionable as it might seem, I can say with absolute conviction that my time in the Falklands War was probably the most exhilarating, exciting and professionally rewarding time of my whole time in the Royal Navy. Indeed, my experience ensured that I would continue with a naval career that I had been on the verge of ending. Every day brought a new challenge, the chance to put all the training one had been given into practice and the need to deal with issues of real consequence. In this sense, there was a tangible feeling of personal involvement in national affairs and in historic events that never really seemed likely during the Cold War. Most important of all was the sense of responsibility and attachment one felt to one's fellow human beings, involved in the same fight and sharing similar dangers, hopes and fears.

The atmosphere and feel of those far-off times are becoming increasingly remote. Many of the senior officers involved in the conflict have since died or are in retirement; those of us who were young are now older. However, it is difficult not to feel a thrill when one recalls days when there was so much idealism, adventure and purpose in the air; it was an exciting time, with a distinctive character of its own. For the UK, the 1980s started as a gloomy, straitened decade, characterized by low levels of national confidence, morale and social cohesion, as well as economic stagnation. That was the UK from which we sailed in March 1982; we returned in July to a country transformed and reinvigorated, with a renewed sense of purpose and spring in its collective step.

My Life and Career

After school, I had gained a place at Jesus College, Oxford, to read Modern History from September 1972. I also decided that I wanted to join the Royal Navy as a University Cadet, as this would mean that the Service would pay my tuition fees and afford me a little more than the average Local Authority student grant while I was studying. In return, the Navy invited me to undertake basic training at Britannia Royal Naval College Dartmouth before university, continue with training at sea (HMS *Intrepid*, an amphibious assault ship, and HMS *Enterprise*, a small hydrographic ship) during the summer vacations and return to complete naval training for a term in September 1975. I went off to sea, in HMS *Ark Royal* and HMS *Alfriston*, in early 1976.

Once I had passed my Fleet Board examination on the basis of what I had learned – and forgotten – I completed professional Seaman courses and was selected for training as aircrew. I then served in HMS *London* from 1977 to 1978, to gain my Bridge watch-keeping and ocean navigation qualifications, before undergoing the demanding Observer course, with 750 Squadron (Sea Prince aircraft – Basic Flying Training) at Culdrose, in Cornwall; 737 Squadron (Wessex 3 – Advanced Flying Training) at Portland; and 706 Squadron (Sea King 2 – Operational Flying Training) at Culdrose. I finally qualified as a Sea King Observer towards the end of 1979 and was appointed to 826 Naval Air Squadron, comprising four aircraft that normally embarked in the helicopter carrier HMS *Bulwark*. I was there to achieve certificate of competence on type, train hard on NATO exercises and make life thoroughly unpleasant for Soviet submarines.

At the start of 1981, I was appointed to HMS *Antrim* as the Flight Observer and, after a quick re-familiarization course with the Wessex 3, joined the ship at Funchal in Madeira in February. I had a year of exercises and deployments embarked in the ship within the NATO region, a tour in Northern Ireland and a Fishery Protection period, before 1982 brought new and unexpected challenges.

I should perhaps mention my family circumstances. In 1982, I was twenty-eight years old and Alison, my wife, twenty-four. We had been married since December 1979 and lived at our own house in Broadmayne, Dorset, within daily distance of Portland Naval Air Station where 737 Squadron and 406 were based. Alison was the daughter of a Brigadier, who had recently retired as the Defence Attaché in Athens and lived in Worplesdon, in Surrey.

My own parents lived in Liverpool, where my father, who had retired from the Royal Navy in 1980 at the age of fifty, after thirty-five years' service, man and boy, and with an OBE, was Permanent Secretary and Bursar of the University of Liverpool. They retained the family home in Portsmouth, where my younger sister, Ann, and I had grown up and been to school.

My dad had served at the end of the Second World War. My great-grandfather's brother, David Henry Parry, was a sea pilot at Liverpool and served as a master in the First World War, until he was torpedoed and killed by a U-boat south-west of Ireland in April 1917. His ship was called the *José de Larrinaga*. My grandfather's two brothers were soldiers in the Great War, one of whom was one of the first of the Welsh Guards in 1915 and was killed on the Somme in 1916.

The Falklands War: The Context

The background to the Falklands Crisis of 1982 was a long-standing dispute between the United Kingdom and Argentina about the sovereignty of the Islands and their dependencies, South Georgia and the South Sandwich Islands. Over many years, the United Kingdom's Foreign Office had seemed disinclined to make much effort to retain the Islands and, but for the stubborn commitment of the Islanders themselves to remain British, would have probably been prepared to negotiate away sovereignty long before, most likely under a lease-back arrangement. By 1982, no mutually agreeable formula had been established to retain, transfer or share sovereignty that took into account the opinions and aspiration of the inhabitants of the Falkland Islands.

Political and economic factors dominated the background to the war, its character and its timing. In 1979, the incoming Conservative government had inherited an economy with an annual inflation figure of 27 per cent. Its overriding macroeconomic objective was to reduce this inflation. It raised interest rates and tightened fiscal policy to reduce a significant budget deficit, as well as increasing taxes, restricting government spending and controlling the growth of money supply.

Consequently, consumer spending, investment and exports declined, along with overall economic growth, and this was accompanied by an increase in the exchange rate, to the detriment of exporters. 1981 was a period of deep recession and, although inflation was eventually brought under control, unemployment rose to over 3 million and real GDP fell by 2.2 per cent in 1981.

Margaret Thatcher's tough fiscal and monetary regime of 1981 included substantial reductions in public spending and, more significantly, measures to reduce Defence expenditure. These measures threatened to severely restrict the ability of the Armed Forces to intervene outside the NATO area.

The Nott Review

The 1981 budgetary provision led to a Defence Review under the Secretary of State, John Nott – *The United Kingdom Defence Programme: The Way Forward*, published in June 1981. At a time of rising Soviet capability and tough resource provision, Nott and his advisers concluded that the UK should concentrate on its commitment to NATO at the expense of its role and influence in the wider world. This echoed and extended the retrenchment by previous, predominantly Labour, governments.

As part of this approach, the Defence Review confirmed the development and deployment of a new ballistic missile system, Trident, and its associated submarines. The UK would contribute a maritime capability that would specialize in anti-Soviet submarine operations, in the North Sea, North Atlantic and the Greenland–Iceland–UK Gap, by focusing investment in submarines and maritime patrol aircraft. The British Army of the Rhine, the centrepiece of the British contribution to NATO, was capped at 55,000 men.

As a result, the Royal Navy was scheduled to lose one fifth of its 60 destroyers and frigates. The aircraft carriers (*Hermes*, *Invincible* and the new *Illustrious*), despite their role as anti-submarine helicopter platforms, were to be sold. Similarly the amphibious capability, based on the assault ships *Fearless* and *Intrepid*, and on 3 Commando Brigade Royal Marines, was to be relinquished.

At the same time, the capacity of the Royal Dockyards was to be drastically reduced and their work largely privatized, resulting in significant redundancies, and Chatham Dockyard would be closed. Finally, the Antarctic Patrol Ship, *Endurance*, which been under resource pressure for five years, was to be withdrawn at the end of her 1982 deployment.

Meanwhile, in Argentina . . .

The authority and credibility of the military Junta, led by General Leopoldo Galtieri, were being challenged daily by the impact of a worsening economic crisis, an unstable currency and increasing civil and social unrest, despite a systemic campaign of repression by the regime and the Armed Forces. The senior members of the Junta needed a cause that would distract and fire the imagination of their people, to rebuild confidence in the regime, encourage social cohesion and restore national pride.

With the benefit of hindsight, it is possible to discern that the Argentinian Junta was planning to engineer a military confrontation to boost national morale and divert domestic opinion at some stage late in 1982, either with Chile over the Beagle Channel or with the United Kingdom over the Falkland Islands. The ambiguous diplomatic signals emanating from the United Kingdom's Foreign Office about the country's commitment to the Falkland Islands and the planned cuts to the Armed Forces, especially the swingeing reductions in aircraft carriers and the amphibious capabilities, were, just before the conflict, leading the Junta to conclude that the Falkland Islands option carried less risk and greater long-term benefits. An operation to seize the Islands was envisaged in May–June when the onset of the Antarctic and South Atlantic winter would make a recovery operation extremely difficult and hazardous.

The train of events that triggered the conflict – and encouraged the Junta to proceed earlier than it had planned against the Falkland Islands – began with an unlikely incident. An opportunist Argentinian businessman, Constantine Davidoff, landed with a working party – and a party of marines – from the Argentinian Navy auxiliary ship *Bahia Buen Suceso*, at Leith, in South Georgia, on 19 March 1982, to dismantle the old whaling station. The estimated scrap value of the materials and buildings was in the region of £7.5m.

While ashore, Davidoff and his workers continued to be supported by the *Bahia Buen Suceso*. Along with marines, who hoisted their national flag, they refused to register their presence with the local British official representative and magistrate, the British Antarctic Survey (BAS) Base Commander, at Grytviken. The illegal landing, and further unlicensed activity, led to formal diplomatic protests by the Foreign Office to Argentina, especially in relation to the presence of the marines and the support given by the Argentinian Navy. The Foreign Office ordered the despatch of the United Kingdom's Antarctic Patrol Ship, HMS *Endurance*, with her embarked marines and helicopters, from the Falklands to South Georgia, which she reached on 24 March. In response, Argentina announced the sailing from Mar del Plata of two missile-armed frigates to support 'the civilian workers' in South Georgia. On 25 March, a second armed Argentinian auxiliary arrived, the *Bahia Paraiso*, which unloaded stores and men and remained on patrol to the north of Cumberland Bay and Grytviken.

It seems likely that a decision to exploit the stand-off at South Georgia with a full-scale invasion of the Falklands and South Georgia was made by the Junta between 26 and 27 March, to take advantage of ships and units that were already at sea as part of a scheduled exercise. Over the next two days, it became clear to the British government that Argentina's attitude was hardening and the crisis escalating, and *Endurance* was ordered back to the Falkland Islands. Her marines were landed into defensive positions at Grytviken, in the vicinity of the BAS base at Shackleton House on 31 March and, after dark, *Endurance* left for the Falklands. By the following morning, the ship was heading into a Force 9 gale.

Meanwhile, Operation Rosario, the Argentinian operation to invade and seize the Falklands, sponsored and spearheaded by the Argentinian Navy, was already under way. Most of its major operational ships, including its aircraft carrier, the *Veinticinco de Mayo (25th of May)*, were at sea off the Islands and positioning for the assault. What had started as a speculative naval venture to test British resolve at South Georgia had given the Argentinian Navy the opportunity to assert itself amid the tangled politics and inter-Service rivalries that characterized Argentina's governing elite at the time. The situation also served to distract and inspire a people desperate for good news and provide a welcome boost to national self-esteem. Ironically, the situation offered the same opportunity to a beleaguered and unpopular government in the United Kingdom and to a country weary of a prevailing sense of national decline.

Overnight, on 2 April, Argentina invaded and occupied the Falkland Islands, having overcome the small Royal Marines garrison with the use and threat of overwhelming force. The following day, on 3 April, South Georgia was also attacked and occupied, after a sharp exchange of fire between Argentinian naval forces and the Royal Marines detachment from HMS *Endurance*.

A Brief Chronology of the Falklands War

2 April 1982	Argentina invades and seizes the Falkland Islands. British naval units operating off Gibraltar in Exercise Spring Train are sent south.
3 April	Argentina invades and seizes South Georgia. United Nations Resolution 502 condemns Argentinian aggression, and calls for an immediate withdrawal of Argentinian forces from the Islands and for a peaceful settlement of the dispute.
5 April	Main UK Task Group, including the aircraft carriers *Hermes* and *Invincible*, departs from Portsmouth.
12 April	UK imposes a Maritime Exclusion Zone 200 nm in radius around the Falkland Islands.
21–23 April	UK forces start preliminary operations off South Georgia.
23 April	UK declares that any Argentinian forces which are assessed to be in a position to interfere with the mission of UK forces in the South Atlantic will be dealt with appropriately.
25 April	Argentinian submarine *Santa Fé* is crippled by UK helicopters off South Georgia. South Georgia is recaptured by British forces.
29 April	UK declares that any Argentinian forces shadowing the Task Force are liable to attack.
30 April	UK declares a Total Exclusion Zone around the Falkland Islands and South Georgia.
1 May	Port Stanley airfield and adjacent military sites are bombed by an RAF Vulcan and Sea Harriers, and bombarded by British warships.
2 May	British submarine *Conqueror* sinks the Argentinian cruiser *General Belgrano*.
4 May	British destroyer *Sheffield* is crippled by an air-launched Argentinian Exocet missile.
7 May	UK warns that any Argentinian warship or aircraft operating more than 12 miles from its coast will be treated as hostile.

9 May	Argentinian surveillance vessel *Narwal* is badly damaged by Sea Harriers.
11 May	Argentinian supply ship *Cabo de los Estados* is sunk by the British frigate *Alacrity*.
14–15 May	SAS raids Pebble Island airfield and destroys 11 aircraft.
20 May	British landing force crosses the Total Exclusion Zone.
21 May	British forces successfully land and establish themselves ashore at San Carlos Water. British frigate *Ardent* sinks as a result of an air attack.
23 May	British frigate *Antelope* sinks after detonation of an unexploded bomb.
25 May	Argentinian air attacks sink the British destroyer *Coventry* (bombs) and the merchant ship *Atlantic Conveyor* (Exocet).
28 May	Darwin and Goose Green are recaptured by 2nd Battalion, the Parachute Regiment.
30 May	45 Commando recaptures Douglas settlement, 3rd Battalion, the Parachute Regiment, regains Teal Inlet and 42 Commando reaches Mount Challenger and Mount Kent.
1 June	5 Infantry Brigade (Scots Guards, Welsh Guards, the Gurkhas and supporting units) lands at San Carlos.
8 June	British landing ships *Sir Galahad* and *Sir Tristram* are crippled by an Argentinian air attack at Fitzroy.
11–12 June	Western approaches to Port Stanley (Mount Harriet, Two Sisters and Mount Longdon) are captured by British forces.
12 June	British destroyer *Glamorgan* is damaged by a shore-based Exocet.
13–14 June	Mount Tumbledown, Wireless Ridge and Mount William, all overlooking Port Stanley, are captured by British forces.
14 June	All Argentinian forces in the Falkland Islands surrender.
20 June	South Thule in the South Sandwich Islands is recaptured.

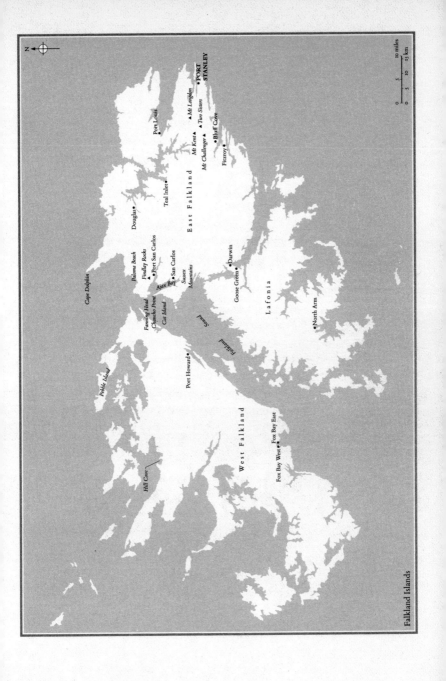

Falkland Islands

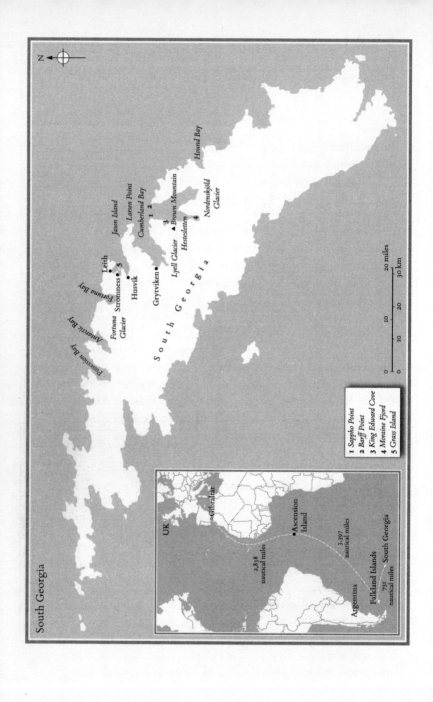

South Georgia

N

Possession Bay
Antarctic Bay
Fortuna Bay
Fortuna Glacier
Leith
Stromness
Husvik
5
Jason Island
Larsen Point
Cumberland Bay
1 2
Grytviken
Lyell Glacier
3 Brown Mountain
Hestesletten
4
Nordenskjöld Glacier
Hound Bay

S o u t h   G e o r g i a

0   10   20 miles
0   10   20   30 km

1 Sappho Point
2 Buff Point
3 King Edward Cove
4 Moraine Fjord
5 Grass Island

UK
Gibraltar
Ascension Island
3,397 nautical miles
Argentina
Falkland Islands
751 nautical miles
2,858 nautical miles
South Georgia

HMS *Antrim*: January to March 1982

Antrim spent the last three months of 1981 in a period of planned and routine maintenance at Portsmouth. Meanwhile, we in 406 – a Wessex 3 single-engined helicopter, known to *Antrim* Flight as 'Humphrey' – were either based at RNAS Portland, or employed on Fishery Protection off the Scottish east coast, or deployed to Northern Ireland, conducting offshore anti-terrorist and covert surveillance operations.

The ship sailed in early January 1982 for sea trials on her equipment and systems and in order to complete an intensive programme of ship-organized departmental and individual team training for the ship's company. 406 embarked and we went to the Flag Officer Sea Training (FOST) facility at Portland for most of February. A serialized programme enabled the ship, her ship's company and systems to be exhaustively trained and tested in all her peace and war roles in challenging multi-threat warfare scenarios against aircraft, ship and submarine opponents. By the beginning of March, *Antrim* was back in Portsmouth and the local sea areas, having 'worked up', to the satisfaction of the FOST staff, and was declared ready to rejoin the Fleet again. We just had to complete collective training with other ships and high-seas firings of our weapon systems to be fully operational.

To this end, *Antrim* sailed from Portsmouth on 17 March for Exercise Spring Train, that took place annually in the Gibraltar exercise areas. It enabled warships of the First Flotilla to conduct sophisticated warfare serials, weapon firings and collective training in good weather, in deep water and in seas uncluttered by shipping.

In all, 18 British frigates and destroyers, three submarines and six Royal Fleet Auxiliary vessels would take part, together with two American frigates, RAF Buccaneers, and US Navy Lockheed P-3 Orion and UK Nimrod maritime reconnaissance and anti-submarine aircraft.

As the flagship of Rear Admiral 'Sandy' Woodward, the Flag Officer First Flotilla, *Antrim* led the destroyer *Coventry* out of Portsmouth harbour and along the deep-water channel past Southsea Castle, the Nab Tower and beyond. As we passed between Palmerston's forts in the

Solent, HMS *Speedy*, the Navy's hydrofoil, overtook us on the starboard side (without paying her respects to the Admiral's flag and dignity). The Admiral affected not to notice, while a couple of his staff urged him to send the cheeky subordinate a 'Negative BRAVO ZULU'* – a bollocking. I'm not sure whether *Speedy* actually would have cared as she ostentatiously powered quickly and noisily ahead.

On the helicopter Flight, we had to take a temporary Senior Maintenance Rating along with us to replace Mel Camp, who had to stay behind because of an administrative mix-up at Portland. In his place, we had Fritz Heritier – and his beard – from 737 Squadron, who appeared to be a robust, no-nonsense individual who immediately took firm charge of the maintainers. He was efficient, quick to adapt and very professional, but we were not sure that he wanted to be in *Antrim* a moment longer than he had to be. He was a passionate, highly experienced sports diver and I think that there was a wreck off the Dorset coast that was missing him.

On the way down to Gibraltar, we had a packed programme of warfare serials in conjunction with the other ships, with the weather proving warm and clear. The ship's company started a beard-growing competition, to be judged before our return to Portsmouth. On 21 March, we began to hear reports of a situation developing at South Georgia (where?), which involved scrap dealers, the Argentinians and the British Antarctic Survey. Later that evening, we read signals indicating that *Endurance* would be tasked to sort things out. The to and fro of events and the seemingly petty discourse had the air of pantomime diplomacy, reinforced by the fact that nobody really had any idea of where the places involved actually were.

We spent 24–29 March in Gibraltar, during which we had the sort of experiences that always come with a 'foreign' port packed with sailors from a large number of ships, determined to enjoy themselves and out to prove that their ship is the best in the Fleet. Gibraltar, with its pubs and various establishments, mainly around Engineer Lane, is geared up and braced to deal with this annual invasion of barbarian hordes. The problem is that there is a distinct shortage of females. Gibraltar's police generally understand and control the situation, but are pretty rigorous and uncompromising in the face of trouble that involves Gibraltarian citizens or property, or embarrasses the locals. The threat of imprisonment – in the

---

* 'Manoeuvre not well executed!'

Moorish Castle (equals primitive, rigorous, nasty, brutish and not short) – is the way in which we try and forestall trouble, although our maintainers were always well-behaved and good-natured ashore.

As it happened, we had the usual crop of drunken incidents and assaults, almost exclusively involving ratings from other ships, but a few of our own. The Doc had to treat a few cuts and bruises on people who all seemed to have accidentally fallen down or walked into something solid. The sport of choice was, inevitably, 'Let's see if we can get across the border into Spain and get back again', with the usual Steve McQueen, Richard Attenborough et al attempts – and the predictable results.

Another craze emerged this time. It involved the dry-docks at Gibraltar that were designed and built to take the Queen Elizabeth Class battleships. The docks are about 70 feet deep. The game involves two sailors, about 10 pints of beer and a camera. Jolly Jack gets himself into a position where he is hanging by his fingertips from the lip of the caisson while the other takes his photograph looking down. The manoeuvre is repeated so that the other chap can have his photograph taken too. We had two incidents the night that I was on duty as Officer of the Day.

The day that I was on duty – Thursday, 25 March – we also had a group- and dockyard-wide Operation Awkward, to practise our defences against terrorists, rioters and other ne'er-do-wells. We had car bombers, snipers, rioters all played by the Staffordshire Regiment soldiers, who were the resident garrison troops. We were attacked by a group of about 40 who stormed up the gangway, throwing bricks, bottles and bits of wood. There was nothing else for it. We turned on two high-power fire hoses and cleared the gangway instantly; the wet and disgruntled soldiers went off seeking easier prey along the jetty.

Much of the time was spent planning for the next phase of the exercise and, by the Saturday, we had a briefing on the forthcoming exercise programme from the Admiral's staff on board *Antrim*.

On the evening of Saturday, 27 March, we all attended a fancy dress 'what you were wearing when the ship went down' party in the caves deep in the Rock, something which struck us afterwards as ironic, in view of subsequent events. The Doc narrowly avoided the aggressively amorous attentions of a WRNS officer who said that she fancied doctors and he was THE ONE. As we said, 'It's not you, Alasdair, it's because you are a doctor', and added, 'Aircrew have to deal with it all the time.'

Sunday saw the culmination of a Major Sporting Olympiad that had taken place during the visit, involving all the ships' companies. *Glamorgan* won the Maxi-Ship Cup and *Plymouth* the Midi-Ship competition, 12 Squadron RAF won the Mini-Ship (!) trophy, and *Rooke*, the local shore establishment, unsurprisingly won the Top of the Rock Race. The route is 2.5 miles long and climbs steeply to about 1,250 feet. I managed 27 minutes and 38 seconds and was struggling from the time I passed the Casino.

Sunday's fun and games ended with the Chain of Command relay, designed to introduce a handicap system based around a relay race of six different ranks and ages from each ship, from junior up to the Commanding Officer, who had to run the last lap. The funniest sight was the tiny CO of *Sheffield* running for all he was worth being pursued by the elegant-looking, tall CO of *Coventry*. *Sheffield* won it, should I say, by a head?

I also conducted an interview with BBC Radio Solent. The reporter asked me about how I enjoyed the Royal Navy, where I went to school, who my teachers were at Portsmouth Grammar School and whom I admired. He asked me if my teachers had any nicknames – I told him some (*Bomber* Ive – his initial was 'D', *Gino* Washington, *Old* Stoneham and *Boggy* Marsh) and then felt guilty about telling him. Goodness, they might hear the broadcast!

Two strange things happened over the weekend. The submarines departed from the exercise – *Spartan* went off at the rush – without warning and *Brilliant* sailed early at 1800 on Sunday, 28 March. At the same time, the Admiral's staff decided that they were not going to plan and run Spring Train and that *Antrim*'s officers would have to do it, in addition to their normal duties. *Antrim* Flight (that meant me) was given the dubious honour of organizing and signalling all the aviation and flying programmes for the rest of the exercise. As Ian had said, 'The Admiral's staff have just fucked off.' We saw them at meals, when, at best, they just looked shifty, slightly guilty and secretive.

We sailed from Gibraltar on 29 March, to conduct a programme of collective training serials, anti-submarine exercises and high-seas firings of the Sea Slug and guns, before the passage home, to disembark at Portland at 0930 on 6 April.

In fact, we had already booked the transport from Portsmouth for the ground equipment and the lads, and had sent our disembarkation plans off to Portland. Alison and I were due to travel up to the ship in Portsmouth on 7 April for a Ladies' Night dinner onboard, just ahead of Easter leave and Good Friday on 9 April.

However, from the radio and the reports sent by signal, we were progressively picking up evidence of increasing tension and the escalation of events in the South Atlantic, almost every hour. We were busy and very active on the exercise, but there was frequent discussion about Argentinian 'will they, won't they, can they, dare they?' intentions. We challenged the Admiral's staff regularly in a light-hearted sort of way – 'Come on, we know that you are doing contingency planning', 'Will we need to get charts for the South Atlantic – just checking', 'What about needing tropical uniform?', 'Can you show me where South Georgia is – on the chart?' They just got irritated – they had a total sense of humour failure – and we thought, 'We know what you are doing!'

The Admiral spent the day flying around the ships, dispensing leadership largesse, and went to *Glamorgan* to confer at length with Commander-in-Chief Fleet.

On 30 March, we had a full day of various warfare serials, including low-level attacks by the Buccaneers. We also prepared for the Sea Slug firings on the morrow.

On 31 March, we did an anti-submarine exercise with *Oracle*, seemingly the only submarine left in the exercise. We were bounced by the Buccaneers again over breakfast. At 0930 and 1020, *Antrim* fired two Sea Slugs at remotely piloted Chukar targets and hit them both. *Glamorgan*, *Glasgow* and *Sheffield* all fired and scored hits as well. We then all had a crack with our 4.5 inch guns.

We were hearing regular updates from London about diplomatic moves to pressure the Argentinians to back down. A signal said that Lord Trefgarne had announced in Parliament that 'the Argentinian Foreign Minister has said that Argentinian personnel in South Georgia would be given the full protection of the Argentinian government. The despatch of Argentinian warships to the area has been reported.'

He also talked about 'a situation which, in itself, is of relatively minor significance. South Georgia is an uninhabited dependency of the Falkland Islands Territory.' It might have been me, but I remember thinking at the time that, if I had been an Argentinian, the UK did not really seem to care about South Georgia.

Later, there was a night anti-surface engagement with the USS *Samuel Eliot Morison* and several serials that involved replenishment and manoeuvring ships in formation in response to various simulated threats.

The Diary

I am starting this diary because I suspect that we might be embarking on an unusual deployment that could result in a shooting war. It may come to nothing and, after a good deal of posturing and threatening, things might just settle down. However, just in case, I thought that I might just commit to the record anything notable or unusual that happens.

We have been told that we are not permitted to keep diaries, apparently in case they fall into enemy hands. What a load of cobblers! There is a lot more interesting stuff – cryptographic materials and Confidential Books – before they get to have a look at my musings and scribblings. I suspect that this instruction has more to do with information control, ensuring that the official version has authority and that things stay secret.

The aircrew

Before I start my diary, it is probably worth me saying something about the previous careers of people with whom I fly:

Lieutenant Commander Ian Stanley (36 years old)

The Boss entered the Royal Navy as an Artificer Apprentice in 1963, but was selected for officer and helicopter-flying training in 1967. He then served as the 2nd Pilot in HMS *London* Flight between 1969 and 1971 and as a staff pilot on 737 Squadron (both equipped with Wessex 3s) from 1971 to 1973. After a tour as a flying instructor on 705 Squadron (Gazelles), he was the Flight Commander of HMS *Ajax* Wasp Flight from 1975 to 1977, before an exchange tour to Australia and an appointment as Senior Pilot of 771 Squadron at Culdrose. He joined *Antrim* Flight in November 1981.

Sub-Lieutenant Stewart Cooper (27 years old)

Stewart joined the Royal Navy in 1974 as a Radio Electrical Mechanic (Air) and served in technical appointments at Portland and Lossiemouth, as well as with 849 Squadron in HMS *Ark Royal*. He trained as an officer in 1977 and, after a brief spell out of the Royal Navy, re-entered in 1979 to undertake flying training and was appointed to *Antrim* Flight in December 1981.

Petty Officer Aircrewman David Fitzgerald (34 years old)

David entered the Royal Navy in 1965 and initially trained as an anti-submarine and torpedo rating, serving in a variety of warships. He trained as an aircrewman in 1974 and served in different anti-submarine helicopter squadrons and flights, before joining *Antrim* Flight in January 1982.

My friends

Also, the officers onboard with whom I have the most in common and whom I count as my friends are Declan Ward (one of the Bridge watch-keepers), Alasdair Maclean (the Medical Officer) and Carlos Edwards (the Deputy Supply Officer). We are all about the same age, have a lot in common and go on runs-ashore together. We form a tight little group/ solid phalanx within the Wardroom and we stick together in the face of bullshit and official irrationality, sharing a similar line in humour and combative banter. Above all, we are known for our nightly, highly competitive games of 'uckers' (a boardgame like ludo) before and after dinner at sea in the Wardroom; I play in partnership with Declan, Alasdair partners Carlos. In real life, Carlos and I are married; Declan and Alasdair are single, but attached.

Thursday, 1 April

There was a flood of signals about the deteriorating situation in the Falklands and South Georgia, with all the indications that the government does not want to do anything that might provoke the Argentinians. The word 'appeasement' was on everybody's mind today and those that actually cared about the issue were pretty indignant and reckoned that the government needed to be robust with the Argentinian Junta, not conciliatory (equals weak). There are some lessons for history that are relevant here.

The Wardroom is split on whether the Argentinians will invade, or are just huffing and puffing. I reckoned that they would, but would do it just to show they could do it any time they wanted in future. They probably wouldn't stay if we kicked up a serious fuss and deployed some ships (and an SSN*). John Archer pointed out that we have a ready-made Task Force here at Gib and we were all wondering whether *Antrim* would go down there.

Today was High Seas Firing Day for the Spring Train Group destroyers, firing Sea Slugs and Sea Darts against remotely controlled Chukar targets. Our job in 406 from about 1000 was to locate and recover the targets once they had dropped into the sea and return them underslung to RFA *Tidespring*,† where they were based and maintained. The targets floated either on the surface or just below it and we were given a reasonable steer from the ships about where to look. Mostly, it meant doing an expanding square search around a last known position.

We had picked up three targets at various stages during the firings and were going after another when I spotted what I thought was a target. We closed to the on-top, but, when we arrived, it wasn't a target at all, but the upturned hull of a large – about 60 feet (19 metres) or more – ocean-going yacht, completely 180 degrees capsized, with its sails set, a hole in the hull and its rudder broken. It had a single outrigger, with the remains of another hanging off. It was positively eerie and very *Marie Celeste*.

We reported it to *Antrim*, but no one seemed interested amid all the missile and exercise action. When we next refuelled, I made the point to the Captain that it might answer questions for people who were perhaps missing their loved ones. It could have been some long-lost round-the-world yachtsman. Also, the historian in me imagined this hulk to be the missing piece in a mystery that had probably been running for ages. The Navigator usefully added that it might be a hazard to navigation. It was in position 33° 44´ N 010° 24.5´ W.

As a result, the Captain got permission to close the yacht and we put

* Nuclear-powered submarine.
† Royal Fleet Auxiliary – a civilian-manned, UK government-owned tanker and support ship.

divers down. They recovered the yacht's brass wheel, its sail number and a camera, but no clues to its identity. They then sank it with demolition charges at about 1600 and that was that. I just hoped that someone would do something about following up the incident once we got back to Portsmouth. We finished flying and conducted various passenger transfers [SOOTAXs] and load-lifting serials [VERTREPs (Vertical Replenishments)] between *Ariadne*, *Sheffield* and *Tidespring* at about 1915. It was a longer and more interesting day than I would have thought possible when we had briefed at 0800.

In the evening, the Admiral's staff had dinner together in the Admiral's Day Cabin and did not come out. Something was going on. All the discussion in the Wardroom was about whether the Argentinians were about to invade the Falklands. The exercise carried on regardless and I drafted and authorized the operational tasking for the air assets for tomorrow and the day after.

During the night, we conducted an anti-submarine exercise in company with *Brilliant*, *Battleaxe*, *Coventry*, *Sheffield*, *Ariadne*, *Aurora* and *Tidespring*. We did not fly.

I always have a technical and intellectual problem with the way in which we fight submarines. Most of the time, because of the limited ranges technically achievable by our ships' active sonars, we only detect submarines well inside the range at which they would probably want to fire at the ships.

There is this theory that all submarines want to do is go for the high-value targets and bypass the escorts. That seems to hobble our thinking. Confronted by Soviet nuclear submarines, we are stuck in the ASDIC era of the Second World War. My view is that, with the current state of our surface ship sonars, serious ASW [Anti-Submarine Warfare] should be left to helicopters (the Russian submariners hate Sea Kings apparently) and Nimrods, both invulnerable to submarines, and friendly submarines. Most of our tactical instructions for surface ships in tracking and engaging submarines (especially the nukes) look like recipes for suicide.

Successful ASW should be determined by the submarines that you do not find in your way, rather than the ones that you do find! We need to avoid them. The lesson from the Second World War convoys seems to be that it is all about routing – not putting yourself in the same time and space as the submarine.

I wrote this entry on 3 April.

Friday, 2 April

I was shaken by the Captain's Secretary, Jeremy Lindsey, at about 0515, who said:

'I am just checking if it's true that you speak Spanish.'

'Have they invaded the Falklands then?' I asked.

'I've just got to ask whether you speak Spanish,' he said.

'Well, I do a bit,' I said. 'Don't be a tosser, Jeremy! Have they invaded, or not?' I was thoroughly awake now.

'If you want to know, go down the Ops Room,' he said, shutting the door behind him.

I went to the Operations Room, to find Pat Brown, the SCO (Tony Dymock) and the Captain deep in conversation with members of the Admiral's staff. I hovered around the edge and earwigged. The discussion concerned a signal from CINCFLEET [Commander-in-Chief Fleet] saying that certain ships would be selected to deal with 'the crisis' and that these should be fuelled and stored to full operational capability. From what was being said, it was clear that an invasion of the Falklands had taken place and that ships were being selected for deployment on the basis of their utility and serviceability.

I went back up to my cabin and read until breakfast, where the conversation was all about whether *Antrim* would be chosen to go and deal with the crisis, which now involved an invasion according to the World Service. The Heads of Department were nowhere to be seen – they were having breakfast, around discussions and briefings, with the Captain and the Admiral. The younger officers (including me) were all energetically and noisily up for it (it sounded like an adventure in distant parts), while the more senior (SCO, Duncan Ford and the Senior Engineer) were more cautious and doubtful about whether a military response, with all the expense and hassle, would actually be needed or required by the politicians. The old hands (Dave Barraclough, Roger Insley and Steve Berry) wanted to get back for the Easter holidays and expressed the view that we would just posture for a while, mess up leave and return home about two weeks late. I had a brief thought about Chief Heritier not getting back – he would not be happy! Ian can tell him!

We very soon found out that the majority of the ships on Spring Train would be going south (*Antrim, Glamorgan, Coventry, Sheffield,*

Glasgow, Arrow, Brilliant, Plymouth and RFA *Tidespring*). Those with major engineering defects or incomplete/unsuitable sensor and weapon suites would go home. As a result, each deploying ship was allocated a 'buddy ship' and ordered to go alongside for a jackstay and helicopter transfer of as much ammunition and as many stores as she could take. Meanwhile, we in 406 were to do load-lifting, or VERTREP, aft on the Flight Deck, mostly ammunition, but also pallets of stores and provisions. Our buddy ship turned out to be *Ariadne* and we started replenishing at about 1000.

Antrim and *Ariadne* were alongside for a good six hours while we lifted loads from Flight Deck to Flight Deck. Unbelievable quantities of stuff came on board. For four hours, palleted loads of food, stores and equipment were being passed on the heavy jackstay forward. We in 406 spent all day transferring torpedoes and 4.5 shells in netted loads between *Ariadne* and *Antrim*, together with other gear that was inconvenient or too heavy for transfer by jackstay. We had in place the sensible precautions – shot mats, earthing poles, protective clothing – but the shells were just placed higgledy-piggledy into the nets, while the torpedoes, with some token padding, were also put singly into nets and lowered by us onto shot mats or torpedo trolleys on the Flight Deck. I have never seen the normal rules interpreted quite so liberally and suspended so quickly. We also carried Sea Cat missiles in nets, 4.5 cartridges in RAS bags, the torpedoes on torpedo recovery strops.

The most remarkable sight of the day was *Ariadne* steadily rising out of the sea as she was relieved of her stores and ammo while *Antrim* was getting deeper in the water as she took on the weight of the additional materiel. All the while, Nick Bracegirdle (the DWEO [Deputy Weapons Engineering Officer]) and his team were fussing around trying to get the ammunition and missiles stored in the most convenient and efficient fashion, not quite as fast as we were throwing the stuff onto the deck.

We also had to say farewell, via a jackstay transfer, to Rob Freeburn and Bob Cody – our American NBCDO and Australian exchange officers. They both desperately wanted to come with us, but of course their countries have not declared their hands yet. They were looking forward to coming back to us soon. Between 1700 and 1800, we topped up with fuel from *Blue Rover*, while we transferred five Sea Cat missiles from *Euryalus* in individual netted loads and completed flying operations at about 1910. When I made my way forward to my cabin, I could see that the ship was littered with all sorts of stores – tins of everything, bog rolls, gash bags, beer and polish were evident everywhere. All the passageways were full of kit and stores that needed to be struck down and stowed. Half of the Wardroom cabin flat had a layer of boxes full of tins and I only reached my cabin by walking over tins containing peas, beans and potatoes. The Canteen is apparently overwhelmed with boxes of Mars Bars, Smarties and other 'nutty' – that's good!

Finally, we had a sea boat transfer with *Aurora*. We inherited a Bridge watch-keeper, Keith Creates, a mild, lean and quiet-looking chap, from *Aurora*. We also sent some mail and I wrote quickly to A from 'off the Azores', saying that we had been detached and would probably be away for about six weeks, based on going down south, touching the wall and coming back again. I also had to make some provision for her to be able to access our bank account and move money around. I thought that we were going to be decidedly short of post-boxes in the South Atlantic.

I was Officer of the Day today. I did my rounds and security duties once we had finished flying and mustered the Confidential Books and crypto in the MCO. Declan, Carlos, the Doctor and I had a game of uckers before dinner, which Declan and I won. We have decided that we will play at least one game a day for as long as this deployment lasts, with a prize – yet to be determined – for the winners.

The details of the Argentinian invasion came through this evening. It appears that their Navy spearheaded the assault using their carrier, a submarine and a wide variety of escorts and transports. They attacked the Royal Marines barracks at Moody Brook and destroyed it while other troops surrounded Government House, until the Governor ordered the Royal Marines to surrender, in the face of overwhelming odds. It seems that the Argentinians could have lost about half a dozen killed, because the Royal Marines had deployed in time to counter the invasion and resisted strongly. It's just as well that they were not at Moody Brook. They will be hopping mad about having to surrender.

I have no doubt that we need to get the Falkland Islands back. We cannot allow a vile military dictatorship to grab a chunk of British territory against the will of the inhabitants – and the British people – and expect to get away with it. The Junta cannot just throw its weight around in order to deflect public attention away from internal problems, mitigate the kidnap and murder of its own people and override the rights of people under international law. 'War is a cowardly escape from the problems of peace.'* The invasion is such an obvious ploy to gain favour with their people. I am sure that they feel really great and are crowing about pulling the lion's tail. I reckon that the Argentinians calculate that they might get away with it because we have a woman Prime Minister. They need to think about Philip II and Elizabeth I there!

I just hope that the government at home does not fold as a result and we end up with the peaceniks of the Labour Party, although our current politicians, civil servants and diplomats should be thoroughly ashamed of themselves for letting this happen in the first place. Announcing the withdrawal of *Endurance* wasn't a great idea; coupled with the imminent Defence cuts, it must have given the Argentinians a strong hint that we were not going to resist any move on their part. In fact, our government has to do something pretty quickly or it is likely to lose credibility and the public's confidence. They have to halt or reverse the Defence cuts and show that the UK is capable of deterring threats to its citizens and to its dependent territories wherever they are. If we do not do something, what price Spain and Gibraltar and China and Hong Kong? And what message does it send to the Soviets?

Needless to say, the ship's company are not exactly over the moon about being diverted just before Easter leave and the general mood is that the whole thing will prove to be a wild goose chase. The boys on the Flight think that we will huff and puff politically and the Argentinians will get away with it, as the United Nations acquiesces in the fait accompli. The annoying thing is that we knew what the Args were up to a week ago and, if we had been sailed, could have been halfway there by now. As it is, it will take us about two and a half weeks to travel down there, pausing to resupply at Ascension Island. If we had gone when all this started to blow up, it might even have deterred the Argentinians from invading.

I recalled a couple of odd things today. When we looked at the Admiral's staff intelligence file on the Argentinian Navy, all it had was photocopied pages of *Jane's Fighting Ships*. The files were contained in pack covers that had been used by the Admiral's staff as part of their recent 'contingency' exercise, when they dumped the conduct of Spring Train onto *Antrim*'s officers. That is why *Brilliant* had sailed early from alongside us in Gibraltar! So somebody at CINCFLEET or the politicians had had some advance warning of the Argentinians invading: that

* Thomas Mann.

is why the staff hid themselves away in the Admiral's cabin flat and would not talk about what they were doing. They were planning in case the capture of the Islands went ahead! They knew about this when we were in Gibraltar and that is why the nuclear submarines had thinned out from the exercise without warning on 29 March.

The other, weird, thing is that when we were part of Navy Days in Devonport last August, we had been chatting in the Wardroom at the end of one of the open days.

A lady naval dentist whose Royal Marines husband (Andy MacDonald) had been killed in a Gazelle crash with Dave Dunne and Charley Farley in September 1980 was there. In conversation, she said that her husband had ordered a new car in June 1980 for the following September. The next month they had been to a fortune teller, who looked straight at her husband and said, 'I know that you are planning to buy a car in the near future. Don't buy that car – you are not going to need it.' Bloody hell!

That seemed to set the tone for the conversation and we went on to discuss the forthcoming Defence cuts and remarked that the government really did not appreciate the RN and all it did. We were also reflecting on the fact that we would lose our fighting edge in the wake of the cuts and would have to accept increasing levels of obsolete weapons and dilapidated equipment. What we needed, said someone, was a war to sharpen everyone up and remind the public why a strong Navy was necessary for the nation's security and prosperity.

We then started talking about potential people to have a war with – no one too difficult, but enough to have a reasonable ding-dong and to make the public and the politicians appreciate us a bit. Hopefully, John Nott would get the sack and the Crabs* would stop sniping at us. John Archer and one of the Admiral's staff onboard mentioned that, when the carriers were cancelled in the 1960s, the RAF had produced a map which demonstrated how they could provide air cover for the Navy anywhere in the world. To do so, they had apparently moved Australia a thousand miles on the map that they showed the politicians. That is how the relationship is viewed in the RN!

Amid additional rounds of bitter and lager, we agreed that we did not fancy taking on the Soviet Union ('Save them for the final,' said one wag); there were the usual jokes about the French. What about Iran,

* Derogatory naval expression for the Royal Air Force.

Libya . . .? We traded suggestions around the world – too difficult, too easy, too nice, too many good runs-ashore, too many British citizens there – until we lighted on and agreed on – surprise! – Argentina! That was spooky!

Well, now it had happened! We could seriously have a war coming with Argentina, if they do not turn round and go home.

This evening, before writing this account, I looked at the *Philips World Atlas* that I had among the Flight books, just to see where the Falklands and South Georgia were exactly. There they were – two tiny splodges of red, the Islands themselves, which were, of course, not politically 'red' at this point, and another island clinging to the edge of Antarctica, with the unfamiliar, but romantic-sounding name of Grytviken on its northern shore.

I briefly reflected on what I knew about the Falklands: they are near Cape Horn; battle-cruisers *Invincible* and *Inflexible* sailing down there to deal with the German *Scharnhorst* and *Gneisenau* and their cruisers in the First World War; distinctive stamps; whaling and sheep-farming. South Georgia – all I knew was that Ernest Shackleton escaped from Elephant Island to there and what I had learned during the past few days about what was going on with the scrap dealers. As I gazed at the place-name on the map, I tried to conjure up in my mind what sort of barren, ice-rimmed and remote place it might be and what might be going on there right now. At least I knew roughly where the Islands were – most of the Wardroom had been pretty hazy about the precise location of these (suddenly prime) bits of real estate.

Declan has just popped his head round the door on the way to standing the Middle Watch on the Bridge.

'Guess what,' he said. 'I've just been asked to go and see the Commander.'

'Oh, yes,' I responded cheerfully. 'Good news?'

'Well, when I knocked on his cabin door, he said, "Do you want the good news or the bad news?" '

Declan had then said, 'Is the bad news that you want me to be NBCDO, now that Rob Freeburn has gone?'

'Yes,' the Commander had said, gleefully, 'I am glad to see that you are a volunteer.'

Of course the job of NBCDO is an onerous and time-consuming one, in ensuring that all the Damage Control preparations, stores, materials and training are kept up to the mark. It involves continuous liaison between the various departments and is even more vital – and onerous – if you think that you might be involved in any sort of coercive operation soon. In action, you are supposed to assist the Commander, WEO and MEO,* in dealing with incidents and damage, making sure that the ship continues to float and move, while continuing to fight. On top of his watch-keeping on the Bridge, these duties would conspire to lose Declan even more sleep – and also constrain the time available to play uckers.

'What's the good news?' Declan had asked.

'There is no good news,' the Commander had said.

However, for me, the good news is that we are doing something out of the routine, something out of the ordinary, which already has the potential to offer new experiences and challenges, both professional and personal.

Come, cheer up, my lads, 'tis to glory we steer,
To add something more to this wonderful year.†

Or will we get halfway down there, only to find it all settled by the politicians and diplomats? Odds on, I reckon, that someone will back down. If it is the UK, I will leave the Royal Navy; what would be the point of staying? Why have a Navy, if you are not prepared to use it in support of your interests, to deal with the bully-boys of the world and to maintain national honour?

Saturday, 3 April

It's been very busy indeed today. The ship has adopted a largely silent posture on its radar and communications emitters, to avoid detection, and the weapon systems are being brought to 30 minutes' notice. We aim to be fully prepared for war by the time we reach Ascension Island.

We have been trying to find out as much as possible about the Falklands, what happened during the invasion and the Arg capability. The ship exercised the Oerlikon guns on both sides against floating targets, while the boys on the Flight had a maintenance day. The aircrew had a

* See 'Command structure and leadership', pp. 333–5.
† From the naval song 'Heart of Oak'.

chat about how we would play things for real. In particular, we decided that we would start each day with a surveillance and surface search sortie, allowing the ships to build up the surface picture ahead and around, while we practise coordinated Exocet missile and gun engagements with each other.

We attended a brief by the Admiral's staff about how the Admiral and they see any military action going. The Admiral has said that he is not anticipating a conflict that will involve much action against their aircraft and submarines, but one that will be almost exclusively fought against their surface ships. The implication is that we will draw their ships onto our SSNs, sink them and then sail into the Falklands with trumpets sounding and flags flying. He also seems to discount a cameo appearance by their carrier, the *Veinticinco de Mayo*. I queried this approach in questions and was treated to the 'you are just a junior officer; we have seen the intelligence and you have not' treatment. Did I feel patronized? Yes!

I then read a strange assessment by the Admiral's staff about the capabilities and ranges of Arg aircraft. They had underestimated their capabilities, so I went to see Ian, clutching the ship's *Jane's All the World's Aircraft* and showed him that the Arg Daggers, Mirage IIIs and A4 Skyhawks can make it to the Falklands from their mainland bases with a decent bomb load. The Etendards definitely can make it with an Exocet. The Args also have C-130 Hercules tankers, so they could top up with fuel once airborne. If they extend the runway at Stanley while we run south, they can make things very difficult for us. We went to see our own warfare officers, who all agreed with our estimation of Arg air capability.

We therefore collared the Admiral's RAF Staff Officer and Air expert who told us that we were wrong and emphasized, once again, that he and the staff had access to intelligence that we were not cleared to see. This seems to be the ultimate trump card for people that haven't got the right arguments. So, Ian and I went to see the Admiral and he is sticking by his staff. He politely, but firmly and definitively, told us to go away and implied that we should stop bothering his busy team. What does he know? He is just a submariner; it's not his fault really. But the Crab should know better. I wonder if he appreciates the real risks in his Admiral's plan.

It got worse. Later this evening, we were told to remove all 406's cabin equipment, the radar and the sonar, to optimize it for load-lifting and troop transport. That would have effectively made me into an aircrewman for the duration of the deployment and would have deprived the ship of a major targeting platform for its Exocet missiles. We went to the Captain, both to explain to him about why the Admiral might be somewhat cheesed off with us and to say that, without telling the staff or the Admiral, we would be keeping the radar in the back of 406 and having the sonar and its winch mechanism stowed and configured in the hangar ready to refit as need arose. He said that perhaps that needed to be our little secret.

It helped that the Admiral has decided that he wants to go to *Glamorgan*. We reckon that the Admiral prefers *Glamorgan* anyway. He and *Glamorgan*'s Captain, Captain Barrow, apparently joined the RN together and were close chums at Dartmouth. He also had *Glamorgan* as his flagship out in the Persian Gulf and in the Indian Ocean late last year, when they unfortunately hit a rock off Oman. I think the CO and the Navigator – and I suppose the OOW – are still waiting to hear whether they are going to be court-martialled. They scraped their propellers and had to make the passage back to the UK at slow speed to avoid incurring further damage.

What is immediately noticeable here in *Antrim* is that the Admiral and the Captain do not look easy in each other's company; the Captain looks uncomfortable and the Admiral indifferent – and there is no eye contact. The chemistry is not right and some of the Admiral's staff officers seem to be in a permanent state of irritation every time that our officers suggest anything.

In fact, we thought it strange that, when the Admiral invited every other CO round for dinner in Gibraltar, our Captain – the Flag Captain – did not appear to have been invited. The Captain's PO Steward came down to the Wardroom and asked the Commander if he would invite the Captain for the evening. He came to the Wardroom for dinner and a film.

It must be that our Captain is a different generation and mentality to the Admiral (the latter is younger) and they have different points of reference, or it's an aviator/submariner thing. I would assess that the 'band of brothers'* is pretty clearly not going to include our Captain. In fact, I think that this Admiral probably only trusts people that he has worked with before and knows. He and Captain Coward were very chummy when *Brilliant* slipped out of Gibraltar and they were chatting in a very

* A favourite phrase of Nelson's, taken from Shakespeare's *Henry V*.

animated and friendly fashion before he left. They are both submariners, of course.

Most of the ship's company do not yet seem to realize how far away the Falklands are. The big surprise for everyone is that they are roughly the size of Wales, not at all the same size as the Orkneys or Scillies, which has been the prevailing misconception.

Remarkably, within the ship I have not heard anyone say, 'This is not what I joined for.' Everyone seems pretty much up for doing whatever is necessary to return the Islands to UK control and give the Args a good kicking in the process, so that they don't come back any time soon. We have had no pacifist or fatalistic talk, although the Padre has been 'right on' with some – fairly unconvincing – stuff about how sad it all is and how we need to be hopeful about the diplomatic efforts.

Also, there is a great deal of barely disguised contempt for the Arg national character, based around stereotypes of the volatile, untrustworthy and emotionally unstable Dago. The boys have distinctly gone off Arg footballers as well, despite the popularity of Ardiles and Villa at Tottenham, and with the World Cup due this year this is one ship that hopes that Argentina do not make it to the final.

The unluckiest guy onboard – or luckiest, depending on your point of view – is John Saunders. He was due to get married at BRNC [Britannia Royal Naval College] Dartmouth in a week, on 10 April! The Captain let him send a signal to BRNC asking them to cancel the arrangements, but, because of security, it needed to be short on detail. John wanted to include a message along the lines of 'let the other half know', but the Captain thought 'the other half' was rather vulgar and harrumphed about it. Apparently, a form of words was agreed, with suitably cryptic expressions indicating that John would not be making the event.

By coincidence, about an hour later, John S received a fax via Portishead Radio from his fiancée saying simply, 'Are you going to make it to the church on time?' We cannot reply and John hopes that she gets the message from BRNC. Meanwhile, we keep reassuring him that she is sure to find someone else to keep her company and her toes warm while he is away.

About a dozen other lads are in a similar position, mostly with weddings planned for the summer.

The beard-growing competition is continuing as we deploy south, with a fine of £1 to the Guide Dogs for the Blind if anyone shaves it off. There has been a discussion about beards because they affect the integrity of the seals around the respirators. I do not usually sport a beard, but I must confess to becoming a bit superstitious about shaving it off. It is totally irrational, I know, but, for now and until I hear that there might be an Arg chemical threat, it is staying put. Ian has decided to shave and pay up.

The last time that I wore a beard was when I was in Northern Ireland and, before that, when I was under training in HMS *Ark Royal*. At the time, we had a BBC team onboard filming the series *Sailor*. It was decided that an episode following the Captain around for a day and contrasting his responsibilities and preoccupations with the life of a junior officer would make good TV. I was chosen as that junior officer and was invited to walk through a number of set-pieces for the sake of the cameras. One included a complement engineer officer pretending to explain to me the delights and intricacies of a switchboard – a switchboard!

He was briefed to talk for three minutes, but, exploiting his moment of fame, he was still rambling on and on after about 20 minutes. My eyes started to glaze after about three minutes (it's tough being 22) and, when we looked at the results, the camera, as if in sympathy, blurred and lost focus after about five minutes too. I was subsequently asked to comment on this incident by the producer and the programme had me saying, alongside the (edited and shortened) scene, something like: 'With such dramatic things happening up on the Flight Deck, some people might think that switchboards are a bit boring . . .' As a result, I received a load of post from 'disgusted' engineers, including one Admiral, who said, implausibly, that what I had said about switchboards would have a devastating impact on recruiting and engineering branch morale.

However, that was not the only albatross that I carried around my neck as a result of my appearance on TV. I had volunteered to teach sailors O-level English, in order to improve their chances of promotion, and had a class of about 20 all heading for examinations in about a month. I was surreptitiously filmed during one of my classes – all good stuff, as it happened – and I wanted to reinforce the points about reading and mental preparation. I was talking about the need to have a book on the go at any one time and said that it was most important to read something just ahead of the exam – 'even if it's the letters page of

Mayfair, because you get some really descriptive language in those letters. You could not make it up – some of the best prose in the English language.' Lots of laughs – point made.

When the episode went out, *Mayfair* was so impressed with my endorsement that their next editorial singled me out for particular praise. The reason that I knew this was because they also sent me a year's free supply of the magazine, which dutifully dropped onto the mat of my parents' home for the next 12 months. My mother's comment: 'We did not think you were like that, Christopher!' Of course, the 'Christopher' as opposed to 'Chris' conveyed a subtle emphasis and message.

Commander E came into the Wardroom after the evening command meeting saying that the HODs had just had a pretty frank discussion with the Admiral and his staff about the material state of some of the ships. They said that *Sheffield* and *Coventry* are 'fragile' mechanically and in need of extensive planned and other maintenance on their main systems and auxiliaries. *Sheffield* has a completely knackered diesel and has just finished a six-month deployment. The staff view was that the Sea Dart ships had proved their missile systems on the Spring Train high seas firings and that the Args would be concerned about them – they had to go south.

The Type 21s* are also a cause for concern because of their aluminium superstructures, introduced in order to reduce top-weight. The suggestion is that they will burn easily if exposed to action damage. The MEO is more concerned about the possibility of bad cracking in the vigorous weather and seas of the South Atlantic. He was also saying that they might have a tendency to plunge suddenly by the stern if too much water gets into the after end.

During the Last Dog, with Richard Hurley on the Bridge as OOW, we altered course to identify an object in the water. It turned out to be a dead cow!

A junior rating, aged 19, put an official request in to his Divisional Officer for 'a gratuitous issue of 1 Cadbury's chocolate creme egg for having to be at sea on duty on Easter Sunday'. The Divisional Officer has approved the request and it has now gone to the Captain!

I have decided to read a Shakespeare sonnet and a psalm every day,

---

* Amazon Class frigates (*Ardent*, *Alacrity*, *Arrow*, *Active*, *Antelope* and *Ambuscade* were all in the conflict).

along with some other Shakespeare and Gibbon, just to establish some sort of routine.

Sunday, 4 April

We passed between Gran Canaria and Tenerife in the night.

Normally, Sundays at sea are programmed as less intense than other days of the week. Not today! We did have church on the focsle, with the reappearance of the Padre's 'organ, portable, small' as it appears in official naval stores inventories, which had been down for maintenance and was played by Commander S.

Overnight and during this morning, 406's sonar was removed and the aircraft converted to a long-range surveillance/load-lifting role with the addition of a fuel overload tank. We can also squeeze in a few more people – standing room only!

We were airborne in 406 for a surface search and over-the-horizon targeting serial between 0600 and 0800, providing contact details to the warships, and finished with a coordinated, dummy missile attack on an unsuspecting, innocent merchant ship. I also practised the low-level transit, pop-up, one sweep on the radar technique that we have devised to minimize our exposure to enemy radars and to electronic intercept.

The drop tank on the port carrier gives us greater range and we can cover more sea in a single sortie. We have also been developing special techniques to deal with Arg surface ships, especially the Type 42s. It involves staying low – down to 15 feet – for as long as possible and then popping up for a single sweep of the radar every now and then, to record as much as possible before the trace fades. Being in a single-engine helicopter at that altitude is an experience we are going to have to get used to. Ian reckons that we will not have much of a chance if the engine stops, even if we trade speed for height. Let's say that it's concentrating the pilots' minds a little. Fitz and I are just getting on with things; there is nothing we can do – if it happens, it happens – do you want to live for ever? However, it would be a shame and a waste to stoof in, practising for an operation that might not even happen further south though.

Having said that, I used to fly this type of profile when Laurie Hopkins, Pat Cosgrove and LACMN McDougall were on the Flight, and that was just so that we would win on NATO exercises – and it was good fun. It used to really piss Pat – as an American – off; he did not see the point in peacetime. We used to say that if you do not practise a bit on the edge, with the chance of an accident, in peacetime, you won't be able to do it in wartime. To his irritation and annoyance, I used to quote Rommel at him, 'Sweat saves blood, blood saves lives, and brains saves both.'

After refuelling and a brief pause, we spent the forenoon transferring the Admiral's staff, their baggage and copious files to *Glamorgan*, while she and *Plymouth* refuelled, and finally took the Admiral to *Glamorgan* at 1200. As he sat alongside me in Fitz's seat, he seemed to be happy to be going and *Glamorgan* had a huge reception committee waiting for him on the Flight Deck – Captain, Commander, Flight Commander and half a dozen other officers. It was just like a wedding meet-and-greet.

So, the Admiral has left us for *Glamorgan* and we hope that he is happy. We are!

Admittedly, *Glamorgan* does have a better communications fit than we do. She is our sister ship and is colloquially know as the 'Glamorous Organ'; consequently – or coincidentally – their aircraft is called 'Willie'! We get on well with our fellow Wessex 3 Flight aircrew, led by Lt Cdr Gerry Hunt (who is an Observer) – we are from the same squadron. However, there is considerable friendly rivalry between us. During a recent exercise off Scotland we were very competitive in trying to detect the 'enemy' submarines and were striving to outdo each other on virtually every occasion. We were probably more aggressive than them and, during some of the sorties, when life was a bit dull on the ASW screen, we used a battery-powered laughter generator on the air to distract them and to liven things up when they put out low-level contact reports.

Glamorgan Flight: 'YV1 – POSSUB Low 2 in position etc. over.'

406 (but unknown): 'Ha, ha, ha, ha, ha!'

Glamorgan (the ship): 'This is YV – say again, over.'

Glamorgan Flight YV1: 'I say again POSSUB Low 2 . . .'

406 (still unknown): 'Ha, ha, ha, ha, ha!'

Admiral (recognizable on the radio): 'Whoever is making this ridiculous noise on the circuit, you are to stop. You will be found with direction-finding equipment and will be disciplined!'

406 (anonymous): 'Ha, ha, ha, ha, ha!'

At the end of one sortie, we both returned to our respective ships. When we arrived at *Antrim*, having conducted a radio and radar silent approach, we found 'Willie' hovering astern of her and looking like he was shaping up for an approach to his own ship. The two ships were about two miles apart so it was a reasonable mistake to make, but finding your way back to your own ship is a real manhood issue for Observers. The letters 'A' and 'N' painted on the Flight Deck were a bit of a give-away, I would have thought!

I transmitted: 'DOLPHIN 117.'*

He flashed back: 'DOLPHIN 159.'†

We replenished from *Tidespring* this afternoon and passed mail and stores before breaking away at 1500. We have started to move ahead of the main force and are positioning for an anti-surface exercise tomorrow.

I offered to run some circuit training for officers who might want to get fit as we go south. I have called it FOCCIF (Flight Observer's Crash Course in Fitness) and, after a warm-up, it consists of repetitions of six basic exercises: press-ups, star-jumps, sit-ups, burpees, squat-thrusts and running on the spot. The idea is that you start off with 7 of each, then do 6, then 5 and so on and work down to 1 of each. We will progressively increase the repetitions by one every couple of days as people get fitter. I have ambitions that we might make it to 20 and hold it there. I ran the first session today and 11 officers turned up, including the Padre, a couple of the Greenies, Dec, the Doc and Carlos, who then went away to do some serious man mountain stuff on his own. We wear sports shoes; he wears DMS [direct moulded sole, but known to the boys as 'dem's my shoes'!] boots. I did my own session afterwards, while the Clubswinger‡ offered beginner and superstar variants.

We are struggling to get any decent intelligence about Argentina and the capability of her Armed Forces. Precious little has come by signal as yet and most of the information that I have has come from unclassified

---

* 'There's something you've forgotten/fucked up: cast an eye/ear round and see if you can sort it out before someone important notices.' The Dolphin code was a private code used by aviators for passing discreet messages.

† 'You're right, I blew it, but that doesn't entitle you to be cheeky. Stick in future to DOLPHIN 153.' ('You are far too senior for me to use anything else, but you can imagine what's going through my mind, can't you, sir.')

‡ The ship's Physical Training Instructor, a Petty Officer. 'Clubswinger' or 'Clubs' derives from the traditional formal exercise routine of swinging clubs in each hand onboard ships of the Victorian Navy.

books onboard (the encyclopedia and various ship's library books), as well as the navigational publications, including the Admiralty Pilot. *Plymouth* went back to Gibraltar and picked up some South Atlantic charts for everyone.

We lost South Georgia yesterday, but not without a fight by the sound of it. The signals indicate – and the World Service has confirmed – that *Endurance*'s Royal Marines detachment put up stiff resistance, fired a Carl Gustav missile and loads of small-arms rounds into the Arg A69 frigate *Guerrico* and shot down a Puma and possibly another helo as well. Well done, them! The Args seem to have had a lot of firepower and the Royals have all now been captured.

We are still not entirely confident that the government will not give in to American pressure at the moment, either to please them, or because they – the government – do not have the balls for a fight when it comes to it. The discussion in the Wardroom was that the government is bluffing in order to get a good deal in any negotiations. Nobody trusts the civil servants – the same ones who would have let the Nott Review cuts and stupidities go through on the nod. We reckon that the government cannot survive if we end up with any situation in which the Argentinians stay on the Islands.

At church, we prayed for a peaceful resolution, but I did not see much Christian charity on display around the ship, more like 'hard-favoured rage'.

The Admiral is firing off signals like there is no tomorrow, including one which states, 'the worst case which must be assumed is that by the time we get to Ascension, we could be in a state of war with Argentina.' Let's hope that gets people thinking about what is required.

I have worked out how far it is to Ascension from the UK – 4,200 miles – and from there to the Falklands – 3,750 miles. That is 7,950 miles!

Monday, 5 April

Today, we went into our tropical rig: short-sleeved shirts and 'empire-building' shorts, with sandals. Apart from official signals, our two main sources of information are the *Daily Oak*, which is a compilation of the newspapers at home put together by the watch-keepers at the satellite ground station at Oakhanger, and the BBC World Service. The *Daily Oak* is produced during peacetime, normally in the silent hours by the night watchmen, and is a really good synopsis of the day's news and a summary of the sport, including the football results.

Amazingly, two politicians – Lord Carrington and Richard Luce – have done the decent thing and resigned over the Falklands fiasco. I am not sure whether they are fully to blame, but their resignation would seem to be a lightning conductor for the rest of the government. The Prime Minister should really take some responsibility (it's her government, after all), together with the Foreign Office senior civil servants who were handing out the advice to appease the Junta and sell out the Islanders. Appease is the right word – giving in to fascist dictators is something, up to a point, that we have tended to do for too long in the past. And what message does it send to other countries which might want Gibraltar, Hong Kong and our other far-flung dependencies? No one will take us seriously in future.

We also heard that *Hermes* and *Invincible* are on their way, to a terrific, flag-waving and emotional send-off. This is getting serious and the Args are about to get their bluff called. *Fearless* and *Intrepid* are following with 3 Commando Brigade. I'd say that the despatch of a Task Force is a real risk. We are all up for it, but we are at the limits of our capabilities and I am not sure that we have the logistic resources to sustain a campaign for long.

So, having messed things up, I suppose that the government has no choice but to do something pretty decisive, maybe forceful. The diplomatic stuff now under way could be tricky for the UK and it could still mean the end of this government if we end up losing the Islands. I get the feeling that the rest of the world, especially the US, just wants a quiet life with this one.

We flew a two-hour sortie of surface search and over-the-horizon targeting during the night/day period this morning. It seems strange not to have the sonar in the cab, but the new arrangements mean that we can stay airborne for longer.

All day, the ship's company conducted a lot of operational and general training, especially section and team drills, in the areas of Damage Control, electrical and emergency power runs, and mechanical failures. The Ops Room has been sorting out the required reactions to likely Arg threats and practising coordination of chaff* and other complicated drills designed to make us look a less attractive target. While we were airborne, the ship conducted gunnery drills and the Royal Marines did their thing with their rifles and support weapons.

At the command level, we have general briefs every day now, which start with the political, diplomatic and military situation as it unfolds. They also include meteorology, whole ship training, lessons from FOST [Flag Officer Sea Training] and other sources, intelligence and warfare preparedness. The MEs and WEs also give us remarkably candid (first time that!) assessments of the state of the various engineering and electronic systems, weapon effectiveness and operational deficiencies. The whole thing is wrapped up with an assessment of logistic sustainability, personnel issues and morale. Afterwards, I give my fellow officers instructions in how to recognize Arg ships, submarines and aircraft. The level of detail and immediate recognition are second nature and necessary for aircrew, but something new for the fish-heads,† who normally have the ability and leisure to reach for *Jane's Fighting Ships* whenever they see an unfamiliar vessel.

A programme of specific briefs has also been arranged, to orientate ourselves as we head south. Various officers have been lurked to prepare talks on South American countries, the Falkland Islands, the environment and other related topics. The Doctor is scheduled to give Teach Yourself First Aid and Resuscitation, as well as specific briefs on cold weather precautions, burns and wounding, not just to us, but to the ship's company as well. Not surprisingly, emergency stations, life raft drills and survival techniques have become subjects of fascination too, all of a sudden.

I have to prepare presentations on Prisoner Handling and Tactical Questioning, Arg air assets, our own air assets and a big one on Argentina and its culture. In addition, owing to popular demand, I am preparing two sessions of Beginners' Spanish. I can't wait!

We flew another surface search and over-the-horizon targeting serial between 1830 and 2030, during which we checked the ship's darken-ship routine and deceptive lighting (this has *Antrim* rigged to look like a

* Decoys comprising hundreds of thousands of metallic strips, fired from special rockets or the 4.5 inch guns and dropped manually by helicopters, designed to confuse and distract radars and missiles.
† Seaman officers, as opposed to aviators.

merchant ship at night). The deceptive arrangements – displaced navigation and steaming lights and a necklace of white lights either side of the Flight Deck – looked pretty convincing and would fool anyone without a good night vision device. We had just enough time to shower, catch a late dinner and the film (we missed the Mickey Duck). The film was the Michael Caine war film *Play Dirty*. A Second World War drama, exciting – but not a great ending!

We received a nice signal from the CO of the QRIH[*] – 'our thoughts and best wishes are with you in all your endeavours' – and from 2 Royal Irish[†] – 'To Flagship Irish Navy. If you are on your way to the South Atlantic, suggest you offload all corned beef, and re-supply with Irish Stew! There are 650 of us here willing to help peel the spuds for you! Good Luck. No Surrender and *Faugh a Ballagh*.' From 5 Royal Irish – 'Good luck and God speed, we are cheering you all the way. *Faugh a Ballagh*.'

The Commander told me that *Faugh a Ballagh* should be *Fág an Bealach*. Meaning 'Clear the way!' it originates with a battle-cry of Sergeant Patrick Masterson at the battle of Barrosa, when, with an officer, he captured a French Imperial Eagle. He was supposed to have cried, 'Be Jabers, boys, I have the Cuckoo!' I hope that this is true!

I could not help noticing that the Commander had a book on his desk about camouflaging ships in the Second World War.

FOCCIF is starting to catch on – we had a few more join us just before flying. Meanwhile, the Clubswinger's fitness sessions for both superstars and ordinary mortals are attended by more and more people now. The 'Fight the Flab' campaign is picking up too. Be Jabers!

I have brought a Bullworker with me, initially to help with fitness while on Spring Train, expecting to be back for Easter. I remember when we were operating in Northern Ireland and had to refuel at Bessbrook, behind an RAF Wessex 2 which was emplaning soldiers in civvies, obviously just off for some R&R. They each had a tightly packed holdall with their kit and, as they ran out, suddenly the rotor blades on the Wessex started breaking up. What had happened was that one of the soldiers had compressed a Bullworker into one of these holdalls and the thing, under pressure, had broken the zip and flown up into the blades. Did we laugh?!

[*] Queen's Royal Irish Hussars – a twinned Army regiment.
[†] Royal Irish Regiment – another twinned Army regiment.

Tuesday, 6 April

Overnight, the ship opened out ahead with *Plymouth* so that we could conduct a simulated attack against *Coventry* and *Brilliant*, which were posing as Arg destroyers. The Admiral of course still thinks that this is what we will be doing later this month. We flew a double-hop surface search and targeting mission from 0600 to 0930, during which we successfully located and 'engaged' the opposition with Exocets and used *Plymouth*'s Wasp to attack with AS-12s. We also laid three dummy formations with Chaff Hotel to confuse *Coventry*'s Lynx, which was targeting for the other side. We watched him go round and waste his time looking at nothing in particular and the tactic gave us more time to work out a firing solution before the opposition knew where our ships really were. I had a slight personal interest as the Observer of the *Coventry* Lynx is Alvin Rich, who was one of my instructors on 737 Squadron. I do not think that he rated my abilities as a trainee Observer very highly, so it was time to show him what I have learned!

The surface action exercise ended with an offset shoot by the 4.5 guns against *Coventry* and *Brilliant*. These firings use real shells, but are offset from the target by 6 or 12 degrees so that you do not actually hit the ships, and there are numerous safeguards built into the checks. That's the theory anyway! We sometimes practise using the helicopter as the target and it is pretty unnerving to have guns pointing almost at you and seeing the shells explode close by!

The Captain and the Padre went to *Plymouth* today, using her Wasp, but I am not sure why. The Royal Marines have been calibrating their weapons again and blazing away off the back end. It's pretty warm now, but we had a steady 20 knot breeze from the south for most of the day.

Now *Fearless* has sailed – that is the first clear indication to the Args that we intend to retake the Islands rather than blockade them.

Thank goodness – a signal has come in from CINCFLEET, oddly addressed to everyone, telling the Admiral in words of one syllable to reassess the Arg threat. It's a bit of a public rebuke. Hopefully, his obsession with anti-surface operations and his state of denial with regard to the air threat will end now.

The big question is whether the Args have extended the runway at Stanley, to permit staging and refuelling operations by their Mirages, Daggers and Skyhawks; the Navy Trackers could also operate from there. They would be absolutely negligent in not doing it. We have had intelligence reports that 'swept-winged' aircraft have been detected there, but SCO and Duncan Ford think that these might be decoys or dummies. I reckon that they might be Aermacchis.

We are now gearing up for something. Recognition training – learning to differentiate friendly and likely hostile ships and aircraft – is being stepped up (I have been conducting most of it, for the officers and the ship's company); the maintainers are very active in repairing and restoring equipment that has been left unserviceable in the light of other priorities and beer is being rationed (senior rates two pints, junior rates two cans per day).

Alasdair is lining everyone up to have jabs – mostly yellow fever and tetanus – and ensuring that everyone's blood group is known. From Ascension, all compartments will be routinely unlocked, or, if containing valuable, attractive or confidential material, secured with a padlock. People are also being urged not to tamper with or damage kit that might save their lives if it comes to a fight and report defective items. Someone who is bored keeps unpicking wires in the queue for meals in the Junior Rates' Dining Hall!

On a hot, hazy day, people have been out on the upper deck in the sun, but there is no sun cream in the NAAFI! We also saw lots of flying fish. Someone pointed out that Exocets are flying fish and we all hoped that it was not a bad omen.

The Commander is trying to get the ship as squared away as possible before we reach Ascension, with pleas to huck out compartments, deep-clean the ship and ditch unnecessary items. There will be an extensive Rounds routine in four days' time to inspect the results and check where the ship needs further work to secure it for action. Tonight, Daily Orders pronounced, more in hope than expectation, 'Neptune only visits clean ships', in anticipation of the Crossing the Line Ceremony at the Equator in a few days' time. In my experience, His Majesty is not that fussy!

We heard today that a forward supply base has been set up on Ascension Island, with a Naval Party and that air groups have embarked in their ships in the UK. We are speculating whether the Chileans are going to let us use their air bases for stationing aircraft. I bet that they won't. It would invite attacks on Chile by Argentina and the Chileans have to live with the Args even after it is all over. If the Args manage to face us down, that would make it difficult for the Chileans.

A lot more people are attending keep fit in the Dogs, both the beginners' and the superstars' sessions.

Wednesday, 7 April

We had a really early Call the Hands this morning, in order to conduct a VERTREP and RAS with *Tidespring*. Stewart and Fitz flew the sortie, between 0645 and 0830, while Ian and I had briefings and meetings with the ship's warfare team to iron out a few procedural and operational wrinkles. The RAS was between 0700 and 0800. From 1200 to 1430, we conducted another surface action, with *Plymouth* as the target.

There has been lots of talk on the World Service and on the news signals that merchant ships are being requisitioned, including *Canberra*, for war service. I wonder if it will actually come to anything, although I am not sure how the Args are going to back down without losing face. Still, if the US tells them to do it, surely they will.

I read in the *Daily Oak* that the Soviets reckon that Argentina is striking a blow against imperialism and colonialism in capturing the Falklands. Well, I'd say that that is pretty predictable. The US is now calling for discussions with both ambassadors separately in Washington. The Args have offered compensation to all those Islanders who are willing to leave and have said that they are unlikely to remove troops before any negotiations. Are they just posturing or do they mean it?

It seems that the US Secretary of State, General Haig, is planning to visit the UK and Argentina. Why is the US sitting on the fence? Surely, they are going to support us – we are the wronged party and one of their staunchest allies. I hope that they do not think that they can play the honest broker and still have a good relationship with the UK afterwards.

Also, the government has declared a 200-mile maritime Exclusion Zone around the Falkland Islands from 0440 on 12 April. That must coincide with when one or more of our SSNs can reach there. The diplomats will have to get their skates on if conflict is going to be avoided, although the view in the Wardroom is that the government will not have the will to start a shooting war even if the SSNs are in position.

The big news this afternoon was that Operation Paraquet has been announced. *Antrim* has been designated as the leader of Task Group 317.9 and ordered to go ahead and recover South Georgia, along with *Plymouth*, *Tidespring* and possibly *Endurance*. We have been ordered to proceed with despatch – flat out – with *Plymouth* and *Tidespring* to Ascension to meet up with *Fort Austin* and *Endurance*. We are going to receive some troops at Ascension. There has been discussion about what this might mean and some of our TOP SECRET-cleared senior officers (dubbed the 'Secret Squirrels') seem to know.

We detached and went ahead at 1600 and at 1800 passed *Sheffield* heading back north towards the main force.

Tonight, the Supply Officer sent a memo around telling everyone that they should make a will. This has suddenly focused attention on reality and a couple of the lads on the Flight want my help in formulating their wills. Interestingly, the memo says, 'sending wills to your immediate family in the current circumstances may cause unnecessary anxiety' – no kidding! The recommendation is that they are all collected and held centrally ashore at HMS *Centurion*.

We are pretty sure that it will all be over soon and that this run down into the South Atlantic will be an exercise in showing that we are prepared to do something about our far-flung dependencies. None of us can believe right now that it will come to blows. This sort of thing just does not happen between countries in the Western world.

However, you could not pick a more convenient foe – a military, tinpot dictatorship, with an appalling record of treating its people badly. Even so, I thought that, with all the English investment in Argentina since the 19th century, we rather got on with the Argentinian people and that they actually liked us, except for that match in the 1966 football World Cup.

We are not sure how to assess the Argentinian capabilities. They seem to have had a border war with Bolivia in the nineteenth century, but, apart from murdering their own people, have not had any experience of modern war. Intelligence indicates that their aviators might be pretty competent; the Israelis trained them and appear reasonably impressed, although they think that natural flair is constrained by over-rigid command and control and corrupt practices. Their jets don't seem to fly at night. We are uncertain about whether they have managed to hook up the Exocets to their Etendards.

The boys onboard are saying that the Argentinians mostly descend from Italians and that this accounts for various national characteristics. Let's hope it extends to fighting at sea, which, on recent history, would help a lot.

I have been giving some thought to going into action. It is quite exhilarating in a way. You spend most of your career training for something that might never happen. If you do not see action, then it's like being a doctor who trains for years and never has the chance to make a diagnosis or cure anyone. So, what am I thinking?

- I will find out whether I actually have the balls for this sort of thing. You assume that you do when you join up and sustain the belief or illusion though all sorts of rituals and routines, but deep down you never really know until it happens. You cannot tell if you have never been in danger.
- Perhaps some things – duty, honour, loyalty and getting the job done – appear more important – at the time – than survival.
- Mark Twain said that courage is resistance to fear, mastery of fear – not absence of fear. In *Julius Caesar*, Shakespeare says, 'Cowards die many times before their deaths; the valiant never taste of death but once.'
- Flying operationally helps test your assumptions. You always have to perform well in the air and if you do not your chums are quick to spot any weaknesses and tell you about it. You can also get yourself killed!
- When we were in Northern Ireland, we had a number of hairy moments, mainly implicit rather than explicit, but the sense of threat was always there, especially when we operated in South Armagh or were taking under-slung fuel down to the boats on Carlingford Lough.
- I think that very few are actually brave by nature. Discipline, routine and training seem to count for a lot, together with a sense of responsibility to your country and people around you.
- I remember reading one of Nelson's letters to his wife, which expressed the view that the brave man dies once, but a coward knows he's been a coward every day for the rest of his life.
- If your number's up, it's up.
- No excuses if you are not as fully prepared as you need to be when you meet the enemy.
- We have the finest naval heritage in the world – what would Blake, Nelson, Drake say if you screwed up?
- You cannot take the Queen's shilling and bale out when the time comes.

Guide me, O Thou great Jehovah,
Pilgrim through this barren land.
I am weak, but Thou art mighty;
Strong Deliverer, Strong Deliverer,
Be Thou still my strength and shield.

The thing about being at sea and flying is that you never do it for practice. You never put to sea or go flying except for real; it's the same with submariners, who never dive for practice. That means that we exercise in peacetime pretty close to our wartime limits. I suppose that it is the same with the RAF.

It does not make any difference to your chances whether you are scared or brave, so you might as well be brave and do your duty.

You do not know how you are going to react until the moment comes. Of course, you assume that you will be OK when you put the uniform on, go through all the training and prepare for things that are a distant, doubtful prospect at best. Have you got the bottle, that's the nagging question?

The present worry onboard is that we are used to dealing with the Soviets and their allies, not people fitted with Western kit or using our tactics. Nevertheless, we do a lot of exercising in the North Atlantic and we are used to being at sea under challenging conditions, so that has to count for something down there. The Schoolie* said that the weather is likely to be absolutely dreadful one day in three down there and will severely affect our operations. Sounds like the submariners will dip in and benefit big style!

I am pretty optimistic about our chances and am not concerned about what will happen. I am sure that we will be fine. If you are a good person, good things happen to you. If they don't, that's just the breaks. I just have to make sure that I have all the skills necessary to give me the best chance of success and survival in any situation and to make sure that I do not let anyone down.

Thursday, 8 April

The details of the South Georgia operation firmed up this morning. We will take *Tidespring* and *Plymouth* to collect a company of marines,

* David Stanesby, the ship's Instructor and Education Officer, who was the Meteorological Officer as well.

ammunition and stores from Ascension, as well as two Wessex Vs (for *Tidespring*) and meet up with *Endurance*. Apparently, *Fort Austin* is already well ahead, down track and almost at Ascension and is going to rendezvous with – and store –*Endurance* on 11 April. We have been told to be at Ascension by first thing on 10 April and off South Georgia by 21 April, ready for an immediate landing and assault.

The day has been spent sailing in company with *Tidespring* and *Plymouth*, with the Master of *Tidespring* (Captain Redmond) and the CO of *Plymouth* (Captain Pentreath) coming over for lunch and a chat with the Captain and the Heads of Department.

At midday, I went out on the upper deck and saw two Soviet Bear D maritime reconnaissance aircraft at about six miles and 200 feet, probably operating out of Luanda, which clearly wanted to identify our individual units.

The boys on the Flight have been painting the aircraft all blue to reduce its visibility and have suppressed the roundels and other features that previously stood out. The distinctive yellow top, designed to allow other aircraft to see the helo when it is in the dip or at low level, has gone. The cab looks much more war-like now.

Meanwhile, we have been trying to work out how the Args might play it if we do actually go all the way down to the South Atlantic. The SCO, Duncan Ford and the Captain seem to think that the Args will see how the even-handed, sit-on-the-fence approach of the US goes, relying on the fact that the US needs them to stave off Communism in South America. Most of us in the Wardroom reckon that now that they have got hold of the Falklands, the Args will not want to let them go. The big question is whether our SSNs will be allowed to start operations against the Args when they arrive and stop them consolidating their position on the Islands by bringing in more and more men, equipment and weapons. The press are pessimistic about a diplomatic solution, even though the US is trying to broker a deal that will avoid conflict.

Also, we have been trying to get some information about South Georgia. CINCFLEET has promised to glean information from the BAS [British Antarctic Survey] scientists who are supposed to be there still, in and around Grytviken, and out in various huts, taking readings and samples, getting cold.

Friday, 9 April

We crossed the Equator in the early morning and, of course, we awoke with the knowledge that we would be visited by King Neptune in the afternoon, culminating in the traditional Crossing the Line Ceremony. Actually, his intentions in this regard had been signalled in a temporary memorandum on 7 April.

I received a telegram from A saying that I had been selected for this year's BBC *Mastermind* competition; hopefully, the crisis will peter out and we will be turned around in time for me to be able to take part this year. I have started, but I might not get the chance to finish!

Ian and I lifted and shifted various stores around *Antrim*, *Tidespring* and *Plymouth* between 0900 and 1000, after which the ship was replenished with fuel from *Tidespring* between 1045 and 1200. I was not able to go to Good Friday church. At 1300, I gave a brief to the senior rates about Argentina and the threat posed by their Armed Forces. I also gave them some handy Spanish phrases, the most popular of which were '*¿Tiene una hermana?*'*, '*Mi bebida se siente sola. ¿Te gustaría acompañarme con la tuya?*'† and '*¡Mi amigo pagara!*'‡

Breakfast conversation in the Wardroom centred on those officers who had not crossed the Equator by sea before – quite a few as it happened. It was evident that Declan, Alasdair and I were all going to get our hair wet that afternoon. I reconciled myself to the ritual humiliation, good-natured joshing and dunking that normally accompany these occasions. The event is a combination of initiation rite and a caricature of baptism, all good-humoured, enormous fun for everyone and with scrupulous attention to the ceremonial, sequence and detail. I am not sure about its origins, but the characters and ritual are set in stone, with all the authority of folk-memory and tribal attachment.

As is traditional and proper, the Chiefs, under the direction of Chippy Gent, have been putting it all together. It's an interesting time for an officer, an occasion when you get to find out what the ship's company thinks of you – good or ill!

---

* 'Do you have a sister?'
† 'My drink is getting lonely. Would you like to join me with yours?'
‡ 'My friend will pay.'

King Neptune (Chief Oliver) arrived on board (he actually emerged from the Hull Office after a few beers) at about 1430, with appropriate faux deference and ceremonial, was greeted by the Captain and processed, with his entourage, to the Flight Deck, where a large timber and canvas pool filled with sea water about four feet deep had been erected, courtesy of the shipwrights. It was made out of Damage Control timbers, Buffer's rope and cordage, as well as spare canvas.

The burlesque entourage consisted of King Neptune himself, Queen Amphitrite (Chief Osborne, for crying out loud!), complete with fetching attire and manmade-fibre wig, a Lord Chancellor (Chief Marshall), a Royal Physician (Chief Woods), a Chief of Police (MAA Quade, appropriately!), Sweeney Todd the Barber (Chief Ellis) along with his assistant (Chief Godfrey), four policemen (to round up the miscreants who have offended the Court) and the Bears (on duty in the pool, to ensure everyone is well and truly dunked/drowned). These included the formidable quartet of RPO Key, the Buffer (Chief Graham), Chief Yeoman Cosker and Daisy Adams. The Court was accompanied by a bevy of elders (various Chiefs, looking alternately sage, shifty, conspiratorial and unsteady, or was it the booze?) and a set of six 'sea-nymphs' (sourced mostly from the younger junior rates), dressed and made up rather too convincingly among a ship's company that had not seen a woman for a while. I was left wondering where all the kit (stockings, suspenders and slinky dresses) came from and, more to the point, where it was stowed onboard!

I noticed that the Buffer was still wearing his beret right up to the time that he had to don his 'bear' mask. The thing is normally moulded to the contours of his head and I have always thought that it would have to be surgically removed. He really never gets separated from it!

I should record at this point that the ship was passing through a rainstorm of tropical proportions and we were all soaking wet from the start. But it was warm and, while the fun was proceeding, no one really cared about the weather.

The disappointing thing was that the Padre had a walk-on part in the Royal Entourage as the Chaplain Royal and wasn't scheduled to be given the treatment. I was sure that he had not crossed the Line before and harboured dark thoughts.

Happily, I was not designated as one of the defaulters, singled out for particular attention and treatment, so was happy to join the enthusiastic throng who gave a good pantomime impression of what their forebears would have been like at public executions. However, I was on the list for mass baptism and humiliation and took my turn in the queue, thinking that it must have been like this waiting for the guillotine. When it came to my turn in the ducking stool, I was doused in a dye-coloured, flour-based substance that immediately stuck fast to my clothes and skin and I was covered in foam. We went through the motions of a mock shave; I had revolting pastels put in my mouth and Swarfega was combed into my hair. The Padre thought that it was great fun and was laughing.

Just before I went backwards into the pool, I grabbed the Padre and in we went in together. I was given a few friendly dunks (thanks, guys) in the 'green mantle of the standing pool'* that passed for water, but the Padre made the mistake of protesting and struggling. The Bears did not seem to care who they dunked, so the Padre got the full treatment and I joined in to help dunk him. After all, how many children has he dunked/dropped during christenings?! I climbed out, my mouth feeling like it was on fire and wondering how many microbes and unmentionables had been in that water.

Later on, while we were playing uckers before dinner, a sonar contact was called by *Antrim* and we and *Plymouth* went through the motions of investigating, while *Tidespring* was told to move away rapidly from the area. I would love to help, guys, but you've taken the sonar out of my aircraft. I am still not happy about that, especially as we are now heading off on our own away from the ASW support available in the carriers and the Main Group.

There has also been a serious disagreement between the Captain and the Royal Marines, in the form of Major General Royal Marines back in the UK, over the embarkation of men, stores and ammunition for the South Georgia operation, which became rather fractious. It's all been agreed now, but the Royal Marines were being a bit precious about what they see as their specialist area.

The Commander in his evening chat to the ship's company emphasized the importance of preparing ourselves for extreme cold, foul weather and the heavy seas in the South Atlantic.

Commander E, in the meantime, has been doing his bit to get his department in the mood. He issues daily short situation reports – in words of one syllable, very readable and succinct – to the officers and

* From Shakespeare's *King Lear*.

ratings, interpreting everything from the diplomatic efforts to important issues onboard. In anticipation of us having extra personnel onboard, he has a declared a 'be nice to Booty week', encouraging his people to make the visitors welcome and show them the ropes (very traditional!).

We heard some interesting comments on the World Service this evening describing our military deployment, with various experts saying that even the US would think twice about mounting such an operation. I am not entirely sure that assessment is accurate, but it is good that we are reacting in ways that people did not expect.

I have just written to A, 'a jumble of instructions, emotions and thoughts', enclosing some 'Familygrams' and details of concessionary telegrams for her use, in anticipation of mail getting off at Ascension. The Familygrams, one a week and a maximum of 30 words, are transmitted by CINCFLEET when operational traffic on the communications system allows. I have said that we ought to use them for news of major events and emergencies, rather than chit-chat; it seems a bit mean, but I really do not want details of our personal life available to be read and discussed by the ROs down in the MCO.

I explained why I could not tell her anything about what we might be doing. I said that I thought that the government was committed to a hard line, with an ultimatum coming into force on Monday, and that everyone was apprehensive and excited about what we might be doing in future.

I also had to explain what we needed to organize with regard to money matters and savings, which have been thrown completely by this sudden diversion south. I included some signed cheques and my Cashpoint details. I asked her to organize a holiday to Spain in August, booking now, at a time when the Apex flights are cheap, and gambling on us being able to take leave when she is off work. I needed her to go and explain about my library books, which are overdue and I do not want to be hammered by the fines. I wanted her to write to *Mastermind* explaining my predicament and also told her that I had made a will today that was witnessed by Stewart and Carlos. It will be despatched from Ascension to my parents. I pointed out that this might be tempting fate and was a bit morbid, but that this simple form was recognized in law as a binding will – and costs nothing!

Finally, I said that I was realistic but confident about what might happen, but that I felt, genuinely, that everything would be all right. I appreciated how rotten it must be for her, not knowing what was going on and having to deal with so many things on her own down in Dorset. What can you say really, though? I cannot write and say that it all seems a tremendous adventure – a real break with expectations and the routine of normal life – and that I would not miss it for the world. Is it a man thing? I am sure that no one in his right mind would wish himself in harm's way, but the prospect of action and the chance to prove oneself in the most testing of circumstances do give a definite edge and meaning to one's life. It's crazy, but I will be disappointed if this crisis fizzles out. I would probably need to look for new challenges outside the Royal Navy.

Saturday, 10 April

We are in the South Atlantic! That has an exciting ring to it, suggestive of adventure and the romantic days of exploration, and, for those of us used to operating in the North Atlantic, it seems somehow liberating.

I woke up with the lingering, bitter taste of whatever had gone into my mouth during the Crossing the Line Ceremony the previous day. It felt like it had taken the enamel off my teeth. Despite this minor inconvenience and the worry that my breath might knock down a tiger at 20 yards, Ian and I took the cab into Ascension, taking off at 0705, with the Commander, Commander S, Mike Petheram and the mail, and returning at 0925. Whilst ashore, I intended to scrounge charts and maps of the South Atlantic, as well as anything else that I thought might be useful. As we transited, the volcanic island emerged shimmering out of the early-morning haze, looking like it was floating in the middle of the ocean. In fact, it looked smaller in area than its 62 square miles, but higher than its nominal 2,700 feet.

The scene at Wideawake airfield (named after a tern) was remarkable and I was surprised by what I saw. The runway is huge and has a pronounced dip in the middle, so you cannot see the end when you land. Apart from the US presence, the UK organization ashore had been up and running for about a week, based around a Naval Party. As well as routine US aircraft that seemed to be there to refuel as they crossed the Atlantic, there were Belfast and Hercules transports on the tarmac. A VC10 arrived while we were there and disgorged a lot of mail and people. The island was also bristling with communications masts and aerials and I wondered whether I would get the chance to phone home.

Most importantly, Wessex Vs were already flying around and these started ferrying stores – mostly cold weather clothing, specialist Arctic warfare equipment and miscellaneous ship's stores – and military personnel – out to *Antrim* while we were ashore. Two Wessex Vs from 845 'C' Flight were to embark in *Tidespring*; they had been transported down to Ascension by a Short Brothers Belfast that had been chartered from a civilian firm from Stansted in Essex.

Ian and I completed two separate two-and-a-half-hour load-lifting and transfer sorties, bringing stores, goods and people from Ascension out to the ship. Stewart and Fitz cracked on with Flight chores, paperwork and returns and did some ground training, as well as assisting with the management of the loads and other Flight Deck activities.

We brought some Army officers and other ranks onboard, who all looked and chatted like part of a team. There's an eccentric but extremely amiable Lieutenant Colonel, called Keith Eve, and two fit-looking, younger officers, 'Chris' and 'Willie' and a heap of kit, which included Bergens★ and Arctic clothing (a clue there, I think!). They looked knackered when they arrived and promptly disappeared, although they emerged pretty promptly for supper that night, saying that they had come down on a VC10 to Ascension. Everyone was thinking that they were SAS and nobody in the Wardroom wanted to ask. Then the Doctor said, quite unexpectedly, 'If you are SAS, I need to know, because I might not have enough security clearance to treat you if you get ill. After all, you guys have to get ill sometimes!' Everyone held their breath waiting for the put-down.

'No,' said 'Chris'. 'We're Naval Gunfire Forward Observers and the colonel is a Naval Gunfire Liaison Officer.'

'Right, of course, I thought that you were,' said the Doctor, confidently, without knowing what the hell he was talking about.

Also, we picked up a fairly taciturn RM Major Sheridan and Captain Chris Nunn, who looked at me as if he recognized me. He should have done as he was a Staff Officer at Dartmouth when I was there, with a not too sympathetic or supportive view of 'grads' [graduates], as I recall. He still has not worked it out. Sheridan has taken the cabin formerly occupied by the Admiral and the Admiral's Day Cabin is now appar-

---

★ Rucksacks configured for Arctic conditions.

ently transformed into an Operations and Planning Room that is off-limits to mere mortals.

By the time that we finished, the ship had anchored in the one place that was shallow enough (the anchor was out to eight shackles). In the meantime, we had acquired about 30 decidedly fit, quiet and determined-looking soldiers or Marines who were not immediately keen to let us know who they were. The word went round that they were Special Air Service.

As I was not going to fly again that day, Declan, who had done the Middle the previous night, and I decided that we would help around the ship. We volunteered to paint out the ship's pennant number on the port side. We went down a ladder onto a paint stage that had been rigged over the ship's side and, to the amusement ('Officers getting their hands dirty!') and bemusement ('Why volunteer for anything, especially if you are an officer?') of the part-of-ship seamen, did our bit for the 'war effort'. In the sun, the colour of the sea was a deep, translucent blue and one could see clearly down to about 30 feet.

While we were over the side, we joked about the ship moving under the South Atlantic swell, with the boyish excitement of people who had never been in the South Atlantic before. We also chatted about whether we would actually get to go down to the Falklands. We discussed whether we would actually go to war and decided on balance that it would not actually come to any fighting – it would all blow over before we got to go anywhere near a crisis. That would be disappointing, but that thought is pretty silly. You would have to be bonkers to wish yourself in a war, wouldn't you? But that is what we have been trained to do and there are questions that need answering. How would we react? Have we got what it takes? How good is the RN? Really?

What I particularly remember was a mass of small black fish coming up to the surface to feed on what was coming out of the outfall from the ship's heads. We both saw bigger fish lurking in the depths, seemingly waiting for us to fall off our perch. This induced a serious attack of 'let's get the job done' and a swift displacement away from the scary-looking fish – and those teeth!

Stewart and Fitz flew a long three-hour, day-night VERTREP and passenger serial from 1730, but the transfers continued well into the night using the Ascension-based helos. Meanwhile, the Wessex Vs were ferrying a whole company of Royals out to *Tidespring*, again with all their kit.

The Chinese laundry guys are not keen to stay and will be taken off before we leave Ascension, although Number One (Mr Suen Ling Kan) is prepared to stick around with us. The Junior Officers Under Training (JOUTs) are happy to stay, especially Mike Petheram and Bob Tarrant, and are anxious not to dip out by being sent home for their Officer of the Watch course. They are keeping very quiet and out of the way, so that they are not noticed and cannot be found. Fritz Heritier is making noises about going home and doesn't understand why Mel Camp has not pitched up – I reckon that he is in for the duration. No bad thing, though, he's good, if a bit grumpy about still being here.

Sunday, 11 April

Today was Easter Sunday and we each had cream eggs on our plates at breakfast. We in the Flight have been flying VERTREP and other transfer serials all day. It has been quite tiring one way or the other, but I now have some half-decent charts of the South Atlantic and maps of South Georgia. I am not sure how accurate they are though. Miraculously, we received mail, but, as I was busy all day, I did not have time to dash off a letter to A or anyone else. Our Land Rover has been put ashore – bet that is the last we see of that!

Plymouth and *Tidespring* departed late this morning, while *Antrim* remained behind to complete the transfer of stores (cold weather clothing, medical) and personnel that had not yet arrived by air. I did not even have the chance to go to church. The ship weighed anchor at 0915 and has been steaming a racetrack just off the runway to the west all day, apart from a top-up replenishment this afternoon. *Glamorgan*, *Sheffield* and *Appleleaf* appeared at about 1700 and 'Willie' landed on deck, to pick up some spares, before departing, plastered with *Antrim* Flight and Humphrey stickers. Ha-ha! Well done, boys.

Ian and I did most of the flying throughout the day, with the last serial completing at 0100 just now.

About 1930, we were just about to lift from the airfield to return to the ship on one run, when a dishevelled-looking Army type, dressed in combats and a smock, jumped in the aircraft and simply, amid the noise, shouted: '*Antrim!*', in the manner of someone jumping into a London cab and shouting: 'Waterloo!' He sort of strapped himself in, looked around as if to say 'Does this thing really fly?' and seemed not to care for ear defenders. He had longish, gingery hair and cool, intelligent eyes and looked like the sort of chap that did not give a toss about anything. While I sat in the door, he came up to join me and watch as we approached the ship.

It turns out that he is an SAS Major called, improbably, 'Cedric', and he is coming to South Georgia with us. I am glad that he is on our side. He disappeared as soon as we handed over to the Flight Deck team and we have not seen him since.

We have also picked up the *Endurance* survey team that was left behind on the Falklands when the ship dashed off to try and support Keith Mills at South Georgia. We are going to return them to their ship. I know Chris Todhunter and there is another officer, Lieutenant Richard Ball, plus one senior rate and four junior rates. They have been telling us how they were included in the defence of Stanley and Government House. Interestingly, they reckon that the Args have brought in enough kit, vehicles and stores to enable them to hold out in the long term and that they were unlikely to give up without a fight. They also said that they had been treated well by the Args when in captivity and while on their way home. We have been asking them about conditions in the Falklands and South Georgia and the Commander has asked them to give a couple of briefs to the officers and the warfare teams.

Our Chinese laundry team did decide that there is going to be a war and have left. Number One has opted to stay – good for him – and it looks like members of the ship's company will have to do their bit, if we are to maintain any semblance of good order and decency in our uniforms, flying garments and other working clothes, not to mention sports kit!

A's letter said that she had contacted Portland for information about whether *Antrim* Flight was going to be back as planned or would be away a bit longer. She did not press for details. Apparently, she received a decidedly rude and dismissive response from the duty staff in the Operations Room. I need to sort that out somehow, especially if this situation deteriorates. Also, it seems that A has had to enter into negotiations with Lloyds in Dorchester in order to access my bank account and pay. Happily, I sent some cheques from Gibraltar before we left and, now that I have sent my PIN, she can use my new Cashpoint card, which should have been waiting for me at home.

12 April – Easter Monday

We are now about 16 degrees south, but, during the night and forenoon, ran into a heavy sea, with winds of 35–40 knots ahead. We did not fly as the boys needed the cab for routine maintenance. At 1330, we went to Action Stations for the first time since Spring Train, to test the procedures, check that all the necessary kit was in place and to practise drills. Most of the time was spent ensuring that we had full watertight integrity and that our hatches were all serviceable. It is amazing that people are suddenly keen on snug, tight-fitting hatches and watertight seals, as well as clips that do not need too much brute force to operate!

We also had a Damage Control exercise while at Action Stations, as part of our preparations for war. The assessment is that we have a lot more to do to get up to scratch – we have not quite covered the requirement to Float, Move and Fight under conditions of damage and other pressures. The Rover Gas Turbine pump, as usual, refused to run up on demand. We need it, as it's the only stand-alone pump that can support our fire main if we lose all the other main pumps or have a major breach.

It is interesting that people are taking it really seriously. You see none of the loafing and going through the motions that characterize the routine Damage Control exercises and training in some of the remote areas of the ship. I have never seen the lads take so much care over their kit – they are really keen to know how to use the pumps and all the other stuff. Other people are very relaxed about it all – I went down to the 4.5 turret to talk to the boys there and found them all playing with Rubik's cubes, even the Leading Hand in the visual position.

We finally caught up with *Plymouth* and *Tidespring* in the late afternoon. *Plymouth* passed by light: 'Is it Paraquet or Paraquat we are doing?' The operation is called Paraquet, although everyone is saying Paraquat, because a proprietary weed killer somehow seems more appropriate in the circumstances. Paraquat is already appearing in signals!

The Marine Engineering Officer from *Plymouth* came across to give us a brief on the Falklands and South Georgia, complete with slides. He had spent time with the BAS before and was good. We are continuing our preparations to be fully ready for war and cold weather operations, topping up with different oils and fluids, by 15 April.

The World Service seems to think that there is likely to be a diplomatic settlement. The view in the Wardroom was that we would probably continue heading southwards anyway because the government would want to demonstrate some 'presence', even if the Args decided to pull out for now. It looks like we will reach South Georgia on or about 21 April, if the weather does not get too stiff and *Endurance* can keep up! The main worry is the prospect of damage from the heavy weather and collisions with icebergs, although the METO thinks that it is too early in the season for the big bergs to be floating north. We are dispersing equipment around the ship to ensure that it is not all lost in one incident.

I saw a signal today that gave an assessment of what the Israelis thought of the Argentinian Air Force, especially with regard to the Skyhawks. The word is that the pilots are professional, proficient and pretty gutsy when it comes to flying and fighting the aircraft, prepared to take risks. The aircraft themselves are fairly basic types, but their routine maintenance falls well below our standards because of skill levels among their maintainers and shortage of spares. It was noted that this made the Air Force fairly resourceful when it came to making do and keeping the aircraft in the air. They also do not seem to be able to do a lot of night training and flying. We have not had too much intelligence with regard to the Mirages and Etendards, with still less about the AM-39 air-launched Exocets.

Nobody is quite sure whether the Etendards are able to carry the Exocets or not and how many they actually have. Current estimates are about a dozen. Discussion centres on whether the French would have a technical team in Argentina on the quiet in order to help the Argentinians fit the missiles to the aircraft. Most people think that the French are commercially cynical enough to do just that in order to see how the missile performs under combat conditions.

It's possible, I suppose, but there would have to be a reckoning afterwards, with them being our allies and partners in Europe. Also, it cuts both ways. If the missile is used and does us over, it will be a big commercial success. On the other hand, if we manage to deal with it, it will be a commercial disaster. It's a worry, though, for two reasons. It is a good missile, as we know, with our variants. Secondly, our missiles and systems are procured and configured against Soviet high-flying and large missiles, not the sea-skimmers.

The Exocet is a particular worry for us in *Antrim*. If it came inboard, it would come in roughly at the height of the Sea Slug magazine and, given its kinetic, let alone explosive, force, it would almost certainly penetrate right through to the magazine. That is not a good thought, as the configuration of the main magazine, running virtually the whole length of the ship, would probably mean a massive detonation that would take us out instantly and spectacularly.

One thing that is frequently discussed is the possibility that the Argentinians might launch the Super-Etendards on a one-way mission to extend their range to get at the carriers. In that way, they could achieve the range they need; the pilots could then ditch in the vicinity of one of our ships, in the knowledge that they had a good chance of being picked up. It depends how committed they are and whether all the bluster from their Junta translates into the sacrifice that is implied by their statements.

We will shortly be assuming a 'silent' procedure with regard to our radars and distinctive communications and sonar emitters, as well as darkening ship every night and rigging deceptive lighting for real when we cross shipping lanes or come across merchant ships.

We do not want to use HF communications, unless we have to, for wide area fighting nets, because they provide opportunities for intercept and location of our forces. HF signals bounce around the world and can be detected from thousands of miles away. If the intercepts are received by a number of stations that are separated geographically, the transmitting unit can be fixed and possibly identified by using triangulation techniques. We are thoroughly familiar with − and have grown up with − the need to minimize HF communications because of our experience in countering the Soviet Union and their massive intercept and location capabilities, which include satellites and intelligence-gathering vessels.

Of course, we will be systematically exploiting any carelessness on the part of the Args in this regard and HF direction finding and intercept will be playing a major role in both intelligence gathering and the appreciation of overall force disposition. I do not expect that they are as disciplined as we are and there will be lots of opportunities.

Intercept also allows the enemy to conduct jamming of our frequencies and spoofing, either putting false information into the system or playing back your own communications that have been previously been recorded and contain voices that are recognizable ('spoofing').

There is also a real drive – and need – to minimize the communication load because the satellite and long-haul systems cannot cope with the massively increased traffic. Therefore the text has to be ruthlessly précised and maximum use made of pre-formatted signals [OPGENs and OPTASKs] that compress the detail and words while giving enough information to inform people or order tasking.

Even some of the Special Forces guys have started to come to FOCCIF – they see it as being part of the team and as a bit of social engagement. I now know some names – Danny, Chris. The sinister Major never comes, nor the SAS Captain. Carlos always does twice as much as anyone else and the Doctor is looking pretty fit, too.

A brief word about naval doctors: known as 'scab-lifters', Royal Navy doctors consider themselves a breed apart, with all the diversity of character and idiosyncrasies that one would expect to see in Civvie Street. The usual complaint from them is that all they get to deal with at sea is colds, drunks and venereal disease, so the prospect of a shooting war opens up all sorts of possibilities for their talents and skills.

The vast majority are independent-minded, plain-speaking characters, cheerfully unambitious and unconstrained by the usual hierarchical deference, and – onboard – unchallenged experts in their specialist field. In any case, no one wants to upset the Doc, with his power over life, limb and reputation! However, the Royal Navy seems to attract more than its fair share of eccentric types.

I served in a large ship where the Doc was decidedly odd. He was an accomplished, very able surgeon, but the rumour about the ship – rightly or wrongly – was that he was attempting the deployment record for the removal for appendices.

This rumour gained significant credibility because of interchanges such as:

Young pilot: 'I think I have strained my stomach muscles doing sit-ups.'

Doc: 'Well, let's have a look. Ah, yes, seems like it might be your appendix. We'll whip it out tomorrow. Better safe than sorry. You don't need it anyway.'

Or again:

Engineer: 'I have the runs. I think it might have been the curry I had in Pompey last night.'

Doc: 'Well, let's have a look. Ah, yes, seems like it might be your appendix. We'll whip it out this afternoon. Better safe than sorry. You don't need it anyway.'

As might be expected, anyone who had an ailment that manifested itself between the neck and the testicles didn't dare go near the sickbay, out of fear of instant weight loss at the hands of a scalpel-wielding maniac.

Just before my qualification courses as an Observer, I was really pleased to have passed all my medical tests for aircrew and went to Seafield Park in Hampshire for my final examination by the doctor. I was called forward and made my way along to the surgery, knocked on the door and opened it.

No one was there; I was reluctant to enter an empty surgery, with all the confidential documents lying around and went back to the waiting area. I told the MA that the doctor was absent, but was told to go back and wait in the surgery.

I returned, opened the door and walked in. BOO! A figure leapt out from behind the door, dressed, as I recognized shortly afterwards, in the uniform of a Surgeon Commander Royal Navy and a facemask. By pure reaction, I had leapt sideways and turned round sharply to confront this unexpected threat.

'Good, good, that's the reflexes sorted out,' said the figure.

It was the Mad Doctor. Fuck!

'Right, let's get started. Down to your underpants. We'll do your blood pressure. Have a look at these while I sort a few things out.'

He handed me some photo albums. I turned the pages, which were full of pictures of his surgical operations over the years. They showed in graphic detail the Doc manoeuvring his way around the insides of various anonymous torsos — fingers in this, medical instruments in that — blood everywhere. Now, oddly, I'm normally OK with the real thing, but representations on the TV or in pictures tend to make me feel squeamish.

'You don't look well,' he said. 'Anything wrong?'

I was still smarting from the ambush and there was no way that I was going to let him win this round. 'Fine, sir,' I croaked, sitting in my underpants, with my stomach churning and my left hand casually flicking from page to page. 'It makes it look like a work of art. These pictures are simply amazing,' I blathered, as my eye lighted on a photograph of a patient with the medical team posing like big-game hunters with some trophy that they had just bagged.

He took my blood pressure. 'A bit high,' he said. 'How old are you?'

I told him, reflecting to myself that I was surprised that it was not off the scale.

After this, things settled down as he methodically went through the rest of the checks, including the more intimate stuff. Then, in a matter of fact way, he asked:

'Do you get shortness of breath?'

'No.'

'Night sweats?'

'No.'

'Giddy spells?'

'No.'

'Any tension in the chest?'

'No.'

'Any stomach complaints, problems with digestion or strange movements?'

'Sorry?' I stalled.

'Any stomach complaints, problems with digestion or strange movements?'

I felt a sudden psychosomatic panic in my right side and shot out: 'NO! NO!' shaking my head vigorously in a way that conveyed 'No bloody way do I want to be centre stage in one of your trophy photos.'

He scrutinized me closely and looked at the checklist for a long while.

'Well, that's all right, then. You are cleared to fly. I hope that it all goes well and that you don't kill yourself too soon.'

Tuesday, 13 April

We are now 23 degrees south.

We briefed early this morning for an early-morning/dawn push at 0630 for surface search and over-the-horizon targeting practice, ahead and to the flanks of the Force. The ship is of course in radar silence as far as possible to avoid giving out gratuitous information about our position and movement.

We have been told by FLEET to look out for a Soviet Krivak Class frigate that might be moving to intercept and shadow us. Just before we manned the aircraft, two contacts were detected on the horizon and we thought that it might be either *Plymouth* or *Tidespring*; they were told to burn stern lights. It was them and we passed them on the way out to our search area.

We landed back on at 0730, to take some passengers across to *Tidespring*, did some more surface search and targeting and were back at Alert 30 on deck by 0825. We then stowed the aircraft in the hangar in anticipation of the day's load-lifting on the Flight Deck.

A replenishment of stores and solids – an RAS (S) – with *Fort Austin*, while *Plymouth* and *Tidespring* continued ahead, went on all day and into the night, starting with a major jackstay transfer between 0900 and 1400 and replenishing stores, ammunition and food. The two Wessex Vs from *Fort Austin*, backed up by her Lynx, transferred a large number of under-slung loads.

Just before the RAS (S), Major Delves told the Captain that he wanted to get his SAS Squadron across from *Fort Austin* with their kit. So at about 1500 we started the transfer of the SAS and their kit from *Fort Austin* to *Antrim* and *Plymouth*.

In and around the transfers, the Captain has been on the 'Growler'* talking to FLEET about various aspects of the Paraquat (which we are now calling it!) operation.

After dark, at about 2100, the flying was becoming decidedly marginal for the Wessex V and Lynx of *Fort Austin*. Firstly, a Wessex V dumped his load (meat; comment on deck, 'Good thing it wasn't the beer!') and needed a precautionary landing on *Fort Austin* because of a technical emergency. The VERTREP needed a second Wessex V to get airborne and the transfer continued with the Lynx. At one stage, the Lynx completely lost control of a load as he was coming in to *Antrim* and had to jettison it in the sea. It was just as well because it contained 81 mm mortar ammunition. We decided to fit all subsequent loads with luminous strips. Flying finished around 0015, *Fort Austin* went on her way and I am knackered. We received about 300 under-slung loads today, including 15 tons of SAS kit – and we took the SAS personnel too – all to be spread around *Antrim*, *Endurance* and *Plymouth*. We also have a surgical team embarked with their equipment.

---

* Secure satellite communications phone.

Carlos told me tonight that we have over 600 souls onboard. The good news is that, after our dalliance with *Fort Austin*, we are stored for 60 days with victuals for our own ship's company and an embarked force of 150, but we did not receive any fresh food, vegetables or eggs and very few potatoes. Eggs will last for another nine days and the potatoes another 30 days, they say. We are going to be into rationing immediately: cereals and something on toast for breakfast, soup and a roll at lunchtime and some sort of pot mess or stew in the evening (and no pudding). The Pusser's propaganda line is that this is how we are going to have to eat if we go into combat anyway, so we might as well get used to it.

The word has gone round to the ship's company that we have inherited the SAS from *Fort Austin*. The Commander has decreed that they are not to be photographed or asked about their previous existence, especially in Northern Ireland. Commander E helpfully suggested that 'for their safety AND YOUR OWN safety, stick to safe topics, like religion, sex and the movies'!

Wednesday, 14 April

We are now 28 degrees south.

Once again, we briefed and manned early to undertake another surface search and targeting serial with the ships. The briefing contained news that two Soviet Bear long-range maritime reconnaissance aircraft were again airborne at 0430 from Luanda and were likely to have been tasked to locate us. We therefore took plenty of chaff with us and climbed to height while on our surface search to dispense enough skillets to impersonate a four-ship-sized formation in three different places at a radius of about 60–80 miles from the real ships. They might not be fooled in the end, but it makes their job a lot harder and they might think that there is something wrong with their radars.

We have actually been very careful about concealing our position on the way down. The Emission Control plan has restricted our high-power radar and radio transmissions to a bare minimum and every time that a Soviet radar satellite passes overhead we take the ships of the formation out to distances of up to 50 miles so that we cannot be associated with each other.

We caught up with *Plymouth* and *Tidespring* in the Morning Watch and we were airborne at 0920 for our surface search and targeting serial, with the specific intention of finding *Endurance*. We found the 'Red Plum' easily and Ian, as a welcome, rattled close down his starboard side at high speed and very low, before climbing into a spectacular wing-over that came down to a hover on *Endurance*'s port beam about 50 yards away. Very impressive, Boss! I'll just collect my things from around the cab.

We were back onboard in time for *Endurance* to pass down our starboard side. The Commander thought that it would be a good idea if, as she passed through our formation to take up station and in view of her exploits, we should clear the lower deck and cheer ship. This the boys did with vigour and enthusiasm and, with her being red already, it was difficult to see whether the little ship blushed at the unexpected honour paid to her.

Her Commanding Officer, Captain Barker, came across by helo to have discussions with the Captain, the command team and the embarked forces about what had happened in South Georgia. He also updated everyone on the likely situation and conditions on the island ahead of our arrival. Most importantly, he was able to give us an indication of the incidence of icebergs further to the south. As I walked him back to the Flight Deck, I tried to engage him in conversation; he wasn't really interested and I gained the distinct impression that he seemed rather smug and pleased with himself.

Endurance then refuelled from *Tidespring*. Instead of going alongside while the RFA was stopped and using the Yokohama fenders that *Tidespring* had onboard, they managed to complete a stern refuelling with a modified rig. Fortunately, the conditions were very suitable, with the wind light and the sea reasonably calm.

Stewart and Fitz flew two hours of passenger transfers – reuniting the *Endurance* survey team with their belongings – during the Afternoon and First Dog, as well as doing round-robins around the ships with stores and other chores.

In *Antrim*, we went to Action Stations again this afternoon and closed down to manning state 1 and watertight condition ZULU. We still have more to do.

The World Service said that the Arg Navy has been put on alert and their Commander-in-Chief has formally bid farewell to the sailors. Surely, this is politics by gesture and emotion – straight out of Dr Goebbels' book of practical propaganda. The Commander is now referring to any confrontation as 'Argy-bargy'.

Also, through our signals, we heard that we have requisitioned four trawlers to be converted to minesweepers, because of the threat of mining by the Args in the approaches to the Falklands. I would do it if I were the Args – it would prevent our submarines, especially the nuclear ones, probing too close and certainly complicate things if we have to do a landing and assault from the sea. Also, some RAF Harrier GR3s – presumably for land attack – are coming down on a container ship. These preparations must be giving the Args a pretty accurate timeline on when they have to be ready to receive us. They will, of course, have home advantage and must be rapidly fortifying the Islands. Have they extended the runway?

These issues came up at the evening briefing, but the discussion was all about what we would do if we were them. We must think what they are likely to do, on the basis of the information and perceptions that they have, not as we would think and do under the circumstances, and consider their cultural frame of mind. We must not judge them by our standards and assumptions. The historian is used to this discipline and detachment; a lot of my fellow officers are not, it seems. That sounds so pompous!

Thursday, 15 April

At the end of the day, we are 33 degrees south. Today was designated a maintenance day – fat chance for the Flight!

Stewart and Fitz flew two housekeeping VERTREP and transfer sorties today, first thing this morning and at lunchtime. The Wessex Vs were busy taking people around the ships for planning and briefings and consolidating personnel and stores between *Tidespring* and *Endurance*. *Endurance* can only do 13 knots, so we have all had to reduce speed so that she can keep up.

The part-of-ship hands have been busy painting all the boats, lifeboats and other coloured fittings a uniform grey. The stern pennant number and ship's name letters at the stern have also gone. The boys are calling the ship, 'The Grey Ghost'. Of course, we painted Humphrey a good while ago now.

Highlight of the day was the arrival of a Nimrod with our operations order for the recovery of South Georgia. The Nimrod was way out on the limits of its endurance and I did wonder why it was necessary to deliver the order, which presumably could have come by signal. Perhaps the secret nature of the operation, the need for surprise and operational security mean that it has to be delivered in this way. Given the size of the thing, it would probably be too long to send over the air, by communications.

The Nimrod did a couple of practice runs and on a third dropped a parachute with a canister attached on a final low-level pass, before waggling its wings and departing to the north. It almost seemed unreal to see this large, sleek aircraft appear out of nowhere and I mused how long it would take them to get back to Ascension. I also wondered if they had a second canister and OPORD ready in case the first one disappeared into the sea.

Those of us on the upper deck waved. The aircraft, with its distinctive shape and familiar fuselage markings, seemed like a hint of home and normality in the vastness of the South Atlantic. One almost felt a twinge of sentiment about the RAF!

The sea boat went away to pick up the canister, which had a smoke-and-dye marker attached. Mere mortals have not been vouchsafed the detail of the document it contained yet, but all the 'passengers' have been in huddles ever since it arrived and clearly look motivated about things. Apparently, the operational order was signed off, on behalf of the Commander-in-Chief, by a Lieutenant Nelson!

The ship continued with general and warfare drills all day, but it was pretty routine today. *Endurance*'s Flight Commander came across and briefed us about South Georgia – with slides. Interestingly, there has been a lot of discussion today about options for South Georgia, but no one has deigned to include us or ask our advice. Presumably, they intend to use helicopters to get everyone ashore.

Commander W did magazine rounds today and was complaining about the amount of unauthorized explosives that we have stowed at present – claymore mines, shaped charges, grenades, mortars, 66 mm HEAT [high-explosive anti-tank] rockets and nefarious Special Forces devices, as well as the extra ammunition lying around in boxes in various places. Small-arms ammunition is piled up in (sealed) boxes around the Junior Rates' Dining Hall and the Special Forces guys seem to sleep with their stuff. We are breaking a good few rules – every day.

We were just settling into an evening of chat and uckers after dinner when the emergency klaxon sounded and the ship went to Emergency Stations in reaction to an iceberg. It was a drill, but no one knew that at the time, and all the critical watertight doors and hatches (the so-called 'red openings') had to be shut instantly by the person nearest each opening. The drill worked so well that the Commander decided that we might as well go to Action Stations as well, so we did. It was all over by 2200 and we were back in the Wardroom for our last game of uckers, once we found out where the board and dice had been secured for action.

Friday, 16 April

Antrim and *Plymouth* detached in the night to displace themselves 60 miles from the formation, so that we could run in and practise a simulated attack on *Tidespring* and *Endurance*. We were launched at 0600 to provide surface search and targeting information to set up the attack. We were airborne for just under three hours and managed to provide accurate targeting for the two ships, which remained electronically silent throughout, and took the *Plymouth* Wasp under control for an AS-12 attack towards the end. With the almost non-existent shipping density, it was not too difficult to locate and identify our targets. The Exocet and gun targeting went smoothly, even though I was using 'pop-up' and limited sweep techniques to minimize intercept possibilities for the 'enemy'. The victims tried to make it difficult for us by switching their position in the formation, but, from 28 miles away, I had continuous coverage and tracking.

We were back onboard by 0850 and the Flight Deck was busy for the rest of the day with various personnel and stores transfers, mostly in support of meetings about the South Georgia operation.

While the lads were handling things back aft, we were involved in series of warfare table-top discussions and scenarios, designed to explore and formulate our reactions to various situations. We chatted to some of the SAS about how they intend to get close inshore when we arrive off South Georgia. One of the proposed options seems to be by inflatable boat – Geminis.

We have also been continuing the formal briefings on various topics. I did my piece on Argentina for about an hour and it seemed to go well – I had 20 minutes of questions. I had started with a humorous quiz – '20 questions about Argentina', all good fun to get everyone going.

We replenished from *Tidespring* 1400–1600.

This evening, the ship stopped for Gemini launching and recovery drills, in the hope that we will be able to insert the SAS using silent and darkened procedures. It was not very inspiring and boating is not something that they seem to do very much on the Wye at Hereford.

Having witnessed the debacle, I gently pointed out that it might be difficult to make an accurate landfall at night, amongst the ice floes with poor chart information and dodgy maps, and wondered whether I could control them from the helo on radar. This appealed to them, but I pointed out that rubber Geminis did not give a good enough radar return. I then had an idea. The same problem of radar occurs with helicopters, which are fitted with a transponder that enhances the echo, to assist with control. It can of course be switched off, for tactical reasons.

I went away to see Chief Bullingham and Chief McKee about the practicality of using the spare transponder, hooked up to a battery in a wooden crate, so that could be used as a portable device in a Gemini. That meant that the radar echo from the Gemini would show up clearly on Humphrey's radar and enable me to control the boat from a distance via radio, by giving it compass directions and distances to go. When I mentioned the idea to them, they gave me that weary, knowing look of 'here's another officer's good idea' and the distinct impression that this task might impinge on other things that they might want to do. They are not so sure about the feasibility, but are prepared to give it a go (it's a technical challenge!) and are cracking on with the design and fabrication stages.

Meanwhile the Admiral's Day Cabin is becoming a veritable Operations Room in its own right, with cables being run through bulkheads to new communications devices and maps festooning the bulkheads themselves. The SAS and Major Sheridan seem to spend all day in there, only emerging for meals and sleep, and access to it is denied to mere mortals. The Captain and the Secret Squirrels are allowed audiences every now and then, but it is all rather mysterious and, frankly, not at all how we should be doing business in these circumstances.

As I am the relevant officer and am trained, I had a discussion with the Commander about Prisoner Handling and Tactical Questioning, in case we have to deal with these aspects and ahead of a brief to the Regulators and the officers. We agreed that the Geneva Convention seems only to apply if we go to war, but there is no indication so far that war will be declared. We reckoned that, if it came to it, we would treat all prisoners as if we were at war and that the Geneva Convention provisions should apply.

We have also been allocated a Victor to do a recce of South Georgia for us, both for Arg activity and ice floes. We are not sure whether a Victor has thermal imaging.

We had a signal from FLEET indicating that our covert and deceptive measures were working. The Navigator was particularly pleased.

This is good because the highly qualified and experienced Navigator of a County Class destroyer is pregnantly in zone for promotion to Commander, so he needs to impress and avoid failure. I served in *London* with a Navigator who was so sharp that he never made a mistake: he always knew what was happening and was able to anticipate everything. It was just as well because our Captain at the time was quite demanding and rather severe in his approach.

I was Officer of the Watch on the Bridge one day and the Captain and the Navigator were somewhere around the ship. I had been told by the Navigator to take the ship to a rendezvous position with an RFA tanker, so that we could replenish fuel. I arrived at the rendezvous in good time, but, despite my diligence, found that there was one thing missing – a tanker. 'Anyone seen a big grey tanker around here?' I asked the Bridge team and radio operators, as I quickly checked the signals and positions to make sure that I had not made a mistake. Nobody could see a tanker. I sent the Bosun's Mate to find the Navigator in a discreet way.

At this point, the Captain arrived on the Bridge, with a peremptory: 'Right, Officer of the Watch, ready for the RAS; where's the tanker?'

'We appear to be in the rendezvous, sir, but the tanker does not seem to be here.'

'Are you in the right place? Sort it out.'

'Yes, sir – of course.'

'Well, where's the tanker, then? Fetch the Navigator.'

'Aye, aye, sir.'

I piped over the Main Broadcast 'The Navigating Officer is requested to contact the Bridge' and very shortly Lieutenant Commander 'Wise as a Serpent' arrived on the scene, with a brisk but genial 'What's the problem?'

'The problem, Pilot' (the Captain's traditional term for the Navigator) 'is that we are about to conduct an RAS and there is one thing missing.'

'Oh yes, sir? Can I help?' he asked quizzically, with a hint of humour in his voice.

'We don't seem to have a tanker,' said the Captain. He was showing accelerating signs of irritation and annoyance.

The Navigator made a theatrical show of peering out of the Bridge windows, looked at me as if to say, 'What have you done with the tanker?', and then, sensing from my shrug of the shoulders that everything that should have been checked had been checked, he made his way to the chart table. After scanning the chart, he turned around, leant back on the chart table and said calmly and quietly: 'Sir, I've fucked up. The tanker is at 290, 18 miles. If we come up to 24 knots and head 310, we can replenish at 1415.'

We all waited for the lightning bolt from the Captain and pretended to be busy with other things.

Instead, he replied: 'Very good, Pilot. Make it so.'

I learned a thing or two as a result of that incident. [The Navigator made it to Vice-Admiral and a knighthood.]

Saturday, 17 April

As I write, we are now 41° S 025° W and we reverted to normal uniform today.

We went to Action Stations at 0600 this morning in order to test the system and organize Defence Watch routines. We then reverted to Cruising Watches again.

In the forenoon, we conducted a simulated anti-submarine exercise with *Plymouth*, fired the GPMGs [General Purpose Machine Guns] and practised loading weapons onto the aircraft. We had a steady breeze from the south-west throughout and a long swell and choppy sea-state.

While we were airborne, Chief Bullingham had put together the transponder and the power source in a crate and it was ready for a trial.

In the afternoon, between 1300 and 1700, we had 'SAS and SBS Boating Afternoon', Gemini drills. This included a trial of my special device (dubbed the 'Gizzit') for tracking and controlling small boats. I sat in the aircraft on deck with the power and the radar on and controlled a

Gemini, with the Gizzit embarked, by radio. The ship was stopped in the water and the Gemini went out to about six miles and I was able to control it in course and time right into about 50 yards, which is good enough, I would say. Well done, Chiefs, for making it work, to my relief. I think our Special Forces guys are secretly impressed (they would never deign to tell us though).

We also successfully transferred 16 assault troops from *Antrim* to *Plymouth* by boat, although the Ops Room log noted: 'SAS not very good at getting in and out of boats'!

Ian did 45 minutes of lifting and shifting with Fitz during the Dogs, along with the Wessex Vs from *Tidespring*. This included the transfer of an SAS team from *Endurance*, led by a Captain, John Hamilton. The weather deteriorated markedly during the sortie, so flying was stopped.

We spoke to the Wessex V team in *Tidespring* today about how we might play things. I know Mike Tidd, the detachment commander, and Ian Georgeson, but met for the first time their tame Crab, Flight Lieutenant Andy Pulford, and their newly minted Junior Joe pilot, Andy Berryman.

Yes, I have known Mike Tidd and Ian Georgeson for a while. They are very experienced pilots, both QHIs [Qualified Helicopter Instructors] and Clockwork-trained.* We served together when they and their squadron were based at RAF Aldergrove in Northern Ireland; they were doing the lifting and shifting for the Army and the RUC† on a routine basis in and around the Province, but particularly in South Armagh, where most of the terrorist violence and serious IRA activity outside Belfast and Londonderry were taking place.

We and 406 were there to support operations on Carlingford Lough and to conduct surveillance offshore, to record shipping patterns and search for/track suspect vessels and known bad guys. It was assessed at the time that the IRA was transporting its bombs and personnel to the mainland – and doing practice runs – by fishing vessels working out of Kilkeel, Dundalk and thereabouts.

We had deployed to Northern Ireland with Brian Gell instead of our American exchange Second Pilot at the time, Pat Cosgrove. Brian is a class act as a pilot and had successfully ditched after a catastrophic engine

* Trained to operate over land in extremes of snow and ice.
† Royal Ulster Constabulary.

failure in a Wessex 3. He is also a thoroughly nice guy. Laurie Hopkins was our Flight Commander then. He was a good operator too – a steady, reliable pilot, with a taste for doing things in style and a keen nose for fun. He was also prepared to take reasonable risks when we were on exercises to achieve tactical success. He was – and is – great socially, but he cannot understand why I do not drink alcohol. Nobody does!

While we were in Northern Ireland, Taranto Night, the primary celebration event of the Fleet Air Arm calendar, fell due. The date records and celebrates the successful and innovative attack by FAA Swordfish on the Italian fleet in Taranto harbour on 11 November 1940. It is our Trafalgar. It is also usually a progressively anarchic event, because it involves a fair amount of alcohol, pyrotechnics and a competition, mainly led by squadrons' HWIs [Helicopter Warfare Instructors], to produce the most original functioning weapon from odds and ends. The best Taranto Nights have re-creations of the event, either outside with fireworks or inside with model aircraft flying around on wires, dropping various projectiles.

We tentatively, but with little confidence, explored the possibility of having a Mess dinner at RAF Aldergrove's Mess, but the Mess President's face turned ashen when it was explained to him that the Mess would be full of FAA officers, what might be involved and that Crabs (who were not at Taranto) were not included. I can see a 'no' from a mile away and so it proved.

Happily, we got a phone call from Moscow Camp, the headquarters of SNONI, to say that they would be delighted to host us and that the Army were really keen on the idea. Moscow was in a very secure area and was the base for minesweepers, Fishery Protection and other patrol craft operating around Northern Ireland. SNONI's deputy at the time and President of the Mess was John Martin, who had been my Captain in *Alfriston*. He was a tremendous guy and I had learned so much from him, and I thought at the time that he must be going places fast. He was so laid-back and hated cant and pomposity. While I was under training, he let me do Bridge Watches on my own, gave me lots of responsibility and let me take charge of things above my pay grade. SNONI wanted to invite Admiral Sir James Eberle, Commander-in-Chief Fleet, along, to give the command and base some visibility.

'Are you sure?' we said.

'Yes,' they said.

'No, seriously,' we said.

'Yes,' they said.

'OK,' we said, a little worried about the way this might be going.

So Moscow Camp and their team cracked on with preparations.

Meanwhile, the Junglie detachment at Aldergrove advertised the event at Yeovilton, resulting in massive FAA reinforcements, all of whom had operated in Northern Ireland, being flown in to the Province to support their chums. That was the first unexpected change to the plan. The second was the late (same day) stated desire of the General Officer Commanding (GOC) Northern Ireland (General Sir Richard Lawson) to attend Taranto Night as well, seeing as Admiral Eberle was coming. We tried to brief his office staff and the ADC about the nature of the event, but they seemed to only hear the words Mess Dinner and assured us that the General would be happy.

We took a minibus to Moscow from Aldergrove, with coats over our uniforms and I could not help noticing that there was a cabbage on one of the seats. We arrived to find the pre-Mess Dinner drinks in full swing. The Mess was housed in an extended hut and comprised an ante-room and a dining room, made up for the Mess Dinner with all the usual Mess silver and decorations. During the pre-dinner drinks, I was aware of various packages being surreptitiously imported into the Mess and we heard that the Commander-in-Chief would not now be coming because he had the flu.

The Mess Dinner started with the Padre saying Grace. No sooner had he done so when there was a loud explosion and the Padre disappeared in a dense cloud of orange smoke. He leaped up – cheers and laughter all round – and tried to escape the cloud. He was then seen to dance a jig; in fact he was trying to escape the smoke. He couldn't escape because the smoke generator had been tie-wrapped to his ankle during the Grace and he disappeared into the galley, returning without his ankle bracelet and in good humour, but decidedly dishevelled.

We then settled down to one of the best-cooked and best-served Mess dinners I have had, punctuated by the occasional thunderflash going off and making those in its vicinity jump. Just as the main course was cleared away, there were four simultaneous explosions as one whole table was wreathed in smoke. When it cleared, we could see that a table of 20 officers, mostly Army and a few Navy (not aviators), had had its legs blown off and that the whole table-top and contents, including the Mess silver, were resting on the thighs of those on the seats. The sight of 20 officers desperately trying to maintain equilibrium for the rest of the dinner, while others, with increasing levels of accuracy and impact, were lobbing pepper bombs at them, with all the consequent sneezing, was highly comical.

And so we came to the speeches. These were interrupted regularly by tribal chanting and various (funny) interjections as the speakers droned on about anything but what people wanted to hear. About twenty minutes into the second speech, the General got up and stormed into the ante-room, followed by his ADC, a DSNONI with a fixed grin on his face and a very obsequious RAF Group Captain from Aldergrove. The three senior officers stood in a threesome facing each other.

It was one of those moments when you see things happening in slow motion. A cabbage, which I had seen before, was describing a perfect arc into the ante-room. It landed between DSNONI, the General and the Station Commander of Aldergrove. All three looked down at the cabbage, with an embedded thunderflash, its tip showing and fizzing away angrily. In the space of a second, all three looked at each other and the Group Captain performed a totally comical John Cleese-like back-flip over the sofa just as the thunderflash detonated with a deafening BANG.

Suddenly, the air was full of atomized cabbage and it all fell silent, before peals of laughter rang out, mainly because of the comical sight of the RAF Group Captain's head, hair all over the place, and fingertips appearing from behind the sofa in the manner of 'Kilroy was here'. Both SNONI and the GOC had inexpertly tried to duck out of the way and had fallen over together. The GOC staggered to his feet and standing erect exclaimed in a strident, think-you-might-have-lost-your-sense-of-humour-sir sort of voice: 'I command men of honour, professionalism and loyalty; you are just a bunch of hooligans and . . .' (struggling for another insulting epithet) '. . . naval officers.'

Now I really admire a man who can say that and keep a straight face, when he has fragments of cabbage in his hair, in his rank badges and in his medals.

He curtly turned on his heel, along with his obsequious ADC, who, I recall, looked exactly like the verger in *Dad's Army*. John Martin, still coming to his senses, tried to follow him out, but gave up, when over-taken by a rapidly departing Group Captain, to chants of 'Goodnight, ladies' from a bunch of very happy aviators, who were determined to continue celebrating their heritage.

It all went wrong when the GOC decided that he wanted to complain that night to the Commander-in-Chief about his first direct encounter with the Fleet Air Arm. The result was that Laurie, as one of the more senior aviators, had to stay behind to face the crescendo of music and khaki indignation, while Brian and I flew the cab with Mac the aircrew-man back to Portland the following day. None of us had been drinking, so things were fine from a safety point of view.

When we arrived back at Portland, the Spanish Inquisition was wait-ing for us and Brian and I were each interviewed by a Captain from FONAC headquarters. An FAA Captain – wow, this might be serious! Mine said that senior people were really cheesed off about the events of the previous night and that they wanted to know what had happened. They particularly wanted to know who threw the cabbage ('What?' I thought).

'Did you touch the cabbage?'

'No.'

'We can probably get fingerprints, you know?'

At this point, I struggled unsuccessfully to contain the urge to laugh. I had seen how small those pieces of cabbage were and even a gnat's fin-gerprints would not be available for detection. I got into one of those irrepressible fits where anything sets you off. Just like the Roman sol-diers in the scene with Michel Palin, talking about his friend Biggus Dickus, in *Life of Brian*.

The Captain looked at me, coldly grave – I anticipated a thunderbolt and career termination – and then burst out laughing himself.

'Sorry, sir . . .' I gasped, immediately corpsing with suppressed laughter.

'Don't worry,' he said, 'it was worth a try. We have all been there. You are not going to tell me who threw the cabbage, are you?'

I shook my head, with moist eyes, looking him as straight as I could, in the eye.

'In that case,' he said, 'let's just say that you did not see the cabbage after it left the minibus.'

But the fact is – I know who threw the cabbage: it was Ian Georgeson!

Sunday, 18 April

We are now 45° S 033° W – this is getting seriously south! We are in the 'Roaring Forties' and it feels like it! We have been issued with cold-weather clothing and survival suits.

We have heard that the Arg Navy has made a great show of putting to sea. In response, the submariners would say that there are two types of vessel – submarines and targets!

People have now been told to carry anti-flash hoods and gloves and sleep fully or partially clothed. There has been a purge on nylon or synthetic clothing (why does the Pusser issue it?) and there are some very strange combinations of rig starting to appear. The sports store has been raided for suitable clothing.

I hope that this marks the point when we move from an exercise-plus mentality to one of war-fighting. We should actually feel just a little bit scared of what might happen. It is not some theoretical scenario, a part in some play, and there is every chance that grim reality will trump wishful thinking if we do not shape up. I hope that it will give our subsequent tactical discussions and decisions a keener edge – without some of the bullshit, insincerity and posturing that we have had so far – especially when faced with a realistic possibility of getting killed or dumped into an icy ocean.

We had an interesting replenishment day today. First of all, we did an astern replenishment of fuel from *Tidespring*, with the hose over our bow and focsle, because the weather might be too rough to do the abeam method, and then went our port side to her starboard to take on lubrication oil. The lads call the abeam method the 'missionary position' and the astern – well, the 'doggy position'. The whole business of fuel probes and receptors has a fairly direct sexual innuendo to it anyway.

While this was happening, I went through the arrangements for Prisoner Handling and Tactical Questioning with the Master at Arms and the Leading Regulator, ensuring that we had identified various spaces for holding individuals and the necessary equipment for recording, processing and interviewing them.

We also had another session of Action Stations between 1400 and 1500 to conduct general drills and Damage Control actions. The Greenies are testing and calibrating their missile fire control radars to destruction, with lots of balloon tracking and adjustments.

Stewart and Fitz did the lift and shift today at 1800 for 45 minutes.

Signals indicated that the *Invincible* Group were in a panic off Ascension over a possible submarine contact.

The Captain has been on the satellite phone to FLEET on and off all day talking about South Georgia and getting real pressure from the political authorities to start operations there by 21 April.

It is quite clear to us that the Junta are trying to divert attention away from all their troubles at home, in an attempt to increase their popularity by taking us on and to cover up all their evil crimes against their own people. I reckon that they do not rate us much as a country – although I am sure that we will hear the usual imperialist and colonialist clap-trap again soon – and nothing that our government has done in the past 15 years or so will have convinced them that we would be prepared to go all that way and fight them.

Dec, the Doc and I agreed last night that we will have no credibility as a country if we do not go and sort them out.

This evening, we saw a *Pebble Mill at One* documentary on the Falklands, before the film. Around 2100, in the middle of the film (*Every Which Way But Loose* – 'Before I saw it, I thought it was a Shakespeare play' from Declan. 'Exit pursued by an orang-utan'?), we had a Total Steam Failure and Total Electrical Failure! Normality was restored after nine minutes once the G6 gas turbines were started.

We are in Greenwich Mean Time – three hours ahead of South Georgia. That might give us an advantage as we will be up before the Args every day.

Monday, 19 April

We finally arrived in the area to the north of South Georgia, seemingly undetected since we saw the two Soviet Bears on 12 April. As we are now just within range of the Arg Neptune recce aircraft, we went to Damage Control State 2 Condition Y* and Defence Watches this morning at 0800. I am not sure why the Neptune issue is relevant as we have been in range of the Arg Boeing 707s for some time, but never mind. The ship's company is now wearing Action Working Dress and carrying survival suits and anti-flash hoods and gloves. We aircrew prefer to wear

* Damage control states and conditions related to the manning and equipment regimes in force and watertight integrity configuration (respectively) at various states of readiness.

our goon suits (better chance of survival), use our aircrew life-preservers (lots of kit and toys to play with) and carry the rest as normal.

More to the point, both Sea Cat launchers and the chaff rockets were loaded and the 4.5 gun hoist now contains high-explosive, radar-echoing and star shells – it looks like this might be for real.

The Captain and CLF [Commander Land Forces] (Sheridan) spent the day doing the rounds of the other ships to brief them and the final troop movements have been completed. Captain Hamilton went and did the same for the SAS guys around the bazaars.

The weather has been fairly mild, so we have been able to 'crack on' with our preparations to recover the island. All the NCOs and troopers give the impression of being mentally and physically tough, as you might expect, and certainly the strong, silent types.

We realized that we do not know very much about the SAS, other than what they did in the Iranian Embassy siege two years ago. They are all, seemingly, introverted characters and spend most of their time in the Admiral's Day Cabin surrounded by, and immersed in, maps and photographs. They usually take their meals in there, with the door being opened just wide enough for the food to be passed to them. I had an audience with them yesterday together with Ian, when we were asked a number of practical questions to do with flying over mountainous, glaciated terrain (why?).

Apart from that one brief insight, everything is very secretive. I am not sure why everything has to be so hush-hush – after all, we are supposed to be on the same side and, in any case, who are we going to tell? More importantly, if we are going to go in harm's way together, a little knowledge of how each of us works – and thinks – would surely help. I am just a bit concerned that, at some stage soon, we mere mortals are going to be invited to do something which is normal to them, but pretty hairy in reality.

It does not help that there is a group of officers on the ship – the Commander, the SCO and the Ops Officer and a few others – who, together with the Captain, are privy to the really secret information and what the SAS are planning. The 'Secret Squirrel club' seem to take pleasure in theatrically passing around among themselves the distinctive blue file, containing what must be secret signals, and noting our irritation. It is frustrating not to know the full picture and I am convinced that it is likely to cause problems and misunderstandings if we have to take on the Args and actually get to do some fighting.

On the operational front, we conducted a targeting sortie today in support of an anti-ship serial run by *Plymouth*. We also swept ahead and to the east of the force, looking for enemy (oops, must not get ahead of myself) surface vessels and the incidence of icebergs. Needless to say, we found very few bergs in the vastness of the sea, reflected that we felt a bit vulnerable in a single-engine aircraft a long way from the ship and did not find large numbers of whales heading north (as we had been briefed). They must know that we are coming and worry that they are dead ringers for submarines on sonar! I reckon that, if the conflict really gets going, the whales will need to run for cover once the torpedoes start running in the water!

The other aircraft in the group did the lifting and shifting today.

The daily uckers game continues. Declan and I are 10–8 up!

We are now 48° S 031° W. Visibility is very poor and the Captain is fretting about icebergs.

20 April – a Tuesday

All through the night and into this morning, we were shrouded in thick fog. It was incredibly eerie. We were not able to see the other ships in company. We planned to do a fuel replenishment at 0800 and, when closing *Tidespring*, she loomed out of the fog at less than a cable (200 yards). Very soon after we got alongside, the fog lifted somewhat and we got airborne in 406 for lifting and shifting.

This morning saw a big meeting between the Captain, various officers from the other ships, the SAS/SBS and the CO of M Company (the bulk of which is in *Tidespring*). Most of the forenoon was taken up for us in 406, moving stores, ammunition and personnel between the ships.

At 1400, we went to Action Stations as we entered the 200 nm [nautical mile] Exclusion Zone around South Georgia. It took four minutes to reach Action Stations and 10 minutes to get to 1Z from 2Y★ (five minutes faster than the time achieved during Sea Training earlier in the year). *Plymouth* picked up what he thought might be a radar intercept from an Argentinian A69 corvette or patrol boat. As a result, we flew two surface search sorties, from 1415 for an hour and for 3.5 hours from 1630, to ascertain whether there were any Arg warships ahead and to the

★ Damage Control and Manning States (see 'Watches and Routines at Sea', p. 348).

flanks and to see if there were any icebergs. There were quite a few bergs ahead of the force nearer to South Georgia and later on, as night fell, we took station one mile astern of *Tidespring* and went at 11 knots for ice evasion and avoidance. *Endurance* could only manage 3–4 knots and *Plymouth* stayed behind to look after her.

The weather is getting steadily worse – all the Wardroom furniture is lashed down and the Padre is looking like death warmed up. I keep reminding him that even Nelson was frequently seasick; he says, 'Well, look what happened to him!' Eh?

I saw a signal that indicated that *Conqueror* was off the north coast of South Georgia, but its periscope reconnaissance was being hampered by the fog. She is going to remain off the island to cover us and to provide updates. The RAF also made an appearance today, in the form of a Victor, conducting at long range and vast expense a maritime reconnaissance of the area between us and the island, to check for bergs and Arg ships. I am not sure how effective the radar is at the height that they would have been flying, or their ability to classify contacts anyway. The Wardroom banter is that the RAF is worried that, if South Georgia falls and the Args give up on the Falklands, they will not be seen to have contributed very much.

Looking at the chart in the Charthouse and noticing extra activity among the Secret Squirrels, it seems certain that we are going to do something about South Georgia. So far, there has been no hint of our presence on the BBC World Service. Sure enough, we (Ian, Stewart and I) were called into what we have now dubbed the 'Squirrel Operations Room' (Admiral's Day Cabin) for a special briefing.

The plan is to insert a 16-man SAS reconnaissance party – apparently they are the Mountain and Arctic Warfare specialists (just as well) – on Fortuna Glacier by helicopter (our own cab and the two Wessex Vs in *Tidespring*) the following day. As we scrambled to find the place on our maps, we realized that we had been brought into the forefront of the game. We were asked what we thought and I wondered whether we were meant to respond – after all, they are the SAS and must know what they are doing. None of us wanted to say anything in front of our Captain and the rest of the command team, but it looked risky and unnecessary. Having said that, not one of us had any experience of conditions on South Georgia and of its topography and – well, they must have thought about all this on the long passage south, ensconced in their own special place.

Later we asked for an informal meeting in the Wardroom. We tried a few oblique questions like 'Are you happy with being that high on the glacier?', 'You know that we are going to be well above the freezing level?', 'The katabatic winds are likely to be severe, you know.' They looked at us as if we were wimps and the word 'katabatic' did not seem to be in their lexicon.

We explained that we were not entirely happy about the choice of landing site due to the difficulties of flying in Arctic conditions, possibly in conditions of severe turbulence and zero visibility, if the weather was bad. However, we would do what the Fleet Air Arm always does and get on with it. Ian is always philosophical about these things – he thought that if other people were going to risk their lives, they had a vested interest in getting it right. And, of course, he has quiet confidence in his own flying abilities and he has stacks of experience, not least in flying at the edges of the envelope.

The SAS repeated that the Fortuna option was the best landing site from their point of view, as the Argentinians would not expect them to come from that direction (shades of Wolfe and the Heights of Abraham at Quebec, I suppose). At this point, the normally reserved Stewart said, in all seriousness, 'They won't expect you to come in by Polaris missile either, but that is not a good reason to do it.' I almost laughed, if only to show support for Stewart, but I saw that I would be the only one amid a group of men whose faces looked like they would melt steel at 10 yards.

Ian and I went away to discuss how we would put this plan into operation. I had a closer look at the black-and-white maps of South Georgia that we had. From the contours and other topographical features, the landscape looked decidedly forbidding and rugged, although the various names of places had a romantic appeal – Possession Bay, Doubtful Bay, Cumberland Bay, etc. There was a certain thrill about being associated with it all. Unfortunately, the detail to support flying was not exactly encouraging, but there was enough to see how we might approach the proposed landing site. We have decided that the best option would be for us to lead the two Wessex Vs from *Tidespring* up to the glacier, rather like a mother duck and her ducklings. As we have radar (and me), Doppler and a better altimeter, we will be in a far more comfortable position with regard to navigation and the avoidance of the many large mountains up there. The Wessex Vs will take six men each and their equipment and we will take four, including Captain Hamilton, their troop leader, together with all their gear.

We went and briefed the Captain and told him about our concerns, but he seemed happy that we would do the job regardless. I told him that I was still a bit concerned about not having the sonar in the aircraft as we approached the island. What if a submarine was lurking there already? He did not seem as concerned as I thought he should be, possibly thinking that it was special pleading on my part, and said that the priority was to maximize our troop-carrying capacity for a possible assault.

Also, adding to my concerns about the sonar, we entered the 200 nm Exclusion Zone earlier today which both the British and Argentinian governments have declared around the Falklands and their dependencies, so it seems that the government is determined to see this through. Thank goodness this government is being positive. I can't even begin to think of the confusion we would be in down here if the governments of some recent years were in power. At least Mrs T is making the right noises and is standing firm. I hope that we get some decent ROE [rules of engagement] soon though – in this sort of action, in these remote regions, you can't afford to let the other guy have the first shot free.

MEM Stark got the man of the match prize today from the Commander on Main Broadcast for unblocking the after heads. He was specially selected because of his small hands, which were able to reach into various pipes and drains – and down among . . . (!)

Commander E was heard to assert, 'Jobs like that are just as vital as flying 406.' I know what he was trying to say.

He also said something really smart to his department this evening: 'If some of you are feeling nervous and/or apprehensive about what we are about to do, you are not alone. We all depend on each other at times like this, more than at any other time. Keep alert, keep vigilant, and above all, keep your sense of humour.'

The World Service announced that our government had rejected the US Secretary of State's proposals outright and had insisted on a complete Arg withdrawal and a restoration of British sovereignty over the Islands.

We saw a film tonight, *Five Man Army*, a gold robbery in support of the Mexican revolution. All the furniture was lashed in one corner and people, including the SAS guys, just wedged themselves where they

1. HMS *Antrim* in her pre-war colour scheme, showing the 4.5 inch gun, the Exocet missile launchers, and her radar and communications equipment.

2. HMS *Antrim* from astern, showing the large Seaslug missile launcher on the quarterdeck, Humphrey the helicopter on the Flight Deck and the distinctive round 901 tracking and guidance radar for the Seaslug missile system. The small, cramped hangar for the helicopter can be seen on the port (*left*) side of the ship adjacent to the 901 radar. This required the helicopter, with folded rotor blades and tail pylon, to be manhandled down the port waist and diagonally and nose first into the hangar, while pivoting the front right wheel on a turntable and pushing the tail sideways until the aircraft was secured.

3. The author, in 1982, seated in front of the Wessex 3 radar and control panel.

4. HMS *Antrim* Flight aircrew and helicopter maintainers, with aircrew kneeling, from left to right: Lieutenant Chris Parry, Lieutenant Commander Ian Stanley, Sub-Lieutenant Stewart Cooper and Petty Officer Aircrewman David Fitzgerald. Chief Petty Officer Bullingham is standing third from the right.

5. *Antrim* at anchor off Ascension Island on 10 April, with Declan Ward and the author over the side, concealing the ship's pennant number with grey paint.

6. The 'Crossing the Line' ceremony at the Equator – HMS *Antrim*'s ship's company dress the part.

7. Angus Sandford, during the 'Crossing the Line' ceremony at the Equator, in dubious company.

8. Heading south – *Antrim*'s flight maintainers spread the rotor blades of the helicopter.

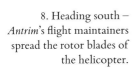

9. SAS troopers mess around in boats.

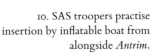

10. SAS troopers practise insertion by inflatable boat from alongside *Antrim*.

11. Humphrey and two Wessex Vs head for the SAS insertion on Fortuna Glacier on 21 April 1982.

12. The face of Fortuna Glacier on 21 April 1982, taken from Humphrey.

13. The first Wessex V (YF) crashes on Fortuna Glacier, with SAS troopers emerging from the second Wessex V (YA).

14. The pilot of the crashed Wessex V YA, Lieutenant Ian Georgeson (*on right*), and two SAS men, with the inflatable life raft from the helicopter.

15. The scene on *Antrim*'s flight deck after the first return from Fortuna on 22 April 1982, with SAS (*in white*) and aircrew recovered from Wessex V (YF).

16. The final return of Humphrey to HMS *Antrim* after the rescue of the SAS and stranded aircrew on 22 April 1982.

17. Major Cedric Delves awaits the return of Humphrey after the rescue of three SAS troopers from an unserviceable and abandoned Gemini inflatable boat on 23 April 1982.

18. King Edward Cove, Grytviken, with the whaling station in the foreground and Shackleton House to the left of the ship alongside.

19. HMS *Plymouth* bombards South Georgia, 25 April 1982.

20. The abandoned Argentinian submarine ARA *Santa Fé* alongside the whaling station at Grytviken.

21. The church at the whaling station at Grytviken.

22. The British Ice Patrol Ship, HMS *Endurance* – the 'Red Plum'.

23. HMS *Antrim* under way in Cumberland Bay, April 1982.

24. Commander Angus Sandford (Executive Officer), Lieutenant Commander Anthony Dymock (Signals and Communications Officer) and Captain Chris Nunn, Royal Marines (Commanding Officer M Company), ashore in Grytviken, 27 April 1982.

25. Lieutenant Alfredo Astiz signing the Instrument of Surrender on behalf of all Argentinian forces on board HMS *Plymouth* at South Georgia. The British officers are Captain N. J. Barker of HMS *Endurance* (*left*) and Captain D. Penreath of HMS *Plymouth*, 26 April 1982.

26. The commanding officers of ARA *Santa Fé* (Lieutenant Commander Horacio Bicain, *left*) and HMS *Brilliant* (Captain John Coward) on the casing of the submarine after the shooting of the Argentinian Chief Petty Officer Felix Artuso.

27. The Executive Officer, HMS *Antrim*, Commander Angus Sandford, in his custom-made 'Hagar the Horrible' Action Stations helmet.

28. The Medical Officer, HMS *Antrim*, Surgeon Lieutenant Alasdair Maclean.

29. The author during the conflict.

30. Lieutenant Declan Ward, as Officer of the Watch on the Bridge of *Antrim*, during the conflict.

31. Officers of HMS *Antrim* about to leave for the 'what you were wearing when the ship went down' fancy dress party in Gibraltar on 27 March 1982, from left to right: Ian Stanley, Declan Ward, Angus Sandford, Alasdair Maclean, the author.

32. Lieutenants Declan Ward and Carlos Edwards (*left and centre*) at the wedding of Lieutenant John Saunders (delayed by the Falklands conflict) at Britannia Royal Naval College, Dartmouth.

could, occasionally rolling around and sliding across the carpet in formation, as the ship pitched and slewed. The projector struggled to cope, frequently breaking down, and there was a lot of good-humoured banter amid the chaos. David Stanesby decided to put on the style, having got his meteorological forecast right, and appeared in Mess Undress (formal) uniform. It did not help his stability, though!

As I write now, the weather is deteriorating rapidly. I went up to the Met Office a while ago and we have a north-westerly Force 6 at present, with a south-westerly Force 9 imminent. Certainly, it feels very lumpy. Uckers was a bit of a trial. We lost and could have sabotaged the game by exploiting the ship's movement to up board, as if by accident.

Wednesday, 21 April

As I said yesterday, for once, the 'Schoolie' got his weather forecast right. Last night, the wind went round to the south-west and blew all night as a Severe Gale Force 9. I don't think that anyone onboard could have slept at all. I tried wedging myself in my 'pit', but even that failed to stop me being shaken about. Everyone who has a motion problem is past the seasick stage now, although mercifully I still continue not to suffer from it.

Right now, as I write, we are in the middle of a Storm Force 10 with gusts to 90 knots outside and today has been very interesting.

This morning, we heard the World Service telling everyone that units of the Task Force could be in position to attack South Georgia tomorrow. Thanks very much for alerting the Args!

We arrived with *Tidespring*, *Plymouth* and *Endurance* off South Georgia, about 30 nm to the north of Possession Bay, well out of sight of any Arg OPs [Observation Positions]. In view of the severe weather, we convinced the Captain that it was worth making a preliminary reconnaissance of the proposed landing site first, before committing all three Wessex and their troops. At first light (0930), we took off in Humphrey (Ian, Stewart, Fitz and myself) with the SAS Major (Delves) and also John Hamilton (I have found out that he will be in charge of the Mountain and Arctic Warfare lot).

For the first time, we went flying with personal weapons – Ian, Stewart and I with 9 mm pistols and Fitz with an SLR [self-loading rifle], to go with the GPMG. I have a Browning 9 mm on a webbing belt worn over the goon suit, along with the lifejacket (and dinghy pack in the aircraft). This really brings things home, I thought, as I slid the bullets into the magazine and checked the mechanism over and over again. I haven't worn side-weapons since our recent tours in Northern Ireland and there seems to be a greater possibility of having to use them on this trip. I'm not a great fan of the Browning; it tends to kick a bit when you shoot it, but better than nothing. I must get some practice off the back end of the ship, although the SAS boys say that I really should get hold of a better weapon than a 9 mm. They have promised to bring back something better for us if they capture any Args (Walther PPK – that would do very nicely, sir – or a Colt 45, apparently). They all seem to prefer Armalites, presumably from their time in Northern Ireland.

We flew low into Possession Bay to avoid observation by any Argentine patrols in total radio silence. The weather was clear and bright and the wind was steady at about 30 knots at the mouth of the bay. As we entered the bay, Fitz cocked the GPMG in the starboard window, while I directed Ian by radar and stopwatch navigation through the gaps in the swirling low-lying cloud and snow.

The geography of South Georgia is staggering and like nothing I have ever seen. The large mountains that rear up like jagged teeth are themselves dwarfed by the enormous glaciers which grow down to the edge of the sea. The whole spectacle has an eerie, other-world atmosphere about it – yes, it definitely has an atmosphere; the predominant colours are the green of the sea, the brilliant white of the snow and the ethereal blue of the old ice in the glaciers. Above all, everything looked cold, very cold, particularly the sea in the bays, which looked menacingly still with vast chunks of ice floating along.

In fact, it was so cold that I could not use the chinagraph pencil on my overlays on the radar. They were too brittle and broke every time I tried to mark anything. It took a felt tip in the end to make any impression at all. Despite all the survival gear and about three layers underneath, it felt cold in the cab too; the fingers and feet seemed to be affected the most and it's strange to see your breath every time you exhale.

It was difficult to navigate over what were in effect uncharted ice floes amidst the swirling snow and the low cloud which formed over the mouths of the coastal bays. The visibility was almost down to zero in parts and the radar was getting considerable scatter from the surrounding rock faces, but we felt our way across from Possession to Antarctic Bay and came to the massive edge of Fortuna Glacier where it fed into Antarctic Bay. Its top was capped with cloud and it was difficult to see how we could get up into the glacier in the prevailing and encircling gloom, but breaks appeared in the weather as we made our way up a winding route between unseen and seen obstructions during an ascent which relied more on blind faith than anything else. All the time the wind swirled around us, giving us frequent, random, seemingly uncontrolled lurches. At one stage, Ian said, 'This is the pilot. You might be experiencing some turbulence, so for your own comfort and safety you might want to ensure that your seat-belts are fastened.' Fitz asked when the film would be starting and complained that he hadn't had any champagne yet.

I say blind faith because the radar is very primitive and not designed for transit or navigation over the land. There was also something else – the topographical features did not seem to be exactly in the positions represented on the map. One peak seemed to be about a mile away from where it should have been and the glaciers could be mistaken for mountains on most days.

As we climbed the mountain, well beyond the freezing level, the prospect that greeted us was quite alarming. The glacier was heavily pitted with massive crevasses about 300 feet deep every hundred yards or so. I was thinking, 'The SAS are proposing to cross three miles of this terrain.' We started chatting among ourselves about how bad it was, just as we were hit by a terrific blast of wind from the right-hand side of the aircraft, which spun us about 40 degrees to the left. 'Ouch,' said Stewart in his understated way. 'What the fuck was that?' he exclaimed, somewhat less phlegmatically, when the next buffet hit us.

Meanwhile the SAS officers had been surveying the scene and had been silent, even though they were on intercom. They took a long, sombre look at the situation and the one said to the other: 'What do you think, John?'

'It's not good,' said the other.

'Well, you've got to get on, John.'

'OK, we'll do it,' said John.

I was watching them as they were speaking. I could detect nothing but quiet resolve and determination to get on with things. I looked at the map and the distance between the landing site and Leith; I looked at the terrain and the conditions. But they know their business, I thought, and, anyway, as one of them said to us yesterday, Shackleton made it across this glacier here when he escaped from Elephant Island (not sure, can't remember) after he and a previous *Endurance* had been trapped in the Antarctic ice. Also, Shackleton did not have the kit, presumably, that these boys have. Not sure about it myself.

So it was back to the ships to refuel and collect the rest of the troops and the two Wessex Vs. The terrain had been uninviting (!), but apart from some driving rain and wind amid the manically swirling cloud the conditions were just about suitable.

When we led the two Wessex Vs (flown by Mike Tidd and Andy Pulford) back to the glacier, we once again crossed from Possession Bay into Antarctic Bay, only to find that the whole area was covered in thick low cloud, made worse by driving snowstorms of amazing intensity. After some circling in Antarctic Bay, we were forced back to the ships to refuel. By 1315Z [ZULU, i.e. Greenwich Mean Time], we decided to have another try. The weather in the bays appeared to have improved by the time we arrived, so the formation penetrated Possession Bay, crossed to Antarctic Bay and climbed up onto Fortuna Glacier amidst enveloping low cloud that became progressively thicker as we ascended. The visibility problem was exacerbated by frequent driving snow squalls and sudden violent changes in wind speed and direction. Luckily, I was too preoccupied trying with the radar and a DR [Dead Reckoning] plot to keep us from crashing into the mountains to worry about it all. It felt very real and immediate, but at the same time very unreal, as if it wasn't actually happening to me. Not sure that sounds right – too late.

However, we managed to reach the landing site and disgorged our men and equipment. Rather them than me, I thought, as Fitz and I helped them out with their kit. I saw John Hamilton give a thumbs-up to us. Even with those three layers of clothing under my immersion suit, I was absolutely chilled to the bone by the cold. In fact, it was so cold that my teeth hurt even though my mouth was firmly shut. I returned to my seat to find that my window had icicles hanging from the frame.

Just as we lifted, the snow was falling all around us and Fitz noticed that we had in fact landed on an ice-bridge between two crevasses that was rapidly disintegrating. Once we were clear of the glacier, the journey back to the ships was uneventful and none of us said anything except to recite the mandatory pre-landing checks. Job done!

Today has not been pleasant; we certainly would not have considered doing that sortie in anything short of operational or SAR [Search and

Rescue] conditions. Ian really did well to get the cab through all the gloop, but I think that four pairs of harrowed eyes in and out of the cab must have helped. I do not think that I have worked harder in the air in my life and it proves why initial and operational flying training need to be so tough. As they say, 'If you cannot take a joke, you should not have joined!' I am just glad that I was up to it. Ian and the others do not need to know how useless the radar is in these conditions. It's not designed for the terrain-following role which we were called upon to perform during that sortie and the 30-degree blind arc through the nose does not help when you are running in towards a mountain. Still, it's all good motivating stuff – a little bit of what I joined the RN for.

Tonight the weather shows no sign of abating. It must be infinitely worse up on the glacier. We have had to leave the cab out on the Flight Deck with the blades spread, and with the gust-lock and tip socks on, as no one dares or is allowed to go out onto the upper deck. Probably another sleepless night is in the offing. It's good that Royal Navy ships have a reputation for being well-built and sound in all types of weather conditions. From the creaking and groaning of the hull, I would guess that she is certainly testing the tolerances. I wonder if the Args are out in this?

Needless to say, the uckers was cancelled again – really, we must get our priorities right! Dinner in the Wardroom was an absolute farce with all the officers sitting on the deck, eating their 'pot mess'. Every time the ship pitched, we were all over the place, with bits of potato, carrot and meat everywhere, as furniture, plates and assorted officers were thrown about and from side to side.

Saw a film and the projector, despite being secured, was wobbling all over the place – surreal. We all had to sit on the deck again because the chairs were lashed to the bulkhead. Just into the second reel, about half a dozen of the lads tumbled away into the darkness and ended up against the port bulkhead. The Padre, to everyone's entertainment and cheers, tumbled into the grate on the port side in an undignified heap.

I am finding that it is good to write everything down. I reckon that, if you have an unusual or alarming experience, it is probably a good idea to get it out of your system as soon as possible. Maybe, that is why people who are in car accidents feel compelled to tell other people about it. If you bottle it up and don't express it, who knows how it will affect you?

Thursday, 22 April

All through last night, the ship was tossed violently in all directions, with the hull shuddering, rolling and plunging as she rode out the storm. I do not think that I have ever been in such conditions at sea and I did not get much sleep. I just couldn't get comfortable in any position and tried to read, but even that proved impossible, as I was continually thrown around. The one time that I did try to get out of my bunk, I was propelled deckwards with considerable force and ended up landing in a heap and crashing into the door. I could hear Stewart next door getting up a couple times and somewhere I could hear another door banging. Often, the impact on the hull was as if it was being hit with a solid object and the seams were creaking continuously. It's a good thing that our ships are designed to such exacting standards and that the old girl is built like a Second World War cruiser in most respects. She feels solid and that's a nice thought.

I heard that the Captain spent all night on the Bridge because he was so worried about the conditions and the violence of the sea (that's what the Naval Prayer★ is for!) and that he was encouraging people to come up and see what really rough weather at sea looked like, 'so that they could tell their grandchildren about it'.

Today was another remarkable day. As I wrote last night, the weather positively worsened overnight, but luckily abated early in the forenoon. We scrambled down to the Flight Deck to see if our beloved cab had been damaged. When you have shared so many trials and tribulations together, you almost anthropomorphize the aircraft and I felt guilty that we had left it down there on its own, left to the worst of the weather. How sentimental is that!? We expected the poor thing to be utterly trashed, but, amazingly, it hadn't been damaged, despite some severe buffeting.

The weather was still pretty rough, with a long, violent swell, by the time that we sat down for the Captain's morning briefing. Breakfast had been taken on our laps as the tables would not hold anything for long, even with the non-slip mats. Everyone looked tired and drawn, with not a lot of banter or humour flying around. During a briefing from the SAS, just after 1000, it was revealed that the group up on the glacier had radioed that their position up there was untenable and they would not be able to survive for long. Apparently, the weather had taken its toll on

★ 'Preserve us from the dangers of the sea and from the violence of the enemy.'

them as well — not surprising considering that they were 3,000 feet above sea level and the temperature has been about minus 25, even without the wind. Ian and I gave each other a long, hard look, both of us remembering the 'challenges' and narrow escapes of the previous day; he then, typically, shrugged his shoulders and smiled in his characteristically resigned, philosophical, half-amused way. He is such a good bloke. Then the Navigator casually said, 'Well, I suppose 406 can go and pick them up — you are serviceable, aren't you?'

'Fancy coming with us then?' I thought.

Ian, Stewart, Fitz and I had a discussion with the Captain to decide the best course of action. None of us really relished the prospect of another trip up onto Fortuna — we joked about just how long our *fortuna* would hold out. *Audaces fortuna iuvat*, I thought, but decided that it was not the time. But we had to do something for the 16 guys whom we had come to know quite well in the past couple of days. It was decided to extract them from their predicament using the same tactics and formation as yesterday and the SAS Major would accompany us.

So we briefed, manned up and took off, but, as we entered Antarctic Bay with the faithful Wessex Vs (this time, flown by Mike Tidd and Ian Georgeson), we realized that the meteorological conditions would be worse than the previous day. Thick low clouds swept across the glacier, interspersed with racing snowstorms. Also, the violent winds, gusting up to 80 knots, would suddenly drop to 10 knots and change direction by up to 120 degrees each time, creating severe mechanical turbulence over the mountains. We left the Wessex Vs circling in Antarctic Bay, while we tried to get up onto the glacier.

We ascended the glacier face and at about 1,000 feet the first attempt ended when we flew into dense cloud just after we reached the glacier edge top and we lost all visual and radar orientation as we entered a gap between the mountains on either side. We had a lot of icing on the front of the cab and we lost tail rotor control a couple of times, while the radio altimeter was oscillating from 30 to 200 feet and back again as we traversed across unseen crevasses. I suggested that the Wessex Vs should land on a spit of land and wait to see how we in 406 got on. On the second attempt, I tried to con Ian through using a combination of DR navigation and any radar clues I could pick up. Stewart and Fitz were keeping a particularly good lookout. Given the inaccuracies of the maps and charts, it did not feel safe and, although I was giving a convincing commentary, I did not feel that I could risk my chums' lives in this way. So we had another attempt, coming to the hover by means of the FCS [Flight Control System] and attempting to wind our way up onto the glacier by using the ASW hover mode. We were defeated by the sudden oscillations in height caused by the crevasses and nearly bounced on the glacier a couple of times.

Having frightened ourselves silly, we decided to take everyone back to the ships (us to *Antrim* and the Wessex Vs to *Tidespring*), in order to refuel. I got out and went to the Bridge. The Captain and the team onboard were surprised that we had come back empty-handed, and when I told them about the conditions, real worry and concern were visible on everyone's faces. 'This is not going well!' said the Captain and headed for the lift to the Ops Room. I was not sure whether he was irritated and blaming us or commenting on the general situation. The Commander took more time to listen to what I had to say and reflected that the SAS would probably die up there if they had to spend another night on the glacier.

Refuelled and with some blankets, we took off, grouped up the Wessex Vs and had another go. At about 1330, our next attempt proved successful as all three aircraft climbed up onto the glacier, to find the SAS half a mile further up the glacier from their original landing site. It took a while to locate them, but Stewart noticed the flares that they had ignited when they heard us coming. By this stage, I think that it is reasonable to say that we were fairly well rattled by the weather conditions and were keen to get back to the ships as soon as possible. We landed into wind, such as we could identify its direction, but I noticed that Ian was having to push the rotor disc forward into the wind to keep the cab on the deck. The SAS were in a bit of a state, with ice flecking their noses and lips and their weapons totally frozen up. They loaded their kit into the back and John Hamilton and three others got into the cab. John Hamilton came onto the intercom.

'Thanks for coming to get us,' he said. 'It's not been great.'

'It's our pleasure,' said Ian. 'We weren't doing anything this afternoon anyway.'

Even as the troops embarked, we could see that the weather was closing in again, with real rapidity and force. It was almost as if the weather had parted to let us in, but was now threatening to swallow us, with the snow being whipped up and the wind blowing strongly. When we landed, I could see about half a mile – now it was about 80 yards. Then it seemed to open to about 500 yards and Mike Tidd, the pilot of YF, one of the Wessex Vs, decided that he wanted to lift before the weather got too bad. Ian and I discussed whether he should go and talked about this being a 'sucker's gap', a brief gap in a period of bad weather that makes you think that you can take a chance. But, in the end, weighing the odds, he decided that, as Mike Tidd was a QHI and Clockwork-trained, he should be able to make a good fist of it. So off he went. Mike lifted, but, as he transitioned forward, he seemed to lose his bearings in a squall-line, wobbled both ways, and momentarily disappeared. As the squall pushed through, the aircraft crashed in some snow, ending up on its side, after a skid of about 50–100 yards. Bits and pieces of the aircraft flew in all directions and a piece of rotor blade narrowly missed the second Wessex V – YA.

'Bloody hell!' exclaimed Stewart. 'He's stoofed.'

'Bugger!' said Ian. 'Why did I let him go? I shouldn't have let him go.'

'Is it bad? Are there any survivors?' I asked.

'Not sure' was the answer.

Then Fitz said that he could see some figures clambering out of the crashed cab. One came over to us – it was Mike Tidd. He was clearly shocked and, after saying that he had nearly made his wife a widow, told us that he reckoned no one was seriously injured. We decided that we would split the survivors between ourselves and YA. Just before Mike unplugged from the intercom to help with getting people clear of his crashed cab, Ian said, 'Mike, just one thing. You've left your wind-screen wipers on, you sloppy bugger!' Sure enough, amid the jumble of wreckage, the windscreen wipers were batting back and forth like billy-o and, in the rush to get out, Mike the QHI had not completed his shut-down checks. We all laughed – nervously – knowing that we still had work to do.

Ourselves and YA, which dumped fuel, cautiously lifted and crossed, being buffeted strongly, over to the third, stricken aircraft to embark the survivors. I could see all around me some very worried and shocked faces, all of which seemed to have gashes and bruises from the crash of YF; one of them (I think I heard him called 'Phil') had a pronounced gash across his forehead. It's funny how you notice these things in detail when things are tense. We each took half of the remaining survivors and prepared to lift. The meteorological conditions were still severe, with visibility down to virtually nothing. We would have to rely on the route that I had recorded in brittle chinagraph and permanent felt tip on my overlay on the way up. At this point, I realized how cold I was, despite the adrenalin. Before I could turn the range scale on my radar, I had to clench and unclench my hands several times; I could not feel my toes in my boots. Concentrate!

We were now carrying 12 souls onboard (four crew, Cedric Delves, Mike Tidd and two troopers from YF, as well as our original four troopers), so it was pretty crowded in the back of our Wessex 3, designed to take two crew only (with two pilots up front), with space for a couple of others at a pinch. Both helicopters lifted, despite their heavy loading. We certainly staggered into the air and, from the whine of the engine and gearbox, it seemed that Ian was using a lot of power and torque. We lurched a couple of times in the wind and started to make our way down the glacier at a height of about 30 feet in appalling conditions with YA in line astern. Ian said that he could see the way ahead intermittently and Stewart was keeping an eye on the second cab about 50 yards behind, to port and slightly above us. We were being knocked about by the wind and the squalls were rolling through dramatically, with periodic total white-out conditions. I carried on giving Ian positional information and courses to steer, with height information cross-referred to the radar altimeter. As long as Ian Georgeson was able to keep us in sight, he would be OK.

Unfortunately, soon we were in total whiteness and what none of us could see was that there was a raised ridge of ice and snow running across the glacier, no doubt built up over days by squalls. We cleared it and continued our descent unaware that Ian G had just lost sight of us and all visual references. Stewart was keeping an eye on the second aircraft through his rearview mirror and what he could see out of his window. He was saying something like: 'He's good, OK, about three lengths astern. Steady, steady, still in sight – oh God, he's gone in!'

'Fuckin' 'ell,' said Ian and he momentarily considered turning around.

'Boss, we can't,' I said, 'with all these onboard. Let's go back, refuel and have another go. I'll try and raise them on Guard.'*

We had not wanted to use the radios in case we alerted the Argentinians to our presence. I called, but there was no reply. Fitz told me that at this point Cedric Delves – who was listening on a headset – looked straight at John Hamilton and drew his right hand across his throat.

* The International Emergency Frequency.

Once we reached Possession Bay, I could use my UHF radio to the ship with little chance of intercept and clear of the deadening effect of the mountains: 'Feet wet [departing coast now]. ETA one-five [minutes]' and I added 'Regret we have lost our two chicks.' I was amazed by the HC's response – he simply said, 'Roger, out.' A couple of minutes later, obviously after he had passed the message to the PWO, he came back with: 'Confirm what you have lost.' 'Our two chicks,' I repeated, trying not to give too much away on an open circuit. 'Oh . . .' said the voice on the other end – and that was it.

When we got back, there was consternation onboard at the news, as we announced our intention of going back up the glacier immediately. The Captain looked very worried and hurried down to the MCO, presumably to talk to Whitehall. We refuelled, while Cedric Delves went off to do something, and loaded up with blankets and medical supplies. The POMA jumped in the cab (the cheeky bugger was actually sitting in my seat!), but we told him to stay in the ship. We had got through a lot together and we were determined to continue flying as a crew. The weather was getting worse all the time. There was no question that we wanted to rescue our fellow aviators and the rest of the troopers, but you would never have operated in peacetime in conditions like that. Of course, technically, we are in peacetime!

Off we went again, and found the edge of the glacier by radar. We briefly saw its top just below a highly active cloud and squall line and squeezed through the gap. We heard ice breaking off the front of the cab, while Ian tried to hover-taxi and use the FCS to feel our way in the gloom and cloud, always conscious of the fact that, unseen, there were mountains all round us. These attempts to get up onto the glacier were somewhat harrowing. We had two bashes at it. The first attempt nearly ended in disaster as we flew out of a cloud to find a huge white mountain rearing up in front of us, which we avoided thanks to a spectacular flare by Ian. On the second, we totally lost tail rotor control and spiralled down towards the glacier. Luckily, we pulled out before striking the surface. We were knocked about by some seriously violent gusts, which on one occasion spun us around about 240 degrees. Another katabatic down-draught nearly slammed us into the glacier. We could not find the rest of the lads and, in the conditions, we could not have landed anyway.

All the while, I was trying to contact any survivors on the emergency radio frequency. We heard someone calling faintly on Guard. It was Ian G, who said that he thought that he could hear our helo – from our position I was not sure that he could. He confirmed that everyone with him was alive and that there were no serious injuries among the passengers and crew.

After these fruitless and distinctly challenging efforts, we returned to the ship to wait for a break in the weather. I went to my cabin, to collect my thoughts, wrote two quick letters – to my parents and to A, enclosing my wedding ring.

What can you say? It's been good to know you. Thanks for everything. I hope that things work out for you and that I was worth all the effort! Love to everyone.

Then a prayer: Thanks for looking after us so far. Please let me be at my very best professionally and personally if we have to go back up there again today. Please do not visit all the times that I have screwed up on me right now. If not for me, think of the others. Lord's Prayer.

At 1635, we decided to try once more before darkness fell. Most of the command and warfare team seemed to treat it as just another routine sortie and I am not sure that they appreciated just how hairy it was up there. Maybe they were just trying not to transmit their nervousness and concern to us. After a sombre briefing in the Operations Room, we climbed back into our trusty cab, wondering if our luck would hold out just once more. We all, almost on auto and subconsciously, shook hands before we manned up the aircraft, taking our SAS Major with us, now deeply concerned about his men. I distinctly remember looking hard at – and touching – the reassuring solidity of the cab as I climbed into it and thought how it was going to be the only thing between us and – well, what?

Off we went. It was becoming a matter of professional pride – us against the mountain, as it were. This time, we tried a different approach. We climbed high through the cloud to about 3,000 feet, ignored the icing rapidly and alarmingly forming on our fuselage and found ourselves in clear air about 500 ft above. We could see the mountains all around us and were clear of significant rotary turbulence. I navigated our way to roughly on top of where I had been able to fix the position of YF on my radar when it crashed. We flew around for a while, straining to see anything while I called on the radio.

After about 10 minutes, Ian said, 'There they are. I can see them,' and talking to Stewart, 'Can you see the day-glo orange?' 'They've got their life-raft out and inflated,' said Stewart. There had been a lucky, transient break in the clouds and Ian spiralled down, despite the worry from all of us that it could have been a 'sucker's gap'. In this situation, the cloud closes just as rapidly as you are descending and you end up either crashing as you continue or totally disorientated in the cloud. As it was, we took a serious battering from high winds and turbulence as we went down, with the wind coming from different directions every few moments. I thought, there is no way that we are going to be doing, or surviving, two trips.

In this way, we managed to reach the position of the crashed YA and found 12 weary, battered and cold survivors. In the meantime, the 'gap' in the clouds had closed and we were enveloped again in total whiteness – we would have to go back down a few feet above the glacier. The two Ians discussed the reality – that we could only make one trip back – and that the packs, specialist equipment, Claymore mines and secret communications kit would have to stay. I started working out the weight. It was a real ergonomic nightmare trying to get them all in anyway and we had to force them to leave their kit behind. Fitz was standing by the door saying to these really hard men: 'Either the kit comes or you come, it's up to you, but this is the last train down the mountain.' Good for you, Fitz! Even so, they insisted on taking their beloved Armalites and other personal weapons – no one was going to dare take those off them. In the event, we had to pile them one on top of each other in the back and I will always remember their shocked, ice-fringed faces as they huddled together. It was so packed that we had arms and legs sticking out of windows and the door, while, in order to work the radar and comms, I had to sit on a trooper who was lying across our two operator seats with his head in the port window blister.

Then I completed the weight calculation – we would be a ton overweight, I told Ian.

'We should be OK for take-off in this wind,' he said.

'Are you going to be able to hover alongside and steady at the other end?' I asked, knowing the answer.

'Don't know, let's suck it and see,' he replied. 'Nobody said that it would be easy!'

'That's fine,' I said. 'Just so that I know.'

Just before we lifted, I could feel that the cab was lurching around and we sank abruptly as the load increased. I worried about our air intake becoming embedded in the snow and the engine failing. Just as we were lifting, we jolted down again and, as Ian pulled power and we careered upwards, the snow fell away beneath to reveal that we had originally landed on another ice-bridge across a crevasse which had now given way to reveal a deep void. We had had a perilously close encounter with what looked like a bottomless chasm and I was privileged with the momentary glimpse of the truly amazing, unearthly blue colour of the inside of a glacier. I did not tell the boys about it right then!

On the way down, I thought that I could smell burning and could see smoke. Shit! After all the drama, I could not believe that it would come to this.

'Boss,' I said, 'I think we have a problem back here – can you smell the smoke?'

'What is it?' came the almost resigned, but worried reply.

'It's OK, Boss, I know what it is and it's not a problem,' said Fitz.

'What is it?'

'I had some cigarettes in my goon suit and thought that the lads might appreciate a drag or two,' said Fitz.

I didn't have the heart to scold him. We had survived and still had a way to go and he was passing round the cigarettes while we were cruising along on top of all that very adjacent aviation fuel. Great!

So, having negotiated the glacier, we staggered back to the ship, somewhat overloaded and with a rear cabin like an opium den, and Ian thrust the cab down onto the Flight Deck with very little ceremony. We had been well overweight and we could not hover alongside. We had only been able to take off from the glacier once the wind strength got up to about 60 knots.

Ian's flying today has been quite remarkable, although he is too modest to admit it himself. He has been calm, assured and philosophical throughout. I hope that when they hand out the 'goodies' at the end he will receive something. Having said that, I think that we all did our bit and Stewart and Fitz were terrific. Not once did we lose our cool or our sense of humour and none of us blinked when it came to it. We are a really good team and today's situation has brought out the best in us. It is interesting that the Captain has not said well done or anything and most of the officers seem to think that it is just another day in the life of 406. Declan, Carlos, Alistair and Daddy S were interested in knowing what happened. All in all, I reckon, in complete seriousness, that we earned our flying pay today.

All this excitement and we haven't seen an Argentine yet! I feel sorry for Mike Tidd and Ian Georgeson, the pilots of the Wessex Vs. They are berthed in the gunroom with the officers under training right now. They are very down and depressed about the loss of their cabs and are currently filling out their A25s.* Mike Tidd, especially, is feeling it, saying over and again: 'I'm so sorry, Yankee Foxtrot . . .' Poor chap. However, I think that it took a lot of guts to go up to the glacier today, having seen how bad it was yesterday and how fearsome it was today. I suspect all that will be remembered is that they crashed their helicopters, not that they willingly and bravely went on a very difficult search and rescue mission, with all the odds against them.

The SAS are a strange lot. Before the events of the last two days, they barely spoke to us. Just before supper, all of them, including the troopers, invaded the Wardroom and insisted that we have a drink with them. There they were, toasting the Fleet Air Arm (which I do not think they had considered worth dealing with before) and our good luck, with bandages around their heads, dressings on their faces. They were keen to involve the Doctor as well. They also opened up a bit and told us something about conditions up on the glacier last night. Apparently, as we anticipated, they had been done in by the extreme cold and the numerous crevasses. Overnight, they had dug into snow-holes and had been covered by even more snow. Once they emerged, they had realized that, with the wind chill, they could not survive in the open, still less manoeuvre their kit on the sledded pulks across the deeply crevassed terrain. One chap said that he had never been in conditions like that and that nobody really wanted to leave his snow-hole.

Some of them are entirely cheesed off about having left their personal weapons and kit up on the glacier, including their beloved Armalite rifles, which they seem to have had in missions all over the world. We spoke a bit about operations and mutual experiences in Northern Ireland and the sort of scenarios they usually trained for. Even so, I still do not know any of their names and still less their backgrounds. I think that we are going to have to sort out better ways of the SAS operating with the rest of us mere mortals in the Armed Forces. It would have helped, I think, if we had got to know each other a bit better on the way down and they could have explained where exactly they fitted in.

* Accident reports (see 3 July entry).

Given what they have been through, I was surprised that they were so easy-going and philosophical about things. They really are most impressive and I understand from snatches of conversation that, not to be dismayed by the glacier, they are going to try something else tonight.

One last thing: David Stanesby has started selling (10p a sheet for charity) copies of the plunging barograph trace from last night as souvenirs, along the lines of 'South Georgia, I was there.' They have been selling quite well; I must get one.

Apparently, while we were away today, the ship had a fire in the Exocet bay, which was extinguished after a marine had seen smoke emerging from the compartment below the launchers.

We managed to get in a game of uckers (good therapy), which, thanks to a couple of late blow-backs, we won, but I'm knackered.

Thank you, Lord.

Stop press – I just heard during supper that the SAS have decided that they want to go into Stromness and thereabouts by Gemini now that they have lost the two Wessex Vs. We could have put them in pretty close by helicopter if they had not insisted on going via Fortuna – we still could. I will write about what transpires overnight tomorrow.

Friday, 23 April

It's St George's Day today and Shakespeare's birthday.

I slept well for about four hours, but, having heard about the SAS plan, I thought that I would get up and see what was going on, especially as it involved some risk to the ship.

As I thought, the SAS were up to something. Last night, they talked the Captain into taking the ship into Stromness Bay – right in, opposite Leith – so that they could insert five teams by Gemini. I felt that I had to stay up for this one, not only to witness the evolution, but also just in case we came under fire from the shore. I judged that it was a highly risky manoeuvre in a confined space and I could not help thinking about the fate of the *Guerrico* around by Grytviken at the hands of Keith Mills and his gallant team. If the Args at Leith had 66 mm rockets and recoilless rifles, as well as illuminants, we could be in for a rough ride. I kept on hinting to the Commander that the evolution might be dodgy, but he said that the Args would have their heads down and our gun teams would be fully briefed and ready to act in case.

We went to Action Stations at 0215 and entered the bay, silent and darkened, with our steam plant providing quiet propulsion and the ship closed down to the highest watertight condition, ZULU. The sea was flat calm, the night was pitch dark and the wind still – apart from the inky darkness, not really what we wanted. The Navigator was working really hard to keep us safe in very confined waters and with only occasional single sweeps of 978 radar, in sector scan.

There was a ban, on pain of something worse than death, on the use of intercoms, broadcasts, radios or shouting on the upper deck. The MAA had patrols out looking for any chinks of light – we were on red lighting anyway – and any 'goofers' who were away from their Action Stations. I suppose that I was 'goofing'. The gun crews were briefed and ready to fire if necessary.

From the starboard signal deck, I could see a couple of lights over by Leith and was sure that anyone worth his salt would have posted a guard. Surely, they know that we are here! They must be able to hear the noise of our main machinery and generators – another quick glance over at the lights.

We reached the selected drop-off point, but the Gemini engines weren't ready, so at 0245 we tiptoed away from navigational danger and out of possible range of gunfire. All of us, not least the Navigator, paused for breath, until the Gemini engines decided that they would cooperate and start.

We went back into the bay at 0330, but suddenly realized that we were still making a great deal of noise with our ventilation, which was immediately crash-stopped. We had to restart some ventilation almost immediately because the Ops Room displays and computer promptly crashed because of lack of cooling air.

The SAS were getting ready down aft, with their Geminis ranged on the starboard side of the quarterdeck, working in red lighting. You could discern the activity from where I was standing. I looked over to Leith through binoculars – just the same two lights. Then, from aft, I heard the faint sounds of Geminis being slipped over the side – on an improvised ramp that Chippy and his team had made – and saw in the dim light personnel and kit being loaded.

There was a pause of about five minutes and then 'whirr – wump – wump – wump – wump – wump – wumpa – wumpa – wumpa – wumpa – wump – wump – whirr – whirr – whirr – clunk': the unmistakeable sound of an outboard motor – or lawn mower – that does not want to run up.

Then another one! And another! Each one seemed to be demonstrating its petulant displeasure at being put into the icy water in the middle of a freezing cold night.

Bloody hell – you do not have to be a panel member on the Arg equivalent of *What's My Line?* to know what that noise is, I thought.

Also, why are they running up the engines on the side nearest to the Args? They could have launched and paddled round to the other side of the ship before starting!

This went on for about 10 minutes before at 0415 a couple of the engines decided that they wanted to play and the SAS went off into the night, with the two boats towing the other three.

Rather like ducklings, they seemed rather reluctant to go and within 10 minutes were back alongside again, because they still had technical problems, had forgotten something or did not know where to go. By this stage, the Captain and the Navigator were ageing rapidly by the minute. However, by 0435 the Geminis were on their way and we were heading out of the bay. We were clear by 0445. I turned in, much relieved.

Of course, the engines, which had been carefully stowed and lovingly maintained in converted oil barrels, full of sea water (thought of that), in anticipation of such an occasion, had seriously objected to being taken out of the warmer atmosphere of the ship and to being invited to perform immediately in such extremely cold conditions (didn't think of that).

In the morning, I was just chatting with Ian and Carlos Edwards about what happened when Cedric Delves came bowling into the Wardroom, with a glum, but suggestive look on his face and headed straight for Ian and me. 'We've got a problem; we've lost contact with two of the boats from last night. We don't know where they are.' I remember thinking, this is becoming a habit!

So, I had a look at the charts and calculated the likely drift rates based on the elapsed time, the sea-state, the wind speed and prevailing currents. We launched at 0840 to find them. Visibility was poor at about 100 metres and the cloud base at about 200 feet. After an hour's fruitless search, trying to locate the survivors in the vicinity of the mouth of Stromness and Cumberland Bays and evading any Arg activity ashore, I plotted and controlled a box search down-sea and downwind of where the Gemini should have been. The search legs were getting increasingly longer and we were reaching the limit of our endurance. I was thinking, we don't like to come back empty-handed; it's not our style.

On the last leg, I heard the faint tone of a beacon at extreme range and suddenly Fitz called that he could see something astern of us on the starboard side at about a mile. It was an orange flare. We closed quickly and found the boat, with three frozen yetis inside, looking very much the worse for wear. We winched the three survivors up, with their equipment, instructing the last man to sink the Gemini, in case it was found by the Args. They were not in a good way, with their dry suits brittle with ice and their faces grey with fatigue and cold.

I said, 'You were only supposed to have that boat for an hour. You'll lose your deposit!'

They were not amused and just kept themselves warm. We handed out blankets and gave them a flask of coffee. One man could hardly hold the mug, he was so cold.

They were lucky because they were well on their way to South Africa by the time that we found them.

Boats! In HMS *London*, back in 1978, we were just looking forward to a well-deserved weekend in port when we were told that we had to replace a ship that had been on Fishery Protection patrol, but had become unserviceable. This was a task somewhat beneath the dignity and capability of the 5,000-ton battlewagon, but the Captain decided to give it a go and we went off to the North Sea to look for likely malefactors. Having scanned the horizon for victims, it was decided to board a German, to test the system and exercise the boarding parties. I was Officer of the Watch and we roared up to a German stern trawler and ordered her to heave to and prepare to be boarded. Suitably impressed by the attention and an upper deck bristling with armaments, the German complied and we sat menacingly about 100 yards to port.

Needless to say, all the senior officers mustered on the Bridge wing to watch the spectacle as the order 'Away sea boat' was piped. The trouble was that the thing would not start; nor after 10 minutes did a second boat. The third boat came out in sympathy and the fourth (and final) vessel did not want to feel left out and petulantly refused to cooperate. The boarding party had shuffled round each boat in turn. The air was turning blue on the Bridge wing as the German manoeuvred deftly underneath the assembled senior team and called up, 'Good thing that you are not sinking, ja!' – before speeding off into the distance.

I won the job of Boats Officer as a result of that incident.

The Args have been flying reconnaissance sorties along the north coast of South Georgia today and we think that our presence has been detected on radar. Towards the end of the forenoon, we started picking up strong transmissions from an Arg aircraft, classified as an Arg C-130 to the north-west. At about 1400, *Plymouth* reported that she had detected a C-130 to the west, which coincided with an intercept by *Endurance* of a high-frequency transmission that she associated with a submarine bearing 330 within 100 miles. By 1445, the C-130 was operating in sector scan mode (was he targeting for someone else/cooperating with the submarine?).

The aircraft were careful not to come within Sea Slug range – they stayed at 30 miles – and cannot possibly know what the ships are. That was confirmed later when the World Service reported that the Arg media had claimed that *Exeter* was off South Georgia 'with two frigates'. I reckon this is because *Exeter* was in the West Indies and they have assumed that as the nearest ship she would be here already.

Meanwhile *Tidespring* refuelled *Plymouth* and started a pump-over* with *Brambleleaf* to the east-north-east. We headed towards them in fairly lively, sporting seas.

At 1500, it was decided to remove the covers from the Sea Cat missiles and the 3 inch chaff rockets.

By 1525, the C-130 was within eight miles of the *Plymouth*, *Brambleleaf* and *Tidespring* group and must have identified the types of ship.

By 1630, we had signal intelligence that an Arg submarine might be approaching or already be in the area. The 182 torpedo decoy was streamed and all ships started evasive steering and zig-zags, to minimize the chance of being caught by straight-running torpedoes. In addition, we enforced restrictions on the use of our radars and other emitters, in order to deny the C-130 and the submarine any information about our force composition and the identity and capability of individual ships.

Of course, we still did not have the ROE to engage! Even tonight, a problem we have in considering the ROE is that we do not have any insight into how the political and diplomatic negotiations are going. We are not receiving commentary on this aspect and have to rely on the World Service.

Then *Endurance* wound everyone up by reporting that she had picked up a submarine radar transmission in the vicinity of the pump-over

---

* To top up with fuel from another tanker.

group. The Captain was rather – shall we say – energized by that news, but I offered the view that the racket had to be spurious. I ventured that submarines rarely rig, let alone use, their radars and they have character-istics just like commercial sets. Anyway, just look at the range at which this intercept was supposed to have been detected. I was sure that it was one of the pump-over group ship's radars.

The warfare team did not agree and the 'good ideas in action club' swung into action. The pump-over ships were ordered to break off and depart the submarine probability area as soon as possible, streaming 182s in the process. We were told to get airborne with two Mk 46 torpedoes – never mind that we do not have our sonar fitted, thanks to that stupid decision by the Admiral at the beginning of the month. I want it back – now!

The Captain went to talk to Northwood about the situation and the need to have some more robust ROE, in view of a reconnaissance plane and a submarine possibly being in the same area as us. I pestered him all day to have our sonar refitted. Ian is backing me up. The Captain remarked on one occasion that I was in danger of becoming 'the least popular pork pie in his synagogue'.

The evening briefing was a bit fractious because we cannot get the ROE to deal with the C-130; nor is it certain that we can engage the submarine before it attacks us even if we detect it. There are two dis-tinct camps: the 'the suck it and see' lobby and the 'the war has started, so let's go for it' team. I am firmly in the latter group, arguing that the Args are not over here for their health's sake. The Captain is really wary of letting the group close the coast now and is looking for options which reduce the risk.

We heard some blatant hypocrisy from the head of the Arg Navy reported on the World Service tonight: 'We have peace in our hearts, but hot powder in our cannon.' Hot powder?! Also, the boys are calling the main Task Group the *Daily Mirror* ships, because of all the publicity that they get.

This evening, on the strength of an intercept of a unit communicat-ing on HF Radio Automatic Tele-Type with his base, in both directions, and a signal from CINCFLEET, we deduced, because the signal strength was strong, that an Arg submarine, probably the *Santa Fé*, might be close to South Georgia or within 100 nm.

At this point, in discussions, we pointed out again to the Captain that there was a clear danger that the Hercules could – or soon would – be targeting for the submarine and the ROE needed to be updated to reflect this latest change in the correlation of forces.

The Captain decided to withdraw all warships to a point 40 miles off South Georgia, especially as we really did not have much of an ASW capability and we did not yet have the helicopter lift to do anything about landing. Some people then started talking about capturing Leith, but it all seemed like a futile gesture and not worth losing a ship to the submarine. Nevertheless the Captain wanted to press ahead with planning for it. It's all a bit desperate.

At 2100, we rendezvoused with *Plymouth* and the two tankers at 53° 58′ S 035° 31′ W. *Plymouth* and *Antrim* formed a screen around the tankers and everyone was thoroughly twitched about the possible presence of the submarine.

So, for now, the tankers have been told to clear the Maritime Exclusion Zone to the north, along with *Plymouth* as escort, and *Antrim* is positioning to assault Leith with the Special Forces and any other troops we have to hand. *Endurance* is going to Hound Bay to withdraw some SBS who were landed by them and who are now finding conditions a bit tricky.

What has happened? Did the SAS give our presence away by transmitting while they were ashore? Or more likely is it in response to yesterday's speculation by the BBC (that first B is for British, I think) and the Voice of America that it is probably about time that the Brits were off South Georgia. That seems more likely.

I just broke off to go to Action Stations, which was sounded at 0010, based on a surface contact detected by *Tidespring* eight miles away to the north-east. I have never been so shocked in my life when the Main Broadcast Alarm went off (the submarine has pitched up?) and I got down to the Flight Deck and into my goon suit in record time. In the dark, we had a near miss with *Endurance*, which suddenly appeared at 100 yards on our port beam. We illuminated the reported target with star shell from the 4.5 gun, with two high-explosive rounds ready to follow. Under the descending glow of the flare, we could see the unmistakeable, familiar shape of *Plymouth*, which was no doubt as surprised as we were at the turn of events! At 0030, we fell out from Action Stations and I am now writing it all up before I go to sleep. Boy, are we twitched!

I know that we are operating under silent conditions and without radars, but we have to maintain our Ops Room plot and Bridge awareness better than we have demonstrated in this complete fiasco. We are frightened of our own shadows at the moment. It is because we do not have good enough intelligence about the submarine and the appearance of the C-130 has thrown everyone into a panic. We need to have the ROE and to take the initiative. As an anti-submarine Observer, I am decidedly unhappy, with a submarine in the offing and no bloody sonar in my aircraft – one wheel on my wagon, I'd say, and hardly rolling along!

We reckon that if we have an Arg 707 over South Georgia again, we will put it to Northwood that it could be targeting for the submarine. If I am honest, that is probably not true, although the reconnaissance information could be transmitted back to the submarine once the 707 is back at base. However, it is a plausible scenario and anything that allows us to get the ROE to deal with the submarine or the reconnaissance flights is justified. I am not sure whether the Captain believes it, but he is pushing the justification up the line to Northwood to get the ROE changed.

The boys have started an underground newspaper – the *Daily Scum* (Ship's Company Underground Magazine) – which is a compilation of gossip around the ship, digs at shipmates and comment on what is happening. It is produced during the quieter moments of Defence Watches and keeps people occupied. The first edition was not that good or humorous, but it does reveal what the boys are thinking and indicates their level of tolerance and state of mind as we experience new things and come under more pressure. As such, it is a good barometer of opinion and what is preoccupying everyone. I am sure that the content will pick up – we need to watch out for people being picked on though. We need to be 'all of one company' or we are nothing.

Faux pas of the day on the Growler:

Vice-Admiral Hallifax: 'Good morning, this is the Chief of Staff, I want to speak to the Captain.'

RO Ford: 'Hang on, Chief, I'll let him know you want a chat.'

Saturday, 24 April

We spent the forenoon frustrated at the turn of events. *Plymouth* replenished from *Tidespring* and promptly had a main feed pump failure while alongside. It was very dramatic to watch her falling astern and clear, thankfully not colliding with the tanker.

Tidespring then went off to pump over again with *Brambleleaf* on the edge of the Exclusion Zone. There were also reports that some British Antarctic Survey personnel had seen a couple of Arg warships (corvettes?) off the north coast of South Georgia, towards Bird Island.

This morning brought three pieces of welcome news:

Alleluja One! The Arg Hercules pitched up again in the night and it has been decided that *Antrim* cannot afford to be caught offloading troops inshore, at Leith, with the submarine possibly out and about to get us.

Alleluja Two! The really good news is that I have got my way and the sonar will go back into the cab.

Alleluja Three! We now have the ROE to splash the Hercules or 707 if it comes within range and deal with the submarine if it threatens us.

At last, the submarine is concentrating senior minds. Thanks to the Commander, the Captain realized that the only way that we were going to get onto the island was to dispose of the submarine. *Brilliant* is on her way to help, with a half-decent hull-mounted sonar, and 406 will soon have its sonar back. *Conqueror* has also been moved closer to intercept and, if necessary, deal with the *Santa Fé*, especially if she snorts or runs on the surface with her diesels. It all seemed a bit passive and reactive though, with no sign of a desire to seize the initiative or take the battle to the enemy.

At 1100, there were World Service reports in the Arg press of British ships – two warships and a tanker – already sunk, denied by MOD and reinforced by a signal from *Antrim* saying simply: 'Not us!'

Endurance signalled at about 1430 that she was being overflown and identified by the 707 and we started to move south to ambush it, with Sea Slug. *Endurance* then sent a cry for help – we thought that she might be over-reacting – in response to the 707 and to a BAS report from yesterday that the boffins had sighted two warships and two small jets off Bird Island. We signalled back that we were 'on our way' and the intention was that we would now splash any reconnaissance plane that already was, or subsequently ventured, over here.

Ian and I chatted over the options. We could not get onto the island while the submarine was hanging around and it would be a constant threat to us. 'Let's go after it,' I said, 'rather than sitting passive beyond 200 miles from the coast.' It's just not right! I eventually convinced Ian to go with me to the Captain and put a plan to him. When we went in,

Ian said, 'Flobs★ has got a plan, sir. I will let him explain.' The Captain looked wearily sceptical as I started along the lines of:

'Sir, this is a conventional submarine and he has to have left port a while ago. So, this cannot be a pre-planned mission in reaction to us arriving off South Georgia. The Args clearly did not expect us to come here first and, if he is here, this has to be either a reinforcement or a resupply task. If so, he will want to be on his way as soon as possible, because he will have been told that we are here by his headquarters.

'My guess is that he is already in Grytviken and that he will come out tomorrow morning as soon as it is light. If you consider all the bergs and ice that are around, he will come out on the surface and then dive once he gets clear. I think that we should go and get him.'

'We are too far out,' said the Captain.

'Sir, bear with me,' I said, feeling a bit nervous about pressing the case.

'Go on, then,' he said, but I felt that I was on borrowed time. Ian was shuffling a bit.

'Sir,' I continued, 'if what I am saying is true, we could fly in and put ourselves at the mouth of Cumberland Bay just before daybreak just on the off chance, with a couple of depth charges.'

'It is more important to keep the ships safe right now,' said the Captain. 'We cannot risk getting torpedoed; there is very little chance of rescue if we all end up in the water.'

'Sir, can I? I think that the risk is quite low. I reckon that, if you close to 80 miles, I can DR navigate my way in without using the radar or comms and we might surprise him. You'd be a long way off and you could keep the others further out. If we do not have a go now, we might never see him again until he attacks us. It's classic ASW – catch him when he is at PD [periscope depth] or on the surface!'

'What are you going to do if you find him?' said the Captain, suddenly sounding interested.

'I'll give him the two depth charges,' I said. 'We have the ROE and it would make our job here a lot easier.'

The Captain looked reasonably pleased, or rather amused, and said, 'Is that it then?'

I replied, 'I think that we should have *Plymouth*'s Wasp on alert with AS-12, as well as *Endurance*'s, and we can put *Brilliant*'s Lynx up to the

★ FLOBS – Flight Observer.

north-west along the coast with a Mk 46, in case I miss him. He can also provide early warning if there really are two Arg warships up that way. That means we will have a variety of weapons airborne just in case. The AS-12s will also be available to deal with any Arg surface ships that pitch up, if the BAS reports are true. I reckon that they might have seen *Plymouth* and *Antrim* at long range and misidentified us. Unless they are ship-spotters, it would have been difficult.'

'All right,' said the Captain, 'let's discuss it at the command meeting after the RAS.'

Two hours later, after the RAS and a visit by a *Brilliant* Lynx, we reviewed the day and the future prospects with the command and warfare team. When the submarine issue came up, the Captain said that I had a plan and that I should explain it. I wondered for a second whether I was being set up. I explained the logic and what I planned to do. The Commander thought that it was better than sitting out at sea on the back foot and that we should do it. Tony Dymock said that we had nothing to lose and the Navigator said that he thought I watched too many war films. In the end, the Captain ordered me to write the tasking signal and bring it to him for release.

Ian and I went into the Wardroom to write the signal, to find Major Sheridan, Major Delves and Chris Nunn at the forward table in a reflective mood, that is to say that they had had a drink or two. As they were well out at sea with no prospect of action, they had taken the opportunity to relax a bit. They asked what we were up to and when we explained Sheridan and Nunn were decidedly contemptuous of our idea and scoffed at the possibility of us actually finding and taking the sub out. They were totally dismissive of our plan and pretty fed up with their prospects of getting onto the island. I just hoped that we would find the thing – tossers! Typical Royal Marines! We got on with it and took the signal to the Captain for release, adding that the intention for the submarine was that we would conduct a 'search to destruction'.

I had received, via *Brambleleaf*, a letter from A with some press cuttings and a host of admin problems that need sorting out. I despatched some blank, signed cheques to cover access to my account and asked A to go and see the bank manager to explain the somewhat unusual situation. I have sent another letter to him to make sure that there are no problems for A in getting hold of OUR money if she needs it.

I also wrote home, stressing that I could not say much because of security considerations and that censorship was in force. I said that I had lots to tell her (!), but could not, and added that we had been 'involved in several adventures already' and 'have had some very narrow escapes'. I told her how cold it was, how rough the weather was and how we were into rationing (for the second time in my life. I was born when post-2WW rationing was still in force!).

I promised to see the team at Portland when we got back because people were pretty rude and indifferent when she asked whether there was any news after our sudden departure from Spring Train. From her letters, I am not sure how she is taking this unexpectedly extended separation and the prospect of war; I wanted to sound positive about our future. I said that I was not sure how long we would be 'down here among the penguins'. I mentioned that we had heard that 'relief' ships were sailing from the UK on 10 May, but I assess that if the crisis escalates they will be reinforcements, not reliefs!

All we hear about on the World Service is the progress of the *Hermes* Group (Blah! Blah! Blah!). It says a lot for our ability to stay undetected on the way down and where the focus of the press effort is right now. Surely, the Args must know we are serious now and that we are coming to get them.

It will be good to have the ASW kit back in the aircraft – hope that it works first time if we find the sub. There is also the chance that we might have a go at the Arg recce plane, now that we have the ROE.

Sunday, 25 April

During the night, we had left *Tidespring* on the edge of the Exclusion Zone and closed to within 80 nm of Cumberland Bay, with *Plymouth* and *Brilliant*.

I went to my cabin last night really excited about the prospects of the morning, although I was concerned that the submarine might be cleverer than we thought and was even now on his way to deal with us. I lay on my pit in my goon suit, mainly because I wanted to be ready to go in case the sub was detected and partly because I thought it best to be in my goon suit in case he found us first and torpedoed us. If I was going into the freezing water at night in the middle of the Southern Ocean, I wanted to be as warm and waterproof as possible and have as many survival aids with me as I could. Anyway, it seemed the right thing to do, 'on the vigil', armed and ready. I slept on and off, dozing, throughout the night, but with a real feeling of certainty that we would get the sub in the morning. I just hoped that the cab would be serviceable and that we would not miss this chance.

How long would our luck hold?

We briefed at 0700 and found our cab already ranged on deck with two war shot Mark 11 depth charges already loaded. The only disconcerting thing was the weather and we took off a bit late. It was extremely foggy, with visibility down to below a quarter of a mile. I would not be able to use the radar for navigation as this would alert the submarine to our presence and approach. We launched at 0810 and transited to the mouth of Cumberland Bay, using Dead Reckoning Navigation and fingers crossed, and trusting that we did not run into the land in the thick fog. In the circumstances, I did reflect on why it might be called Dead Reckoning and that you could end up dead as a result! Happily, we arrived spot-on at the entrance at about 0850 and began our search visually, as the visibility had slightly improved. Looking out of my blister, I could see the land features with which we had become so familiar and varying shades of dirty white and grey – clouds, fog, sea and large chunks of sea-ice and bergy bits.

We cleared the bay visually and the boys up front said, 'He doesn't seem to be here.' Bugger, I thought, thinking about having to return to the ship and face the cynics in the warfare team and the landing force drinking club. More than that, it would still mean that the submarine was a threat out there somewhere and we would be stuck about getting onto South Georgia.

So, what have we got to lose? I said to Ian that I would have one sweep on the radar to see if I could pick anything up, in case the submarine had left late or had made it out to sea. I decided to rotate the transmit switch on and off very quickly, in order to deny our potential victim definite proof that we were around. One electronic and aural blip from the radar might be judged by a casual intercept operator to be spurious, but two would certainly identify us as a hostile airborne radar to any half-competent operator.

As it happened, during the previous few days, I had taken the opportunity to plot on my acetate overlay the position of all the major icebergs and significant bergy bits, rather for the ship's navigational safety than for my operational convenience. I had actually given them names, all kings, as it happened – William, Henry, Stephen, Richard, etc., so that if they broke up I could name them Henry I, Henry II, etc. Anyhow, they were there on the overlay.

On went the trace for just one second and, before the background light faded, a small contact briefly illuminated that I instinctively judged did not correlate with any of my ice plot. It was pretty close to Edward III and (in maintaining a cheerful outlook) I wondered to myself whether the Black Prince had made an overnight appearance. Silly – and a bit intellectually pretentious – really! The new contact was about eight nautical miles away to the north of Barff Point and I guided Ian towards the contact, hardly believing that this small, instantaneous apparition could be a submarine. At every mile, I said to Ian, 'Anything?' 'No, it's still clampers, just ice and bergs' was the constant reply.

In reality, I hadn't expected Ian and Stewart to say anything for a while, as we were still in thick gloop. Then, at about a mile to go to the on-top,

'It's a submarine,' said Ian unemotionally.

'You're joking,' I said, thinking that it was a wind-up.

'No, no. It is,' said Stewart. 'Amazing!'

I quickly worked out the ballistic corrections for the movement of the submarine. It was not difficult. He was heading 310 at 8 knots. The forward-through of the DCs was 164 yards and you had to allow 20 yards per knot of submarine speed – 8 times 20 is 160. Talk about making it easy for us – just go to the on-top along the submarine's track and release. I fused both the weapons and was ready to release them (can you believe that this is actually happening!).

Ian then spoiled it for everyone,

'Are you sure that it is not one of ours. It could be *Conqueror*,' he mused glumly.

A little bit of me thought, sod it, it's a submarine and it's going to get away.

'Let's do him before he sees us and dives.'

Then I thought, *Conqueror* should be away to the north-west, looking out for Arg surface ships. The only reason for him being here and on the surface would be that he is in trouble and has had to come up.

By this time, I was craning my neck and head in the blister to have a look. Frustrated and failing to see the submarine, I asked, 'Has he got a flat casing and a tapering flat fin?'

'It's the Argie, no doubt about it,' came the sudden, reassuring call from Stewart in the left-hand seat.

'OK,' said Ian, 'are you sure that we have the ROE?'

'Of course,' I replied, reflecting the briefing and conversations the previous night. 'He's fair game – we might not get a second chance.'

'OK, Boss, let's go for it! Get astern of him and run up his track at 150 feet and we will release when you call on top. That should sort out the ballistic correction.'

What a moment! Every Observer's dream to have a real live submarine caught in the trap with two depth charges ready to go! Momentarily, I thought about the men that we might be about to kill, but Ian started calling down the range. As Ian called, 'On top, now, now, now', I saw the fin of a submarine pass under the aircraft through the gap around the sonar housing and I released both depth charges.

Ian flipped the cab around violently to starboard to see the results of the morning's work. I had told Fitz to man and cock the GPMG and, unstrapped, he tumbled back towards the rear of the aircraft. 'Fucking hell, Boss!' he exclaimed.

While this was happening, I glanced out of the starboard window. As we turned, the whole of the aft section of the submarine disappeared as two large explosions detonated either side of her casing about three-quarters of its length along and plumes of water shot up. It looked like she was in the process of diving when we struck her, but the explosions lifted her after end up and out of the water. She then began careering violently in all directions as I triumphantly reported back to *Antrim* the position of the stricken submarine. The HC didn't get it at first, possibly because we used the brevity codeword for a submarine, and there was no response (!). I was, momentarily, disappointed that the submarine was not sinking, but, at the same time, worried about what it must have been like for those inside. Still, this is war – and things happen, to them and us. It's always been that way. You make your own luck. Luck is when preparation meets opportunity!

I then called in *Brilliant*'s Lynx (Nick Butler and Barry Bryant) to close with the Mk 46 torpedo and instructed Fitz to have a go at the submarine's masts, fin and sonars with the GPMG, in case it looked like diving. Once Fitz had finished, we brought the cab into the dip,* safely out of

* Hover.

96

small-arms range, so that we could track the submarine on the surface and on the sonar if he dived. Simultaneously, as the submarine looked reluctant or unable to dive, I asked *Plymouth* to launch her alert AS-12-armed Wasp, since I believed that the submarine still posed a threat even on the surface. All the while, the visibility and low cloud were lifting dramatically, as if a curtain was being raised on a stage, to reveal a stunning backdrop of snowy peaks, huge mountains and glaciers, to complement the combat of mere mortals below. All the world's a spectacular stage!

I could now see on radar that *Antrim*, *Brilliant* and *Plymouth* were closing at high speed from the north-east and, on its launch, took *Plymouth*'s Wasp under positive control. I was receiving constant calls for a SITREP from the ship, but, hell, I was busy trying to control an ASW action. I tried speaking in brevity codewords, but the HC or the Ops Room team did not fully understand or decode them properly. In the end, I said in plain speech:

'CERTSUB [certain submarine] 320 Barff Point eight miles on surface – attacked with two ash cans [depth charges] and preparing for Bruiser [AS-12] attack by call sign [*Plymouth*'s Wasp]. I am Scene of Action Commander – CERTSUB allocated track 4011.'

After a pause: 'Request DAMASS [Damage Assessment]', from *Antrim*.

I was too busy at this stage, with controlling *Plymouth*'s Wasp and stopping the situation from becoming chaotic, to go into detail and the formal reports broke down: 'He's on the surface and I have definitely winged him. He seems to be down by the stern and there is smoke coming from his fin. I reckon that he is trying to get back to Grytviken.' And, as an afterthought: 'Request two more ash cans on my return.'

We broke dip just as *Brilliant*'s Lynx arrived and I instructed him to drop his torpedo only if the submarine showed signs of diving, as the Mk 46 did not have a capability against surface ships (with good reason, if you are an attacking escort!) or surfaced submarines. Barry tentatively asked to lob the torpedo in anyway, just to discourage the submarine from even thinking about diving. I was not sure, but agreed, thinking that I wanted the submarine to remain on the surface while we lined up the missile attack. 'OK then,' I said, 'let him have it.' So *Brilliant*'s Lynx ran in and released his torpedo, which, as we thought, failed to make contact; *Plymouth*'s Wasp fired an AS-12, which hit the submarine aft on the casing, causing a number of plates to fly off.

Almost at the same time, without warning, the submarine was

attacked, as she struggled to make for the harbour, by Wasps from *Endurance*. One of their missiles had nearly hit John Dransfield in *Plymouth*'s Wasp as he ran in for the attack. I was also aware that the three Cowboys (brevity code for ASW escorts), *Antrim*, *Plymouth* and *Brilliant*, were rapidly closing from the north-east. I was concerned that, if the submarine CO had any balls or he was me, he would turn on his pursuers and fire off as many torpedoes as possible. I tried to assert some control on the action and sequencing for the Wasps as Scene of Action Commander, but it was no use. Everyone wanted to get their name on the score sheet, it seemed. Shambles! We decided to go back and get more depth charges and refuel.

We transited the 10 or so miles back to the ship, feeling pretty pleased with ourselves, and eager to have another go, while the Wasps from *Endurance* and *Brilliant*'s second Lynx continued to fire off pot-shot AS-12s and a GPMG respectively, as the submarine staggered into Cumberland Bay, down by the stern. We thought that she might be sinking. She certainly did not want to play any more. At this point, I heard *Brilliant* announce that she was going to launch her Atlantic sea boat with Royal Marines in it to fire a Carl Gustav rocket at the submarine!

We arrived at *Antrim*, to find her sporting a couple of huge White Ensigns from the foremast as battle-flags, one of which was snagged around the navigation radar. She was creaming along at an incredible lick and you had to admire the elegant design of the County Class – they look like they mean business! Less impressive was the ship's reluctance to alter her speed and course to recover us, as if we were now getting in the way of her drive towards the action. They eventually came onto flying course and we landed on, lashings came on and we asked for fuel and our two depth charges. We quickly refuelled, but there was no sign of the depth charges (after 30 minutes' warning?), and, about 15 minutes later, we relaunched with one depth charge, to witness the final stages of the submarine flopping alongside the BAS jetty and Grytviken, pursued all the while by *Brilliant*'s Lynx and *Endurance*'s Wasps, firing off AS-12s like they were going out of fashion. There was tracer flying up from the ground forces and a Lynx aircraft flying above the scene. I tried to stop the action as it was obvious that the submarine was no longer a threat and her ship's company were streaming off the boat onto the land. The Lynx dutifully pulled away. Then, there was another of *Endurance*'s Wasps firing off AS-12 missiles – what is their problem!? It seemed a bit like overkill to us – literally, as the submarine was knackered from the time that we hit her with the depth charges.

So we again returned onboard and everyone was in high state of excitement. Those battle-flags had something to do with it and it was all *Boy's Own Annual* stuff! We disembarked and shook hands with our Flight members and started relating what had happened. I told Chief Bullingham that both his weapons had functioned perfectly and he gave me one of the fuzing lanyard pins as a memento – he kept the other.

As I walked to the hangar, Fritz the SMR said, cheerfully: 'One-nil to us I would say.'

'Yes,' I said, 'not sure how long we have left to play, though.'

I then asked, 'What happened to the second set of depth charges?' (Two of which I could now see were sitting in their cradles at the front of the Flight Deck.)

He said, 'I think that you had better speak to the Greenies.'

I could see the DWEO and marched over to him. 'If you don't mind me asking, what happened to the second set of depth charges?'

'Look,' he replied, holding up a thick BR [book of reference], 'it says in here that we have 45 minutes to prepare a depth charge, let alone two.'

Only my best withering look – which must have transmitted, 'Don't you know that there is a bloody war on?!' – saved me from committing instant insubordination in front of the boys. I turned away to go with Ian up to the Bridge to brief the Captain on what had happened and to urge him to authorize an immediate assault on the island while the Args were in shock. I had forgotten that most of our troops were well out to sea in *Tidespring*, but – come on – we had our own Marines and the assortment of SAS, SBS and other troops in the three warships.

After the sortie debrief, we then had a discussion with the Captain and the warfare officers, Major Delves and Major Sheridan, about possibilities. There was a quick tot-up of how many forces the Args had on the island and whether we had enough to deal with them, especially as they now had a submarine's ship's company as well, or whether we should wait for *Tidespring* and M Company to come in from the edge of the Exclusion Zone. It was assessed that the weather might change or darkness might fall and we could lose momentum if we did not crack on with the assault today. Sheridan, despite his scepticism the previous night in the Wardroom, was decidedly keen to get on with it, as was

Major Delves, who had the sort of sinister gleam in his eyes which suggested restless impatience now that the game was afoot and that these softy sailors were only getting in the way. There was just the little matter of him getting ashore, of course, although, at this point, I am pretty sure that he was weighing up his ability to walk on water to get at the Args. Lieutenant Colonel Eve was also very enthusiastic and desperate to do something – he's obviously switched on, but very eccentric though!

Anyway, a plan emerged. We would take Chris the 148 Battery NGS spotter and his team ashore and, with *Plymouth*'s and *Antrim*'s 4.5s, give the Args a demonstration of naval firepower on the Hestesletten opposite Grytviken and then follow up with an airborne assault (with just Humphrey and the two Lynx from *Brilliant*). That would take some coordination. The hope was that they would surrender without bloodshed.

In order to sequence the troops and weapon loading properly and to free up space and weight in the cab, we decided for the first time that we would not fly as a crew and that Ian and Fitz would do the short hops in and out of the assault area, once the NGS was over. Stewart and I would run things on the Flight Deck.

Shortly, while the Booties were getting their act together, the three warships formed into line ahead heading west and prepared to bombard the Hestesletten, opposite the Args in Grytviken. Stewart and I then coordinated the complex arrangements on the Flight Deck and made sure that the lift operation ran smoothly, although the superstition about flying together was on our minds. From 1445, we landed 79 assorted SAS, SBS, elements of M Company and our own RM detachment, as well as the 148 Battery teams, using 406 and *Brilliant*'s two Lynx. Once the 148 Battery team were ashore, we started the bombardment. Both *Plymouth* and *Antrim* opened up with the 4.5s, while the troops approached Grytviken on foot. It seemed like an unreal world – we had just disabled a sub and we were doing gunfire support for real! It was a throwback to another era – one inhabited by images and sensations that you normally associate with the Second World War. *Antrim* fired 69 rounds and *Plymouth* 120.

All through, we had lots of problems with communications, because of the terrain and the propagation. During the bombardment, I climbed onboard and we remained airborne to act as a communications relay with the troops ashore. After this initial bombardment, this Captain decided to land us on and bring the ship in close to threaten the Args with direct fire and show them what they were up against. I must say that I was distinctly nervous about this. Surely they must have anti-tank weapons. As we rounded the Point and came into view of the BAS building, I was on the lower Bridge, casually listening to the radio circuits.

The atmosphere was tense, but:

Chief Yeoman: 'I can see an Argentinian flag still flying, sir.'

Navigator: 'Where?'

Chief Yeoman: 'On the flagpole, sir.'

At about 1650, I could hear someone trying to communicate in broken English on Channel 16, with what sounded like a rugby team singing in the background. 'Surrender . . . we have injured . . . *es terminado . . . no más . . .*' I heard. I then realized what was going on and called up to the Bridge and the Captain: 'Sir, I think that they are trying to surrender. They are singing their national anthem.'

At 1705, we could see a white flag flying; our troops held their fire and started moving towards the settlement.

The ship then prowled around off Grytviken, while we got the cab ready for taking the Doctor in to deal with any casualties. Needless to say, having been told to go round to Leith, *Endurance* insisted on making a dramatic entrance into Cumberland Bay, did a flourish off Grytviken and chugged back to sea. Having led the Cowboys' charge against the submarine, *Brilliant* modestly held off to secure the mouth of Cumberland Bay.

Stewart and I flew into Grytviken with the Doc, because of reports of enemy casualties, including an Argentinian sailor whose leg had been badly injured in one of the attacks on the submarine. We heard that areas had been mined, so asked the troops ashore where we should land. A really useful reply came back: 'Your guess is as good as mine.' While we were deciding what to do, we flew over the site and I looked around. There were numbers of dejected, disgruntled Arg submariners on the damaged casing of the submarine, no doubt because they could not be sure where the mines were either. The submarine casing and fin were seriously roughed up with missile strikes and other damage. She had settled by the stern and was low in the water. Nearby, a Union Flag was flying from the flagpole, without a White Ensign, and Cedric was standing near a helo landing site looking as cool, determined (intimidating actually) and sartorially shambolic as you like, hands in the pockets of his combat jacket.

In the end, we decided to winch the Doc down, having told him about the mines, in case the vibration set off the explosives. He wasn't happy initially and I shouted, 'Do you want to live for ever?', knowing that he would be safe if I put him down where people were standing already. He was not impressed and was still remonstrating as I winched him out of the door, pretending in a pantomime way that I could not hear him amid all the helo noise. I gave him a cheery wave as he touched down.

The ship then sent a well-crafted signal, which I think the Commander had had up his sleeve for a while:

'Be pleased to inform Her Majesty that the White Ensign flies alongside the Union Flag in Grytviken South Georgia. God save the Queen.'

It has an authentic Imperial ring and a quiet, unfussy dignity about it.

CINCFLEET came back to all the Paraquet ships with a simple 'Very well done indeed.' The Captain signalled to the South Georgia Ships: 'A good day's work. BZ.'* You could tell that everyone was busy at Northwood.

We came to anchor just off King Edward Cove, with six shackles on deck at about 1900.

Although we should have done it slightly earlier, we deliberately conducted Sunset at 1934, to impress the Args ashore. John Saunders did the honours and we briefed everyone carefully that this would be a formal Sunset, with 'Sunset' played on the bugle. Bugler Brown, the Royal Marines musician who had joined us for three weeks of Spring Train and has stayed in *Antrim* ever since, performed a pitch perfect Sunset ceremony. In the half-light and the clear, cold air, the haunting, insistent sound of the bugle could be heard across the bay, as the flags ashore fluttered in a far outpost of a territory that was once again British. It sent shivers down my spine, as the Ensign came down in time with a bugle whose volume was magnified by the surrounding snow-clad mountains.

I said to the Captain that there was a possibility that the Argentinians might not have all surrendered and that we ought to take precautions against underwater sabotage. He ordered scare charges to be dropped

*BRAVO ZULU, a naval signal of approval from a senior officer, meaning 'manoeuvre well executed'.

over the side to deter underwater attack and I suggested that he invite the submarine CO and the commander of their soldiers/marines onboard. They would be nervous if anything was afoot – I recalled a film about the Italian midget submarine attack on our battleships in Alexandria in the Second World War – and we might gain some intelligence.

Given that I spoke some Spanish, the Captain asked me to be on hand to talk to them when they arrived. The Captain of the submarine was clearly distressed and embarrassed, but well dressed in a Navy coat and cap, when he came onboard and the commander of the marines was impeccably dressed in an overcoat and smart cap (how do you achieve that when you have been in a submarine for week or so?). In fact, they looked incredibly well turned out considering what had been going on and there I was in my flying overalls, looking, in my beard, decidedly piratical (happy with that!).

I introduced myself to the CO and went with him down to the Main Drag. I had no intention of telling him that I was the author of his present troubles, but it felt strange and humbling being in the company of someone whose life I had affected so drastically, and probably for the worse. He will never be able to get over this, I thought, either personally or professionally. His career would be over and the loss of face in Argentina would be huge, in view of their machismo culture. I did, momentarily, feel the thrill of real achievement though at having found him exactly where and when I expected. Great to pull one over a submariner!

I said to the CO in Spanish: 'I am sorry to see you in these circumstances.'

He said (in Spanish): 'This is what happens in war.'

I said (in bad Spanish): 'I hope that your crew is being looked after', but I think that he thought that I said, 'I think that you and your crew did well in getting the boat alongside.'

He said (in English): 'No, I was stupid, but we really did not expect to be attacked by the British without warning.'

He then asked, 'What are those explosions?', referring to the scare charges going off about every three minutes.

'That's just in case some of your men decided that they might attack the ship after you surrendered,' I said.

'Oh no,' he said, 'it's far too late for that.'

They went along the Main Drag under escort to the Captain's cabin for supper – 'I bet it's not pot mess!' I thought.

I then needed to go and help the medics explain to the injured Argentinian sailor what was about to happen to him, before they gave him the general anaesthetic. I was a bit squeamish about this – I hate hospitals and things at the best of times and I could not imagine what a mashed-up leg looked like. Anyway, I went into the Sick Bay and saw Alasdair (all dolled up in the medical gear and mask), who told me what was going on. There were a couple of people in the operating area to the left and I could see Godfrey and the CPOMA [Chief Petty Officer Medical Assistant] helping. The sailor was on the operating table and conscious. He was looking remarkably stoical. 'Is he going to lose his leg?' I whispered to Alasdair. He nodded, but motioned me to say nothing. 'What do you want me to say to him?' I asked, feeling extremely doubtful about my feeble Spanish in a medical situation. I could just about manage '*Me duele la cabeza*', and, if pushed, '*¿Tiene una enfermedad de transmisión sexual?*', but what on earth would I have to say?

The guy was coping well and was impressive in his bearing. He was a tough guy and I admired his gritty stoicism. He was clearly the sort of sailor that every navy cherishes, salt of the earth. I tried not to look at the mess that was the remains of his leg and tried to appear unconcerned.

Tentatively, I said, '*Soy capitán Parry y hablo espanol un pocito. ¿Como esta?*'

He said, '*¿Es de gravedad?*'

I continued in Spanish and was suddenly sad at what I was witnessing. 'You'll be OK. These guys are terrific doctors, you are in good hands.' Phew! That went OK.

Then the masked surgeon, who I think was called Crispin, said, 'We need to put him under, before infection sets in. Can you tell him that we need to put a catheter into his penis and then put him under?'

Inside, I winced at the thought of the catheter and the limitations of my Spanish bore in on me immediately as I struggled to work my way round that one. It ended up with the Spanish for 'They need to put a tube into your dick and you are going to sleep for a while.' Luckily, he got it first time and he gave a determined, grit-your-teeth nod. I said, 'It'll be fine – best of luck' and left it to the experts.

As I left the Sick Bay, I couldn't help remembering that my tenuous grip on Spanish has got me into trouble a couple of times before. I recall that I had to go ashore in some Spanish-speaking port where one of the sailors had misbehaved and nicked a motor scooter as a prank. The police had been officious and could not see the humorous side. They also were enjoying having a British officer at a disadvantage and in their debt. I waited around for about three hours and decided that I need to lubricate the process. I went back to the ship and got two bottles of whisky. This seemed to translate what we wanted better than I could and, after assurances that the sailor would be dealt with in the traditional Royal Navy manner, he was released into my custody. That's a win then, I thought.

The following day, we had a mini-demonstration on the jetty about the barbarity of the Royal Navy and the way it treated its sailors. I was told to investigate and, to my intense embarrassment, discovered that the report of the incident with the scooter had appeared in the local rag. My blood drained from my brain and face, when I read, at the end of the article, in Spanish, 'The officer who took custody of the man assured the police that the offender would be flogged when he returned to the ship.' Brilliant! The Captain really enjoyed that – eventually.

I was on hand to see the Captain of the *Santa Fé* and the marine Captain off the ship at the end of the evening before they went ashore and wished them well. I then wondered whether the Captain wanted to see his man in the Sick Bay, but, when we went down there, the guy was still under the influence – or the knife – and could not be seen.

The Captain of the submarine was clearly upset about it all and simply thanked us, on departure, for 'your humanity and understanding'. Could not help thinking about Nelson's prayer before Trafalgar: 'May humanity after victory be the predominant feature in the British fleet.' Glad that we got that right, then!

All through the day, I was hoping that Stewart would have managed to get the photo of the decade as we winged round on the submarine, but he didn't. He had split a wrist seal on his goon suit that very morning before manning up and, in changing, had inadvertently left his camera in his discarded goon suit.

One of the most exciting moments of today was dinner. As we ate our dinner, the BBC World Service was announcing the first news of the invasion of South Georgia some two hours after the completion of the events. It was a dazzling moment, to be part of history, if only for a few hours, and to hear those events being relayed around the world after that famous and, for me on this occasion, emotionally charged theme tune, 'Lillibullero'.

But, if the kill of the submarine has been the high point of the day for me, I will always remember returning to the ship after the submarine sortie. The Commander had promised me a can of Coke if I managed to find the submarine so I marched up to the Bridge to claim my prize, to find the Padre in earnest conversation with the Commander. Suddenly, the Padre turned round to me and said, 'It's all your fault, Flobs!' and I thought I was about to be on the end of some pacifist, love-thy-neighbour invective. 'Because of what you've done,' he steamed, 'we can't have Holy Communion now. It was on Daily Orders, you know.'

What can you say? Of course, it is Sunday today! And He has been good to me. Yes, He has.

Lost at uckers tonight, not badly, but who cares? We won the real game. I feel pretty buoyant about it all and pleased that I was able to do my bit. To be fair, we have been more at risk from the weather and the terrain than from the Args and we have not actually been on the receiving end of any direct fire yet. They gave up very easily, without even token resistance, except by the injured guy with the rifle in the fin of the submarine, who has probably by now lost his leg. But it is exciting to be actually doing the job for which I am trained and I reckon that I am the only Observer ever to have taken out a submarine since the Second World War. As yet!

No time to read much tonight, what with the day's events and writing up.

Monday, 26 April

Today's priorities were getting M Company ashore from *Tidespring*, containing the prisoners and offloading all the equipment needed to garrison and sustain the island. We also had to ensure that we did not get attacked by Argentinian forces in retaliation for what happened yesterday and to secure our position ashore. We have about 160 prisoners of war and, as well, had at the start of the day the little problem of the Args at Leith, who did not appear to want to surrender. It seemed to be a question of 'Come round and make a show of force and we will consider it.'

So, last night, *Plymouth* and *Endurance* were tasked to go round to Leith to invite the Args there to surrender. Meanwhile, *Brilliant* wanted to come and anchor in Cumberland Bay after *Antrim* and asked permission to do so. The Captain replied, 'There is only one anchorage in this bay and I've got the bastard.'

I just need to record a few things from yesterday evening. I tried to claim the submarine as a naval prize, but apparently the law and regulations allowing this were repealed/rescinded just a few years ago. I am not going to get rich that way. Time was – in Nelson's day – the capture of a French or Spanish 74-gun line-of-battle ship would permit you to retire in reasonable comfort and get a walk-on role in a Jane Austen novel.

I was wondering whether we were going to ask the Args questions. As a trained Prisoner Handler and Tactical Questioner and with my little Spanish, I am surprised that we are not trying to get useful information out of them, all in accordance with the Geneva Convention of course. Apparently, we have received orders from Northwood that we are not to question the prisoners and are to handle them with kid gloves.

The SCO and Duncan Ford went off to see if there was anything in the submarine that might have value from the intelligence point of view. They came back with some souvenirs. I hear that someone lifted an Argentinian national flag in a wooden case and the Wardroom silver. I was given a couple of brass tallies from the torpedo tubes, showing whether a practice or a warhead torpedo was loaded and was told to have a look at some of the books they had recovered, as they were in Spanish. It seems that the soldiers and Marines are going through the submarine and removing all sorts of things. They seem to have an almost medieval attitude to helping themselves.

Duncan Ford and SCO said that the interior of the submarine was a shambles. Gauges, dials and electrical boxes had sheared off the bulkheads – no doubt caused by the depth charges – and the control room was festooned with tomato sauce. Apparently, we hit the submarine just as they were serving from a large bowl of early-morning pasta and sauce – the shock had distributed it liberally around the control room.

I had a look at the books and papers. There was not much of interest – a few tactical procedures and general warfare instructions, together with the engine room log, whose last entry in Spanish was 'attacked by helicopter with bombs' – '*con bombas*'. There was a sheet of paper that had probably come from the control room, with various lats and longs*

---

* Latitude and longitude.

and references to Area Carlota, which seemed to be where the sub had been ordered to go on completion of her excursion to South Georgia. It looked like she had been told to patrol to the north of the island between 20 and 40 miles.

I reckon that they burned all the cryptography, codes and confidential stuff, either on the way in or once alongside. We had seen smoke coming from the submarine late in the action and assumed that this came from the hits on its fin. However, I suggested to the Commander that the Args, in the rush, might have dumped some material overboard when they got alongside King Edward Point. He sent our divers down and they found some British waxed codebooks (in really good condition) from the 1950s, obviously evidence of a previous confrontation.

At 0100 this morning, *Antrim* weighed anchor and left Cumberland Bay. The sea was, as usual, pretty lumpy, with the by now familiar stiff, offshore breeze (40 knots) whipping up the surface of a long swell. Bracing, the Booties would call it! We headed out to a point where we could provide good anti-air defence and cover the seaward approaches to the north-west, up and down a 20-mile racetrack about eight miles offshore. We thought that the only likely threat at this range might be warships or, in the air, Canberras or Hercules dropping bombs out of the back (risky, but possible). Sea Slug would just love to have a crack at them! We spent the daylight hours at Action Stations.

At about 0400, an Arg Hercules seems to have probed from the west to about 35 nm, but did not close to investigate or identify us, particularly after *Brilliant* turned on his radar. Another one came back between 1530 and 1800, but never came within range (to 50 nm) after he was tracked and illuminated by our Sea Slug radar (901).

In the forenoon, *Tidespring* went into Cumberland Bay, to put M Company Royal Marines on the ground by boat and start shifting loads of stores and ammunition ashore. In 406, we spent most of the day taking personnel, equipment and stores from the ships to ashore and around the bazaars, in order to ensure that the garrison is well-founded and that everyone and everything is in the right ship for subsequent operations.

We were glad that *Conqueror* was still around to deal with any intruders, although we were a bit puzzled that she had not detected the *Santa Fé* inbound. After all, the Arg must have snorted or run on the surface on her way to South Georgia, with her engines sounding like a box of spanners in a gale. Perhaps the sonar conditions and the constant growling, cracking and banging from the ice floes and bergs made it impossible.

It felt strange to be busy doing normal things after the excitement of the previous days. Also, it feels good to be in the news, even though we are at the far end of the world. We heard on the World Service that the Args were claiming that the Arg garrison was fighting to the last man and that we had suffered dozens of casualties, not that they have any information about what is really going on, of course. I am sure that this would have resulted from radio broadcasts from the Args who were still holding out at Leith – they would not want to report that they had given up without a fight (bad for the reputation and their future when they get back).

Talking of which, last night, *Plymouth* and *Endurance* were sent round to secure Leith and accept the surrender of the marines and civilians round there. We also needed to recover the SAS teams that had been landed/stranded on 22 April. When contacted by radio, the Arg commander said that the civilians would give up, but that he and his marines were going to fight on. The civilians were told to go to Stromness, while *Plymouth* prepared to land SAS troops at 2300, for a combined bombardment and assault at first light (why is it always first light; it's pretty obvious!). However, by 2245, the Args thought better of fighting to the last drop of blood and said that they would surrender at 0800 the following morning. *Plymouth* and *Endurance* then landed their SAS and SBS troops, who took up marking positions overnight.

At 0900 this morning, there was a white flag at Leith and 12 Arg marines surrendered, along with two others who had to be rounded up. The vicinity of Leith was heavily mined. There was a formal surrender ceremony onboard *Plymouth*. The civilians and marines were taken onboard *Endurance* and *Plymouth*, along with a reindeer that the SAS had bagged and presumably want to eat. The civilian prisoners were reported as being 'extremely smelly, dishevelled and undernourished'. The marines are apparently in good shape, but, again, unwashed. Their commander is apparently a robust, smooth-talking, murderous piece of work called Alfredo Astiz. All the Args seem to be afraid of him and I hear that he might have been a player in the 'Dirty War' in Argentina.

Flying conditions today have been dreadful, with visibility and cloud base at less than 100 feet, blizzards and examples of violent wind sheer of up to 180 degrees. I crewed with Ian and Stewart with Fitz. Around lunchtime, while Ian and I were writing up our reports of the previous few days, Stewart and Fitz were tasked to lift the SBS guys from *Conqueror* and take them and their kit to *Plymouth*. *Conqueror* surfaced a couple of miles away and the transfer started.

While they were winching some of the kit, one of the SBS (called 'Jem') and a sailor from the submarine were swept off the casing, along with a load of weapons, stores and equipment. Stewart and Fitz winched them up in the nick of time. They were bloody lucky – no survival or once-only suits in this environment. They would have been alive for about five minutes at best and Fitz said that he had to make them beat themselves continuously in the aircraft. They were brought back to *Antrim* for treatment and I was on the Flight Deck when they arrived, with the Doc and Godfrey Rhimes. The sailor was blue with cold and almost delirious; the SBS guy looked and sounded a bit better, but not much. Alasdair and the MAs looked after them and they spent time immersed in baths (Sick Bay and Wardroom) to restore their circulation and feeling in their limbs.

'How did it go?' I asked Fitz.

'Unbelievable!' he said. 'The submarine guy was almost unconscious in the water and was not responding when I lowered the strop. I had to get the SBS bloke in the strop and trail him across the water, so that he could put the other guy in the second strop. I brought them up together and then could hardly get them into the cab, what with the sonar and everything in the way.'

'At least the submariner will get a bath – the only one in months,' said Stewart. 'He'll notice how much the other submariners stink when he goes back,' he joked.

It seems that we have about 185 prisoners to accommodate. The total comprises: 48 scrap dealers of various nationalities; 76 crew from the submarine and 20 newly arrived marines; 16 of Astiz's boys and 25 soldiers who were the garrison at Grytviken. Except for the Leith prisoners in *Endurance* and *Plymouth*, they are all in Shackleton House at the moment as we do not currently have any accommodation for them in the ships. It's tight and distinctly unpleasant, but at least it is warm. The word is that they will be going to *Tidespring* and then north to Ascension, for repatriation.

Unfortunately, there was a fatal incident in the submarine, while we were out at sea. Nobody is quite sure what happened, but it seems that

Major Sheridan had convinced Captain Coward from *Brilliant* that the *Santa Fé* was in the way alongside the BAS jetty. She contained explosives and her unstable weapons, and, as she was sinking slowly as a result of the depth charge damage to her ballast tank and after section, she might foul the jetty. This is the main access point for the BAS base at Shackleton House, where we had the prisoners and the captured munitions and stores. Sheridan wanted the boat moved to deeper water and sunk. There was also a discussion about whether the Args could recapture the submarine and use it against us. Given its state, I think it unlikely! I had heard that Major Sheridan had asked the Captain whether this should be done while we were out at sea for the day. The Captain had said that he should put the boat off-limits to the considerable numbers of people who were goofing and souvenir-hunting inside.

Apparently, they did try and move the boat, with Captain Coward and the CO of the submarine and a few Arg sailors, but, in the process, a Royal Marine shot one of the Arg CPOs dead. It seems that a couple of Royal Marines were in the control room with the CPO, while the others were on the fin and that the internal comms and electrics had been knocked out by the depth charges. The Royal Marines had been briefed that if there was any attempt to scuttle the submarine, they were to take the appropriate action. The word is that the Arg moved to correct a list by blowing air into some tanks to increase its buoyancy and correct the list. The Marines then shot him a number of times.

Late on, *Brilliant*'s Lynx arrived with her CO, presumably to report what had happened. Captain Coward is a proper officer, who seems to be a traditional fighting Captain and just wants to stick it to the enemy. Straight out of the Napoleonic period. He said that we had done a good job on the *Santa Fé* and we chatted about Barry Bryant and Nick Butler. I met him with the Commander on the Flight Deck, to take him up to the Captain, who, deliberately, it seemed to me, did not come down to the Flight Deck to meet Captain Coward. I felt a bit awkward, as Captain Coward was obviously worried and upset about what had happened and was clearly a decent man. He has a strong handshake, immediate impact and a real presence. He asked me how things were going, then abruptly inquired: 'What sort of mood is your Captain in?'

'So, so,' I said and then, because that did not seem to encourage him, I added, hopefully: 'I know, sir, that he is really looking forward to seeing you.'

I walked with him up to the Captain's cabin flat and handed him over to the Supply Officer, who was looking decidedly uncomfortable, but, as usual, in control.

It seems hardly possible that we in 406 could have taken out the submarine without anyone getting killed and now we have ended up shooting one of their ship's company. That is not going to look good in the press or at the UN, I'd say. There will be a Board of Inquiry. And now there is more scrap metal alongside the whaling station that needs to be removed!

If all that wasn't enough, the Captain invited the CO of the submarine, who looked subdued and embarrassed, and the Arg marine Major (Lagos), who still looks furious and spitting tacks, to sign a formal instrument of surrender, based on a time of 1715Z yesterday. Critically, it states that their 'forces will be treated as Prisoners of War and afforded such rights as are applicable under the appropriate article of the Geneva Convention provided the above conditions are complied with'. What a rotten way to end a historic document – with a preposition! What did Churchill say? 'Ending a sentence with a preposition is something up with which I will not put.'

Everyone was discussing today whether the Args would now give up and leave the Falklands as well, now that we have demonstrated that we mean business. Given their macho mentality and the forces that seem to be massed on the Islands, they cannot afford to lose face. It would be the end of the military regime in Argentina if they capitulated after the first sign of trouble. At least they now know that we are serious – or do they think that we have just done it as a token gesture to improve the diplomatic bargaining position? Anyway, I reckon from the briefings that it's the Falklands that they want and South Georgia and our other Antarctic territories would be simply a bonus for them. I hardly think that we could hold on to them and sustain them if we lost the Falklands anyway.

The *Daily Oak* has an account of yesterday's action which is not entirely accurate and probably reflects the propaganda pushed out by *Endurance* last night. It says that the *Santa Fé* was attacked by 'two helicopters which inflicted severe damage with rockets', because (according to John Nott) 'it posed a threat to our men and to the British warships launching the landing'. Not quite true, that, Mr Nott – a case of *post hoc* rather than *propter hoc*!

We are pretty fed up with the glory-grabbing and rewriting of history by *Endurance* and her Flight. Someone said that journalism is the first rough draft of history; they have certainly sought to make sure that their version becomes the official line. We understand that the reason the news channels got hold of the spurious account of events at South Georgia, while all of us were in radio silence in anticipation of an Argentinian response to our capture of the island, was because *Endurance* were yabbering away on INMARSAT with their 'story'. It was bad enough yesterday when they forced their way into the action and went on firing well beyond the point when it was going to make any difference. The sub was knackered from the minute that we depth-charged him and he started heading back to Grytviken. What happened afterwards was just gratuitous and unnecessary, frankly. Now, they are seeking to grab the credit and are breaking EMCON [Emission Control] rules as well. Sodding amateurs – they should remember that they are supposed to be a warship, not a bloody cruise liner! From the World Service, the first rough draft of history would seem to give all the credit for the submarine hit to the bloody Wasps from *Endurance*.

We were also pretty surprised – and irritated – at the accuracy of the BBC World Service, which provided the Args with some pretty good indicators that we were off South Georgia on the day that we landed the SAS recce parties on Fortuna.

It is interesting to see that the Args think that *Exeter* (known in the *Scum* as 'pretty blue Pompey ship', because of the trial blue anti-fouling paint around her hull and waterline) spearheaded the retaking of South Georgia, possibly because they think that the nearest ship to South Georgia that could have reached here in the time was *Exeter* (deployed as West Indies Guard Ship).

The *Oak* also quoted the Arg Foreign Minister, Costa Mendez, as saying that Britain and Argentina are now 'technically at war'. The Arg military has sworn to fight 'to the last drop of blood' – not much evidence of that today or yesterday! Our own government is saying that we acted in defence of our possessions and that we still wanted a peaceful solution to the crisis. I am sure that this approach is right diplomatically, but, in reality, the Args will want to get us back for this affront to their 'honour'. They will want, at least, to inflict some damage on us to show that they were not completely cowed by us.

There was some good intelligence in the *Oak* from a civilian just back from the Falklands. He said that the Args have not extended the runway at Stanley and that A4s and Mirages are not operating from there. The Args seem to be concentrating on extending the apron to accommodate transport aircraft and air movements.

The *Daily Scum* commented on a *Daily Oak* report that 'Mr Michael Foot, the Labour Leader, dedicated follower of fashion [nice dig], said today that he hoped that the submarine had fired first and that we were only acting in self-defence – IS HE REAL?' I think that is a reasonable comment from Jolly Jack!

Other notices from the *Scum* included tongue-in-cheek advertisements offering postcard and souvenir runs-ashore in Grytviken from 0800, a reflection that, with the prisoners, we now had more mouths to feed and a rare sighting of the Commander eating a Yorkie bar at Action Stations.

There was also a notice that 'Dog Watch instruction will take place in the Wardroom at 1630 each day for Argies and Jocks – subject ENGLISH.'

In response to a request from the *Daily Mail* for a short pithy line to describe South Georgia, the Commander invited the ship's company to come up with something: '**S**ubkiller **A**ntrim **N**obbled **T**he **A**rgies – **F**air **E**nough!'

I am surprised that we were not allowed to question the Arg prisoners. Most of them seemed very willing, positively eager, to talk in the aftermath of what had been a shocking day for them. The officers, in particular, wanted to explain and justify themselves and seemed apprehensive about what would happen to them back in Argentina. I reckon that we have missed the opportunity to gain valuable insights and intelligence.

Tidespring and her boats did a terrific job today: half of M Company was ashore, along with all stores and 80% of the ammunition in just six hours.

Finally, there is a major run on cutlery at the moment. We think that the embarked Marines and Special Forces have been taking knives, forks and spoons for their adventures ashore, in the absence of entrenching tools and other specialist kit presumably. Carlos proposed an amnesty, but his idea was shot down in mock derision and he is now looking at liberating the BAS stores in Shackleton House.

Faux pas of the day:

CRS [Chief Radio Supervisor] (to *Conqueror*): 'If you can hear me, click once. If not, click twice.'

Tuesday, 27 April

Well, you find out who your friends are on these occasions! The Organization of American States has given 'qualified' support to Argentina, invited the UK to cease hostilities and called on the EEC to lift its trade ban. According to the World Service, Nicaragua and Cuba were applauding Argentina as an anti-imperialist and anti-colonial champion, along with Panama, Peru and Venezuela. Brazil is worried about internal Argentinian stability in case they get thumped too heavily by us. The US has been digging out on our behalf, as have Chile and Colombia. Apparently, the Venezuelans have banned the use of Scotch whisky in their government offices and the Peruvians are supposed to be supplying the Args with weapons. I wonder what? Do they have Exocets? They do have some Mirages, I think.

Most of the employment has involved us yet again doing transfers and stores shifting around the ships and parties ashore. We have had to be flexible today as the weather has been really lively, with 40–50 knot winds blowing consistently from the south-west to west, and frequent snow squalls coming through. Conditions – visibility and wind-speed – at Grytviken were particularly dangerous for flying, but we managed to service both *Plymouth* and *Conqueror* in Cumberland Bay and take a load of M Company kitbags ashore, before all aircraft except us were told to cease flying because of the conditions. We ended up taking Cedric and the SAS team to *Brilliant*, finally securing at about 1930.

Everything ashore is a complete shambles. The Args do not seem to have had a clue about basic cleanliness and tidiness. They have trashed the usable accommodation, including Shackleton House and the Post Office, having rifled through and pilfered anything remotely valuable or attractive. All the files and papers have been scattered. Our maintenance teams, which have been restoring the BAS generators, the water and the electrical supplies, have said that the Args seem to have been incapable of maintaining the equipment and that everywhere looked as if it had been done over by hyperactive burglars. The Args seem to have had no idea about basic hygiene and the basic ergonomics of living in field conditions. I expect it is the same at Leith. All this is a shame, because the whaling stations look to be like little time-capsules from a bygone era.

The 180 or so Arg prisoners have been all transferred to *Tidespring*, under the watchful eyes of our nine-man RM detachment, although Mike Tidd and his maintenance teams are also going to undertake the respective roles of prison commandant and routine guards as we go to our next tasking. *Tidespring*'s forward hold, which has been emptied, and the hangar are being used for accommodation, although it seems that the scrap dealers are being invited to build their own gulches and bunks with timber being supplied from ashore and from the ships. I expect that it will be quite cold, initially. The word is that we are going to have to return the prisoners to Ascension, although no one is quite sure whether we will have to go all the way.

We are still of interest to the Args on the mainland. We detected a 707 today – they are wary though and keeping their distance, now that they know we are serious.

Whilst I was ashore, one of the Args came up to me and said that he spoke English. He told me that he was due to go to university in England the following September and was worried whether he might not be allowed to go as a result of what had happened.

'Which university?' I asked and he replied, 'Oxford.' He was somewhat heartened by me telling him that I had been at Oxford. It was a bizarre coincidence. In my haste and desire to reassure him that as long as the Args now gave up their occupation of the Falklands he would probably be all right (I was not sure), I did not do what any self-respecting graduate from Oxford would do, as an immediate reflex action. I did not ask him the college to which he would be going. I will send across and find out. Perhaps I can help, as long as his chums on the Falklands go quietly.

We found out today that the SAS needed more grenades ashore during our assault, two days ago, which *Plymouth* was ordered to provide. The package duly arrived, but when the box was opened, it contained 36 Wardroom cups – shades of *A Bridge Too Far*! It adds new meaning to 'being in your cups'.

There was an interesting quotation from the Admiral yesterday: 'South Georgia was an appetizer. Now this is the heavy punch coming up behind. This is the run-up to the big match, which in my view should be a walkover.'

I think that it is wise to weigh the enemy as more mighty than he is. There are numerous examples of armies and navies indulging in stereotypical views of their enemies. I am thinking of the Germans' contempt for the Russians – and their Romanian allies – at Stalingrad or the Japanese belief before Midway that the US did not have an admiral who could beat them. I reckon that countries have good, bad and indifferent operators and the outcome depends on whom you actually meet on the day. I know that, if you yourself are as prepared as possible both professionally and mentally, at least you have done as much as you can. It is out of your hands after that.

Wednesday, 28 April

Stewart and I spent the whole forenoon (0915–1245) lifting and shifting all the personnel and equipment that were going with *Brilliant* and *Plymouth* to the Carrier Group.

Midway through, it was all excitement as a Hercules was detected closing from the west and came to 45 miles. They are clearly keen to know what is going on. We are keen to knock him down!

At 1330, *Brilliant* and *Plymouth* departed. We then closed Grytviken for stores transfers and went back to patrol overnight.

Cedric Delves wrote a nice letter to the Captain before he left:

Now that the moment for our departure has arrived I find it particularly difficult to express our regret at leaving you all.

The legacy of events from recent days find us with an indebtedness to you, which, had it been possible to foresee, would have excited incredulity. That the Squadron goes to its next task intact, having lived through air crashes, boats swept out to sea, not to mention operations on land, is the product not so much of good fortune as of your expertise. I believe that there are such as lucky ships – all of Task Group 317.9 must surely qualify.

These days have been full of memorable events. But, if I have to single out one it has to be the sight of HMS *Antrim* entering Cumberland Bay sure of intent, righteous in purpose: for us all, the culminating moment. Hopefully, we will meet up again before long – good luck and thank you.

He also wrote one to the Flight:

Dear Ian and company,

From all of us in D Squadron, many thanks to you all. The events of the past few days might have been lifted from a boys' adventure annual. Rescuing troops from a gale-lashed glacier, from a dinghy swept out to sea, not to mention attacking an enemy submarine, all these have been your lot. Our indebtedness to you is great. There is no doubt that, without you, the successful outcome of the operation would have been soured by particularly high losses amongst the Squadron. So successful have you been that 406 was coming to be viewed as a cure-all. We wish you all good fortune – but take care. With luck, we will meet again before too long. When we get back and if it is possible, we would like to get you up to Hereford and thank you more appropriately.

On behalf of us all, thanks.

Cedric.

I find it amazing that he has had the time and inclination to remember us all in this way. He is mentally and physically tough and I really admire his complete disregard for Service conventions when they do not suit him and for bullshit in general. He is quite unlike any other Army officer I have met. The SAS must select them for their individualism rather than their ability to conform. That probably comes from them having to improvise and solve problems on the spot.

I have secured myself a brass 4.5 cartridge case from the bombardment. DWEO and his boys were ditching them over the side.

Thursday, 29 April

Apart from the activity ashore, it has been quiet today. This morning we replenished from *Tidespring* and anchored at Grytviken 1300–1800.

I went ashore with Kevin White and Stewart to have a look around the whaling station, but was wary about the possibility of residual booby traps. The place is like a museum and you get the impression that you could start whaling straightaway, just by running up the generators and turning on the machinery. There are even classic whalers alongside, with their tall funnels and components preserved by the cold.

The Argentinians had started cutting up some of the buildings and the machinery and had trashed the place a bit. However, there were storehouses full of spares from the whaling period, including huge cables made of hemp and other natural fibre. All the machinery and spares you would need to run a major maintenance facility are here. Quite apart from the metal in the old whale-processing factories, there are sheds and warehouses full of chandlery and spare parts for the old whaling ships.

I told the Senior Engineer and Graham Hockley that there were a huge amount of steel plate, miles of seriously thick cable and hawsers, and rows – and rows – of brass indicator dials and gauges in pristine working condition in their straw-lined packing crates, worth a fortune to the antique dealers, I would expect. There were over a hundred steel harpoon heads. These were really heavy and appeared to be just the tip of the assembly used to spear the whales. I have taken one as a souvenir.

The wooden church was in absolutely top condition, as if people came in and cleaned it every week, just like at home. In the vestry was a library of mostly Scandinavian books, all stowed neatly in custom-made bookshelves and amazingly a card-file index that minutely recorded the details of the books and the times that each had been lent out to various workers and seamen. It was as if the librarian or pastor had just stepped out for a short while. I found one book in English – *Ivanhoe* – that had been taken out of an Edinburgh library in 1902! Against my conscience, I resolved to take the book and return it to the library (I wonder if they will charge me the overdue fines!). I always have a romantic notion that it is sad for English books to be stranded abroad and feel the urge to repatriate them.

I had a chat with some of the prisoners from the submarine, who were part of a working party. They said that a look-out on the Bridge only saw us in 406 at the last moment and pressed the 'combat alarm', just before the two depth charges exploded (they said) on the starboard side towards the stern. This apparently opened up a crack in the pressure hull, through which daylight could be seen and a ballast tank was split. Internal communications broke down, electronic units were wrenched off the bulkheads and all the gauges were shattered, including the depth pressure gauge. The CO assessed that the submarine could not dive and the crew tried to repel further attacks through crewmen armed with rifles in the sail, as the Args called the fin.

An AS-12 missile then struck the intake valve and snorkel mast, but subsequent missiles apparently passed through the GRP [Glass Reinforced Plastic] fin and exploded beyond it, although one crew member, Petty Officer Macias, was the man severely injured in the leg. Once the submarine was within King Edward Cove, a Bantam anti-tank missile was fired by a marine against a Wasp.

They said that they had been sent to South Georgia to ferry a section of marines under Captain Luis Lagos, with about four tons of supplies in order to reinforce and assume command of the garrison of Grytviken. He had 11 technicians and nine marines, equipped with some Bantam missiles and a recoilless rifle.

Finally, they stressed that when they were leaving Grytviken, the *Santa Fé* was on its way to a quiet location to effect repairs to their motors and to damage that had been sustained en route to South Georgia. They had been told that, because of the uncertain diplomatic situation on departure, they would not be allowed to fire first – they thought that this was odd. However, once it was known – from the World Service – that British ships were off South Georgia, they were assigned a 'war patrol' area to the north of South Georgia.

For the past two days, BAS personnel and scientists have been either contacted or have come in from their various out-stations and huts. They were rather surprised to see Grytviken occupied by the Royal Marines. They found Commander E and his merry men (Chief Barker, POMEM Berry and a couple of MEMs) continuing to survey and restore the BAS facilities, workshops and generators, just like in a disaster exercise at Portland. One stroppy bearded thing demanded to know 'What the hell is going on here?' They seemed unaware that the island had been recaptured – one said that he had heard some loud bangs (our bombardment), but thought that it might have been glaciers cracking or rolling thunder!

Once onboard, they said that they had been passing information about the Args at Grytviken and King Edward Point: about their force levels and their positions, as well as the lack of activity in the vicinity of their huts, since 5 April. If they did, we did not receive any of that information.

They also said that it was evident from the start that the Arg Armed Forces had sponsored and deliberately exploited the scrap dealer issue as a cover for building up a military presence on the island and that the Arg Navy had been in the forefront of the escapade. The BAS people thought that the speed with which they undertook operations, including the equipment they had loaded in their ships, indicated that the whole thing was premeditated and planned.

I heard the results of the Board of Inquiry into the death of the Arg CPO in the *Santa Fé*, whose name was, ironically, Felix Artuso. After evidence from both British and Arg witnesses, the bottom line is that his death resulted from a chain of unavoidable events, unfortunate circumstances and misperceptions that made the tragedy no one person's fault. There were a lot of people under pressure in an unstable submarine, I suppose.

Stewart and I felt that the incident had diminished our achievement at South Georgia. Declan and the Doc reckoned that things like this happen in wartime. Personally, I cannot see how it could have been considered sensible to put a single Marine, with the power of life and death over someone who did not speak his language, in an unfamiliar, probably alarming space with no one else to give him moral support. Surely, there should have been a naval officer there, preferably someone with submarine experience, to explain things and guide him. I also have a feeling that, unless they are SBS, Royal Marines and submarines do not go that well together, even though, oddly, they rhyme.

We are going to bury CPO Artuso alongside Shackleton in the cemetery opposite Shackleton House tomorrow, with full military honours and with our attendees in their Number 4/Number 1 uniforms. The Args will send the submarine Captain, to say some words, and some mourners along. The temporary memorandum has been issued, with John Saunders taking charge, two JOUTs (Brook and Worrall) attending, and the Padre for the committal. The contents of the temporary memorandum bring it home: 'Actions – Dig grave – M Company; Manufacture coffin – Shipwright Officer . . .'

The guard and the lowerers (all Chief Petty Officers, the MAA, the Chief Stoker, the Chief Writer, the Chief Ops R, Chief Robinson and the CRS) have been practising the drill and procedures all this evening. They are keen to get it right.

There are also two women, Cindy Buxton and Annie Price, in St Andrew's Bay, who have been making a TV programme about penguins throughout the crisis. *Endurance* is going to pick them up tomorrow and then go up to Bird Island and Schlieper Bay to round up the remainder of the BAS teams.

In the middle of last night, the Captain was given a hard time, at Prime Ministerial level, because Lord Buxton (someone's father) had complained that nothing had been done to contact the BAS personnel or assist them since we arrived. In fact, *Endurance* has been doing the rounds with her helicopters, assiduously sweeping up the assorted boffins, scientists and anoraks over the past few days. The complaint by His Lordship is way out of order – the arrogance of title, the abuse of access and the ignorance of distance! – has his daughter something to do with it?

In passing, we wished *Glamorgan*, currently with the Main Group, heading for the Falklands directly, all the best by signal: 'Good luck. Wish we were with you [a sentiment not actually shared by the ship's company, as some were thinking about going home!]. *Faugh a ballagh* (give 'em welly).'

His reply was: 'Very many thanks. We will try to imitate your Georgian prowess. We also wish you were here, but it is comforting to know that you are volunteers to be our relief!'

We also sent our first anodyne 'newsgram' back for the benefit of our families. We talked about being fit, well and living up to the ship's motto of 'Always Ready'. It talked vaguely about a 'momentous month' and Argy-bashing, the progress towards funding a guide dog, beard-growing and other harmless stuff, all designed to reassure families and friends back home and give nothing away. Humphrey the Helicopter made a non-specific appearance, as if part of Thomas the Tank Engine and Friends, as did Percy the Pigeon, a temporary resident that stayed for a week in the tropics. We mentioned our two Antarctic Teal ducks (called Donald and Daffy apparently), which had appeared onboard with the BAS people, for transfer and breeding purposes in the UK, and asked our loved ones not to spend all our hard-earned cash before we got back.

There is a lot of talk in the Wardroom and around the ship about whether the capture of South Georgia will mean the end of the conflict, as the Args now know that we mean business. I don't think so.

Overall, I would say that the operation, despite itself, has been a success – and it has been achieved in pretty short order. It has to be a tremendous psychological blow to the Argentinians that they have lost it so easily. Their pride and masculinity would have taken a severe knock as well, as I am sure that they would have been playing up to this fighting to the last bullet and last soldier claim. I don't think so. Even Astiz decided that the better part of valour was discretion and gave up. He is not so good when the (jack)boot is on the other foot.

Our Flight maintainers have done remarkably well over the past week, far beyond what would or should normally be expected from them. Keeping the cab serviceable and available despite all the adventures and extreme conditions was positively heroic. To a man, their conduct has been exemplary. Calm, professional and efficient, they have been a great support both technically and psychologically and I am really proud to be serving with them in these circumstances. I know what people mean now when they say so-and-so is someone that they rate so highly that they would go to war with him. Every one of them has just knuckled down and got on with the job, despite the pressures and what must be justifiable concerns.

Fritz Heritier as SMR is a real find and we are lucky to have him – strong, authoritative and pragmatic, he leads the boys with drive, humanity and visible energy. And to think that he was originally only a temporary relief for Chief Camp to Gibraltar and back! No more suitcases in the hangar now! We are all wondering how Mel Camp must be feeling right now, having been left behind. He would want to be with us, I am sure, but I suspect that Mrs Camp will not be complaining.

A couple of things really stand out:

The first is the way in which they all went out onto the Flight Deck and lashed Humphrey to the deck, with as many steel and synthetic lashings as they could, at night in the middle of the hurricane. You could hardly stand up it was so rough and the cold was teeth-achingly intense even before the wind chill was added. Even then one or two of the chain lashings sheered, but it is down to them entirely that the cab survived to fly the next day, although it was encrusted with salt when we went to have a look once the storm had subsided.

Secondly, Chief McKee's re-installation of the sonar back into the cab in just 13 hours, with Chief Bullingham's help, the other night was nothing short of miraculous – that must be a record. It worked first time, when we dunked just after the depth charge attack. What a scenario for a Check Test Flight! And the boys had a full day of flying operations afterwards while we retook South Georgia. So much for Sunday routine!

We returned to sea overnight.

Friday, 30 April

Endurance spent the day round at Leith clearing up the facilities, ammunition and stores left behind in a real state by the Arg garrison there. They have also managed to get an Arg landing craft working and are using it for various chores.

It is pleasant to record that there was very little loss of life or damage to the structures on the island. It means that we can garrison it properly ahead of the Antarctic winter and exploit its wonderful natural harbours. The gear at the whaling stations will come in handy too, although I do hope that the historic significance of what is there is recognized. The sites must be unique – they are time-capsules, frozen in time – and represent a way of life and a heritage that will be forgotten if they are not preserved somehow. The trouble is that Clio is being walked all over by Mars (and probably Hephaestus as well) at the moment and no one is taking any notice (I think I just mixed up Greek and Roman myths there!). It's Ares, isn't it?

Another important aspect of recent events is that we have all now been in action for the first time and are aware of the dangers and uncertainties involved. Those of us on the Flight have had a close brush with danger and I think that we came through it well, relying on our training, regard – even affection – for each other and the Fleet Air Arm can-do attitude to make it all happen. So I know what it is like to be in action and I felt and feel OK about it. That said, I need to bear in mind that I have not yet been directly engaged by an enemy who positively wants to do me harm – no one has realistically been in a position to kill me yet. That's probably the next step. Mind you, the terrain and the climate have had a jolly good go already!

The ship came to anchor at 0925 and stayed at anchor until 1400, so that we could conduct the funeral of the Argentinian Chief, Felix Artuso.

John Saunders came back from the funeral. Not much fun at all apparently. He is number 2 section commander of the ship's Internal Security Section. He and a rifle team in full ceremonials, belt and gaiters, plus the Padre went along with the Chief GI [Gunnery Instructor], in order to conduct full military honours. He said that he went in *Tidespring*'s boat to *Tidespring* to pick up the Captain of the submarine and some of the Arg sailors. They went across to the cemetery on the slope opposite the BAS jetty where Shackleton is buried and the party trooped up to where a grave had been prepared in the frozen ground. Chippy and his team had knocked up a coffin and someone provided an Argentinian flag.

John was given a 9 mm pistol with a couple of magazines, but without any guidance or training about what to do in the event of the Args cutting up. The boys only had blank ammunition and he was the only armed person over there! So there he was in his best No. 4 uniform, with an unnatural, unsightly and loaded bulge in his pocket. Apparently, the submarine Captain did a eulogy, which no one on the British side understood, the Padre did his formal bit and there were some subdued Arg patriotic emotion and male bonding shouts. Also, there were some tears and tearing of each other's clothes (thought that was a Jewish custom?).

John remarked that he spent the whole time of the funeral wondering what he was supposed to do if the Args misbehaved or ran off. He said that he did not have the heart to shoot anyone at a funeral. He also reasoned that there would not be any point in trying to escape in this terrain and weather conditions because you were not likely to survive anyway.

We flew for three hours and 40 minutes today from about 1425, in order to do some transfers around the bazaars, have a look at the Lyell Glacier, collect some BAS personnel and conduct a photograph run of what the ship should have looked like with its battle ensigns flying on 25 April. Who says that the camera never lies?

We returned to find that we had an additional guest in the form of Captain Alfredo Astiz, the Arg commander at Leith, who has a decidedly unsavoury reputation as a torturer and murderer, in some cases of foreign females. The Commander told everyone that he had made a name for himself dealing with the 'enemies of the Republic of Argentina' and had the nickname of 'The Executioner'. Apparently, he was encouraging the Arg prisoners to make trouble in *Tidespring* so he has been transferred to *Antrim*, where he will remain under armed guard in a cabin, until we find out what to do with him. I wonder if he will be treated as a prisoner of war or as someone who has to face justice for his part in the disappearance of all those people. It was a bit careless of him to get captured at South Georgia.

We have just had another submarine scare. While screening *Tidespring*, *Antrim* picked up a pretty convincing contact, but it did not have any course or speed, or Doppler – it was classified as a probable pinnacle, an uncharted rock feature.

We have just heard that the Armed Forces are to be given a 9% pay rise. We have not seen the details yet, but I am sure that the normal procedure will apply. The Treasury will give with one hand and take with another – I expect food, accommodation and other charges will have gone up as well.

Tonight, we also heard that the UK has imposed a Total Exclusion Zone (to replace the Maritime Exclusion Zone) around the Falkland Islands and South Georgia. We also found out that the US has now declared its unequivocal support for the British side (what took you so long?) and that the Args have said that they will attack all British aircraft and ships in the South Atlantic.

Well, the gloves are off now. I am not sure that the Args had any intention of negotiating anyway. It's probably just a question of how soon it all kicks off and who gets hurt. It is quite clear that the politicians – and the useless United Nations – have totally failed to come up with a formula that stops what looks like an inevitable slide into war. I would think that it suits the Russians and the Chinese to see one of the US's major allies and one of their potential friends in South America squaring up to each other. The Russians would also be interested in how we, our ships and our kit do in these circumstances. I wonder if they have any submarines down here, snooping around.

The tactical situation is looking interesting and our intelligence suggests that the Args have most of their fleet, including their carrier, at sea. It is all rather confused, but the Arg carrier and the two Type 42s seem to be to the north of the Islands outside the Exclusion Zone, with the cruiser and a couple of escorts to the south-west. With our carriers and their group to the north-east of the Islands, I'd say that they were a bit vulnerable, but the Admiral seems confident that the SSNs are going to deal with most things. However, if the carrier gives the SSNs the slip, she could launch a strike from a good way away.

I'd also be pretty concerned about the ARA *General Belgrano*. She is an old battlewagon from the Second World War, with armour and 15 big guns, capable of firing 6 inch projectiles 13 miles. That means that, unless one of the SSNs gets her, our destroyers and frigates will be left facing a bit of a problem. The cruiser's armoured belt could probably resist a good few Exocets fired from 20 miles or so and, with the gap closing at say 45 knots, you would have 15 high-explosive London buses falling around and on you within about six minutes. Nor would we want her mixing it close in with our carriers. It would be like *Glorious* facing the *Scharnhorst* or the *Gneisenau* on the way back from Norway in the 2WW. The *Belgrano* also has a pretty formidable secondary battery of anti-aircraft guns that could be used in the anti-surface mode.

This does sound like a job for the SSNs, whose COs need to earn their submarine pay. As the SCO said yesterday, in these cases, it is better to put water into the bottom of a ship, rather than air in the top! I wonder, in fact, if the Args know what they are up against with an SSN. They will be used to operating with conventional submarines and really do not have the kit, the expertise or the collective training to deal with this scale of threat. After all, we practise year-in, year-out in anticipation of the Soviet SSNs breaking out into the Atlantic and, although we are pretty good at it, it needs constant exercising at group level and challenging training and live submarine time at unit level. Well, I expect that the Argentinians are about to get some live submarine time!

It would be great to bag their carrier – it is strange to think that it is the ex-British *Venerable*. Sinking her would make their eyes water and take out a lot of strike aircraft – A4s and maybe some Super-Etendards – as well. It might even make them think that the Falklands are not worth it after all.

We believe that we will be heading north soon with our prisoners, scientists, TV people and the two ducks. We need to get the prisoners into warmer latitudes and on their way back to Argentina (we really ought to make them promise not to fight against us again!). The two women are revelling in being the centre of attention in the Wardroom, but give the impression that they somehow need to be treated as VIPs. It does not help that the Navigator and the DWEO are being unctuously charming to them. Nor do our ladies seem to realize that we are tolerating their ways – and their obvious tendency to treat everything as a TV or book-writing opportunity – out of a desire to be hospitable and understanding. The most irritating aspect is that they have swallowed *Endurance*'s propaganda hook, line and sinker and they parrot the Red Plum version of events whenever they can. I was really surprised to hear how the brave and clever (!) aviators from *Endurance* had detected and disabled the *Santa Fé*.

Of course, it is traditionally considered bad luck to have women onboard warships, but we were more worried about the prospect of over 450 red-blooded males trying to impress the females while they were with us. We need not have worried because the general consensus was that Cindy and Annie were not likely to have responded in any case, because they were only too conscious of the awkward situation and behaved impeccably and also, as the Captain's steward rather fussily and needlessly pointed out on a number of occasions, they chose to share a cabin.

Saturday, 1 May

Mayday seems somehow appropriate for the first major attack on the Falkland Islands. While the choir was presumably singing at the top of Magdalen Tower in Oxford, we started the attack that we trust will lead to the recovery of the Islands. It began in an unexpected way though, with a high level bombing attack by a Vulcan. That must be the longest bombing raid in history.

We have not had any news yet of the damage, but, looking at *Jane's*, we thought that the Vulcan must have been carrying about 20 1,000 lb bombs. We are also trying to work out how the Vulcan could have had the legs to make it down to the Falklands with a full bomb load from Ascension. We reckon that she must have been fitted with a probe and refuelled by Victors – quite a few of them – judging by the distances, unless they were cheating by secretly using Brazil. The raid was followed up by an attack by SHars [Sea Harriers], to ram the message home that we are back to claim our own. The 'Empire is striking back'!

All the SHars made it back, despite the presence of considerable Arg flak and Tigercat/Roland batteries, and are reported to have thoroughly duffed up the airfield and surrounding areas. The discussion in the Wardroom posed the very reasonable question of why it was necessary to alert the Args with the Vulcan attack by waking them up and thoroughly pissing them off before the SHars arrived.

The raid was followed up by *Glamorgan*, *Alacrity* and *Arrow* going in to shell the airfield and Arg defences. These ships were then attacked, in turn, by Arg aircraft from the mainland with bombs. It seems that we splashed two Mirages and a Canberra today and the Args managed to shoot down one of their own over Stanley. Meanwhile the first air-to-air dogfight took place between our SHars and the Arg Air Force. It looks like some Mirage IIIs took on our lads, but turned tail after they had fired some missiles at extended range.

Pat Brown and most of the warfare team think that the Vulcan raid is an RAF plot to ensure that the Crabs get the glory for the first attack, to make up for the fact that they can't deploy their Phantoms or attack aircraft anywhere. No one will have them, although we are hopeful about the Chileans. I cannot see that happening somehow; the Chileans have to live with the Args after the conflict, but, as there is no love lost between Chile and Argentina and they have their own dispute, they must want to help us on the quiet.

The ship spent the day at sea preparing to head back up to Ascension, while completing several transfers and chores, including a replenishment with *Tidespring*. The sea has been lumpy and we continue to patrol a sector offshore, extending along the north coast of the island, in case the Args try something. We are seeing more and more icebergs offshore, including one monster 35 miles long and 15 miles wide.

We have had this idea that we might try a stunt with an iceberg. The idea is that we put someone on a really large iceberg at sea – Fitz is the current favourite – and take a photo to send to Smirnoff Vodka, along the lines of 'I never used to have ice with my vodka, until I discovered Smirnoff!' On the Flight, everyone thinks that it is a great idea, but Fitz, strangely, is not keen. I can't do it – after all, I am a teetotaller!

In 406, we spent the day doing various jobs, starting with a surface search to the west and a sonar Check Test Flight, followed by various stores, load-lifting and personnel transfer serials, around the ships and into Grytviken. The weather has been decidedly rough today, with 20–35 knot winds blowing from the south-west and west. The Bosun's Mate put in the ship's log tonight: 'Main Group heroes eventually did something today.'

Tidespring is heading up track now for Ascension and we will follow her tomorrow, expecting to meet up with *Plymouth* on Monday and *Blue Rover* the following day, when we will replenish fuel.

Sunday, 2 May

We are not that impressed with the Vulcan raid yesterday now that we have had some intelligence about the result. It seems that out of 20 bombs, one might have hit the runway. However, the assessment is that it can still be used by C-130s, Pucaras and Aermacchis, which are pretty much the aircraft that used it before! There is no evidence that the Args have extended the runway or enabled it to be used for combat jets – what on earth were they doing all the while we were coming down to get them? Any sensible military precautions would have included making sure that A4s and Mirages could operate from Stanley. As it is, they have to refuel in the air and then operate at the limit of their range, if they want to have a go at us.

The ship went into anchor at Grytviken to complete the final transfers and left South Georgia in the 'capable' hands of *Endurance*, who, I am certain, are glad to be rid of us. *Endurance* – and her Captain in particular – regard South Georgia as their personal fiefdom and playground and our presence has been jealously resented. It seems to me that they have spent too long operating on their own, without restraint or control, and they have got used to doing what they want. There is no doubt that they were warning about trouble before the crisis, but it is also clear that they got a mite too close to the Args during their runs-ashore and other 'social' activities. Their deployment, until the end, seems to have been one long banyan and their ability to be wise after the event, coupled with their desire to grab any headlines that are going, is distinctly irritating.

We weighed anchor and proceeded on our way at midday and are looking to rendezvous with *Plymouth* and *Tidespring* at 1200 tomorrow, not least because they have mail and stores for us. Stewart and Fitz did one last transfer to Grytviken. The sea-state continues to be decidedly bumpy, with winds to 45 knots, a long swell and big waves.

Today, I tried to teach the Wardroom some Spanish, but the teaching and learning experience was somewhat reminiscent of *Fawlty Towers* and Manuel. Once again, as with the rest of the ship's company, we are not much beyond 'Two beers please', 'Do you have a sister?', 'My friend will pay' and 'Do you know the way to San José?'

Great news tonight – it appears that *Conqueror* has stopped or sunk the Arg cruiser *Belgrano* with a couple of Mk 8 torpedoes. That's terrific, although one cannot help but feel for the poor lads who must even at this moment be in the water. I expect that she had an escort or two with her at the time and there is no indication that we sank any other warship. Still, I bet that it is effing cold and people will not last long. 'So all were lost, which in the ship were found, / They in the sea being burnt, they in the burnt ship drown'd.'*

The word is that she was outside the Exclusion Zone. That does not bother me in the least. She was clearly up to no good and would only have come back in again when it suited her. We sank her while we could. Anyway, the communiqué that went to the Argentinians before we invaded South Georgia in which we set up the Maritime Exclusion Zone around the Falkland Islands quite clearly said that the UK would

* John Donne, 'A Burnt Ship'.

be taking 'whatever additional measures may be needed in the exercise of its right of self-defence under Article 51 of the United Nations Charter'. As I recall, that meant 'that any approach on the part of Argentine warships, including submarines, naval auxiliaries or military aircraft, which could amount to a threat to interfere with the mission of British Forces in the South Atlantic will encounter the appropriate response. All Argentine aircraft, including civil aircraft engaged in surveillance of these British forces, will be regarded as hostile and are liable to be dealt with accordingly.' I noted it down because it was absolutely critical to how we were going to deal with the C-130 and submarine combo over there.

Hopefully, we can now get on with the job, without the distractions and delays induced by continued negotiations and prevarications. I am sure that the Peruvians are just trying to cock us up and keep us down here burning fuel and steadily degrading our fighting capability in the rough seas, without serious maintenance and engineering support. I cannot believe that the Argentinians will give up now. Now that we have sunk the *Belgrano*, we must expect some retaliation. The Argentinian mentality simply will not allow them to take it lying down and they will want revenge. Even now, I expect they are planning something fiendish – hopefully emotion will get in the way of logic.

Mind you, it should make their ships think twice about venturing too far out towards us in future and I am not sure that they have the ASW capability to cope with conventional submarines, let alone our SSNs. Great that we got the thing, though, as I would not have fancied us having to square up to a pretty fast cruiser, lobbing hulking great shells at us from a range of 13 miles. She would also have caused difficulty had she slipped across to South Georgia, with only *Endurance* there, or managed to interdict our supply chain down from Ascension. It makes you glad that we have SSNs – they certainly frighten and intimidate those navies that do not have them. They must be wondering how they are going to cope with them if the conflict goes on.

In *Jane's*, I saw that the *Belgrano* was formerly the USS *Phoenix*. That's ironic – I think I recall that she was the only major warship to escape from Pearl Harbor during the Japanese attack. Well, it took a while, but – we got her in the end! So that is an ex-US Navy submarine and an ex-US Navy cruiser in the bag already. This is getting like a game of 'Battleships'. Two squares, three squares – I wonder where the carrier is? Five squares!

Monday, 3 May

We left the South Georgia Exclusion Zone during the Middle Watch, when we reverted from Defence to Cruising Watches, and rendezvoused with *Plymouth* and *Tidespring* at midday for mail and stores transfers. We employed *Plymouth*'s Wasp and 406 (Stewart and I conducted a load-lifting and stores serial for over two hours). We then detached *Plymouth*, did some more transfers and consolidation of personnel and stores (Ian and Fitz did these) and with *Appleleaf*, which had arrived. We then went on our way to Ascension with *Tidespring*, while *Plymouth*, *Appleleaf* and a civilian tanker, the *British Esk*, headed back south.

Apparently, according to the Arg propaganda people, we have been sunk, along with *Invincible*. This is the first time that we have been named and will cause worry for our families and friends back home. The Master Gunner came into the Wardroom and asked loudly whether this meant that he was entitled to 'survivor's pay' as a result.

More to the point, the BBC World Service confirmed early this morning that one of our SSNs did indeed sink the Arg cruiser the *General Belgrano* yesterday, with no word of casualties.

Also, last night, Lynx from *Coventry* and *Glasgow* attacked two patrol boats north of the Falklands, with Sea Skuas. This is the first time that these missiles have been used in action and we seem to have crippled or sunk the *Comodoro Somellara* and the *Alferez Sobral*.★ That's probably one square each on the Battleships grid.

I hope that we can get the carrier now as well. Hopefully, we can progressively increase the costs for Argentina of their aggression and induce them to back off, based simply on the calculation that their possession of the Falklands is not worth all the damage and losses that we can inflict on them. This is in addition to all the economic impact that trade sanctions will have.

Alfredo Astiz has been accommodated in the Doc's cabin in the lower Wardroom flat. The cabin was stripped of anything that might offer him the opportunity to make a weapon, gain intelligence or interfere with the ship's capability or routine. A gunner JR [Junior Rating] sits on a chair

★ This was not the case. The *Somellara* was to the south of the Falklands at the time and the *Sobral*, although damaged, managed to make her way with her injured crew members back to Puerto Deseado.

and has a loaded 9 mm, which he has been ordered to use if the guy leaves the locked cabin. Calls of nature and meals are dealt with in the cabin.

The word is that he spends the day reading or doing press-ups and pull-ups to keep fit and in shape. Under escort, he is allowed a walk around the upper deck every day, when there is nothing to see.

He looks like a serious customer whose character and demeanour seem to match the reputation that we have heard about. I cannot look at him without thinking that he is a throwback to some former generation, something out of the 1930s or '40s, with a mentality totally unlike ours. We know that he has been involved in the disappearance of loads of people, including women, and in murders.

However, he is maintaining his military bearing, is standing on his dignity and radiates belligerence. I detect a suppressed anger about getting captured and a complete indifference about what might happen to him. He speaks good English and seems pretty switched on. After complaining that he does not have anything to read, he has been given a copy of *Who Dares Wins – A History of the* SAS by Tony Geraghty!

The *Scum* has closed down for the moment and will apparently revive if we head back into action again. After the *Belgrano* sinking, its new banner was Surely Argentina's Navy has Tried And Failed Everywhere.

Daddy S sent a signal today outlining his concerns about the lack of 'farinatory' ingredients available at sea and the shortage of roughage, along with the dangers of constipation if the situation were not redressed. The junior officers inwardly groaned when we read it and awaited the inevitable response. Quick as a flash, back came *Glamorgan* suggesting that a couple of days on the gun line off Port Stanley amid the air raids might help ease matters on the constipation front. Amid the general shortage of vegetables and fresh fruit, somebody produced a spoof notice on the symptoms and treatment of scurvy, something which served to wind up an already irritated Daddy S. Three ratings actually turned up at Sick Bay believing that they had scurvy.

4 May – a Tuesday

People are soberly realistic about the loss of the *Belgrano* and are of the opinion that if you invade someone else's territory, you are likely to be called to account. There is sympathy for any sailors who might be still adrift in the South Atlantic (in what look like storm force winds and seas) but a general acceptance that these things happen and that the Args would do it to us if they could.

Today's sea-state was very rough and the weather severe as we headed for our rendezvous with *Blue Rover*. In the forenoon, we started a replenishment with *Tidespring*, but had to break away after 30 minutes because ship-handling was too difficult and the conditions too dangerous, not least because a westerly sea and wind were forcing the ships' sterns together as we headed north. Ian and Fitz did the obligatory stores and personnel transfers in the afternoon. We had a minor scare during the First Watch this evening based on a passive sonar detection, which was either a surface ship or spurious.

It is astonishing how well the fuel supply has been organized down here. The Captain's policy has been to top up with fuel whenever we can, just in case we need to dash off somewhere. However, the way in which tankers appear whenever they are needed, including the ships taken up from trade, indicates a very sophisticated and well-thought-through operation.

The day started with another Vulcan raid on Stanley, but the word is that the bombs all landed beyond the western end of the runway. We are also suspicious that the Args might be using dummy craters on the runway, which they pull on during the day (to appear on our recce photos) and remove at night, when they have incoming flights.

The big, bad news today has concerned the Arg attack on *Sheffield*, which has confirmed that the Args are, in fact, capable of fitting the AM-39 to their Super-Etendards, with or without French assistance. It seems that the ship was hit amidships and the fire spread out of control rapidly, leading to her being abandoned. We have not received a signal yet and there is no word about casualties at the moment. It does appear that we failed to detect an Arg Neptune aircraft that might have been targeting the Task Force; that's not surprising because I think that his old radar is below the frequency detection threshold of the electronic intercept and support system in the Type 42s.

We also lost a SHar to anti-aircraft fire at Goose Green as well today and the pilot was killed. It is starting to get rough. As Commander E said at dinner this evening: 'Well, nobody really expected it to be a turkey-shoot; it has just got nasty.'

The Commander ordered a random search of Astiz's cabin and we found that he had concealed a knife which he had made out of one of the metal bunk supports. The frame has now been removed and his mattress simply sits on the top of his wooden bunk structure. I have said that if it was me I would try and start a fire by shorting an electrical cable in the cabin. That suggestion, and the means to mitigate it, has been consigned to the all-too-difficult category.

I accompanied him on a walk around the upper deck today. When I tried to talk to him in Spanish, he gave me a look of silent contempt, looked straight ahead, and out to sea, and did not offer to speak. He cannot hear Main Broadcast pipes or the World Service on the SRE,* as the speakers have been isolated and muted where he is living, so he does not know about the *Belgrano* or *Sheffield* incidents.

We think about our other prisoners and how they are coping over in *Tidespring*'s hold. When we replenish, we see them exercising, under guard, on the Flight Deck. We reckoned that they must be getting bored, so the Padre organized a consignment of board games, books and pens and paper for them to write letters etc. It was rumoured that he was also looking for soft porn books as well. When he was collecting as much as he could, LSTD Leckey came to see me this afternoon, in the Air Office: 'Sir, do you know that the Padre is going to send the uckers board across to the Argies?'

'No, bloody way . . . thanks' was all Leckey heard as I departed the office, at Mach speed, to find the Padre. I caught up with him in the Wardroom.

'Padre, have you got the uckers board?'

'Yes, I thought that it was the Christian thing to do . . .'

'Padre,' I said, 'we'd rather lose you than the uckers board.'

'I think that I know a thing about morale; that's my job. Anyway, the Commander has given permission for me to send across all superfluous items.'

'Padre, you can't play uckers, you do not understand.'

'It's just Ludo, there is nothing to it.'

That's it, I thought, he mentioned the 'L' word. It's time to end this.

'Padre, you are not getting this; that uckers board is a key component of our morale and our operational capability.'

'It's only a game,' he said, clutching the board to his chest.

---

* Sound Reproduction Equipment – a ship-wide radio selection box, normally transmitting the BBC World service and another station only.

'No, Padre, it is not just a game, it has become an institution in the Wardroom at night and people are following the scores – it is a way of maintaining normality and a sense of indifference to worry amid everything that's going on. It's a Fleet Air Arm thing.'

'It's childish!' was the last word on the subject as I forcibly reclaimed the board and the bits and marched off with them.

'Padre, if this board disappears over the side, you will get a float test, too. Believe me!'

By this evening, we were continuing northwards in company with *Tidespring*, and *Blue Rover* was heading south. We understand that once we get further up track we might be tasked to escort the Amphibious Group as they head south.

Uckers was played noisily with real feeling tonight!

Wednesday, 5 May

We are still on passage with *Tidespring*. During the afternoon, we managed to conduct a simulated anti-submarine exercise, in order to check the Flight Control System, give the pilots some practice and get the sonar in the water. It's a relief to be back in the ASW business after all those load-lifting serials and transfers.

The ship spent the whole day running through Sea Slug functionality and operational checks. At about 1620, when we were doing FOCCIF, an Arg 707 closed us, and the 4.5s and the Sea Slug crews and systems were stood to. The cheeky bugger closed to visual range and overflew us at low level, but, without the necessary rules of engagement, we were not able to pluck him down, even though he was identified positively as a military variant. We could have got him. Nobody quite understands why we did not splash him – we are clearly at war, the missile system had acquired the target and a 707 would have been a great Sea Slug target. I suppose our lords and masters are worried about misidentification and bringing down a 707 full of innocent civilians or nuns or suchlike. It would be just like the Args to try and tempt us like that, for propaganda purposes.

We have been hearing from Mike Tidd in *Tidespring* that he is finding the Argentinian prisoners a bit lively and troublesome. They are obviously getting bored and they have a copy of the Geneva Convention.

For a start, the Arg officers are whining about being held together with the various other ranks – mostly in the main hold – as being inconsistent with their social status, dignity and honour – they want individual cabins and separate dining facilities apparently. They also seem to be taking the most food, without dividing it up equally among everybody and insisting on being at the head of every queue.

In addition, Mike has to maintain good order among a group that comprises submariners, marines, civilian scrap merchants (some of whom are Paraguayans!), and the diehard Astiz mob from Leith. Apparently, there are numerous set-tos and the occasional punch-up. Luckily, we have Astiz under watch over here – he would have been real trouble over there.

Mike and his team must have done really well, to keep everyone quiet for so long, what with the minutiae of accommodation, sanitation, feeding, exercise, health and dealing with all the complaints. It says a lot for the flexibility, intelligence and resourcefulness of the Fleet Air Arm, both aircrew and maintainers – and without being able to speak the language. The RFA guys would have done well too. I know that Captain Redmond told the Captain that he reckons that he will be handing over the prisoners fitter, healthier and better nourished than when he received them.

We see the Args taking the air and exercising on the Flight Deck when we are close to *Tidespring* and when we are engaged in replenishment alongside. They look pretty cheerful and relaxed during their cruise in the sun. I hope that we give the impression of being professionally warlike and effortlessly competent, so that they go back home and tell their chums in Argentina to give up the fight.

We have been hearing more about *Sheffield*. It seems that two AM-39 Exocet missiles were fired against the Task Force and that all the ships, except *Sheffield*, reacted by firing their chaff. For some reason, the ship was not at Action Stations and various key personnel were not at their posts, including the Captain, who was in his cabin. Rumour has it that she was less prepared for action than she would have been for a typical 'Thursday War' at Portland and that her satellite communications were interfering with her ESM [Electronic Support Measures]. That does not make sense. She was the up-threat ship two days after we sank their second biggest ship. She should have been 'armed at point exactly, cap-à-pie'.*

Some people in the Wardroom are shocked about how the Args could

* Shakespeare, *Hamlet*.

have got through, but others, including me, think that it was only a matter of time before the Args got their act together. After all, they needed to retaliate after the *Belgrano* and to show that they would not be rolled over in the first wave of attacks by us. The other thing is that we all knew that our ships were decidedly marginal when it came to defending against sea-skimming missiles; their design, weapons and sensors are all geared to containing and confronting the Soviets and are not entirely capable when it comes to combating similar weapons to our own. It was deceitful to tell our sailors or the public otherwise and our lack of familiarity with this type of threat was always going to be a risk if we went in harm's way.

I wrote to A today that, after the events of the past few days and our experience at South Georgia, we are fully psyched up for war and that it is difficult to concentrate on anything else. Obviously, the increased tempo and uncertainty are a considerable strain on everyone; tempers are currently shorter and life is – at the same time – more communal, with lots of interaction within the ship's company and with embarked forces, and isolated, with one's own thoughts, anxieties and preoccupations in relation to what might happen. Of course, these things are not discussed and people seem to have a philosophical approach to what the future holds for us.

Also, a lot of comradeship and common purpose are apparent, especially within specialist teams like the Flight, and the usual formality between officers and ratings has weakened. Everyone pulls together, but it is clear that some of my fellow officers are just out for their own careers, putting what would appear good above what is required to make the ship ready for action and do her best. Some of this is clumsy and is easily spotted by the Commander, who tends to disregard such blatant 'brown-nosing', with only the occasional reproof. Also, the 'good guys' are trying to keep the ambitious in check, with ceaseless teasing and practical jokes; we should have driven them insane by the time all this is over.

Over uckers, we talked about the risks of combat:

'You'll be all right, Doc,' said Carlos. 'You're a non-combatant and can claim all kinds of rights under the Geneva Convention.'

'Is there a problem?' exclaimed Alasdair.

'Just so you look after your mates,' said Declan.

'Well, I don't know; it depends how this game goes . . .'

'Just roll those bones!' said Declan. 'Get on with it.'

After the dice have been rolled and before his move, Alasdair says, 'How can I be a non-combatant in a ship? The bomb or missile can't tell the difference between you and me, can it?'

From Declan, wanting to force an error on the board by putting him off: 'Look, move your bits; we don't need your deep thoughts right now!'

Alasdair duly makes the tactical error and piles up a mixi-blob, resulting in jeers and derision from Declan and me.

'I'll remember that if we get captured; don't expect any special treatment,' said the Doc, with mock feeling.

'That's a bit two-faced,' I ventured, 'hypocritical and Hippocratic together then!?'

The World Service this evening reported that Ireland had called the UK the 'aggressor' and called for EEC sanctions against Argentina to be lifted. Who pulled their string?

Thursday, 6 May

Overnight, we were ordered to hand over *Tidespring* to *Antelope*, which would escort her back to Ascension with the prisoners and all our assorted passengers. We are indeed to escort the LSL Group – comprising SIR Class landing ships – towards the Falklands and we will see *Plymouth* again the day after tomorrow.

Antelope appeared just over the horizon today to take over the escort duties for *Tidespring* and return with her and the prisoners to Ascension. Her Captain, Commander Nick Tobin, came across by Lynx to be briefed by our warfare team and the HODs. He is bright and alert and ultra-keen to get to grips with things. He said that while at Ascension they had had to see off an Arg merchant ship that was attempting to shadow and report the ships that were passing through, including *Canberra*. He also said that a Soviet AGI [Auxiliary Gatherer of Intelligence, i.e. a spy ship] was in the vicinity.

We have now received the outline OPORDER for the landing on the Falklands, which will be at San Carlos around 20–21 May, after a daytime transit of the TEZ the day before. The intention appears to be to encourage the Arg Air Force and Navy to have a go at us in the open seas, so that the Sea Dart and Sea Slug systems can have a go at them – hmm, not sure about that. San Carlos looks a good choice – it is sheltered from the weather and the surrounding hills will make it easier to defend against air attack. But the water is deep enough for submarines; it could also be mined and it is a long way to Stanley. Presumably, we are going to make use of the helos to get the troops across the island, which is going to be pretty boggy.

Flying – conducted by Ian, Stewart and Fitz – involved the usual milk-run with *Tidespring*, as well as practice for her Flight Deck crews and helicopter controller, to ensure that he stays in date for control hours. The ship refuelled from *Tidespring* in the afternoon.

I have just written a letter to A. I am being really careful what I write in my letters and giving nothing away about the operational situation. Even though I am sure that by the time the letters get home the information will be tactically useless, I do not feel it right that I should be telling people stuff that is still classified. I am sure that the boys are breaking every rule in the book and we are just hoping that their wives and families do not go to the press with tales from the South Atlantic. We are already pretty pissed off with *Endurance* for their endless self-promotion. After all, the ship has not actually seen a shot fired against them in anger, despite her trigger happy Wasps, and I am certain that they are still trying to grab all the credit for the *Santa Fé* incident.

Friday, 7 May

The momentum picked up markedly today, although it started with the disappointing news that we had lost two SHars late yesterday. The pilots were John Eyton-Jones and Bill Curtis, neither of whom I knew personally. Ian knew John Eyton-Jones and said that he was one of the smoothest operators in the RN; he admiringly said that he thought that Eyton-Jones was so suave that he had his flying overalls made by Gieves! No one can determine the cause of the losses, but it seems that they failed to return from a routine CAP [Combat Air Patrol] sortie. It sounds like they collided somehow in cloud or reduced visibility, got lost (how?) or ran out of fuel. It's a mystery, but it also means that we have just lost a tenth of our fixed-wing capability – and two precious, experienced SHar pilots.

I was on the Bridge at about 0720 when a Lynx flew by, without warning, trying to establish communications it seems – I wouldn't care to do that unannounced at the moment! Shortly afterwards, we rendezvoused again with *Antelope* herself, which did a smart, fast pass down the starboard side, before taking up an assigned station on our quarter. We also found *Uganda* (hospital ship), *Brambleleaf*, *Regent* and five LSLs (*Sir Galahad*, *Sir Percivale*, *Sir Tristram*, *Sir Geraint*, *Sir Lancelot*) in 31° 13´ S 26° 16´ W.

We spent the forenoon transferring the BAS personnel, our two ladies, various Chileans and assorted passengers – and the two ducks – to *Antelope*. We also got our RM detachment back from *Tidespring* after their Stalag guard duties. We put our mail into *Tidespring* and *Antelope*'s CO came across to talk to the Captain again. We also sent three scrap dealers on their way back to Argentina wearing HMS *Antrim* T-shirts!

This afternoon we conducted a massive RAS (S) with *Regent*, topping up with provisions and other stores, with a heavy jackstay and VERT-REP aft using *Regent*'s Wessex V helos. We did not fly as the Flight Deck was needed for transfers and the breaking down of loads. Carlos was saying that, with all our additional personnel onboard, we had been rapidly running out of food, despite the rationing, and that we had only about two days' supplies left. We now have 30 days' worth of eggs and 15 days of potatoes. Unfortunately, *Regent* had technical problems with both her transfer rigs and we did not receive the wide availability of items that we expected – no naval stores, cleaning gear or – most importantly – chocolate and sweets. The Commander will be happy that we did get some Yorkie bars, but chocolate rationing remains in force. *Tidespring* passed water (!) to *Uganda*, which has been told to proceed to a holding area off the TEZ and a casualty came to us from *Sir Tristram* with a broken elbow.

Antelope and *Tidespring* then detached at 1800 and headed for Ascension. *Tidespring* has been very flexible, quietly effective and accommodating throughout. She has supported us really well and reacted to every challenge that we have thrown at her, including being turned into a prison ship!

On the political front, we heard that Argentina has rejected the US/ Peruvian initiative, although the perfectly useless UN might still have a go at brokering a deal. I do not think that likely. If we had gone on sinking their ships after the *Belgrano*, they might have thought twice, but the Args will consider that it's one-all right now and that they have a chance of winning. I reckon that our politicians know that the die is cast and that is why they have turned the screw on the ROE and the exclusion provisions.

We heard this evening on the World Service that any unit of the Arg Navy will be considered hostile if it strays outside their 12-mile limit. That must mean that our SSNs have set up a blockade line to deal with them. I think that we are committed to action now; the talking's over from Britain's point of view. The Commander certainly thinks that we are in for the long haul, although most people in the Wardroom are taking it one day at a time. I did notice that there was a rush among the ship's company today to send 'newsgrams' and 'familygrams' away with *Tidespring*, along with the mail.

Our hardening attitude seems to be borne out by the fact that more Harriers (SHars/GR3s?) are coming south – with AD capabilities and the AIM-9L Sidewinder – as well as Nimrods, presumably to Ascension, with new air-to-air refuelling probes. I wonder if Chile will let us have the use of one of their airfields – Punta Arenas? – so that the RAF can help (they will be desperate to get involved!). Even if the Chileans do not play, I expect that they will be helping us in other ways – my enemy's enemy is my friend – like intelligence. If the Junta had not gone for the Falklands in order to distract their people from the internal problems (just like in Orwell's *Nineteen Eighty-Four*), I reckon that they would have had a go at Chile, over their dispute about the Beagle Channel. I was also thinking that the Junta needed a war to validate and cleanse the military and their regime in view of their vicious, disgraceful human rights record, a sort of atonement process.

While we were doing FOCCIF, an ROE signal came in saying that, in two days' time, we would be able to 'hack the shadower' if the 707 or Hercules came within range. As they are about the only types of aircraft against which Sea Slug might have a fighting chance, let's see the whites of their eyes! Our worry remains that the Args will start putting civilian airliners in our way to try and tempt us to pluck a whole load of innocent passengers of various nationalities out of the sky. What a great propaganda coup that would be! It might even stop the conflict.

For the first time in a long while, we do not have vast numbers of embarked forces, eating their way through our victuals like a plague of locusts. We are now heading north to escort *Tidespring* and to pick up another group of other ships heading south, mostly STUFT and the amphibious ships, as we expected. These might be vulnerable to long-range Arg air attack, or indeed one of their submarines if it were deployed up-track towards Ascension. Among them is the requisitioned liner *Uganda*, which has been converted and designated as a hospital ship. This has produced a flurry of excitement, because, to Jolly Jack, hospital = nurses and the Commander has been at pains to mention that there are NO female nurses onboard (not sure that this is true). He has also pointed out that under the Geneva Convention, anyone transferred to a hospital ship has to be interned for the duration of hostilities. I am not sure that this information would have helped – interned in a ship away from the action with the possibility of females sounds like a double win for Jack. Carlos helpfully pointed out that indefinite internment with a load of male nurses might prove a bit awkward. Jack is not convinced – and remains hopeful.

Saturday, 8 May

After their considerable exertions load-lifting yesterday, the boys had a maintenance day with the aircraft, but took time to take part in a helicopter delivery service around our new group this morning, moving people and equipment around all day. Because the LSLs were in such a rush to load when they left UK, and again at Ascension, I am pretty sure that nobody quite knows what is in each ship and that they are not yet configured for amphibious assault operations.

As if on cue, UA9 picked up a 707 racket late this forenoon, which was detected on 965 at 150 nm and closed to 115 miles before opening again. The group also turned away from a Soviet merchant ship that passed at about 10 miles, in order not to give away the composition of our force.

The fact is that we do not trust the Soviets not to give intelligence to the Args, despite the political and ideological differences. That is why we are taking anti-satellite counter-measures, implementing really tight emission control with our communications and distinctive radars and disguising our formation in the presence of snoopers.

At about 1600, just before FOCCIF, the 707 radar was again detected to the west on UA9 and correlated with a contact that appeared on 965 at 240 range 140 miles. It closed on a steady bearing and we all went to

Action Stations. It closed to 20 miles – well within Sea Slug range before it opened to the NE. We had the perfect firing solution, but no ROE yet to hack it. Are we at war or not? With less than a day to go, enjoy it while you can, *mis amigos*! We also had the ROE to engage Arg ships outside the 12-mile limit of Argentina (and Uruguay and Brazil – that's sensible!).

At this evening's command brief, concerns were expressed by SCO and John Archer that we could be within striking range of whichever submarines the Args have operational. The problem is that the intelligence is really poor.

We have come up with this plan for using the Sea Slug (becoming known as Surface Launch Un-Guided) in a totally innovative, potentially useful way – the GASH mode. GASH stands for GIVE ARGIES THE SHITS and, of course, gash is the naval slang for rubbish, as in 'we need to ditch the gash'!

Basically, the idea is that, because the missile is so useless, we will not get the chance to hit anything except at high altitude and long range. However, the beast is absolutely terrifying when it launches, looking for all the world like a V-2 rocket, going at Mach 2.0 and with the booster rockets flying off in all directions after about five seconds and with stacks of distracting efflux, vapour, shit and derision.

Here's how it works. If Arg aircraft are detected too late for a feasible engagement, the missile gets fired down the bearing in the general direction and scares them off from attacking us. This is like Thomson's Gazelle, which jumps around like a mad thing in the presence of predators, hoping that its appearing fit will make the chasing big cat not go after it.

We also reckon that we can acquire land targets – like Arg Observation Positions on the top of hills – and fire Sea Slug at them as well. Imagine being hit by a two-ton V-2 rocket going at nearly twice the speed of sound!

We had eggs and potatoes for the first time in ages today, with 15 and 30 days' supply now onboard from the replenishment yesterday. We still have to survive on Millac rather than real milk.

The film in the Wardroom tonight was *Coma* – not to my taste, as it involved organ selling, and I left early. It makes me squeamish just to think of it.

Sunday, 9 May

This morning a Nimrod was on task to the south-west of us conducting surveillance and checking for Arg surface ships and presumably submarines on the surface. At this morning's brief, the issue of whether the *Santiago del Estero* was serviceable and out and about was discussed. It was pointed out that, if she left her base at Mar del Plata or Puerto Belgrano on 2 May, she could be with us now, but I said that I thought that she was probably not seaworthy. If she had been, she would have taken part in the Arg invasion of the Falklands. Given the marginal state of the *Santa Fé*, I cannot believe that her sister boat the *Santiago* has not been used for spares and is firmly and permanently alongside the wall. The *San Luis* is the one that looks likely to be out and about.

We think that the air threat is low, although we are possibly within range if aircraft are launched from their northern bases and can use in-flight refuelling. The only surface ship we have any intelligence for is ARA *Hercules*, which seems to be on radar picket duty 300 miles north of the Falklands, no doubt wondering whether the Vulcans will strike the mainland. We are not sure what the Arg Navy is up to, although they largely seem to be skulking close inshore or in harbour, possibly waiting for the chance to sally out when the amphibs and assault forces arrive. As they used to say in archaeology though, absence of evidence isn't evidence of absence and we cannot assume that some of their ships are not out here on the prowl. We thought that we had an electronic intercept of a Tracker land- and carrier-based aircraft – operated by both Argentina and Brazil – late this afternoon. Surely, we would know if their carrier was out again? Perhaps, the Squirrels know; if they do, they are not telling us. It seems totally counter-productive not to give your primary surveillance platform – the helicopter – all the information that it needs to perform its tasks effectively. It's really irritating.

We replenished with *Appleleaf* during the forenoon.

The boys have used the past three days to good purpose in completing some planned maintenance and in trying to get ahead of the game in terms of ensuring that we have enough flying hours on various components at a time when we need to fly the aircraft the hardest.

We did a couple of Check Test Flights including an in-flight tracking serial to deal with a wobbly rotor blade that was out of track, in amongst taxi runs and deliveries around the group. Partly, this was to support a meeting and lunch onboard for all the LSL commanding officers and CO *Plymouth*, which is back with us again. I like *Plymouth*'s CO, David Pentreath. Despite being a senior Captain and a frigate squadron commander himself, he just gets on with things and does not demonstrate the *amour propre* and prickliness that the CO of *Endurance* and others do when tasked by other captains.

News came in this evening that two SHars located, strafed and bombed an Arg trawler inside the Exclusion Zone. When it was boarded, it turned out to be a tattle-tale or spy ship, containing Arg naval personnel. It was called *Narwal*. There are also reports that *Coventry* has engaged what she assessed to be an Arg helicopter (Puma, we think) with Sea Darts near Port Stanley and destroyed it. *Coventry* and *Broadsword* were off Stanley, where the Arg radars could detect them, trying to provoke an Arg air raid, to prove the effectiveness of the Type 42/Type 22 working together and to hack a few aircraft in conditions that play to their strengths, with their radars and missiles complementing each other. It's a gutsy move and, if the weather had not been so bad, the Args probably would have taken the bait, or accepted the challenge, depending on your perspective.

We heard that we are not now going to be allowed to hack our shadowing aircraft. We have to pass details of the tracks that we have detected as part of a brief for the Cabinet tomorrow.

We are now heading south in company with the LSLs, *Pearleaf* and *Plumleaf*. Escorted by *Antrim* and *Plymouth*, the force is conducting very long-leg zig-zags, in a modified ASW posture.

Monday, 10 May

At 0800 this morning, we went back into Full Defence Watches, reflecting the threat assessments and our geographical position, and did a full re-secure of the ship for action. We are still a way to go to the TEZ, but, as always with us in *Antrim*, better safe than sorry – à la *Sheffield*. We are still steering a very long-leg zig-zag for ASW purposes and, for the benefit of any hostile surveillance, making like we are heading for South Georgia, before turning west to rendezvous with the Main Carrier Group on 16 May.

We are all now concerned about the submarine threat, about which the intelligence is pretty poor. We do not even know which boats are operational or even serviceable. As a result, we flew three ASW sorties today, with a Mk 46 and a depth charge, with the accent on locating any lurking submarine on the surface in transit or snorting during an approach to the force. Consequently, we flew at the most likely times – dawn, just after lunch and at dusk. We also located a large oil rig support ship taken up from trade, *Stena Seaspread*, which is on its way south, with eight officers and 150 engineering ratings, to act as a support and repair ship, initially at South Georgia.

While we were away on our first sortie from 0900, the ship went to Actions Stations, conducted a Damage Control exercise and implemented the lessons that have come out of the *Sheffield* loss. Most attention was paid to providing the maximum amount of redundancy and back-up in the event of firemain or electrical system damage and failures. We also had a look at better anti-flash and action clothing discipline, as well as ways in which we can shut down to ZULU watertight status quicker from YANKEE. This has resulted in a new 'Enhanced 2 YANKEE' manning and watertight arrangement. The most important drills related to smoke control and venting, as smoke seems to have done for *Sheffield* right from the start. DMEO reckons that we do not have enough sets of breathing apparatus to fight extensive fires and that we need to reinforce our fire curtains, especially those in passageways that give access to large and operationally vital, densely manned spaces, like the MCR, the Ops Room and the Damage Control bases and parties. The Rover Gas Turbine yet again failed to start first time. As this is our most powerful portable pump and a vital back-up for our man firemain pumps, this is a worry.

There are some people in this ship I do not care to be behind if we have a problem. If I have to escape through a kidney hatch or other confined space, I simply won't get out if I have to wait my turn behind certain overweight individuals. They would just get stuck in the opening, especially with their Action Dress and other accoutrements. The Commander S is helping with his rationing regime, but I can see that a bit more fitness and a little less fatness are needed. You have to be fit to fight. I do always have my aircrew knife, though.

After our discussions about the *Santiago* and the *San Luis*, I am amazed that we have not seen hide nor hair of the 209* yet. He must be about somewhere, between the top of Falkland Sound and Stanley, or probing out towards the Carrier Group. If I were a submarine, that's where I would be, covering the options. In fact, I cannot believe that he will not turn up soon. You have to wonder whether the Arg sub has calculated that life might be nasty, brutish and short if he pops up and attacks something; he has probably decided that discretion is the better part of valour.

The Sea King boys in the Main Group would have been after him round the clock – that would probably encourage him to keep his head down and conserve battery life. Still, he has to snort sometime and it's strange that we haven't had a sniff yet – he also has to communicate, but there has not been any indication of HF transmissions from sea to shore. That is very unusual, unless they are using some sort of relay ashore or with aircraft on a fixed-time basis. That's a bit sophisticated for them, I would think – in fact, it is for us! Maybe that is because he is not there and is further out to sea.

The main worry is those German ST4 torpedoes which would probably break a frigate's back and put *Antrim* permanently out of the game even if it did not sink us. I am surprised that the Argentinians have not made any attempt to attack our lines of communications and supply routes down from Ascension. They must realize that this is our lifeline, which, if cut or threatened, would seriously inhibit our operations and options. We would also have to devote assets to protecting our ships. Perhaps, we will meet him now we are on the way back down (?).

Apparently, we can now engage Arg surveillance aircraft, if we can identify them visually or by radar and flight profile. Pat Brown is happy about this and, in his usual gung-ho style, daring the planes to close on his watch.

Have just heard on the news that *Sheffield* has sunk under tow – I think *Yarmouth* was taking her to South Georgia. It's a pity that we could not save her, but, from the signals, she seems to have been pretty well burned out. It would have been a complete rebuild. The Arg trawler, *Narwal*, has come out in sympathy and sunk under tow as well. The weather – and 'the wild and wasteful ocean' – must be lumpy further south. That is not a surprise!

406 will fly a surface search and ASW serial between 0200 and 0400,

---

* The German-built Type 209 submarine *San Luis*.

both to vary the pattern and hopefully to detect and surprise any submarine that might be recharging its batteries on the surface or snorting ahead of the force.

Tuesday, 11 May

Today has been a really busy day from the flying point of view. We started rather earlier than we expected. Around midnight, one of the seamen was thought to be missing and a search was initiated for him – a standard procedure known as 'Thimblehunt', whereby all personnel are formally checked and every compartment thoroughly searched. By 0120, it was confirmed that a Seaman (EW) was missing and we were launched early at 0150 to search along the ship's wake to see if he had jumped overboard. He was eventually found lurking in the starboard Cheverton motor launch, having completely lost it all of a sudden and not in a good way. He was put in the Sick Bay overnight, under guard and observation, and Alasdair has spent the day sorting him out, with suitable anti-depressants and gentle 'get a grip' messages. The Padre has been hovering, sensing trade and maybe a conversion.

In one of my previous ships, a junior officer decided that he wanted to end it all because he had been unlucky in love and had become rather overwrought. He was an engineer, I hasten to add. We were in the Aegean. He went down to the quarterdeck at night and in the dark where the lifebuoy 'ghost' [sentry] could not see him, attached a concrete dan buoy sinker (weighing over a hundredweight) to his leg and rolled it over the side. The sinker and he hit the water, but not at the same time or rate of descent. The sinker did as advertised – it sank. The baby engineer did not. Everyone knows that engineers cannot tie knots!

A few minutes afterwards, a Chief Petty Officer called at the officer's cabin for a signature and found the officer's farewell note, indicating where he might now be found. Grabbing it, he raced along the passageway to raise the alarm. In doing so, he slipped and knocked himself out.

When he came to, he was in a berth in the Sick Bay, with a bandaged head and in the solicitous company of the Executive Officer, the Doctor and the Padre. He tried to tell them what had happened, but was interrupted by the Padre, 'It's all right, Chief, we have read your note. We understand your pain. Just sleep now.' Just before the Doctor could administer the sedative, the Chief managed to cry 'No, no!' and to blurt out the truth. The helicopter was scrambled immediately, searching back along the ship's track and following the line of gash bags. The errant young man was found – damp, cold and not quite able to remember why he had thought it a good idea to go for a swim. When he crossed the Equator the following year, he was charged in front of King Neptune, in strict accordance with the wording if not the spirit of the Naval Discipline Act, with 'improperly leaving his ship'.

We heard today that Chris Craig's *Alacrity* transited from north to south through Falkland Sound last night and found an Arg supply or merchant ship that she engaged with gunfire and sank, in a driving rainstorm. She did not stop to investigate. We wondered what *Alacrity* was actually doing there and, only half-jokingly, thought that the Admiral had sent her in, as a Type 21, to see if there were any mines there. Chris Craig was my executive officer in *London* – the epitome of a dashing naval officer and a fantastic role model, with real presence, authority, a voice that compels attention and effortless, charismatic leadership ability. If James Bond were real, it would be him!

If a submarine were around, I would have thought that *Alacrity* would have attracted his attention. If I know Chris Craig, he would have been batting along at max chat, zigging and zagging like a demon and with his 182 towed decoy and noisemaker out. So he would have rolled over any submarine if it were there.

At midday, we in 406 completed an hour and a half out screening for submarines ahead of the force. Sonar conditions were reasonably good, with evidence of marine life. We then came back so that the ship could functionally check and fire the 4.5 guns.

At about 1600, we were in position 42° 10´ S 032° 58´ W. We briefed for an ASW serial, having discussed with the Captain and the warfare team that the Args might have sent one of their 209s up track. Stewart, Fitz and I launched at 1600 and went out on the screen ahead of the force, with a Mk 46 torpedo and as much fuel as the cab would take. We had also tasked *Plymouth*'s Wasp to be at Alert 8 with a Mk 46 torpedo, just in case.

We operated in a sector 30 degrees either side of the group's intended track from six to 12 miles. After about five minutes, we had jumped to a position just to the right of the group's track at about 10.5 miles. We lowered the transducer to 180 feet and Fitz detected a contact that looked promising on the sonar display. It was about 3,000 yards away, with Doppler 2 opening, and the more we looked at it, the better it looked, bearing 145, tracking about 090, speed 4 knots. We had some problems at this stage with sonar training noise and slight oscillations around the bearing, so I was not sure about what confidence level I should apply to the contact.

I transmitted: 'X-ray, FIVE, Uniform this is Zulu FOUR Foxtrot – Track 4140 bearing 145, range 30, heading 090, speed 4, classified POSSUB LOW 2, I authenticate BF – OVER.'

From *Antrim*: 'Roger, your track 4140 – OUT.'

I decided to jump to a new position to get a better aspect on the contact. Stewart transitioned up and I directed him to a new position which I estimated to be about 1,000 yards ahead of the contact. We transitioned down into the dip, lowered the sonar and started transmitting. There at about 1,200 yards a large, fat sausage-shaped contact, with good definition. Over the next couple of minutes, the contact demonstrated closing Doppler and steady tracking, now heading 120, further round towards the force, which bore about 045 from us. The dome leakage light was periodically illuminating and I was worried about the sonar degrading on us.

'Fitz, that looks good to me. What do you think?'

'Could be, it's got all the right indicators. Good, firm contact, great shape, steady course and speed.'

'Stewart,' I said, 'we've got a really strong contact here. It could be a submarine and he is right in the grain.'*

Stewart simply asked, 'Is it a whale? Not that I have seen any spouting.'

'What do you think, Fitz?'

'Your call, Boss. He's pretty steady and just look at the good shape of that contact.'

By now the contact was at about 1,500 yards and drawing right and away from us. We then suddenly lost contact for about three minutes. However, with frantic variations of transducer depth, we eventually regained contact with the sonar at 235 feet, bearing 160 range 2,800 yards heading 230.'

'Right,' I said, 'transmitting – My track 4140, bearing . . .', giving all the contact details and concluding with 'now classified POSSUB HIGH 3 – Over'.

---

* The area ahead of a force which gives a conventional submarine its best chance of intercepting and attacking a group of ships.

From *Antrim*: 'Roger, out.'

I then asked them to launch *Plymouth*'s Wasp with the second Mk 46 torpedo.

I thought that at this point they would turn the force away from the threat and while continuing to track the contact watched the radar to see if the ships had altered course beyond their normal long-leg zig-zag.

'If it was a whale, the movement would be more random, don't you think, Fitz? Any sea-noise?'

'Yes,' said Fitz, 'it's too big and smooth to be a whale. Look at the shape. I can't hear anything on passive, no whale sounds.'

'Just give me an update on it,' I asked Fitz, wanting him to pass electronically the sonar range and bearing of the contact across to my radar plot.

'Let's see – bearing 180 range 3,200 yards and now tracking away from us and towards the LSLs. No sign of the ships turning away from the threat.'

I transmitted: 'Track 4140 [position etc.] now classified POSSUB HIGH 4. Intend COBRA* in two minutes – Over.'

I had given the contact the highest level of confidence short of actually hearing machinery noises or seeing a submarine with the Mk 1 eyeball. I had said that I intended to attack it with the torpedo in snake-search mode, meaning that it would run out from the helicopter searching with its active sonar along the bearing of the contact.

John Archer now came on the radio: 'Roger FOUR Foxtrot, WAIT, OUT.'

Now 'intend' in the Royal Navy means 'unless you tell me not to do it, I will do it'.

One minute to go.

'Good contact, now almost stopped.'

I thought, can whales stop or do they have to keep moving? I need to know more about whales.

Thirty seconds to go.

The ships are still coming on without turning. If it is a submarine and I were him, I'd be firing a spread pattern now. He must know that we are on to him; he must be able to hear our sonar.

Time for a heavy hint – I transmit: 'Intend COBRA seconds 15.'

From *Antrim*: 'Roger, Wait – OUT.'

* A Mk 46 homing torpedo, in snake-search mode.

The minute winds down. 'He's off again,' says Fitz. 'He's doing about 5 knots.'

'We can't jump again. We'll lose him,' I said. 'That's it, time up.'

I applied the settings to the torpedo and fused it. I lifted the release cover and my thumb paused for a couple of seconds ('Is this the right decision?') over the button. ('Hell, yes, you've convinced me.') I firmly pushed it and felt the torpedo fall away. There was a little lurch as 406 adjusted to its weight loss.

'Bearing 180 range 3,400 yards,' called Fitz.

I transmitted: 'COBRA loose track 4140 bearing 180 range 34. DOG-BOX* established bearing 180 range 34 expiry time minute 36.'

'Bloody hell!' exclaimed Stewart.

'What's the matter?' I asked, worried that something was wrong with the aircraft.

'No, no,' said Stewart, 'it's the torpedo running down the bearing. It's an amazing sight and it's fast.'

Of course, none of us had seen a live torpedo in snake-search mode before.

At this point, we raised the sonar body to ensure that it did not attract or distract the torpedo in the water. In the meantime, I took *Plymouth*'s Wasp under control and we jumped to the last known position of the contact. On expiry of the torpedo run, we transmitted with no contact gained.

'Right, let's go,' I said. 'Prepare to jump.' We then jumped to a position that I estimated to be the most dangerous from the Amphibious Group's point of view – three miles further east, between the last known position and the group. We detected a good-quality echo bearing 145 range 2,300 yards moving at about 15 knots.

Suddenly Fitz exclaimed, 'I've got two contacts on the bearing.'

'Eh? What is it?'

'It's close to the contact and the contact has wound up to 15 knots.'

'Well, yes, I'd speed up, wouldn't you? And I would dive. Let's have a look,' I said, as I leaned across to look at the sonar.

There, big as you like, was a large echo this side of the contact. What is it?

'I reckon it's a bubble,' said Fitz. 'It's a decoy.'

'You're right. It must be a submarine.'

* An active weapon danger zone within which ships should not enter.

'Or it's the whale's big brother wanting to know why we just fired a torpedo at his brother,' said Stewart with a laugh.

'Anyone heard from the ship?' I asked.

'Nope,' said Stewart, 'but the ships are turning now. They must have gone about 60 degrees to starboard.'

'Great – but wrong way. They are turning across the threat; they should have turned to port. Best not say anything until this engagement is over. It would just cause confusion.'

'What's that noise?' asked Fitz.

We listened and heard faint but distinct sonar sounds in the water bouncing around.

'He's up at 22 knots now,' said Fitz.

'Crikey – he must be at max chat then.'

'Another bubble,' said Fitz.

Sure enough, there was another fat contact between us and the submarine.

By this time, I was wondering what we had here. It might not be an Arg after all.

We continued to hold the contact for about 50 minutes, with the target manoeuvring violently in course, speed and depth, in and below a thermal layer that was at 120 feet. His last known bearing was 235 range 2,900 yards opening from the force to the west at 22 knots initially and then 7 knots when we finally lost contact. All the while, I held *Plymouth*'s Wasp in readiness to attack with a second torpedo if the contact looked like closing the force again. I was pretty hacked off that the first torpedo had not speared him. I expected to get all sorts of aggro and mickey-taking from the warfare team onboard about that.

On the way back to the ship, I tried to work out what had happened. We had held a good, firm and convincing contact. We had tracked it consistently and there were no sign of whales or other marine mammals. After we had attacked with the torpedo, his speed had wound up dramatically and we saw two air bubbles and possibly had a transponding decoy as well. The speed at the end seemed a bit high for a 209, even if he thought that he had a Mk 46 on his tail. Difficult!

I came back from the sortie full of righteous indignation about how slow it had all been, annoyed that we had loosed off a torpedo and did not have anything to show for it. I went to debrief the Captain, who was in his Day Cabin, and he looked irritated.

'Well, what was that?' he asked and I could tell that he was annoyed.

'That, sir, was a submarine and, as captain of the aircraft, I made the decision to engage it.'

'You should not have done. We cannot afford to waste precious torpedoes on false contacts.'

'Sir, it does not get any better than that; that was the best sonar contact that I have seen in years, and we saw some decoys as well.'

'It wasn't a submarine! You really need to be less impetuous.'

Hang on, I thought in a flash, I am one of the guys who got you out of the scrape in South Georgia. Professional pride, the simmering indignation and the perspective of a 28-year-old bubbled away inside, while my brain was working overtime to urge me to stay calm and objective.

'Sir, the contact was a POSSUB High 4, in the grain of the force and was tracking only five miles ahead of the LSLs – he was in the perfect firing position.'

'We could have turned the force in time and you would not have had to waste that torpedo. It was stupid.'

That's it, as an aviator, I don't do 'stupid'! Here we go! No more use of 'sir', now. This is a man-to-man issue.

'I called the PWO twice to check what I should do and the only reply I got was "Standby, wait, over." I then said, "Intend COBRA" in two minutes. Again "Standby, wait, over." Nobody got back to me.'

'Look, Flobs, standby means that you bloody well wait!'

The temperature is rising now.

'If I had waited much longer, we would have lost contact and who knows what would have happened.'

'Listen to me, it wasn't a bloody submarine!'

'It was as good as it gets; I was the man on the spot and I'm telling you [risky], sir [precautionary move], that both my aircrewman and I know our business. We are not in the business of letting you down!'

'Well, you have this time . . .'

That was it; that was a low blow. The pressure valve on my composure – and my career – was about to blow.

'Sir, it was only a fucking torpedo. I am sorry to swear, but that's how I feel about it.'

'Right,' he said, 'That's it then.'

In the awkward pause that followed, I gave a curt, Prussian-style nod and made my way out and into the Wardroom, where I gave the forward table a thump. After a hastily consumed cup of tea, I went to find Fitz, who was in the Air Office, to compare notes and share some of the righteous indignation. He'd obviously been telling Ian about the incident and, as I came in, still furious, I heard Fitz saying, 'Flobs did everything to get the force to move, but the PWO kept on stalling. Hi, sir, I was just telling the Boss –'

'Fuck it, FUCK IT, FUCK IT!'

It was one of those occasions for which God, in his wisdom, had expressly invented the four-letter word. Nothing else would have done.

'Is something up?' asked Ian whimsically, with a look that, annoyingly at the time, suggested he did not feel the need to take this too seriously.

I was disappointed and verging on angry, not only because we had not nailed a second submarine, but because of the Captain's attitude. He had touched a raw nerve, the hot sensation of which was still coursing through my temples and the back of my neck.

I told Ian what had happened out on the ASW screen, Fitz chipped in and then Stewart arrived, to complete the story with his perspective. I said that I had been chewed out by the Captain and that I had probably climbed to the top of his fuck-off list. Ian did not see a problem, just a difference of opinion. Well, it depends from where you are looking.

The Captain's PO Steward came to tell me that the Captain wanted to see me.

I went in to see the Captain. I could tell that he meant to be genial this time.

'Flobs, look, this sort of thing happens every now and then, especially on operations. We do not want to fall out over this disagreement. Do we?'

I shook my head, but with my cheeks burning.

The Captain continued: 'I am going to tell you something, even though I am not supposed to share it with you. The intelligence strongly suggests that the Argentinian submarines are not in this area.'

Well, I know that NOW, I thought, no Arg submarine does 28 knots, even with a torpedo up its duck run.

'So, it could not have been a submarine . . .'

'Sir, where did this intelligence come from? I did not see it on the log, nor was it part of the sortie brief.'

'It is "need to know" – and you are not cleared to this level.'

It's the bloody Secret Squirrel stuff, I thought. I am supposed to be going on anti-submarine missions and I don't get to know all the intelligence that is available.

'Sir, could I suggest that we need to have access to this sort of information before we fly these sorties? Perhaps we could be briefed about the content rather than the sensitive bits about sources.'

But then I thought, as Sherlock Holmes said (I think): 'Once you remove the impossible, whatever remains, no matter how improbable, must be the truth.'

I said, 'You are clearly right, sir, it was not an Argentinian submarine.'

'Good, Flobs, I am glad that we agree.'

'Yes, Sir, but it was *a* submarine,' I said, smiling broadly with lips firmly clenched.

He looked wearily, but knowingly, at me, and with the familiar twinkle in his eye.

That's OK then, I thought, and departed.

Had that gone badly, I have a ready-use device for dealing with out-and-out, unjustified bollockings from seniors, particularly those that choose to rage rather than reason, rant rather than relate, normally closer to you than you would want this side of intimacy. I used to lock my eyes onto the forehead of the person dishing out the third degree and recite Latin verb conjugations in my mind: 'I have (*amo*) never (*amas*) seen such (*amat*) outrageous behaviour (*amamus*) in the whole of my time (*amatis*) as a training Commander (*amant*). What (*amabo*) did you think (*amabis*) you were doing . . .' and so on.

I remember that I managed all the way to the Fourth Conjugation once (*audio, audis* . . .), but the trick is to keep one ear on the monologue, because all ranters need a self-validating affirmation of how they are doing at some stage in the process. Observer training, with its need to listen to and absorb a number of radio circuits simultaneously, is great for this!

It wasn't needed with this Captain. In the first place, he did not rage, and, secondly, his dark clouds never lasted that long. However, just in case, it might be worth switching to Spanish verbs now we are down here!

The Commander in his avuncular way asked me later that night if I was easy about the situation and told me not to worry about it. He gently told me not to argue with the Captain though – in his words – 'it's his train set and he can play with it how he likes'.

I will talk to him about the Secret Squirrel issue tomorrow.

That night, I looked at myself in the mirror and reflected (!):

Full of strange oaths and bearded like the 'pard,
Jealous in honour, sudden and quick in quarrel,
Seeking the bubble reputation
Even in the cannon's mouth.*

Indeed!

Wednesday, 12 May

Overnight, we heard, but did not really give any credence to, the news
that talks at the UN to negotiate a ceasefire were still progressing. There
was no confidence at breakfast this morning that there would be a peaceful resolution and considerable indignation at any suggestion of a
ceasefire now that we had lost people and *Sheffield*. We just want the
Args to leave the Islands, with no strings attached and no promises to
them about negotiations on sovereignty. You invaded – it was wrong –
get out! That seemed to sum up the conversation. Also, Tony Wedgwood
Benn came in for some stick about his confidence that we would get
stuffed if it came to full-blown war.

Also, the Pope might be cancelling his visit to the UK because of the
dispute. I'd say that there is a slight Catholic/non-Catholic edge to this
conflict. I am not sure how much, but Argentina seems to be hinting at that
aspect – along with its traditional, conservative values – in its propaganda.

The ship spent the day in Defence Watches, mostly practising general
drills, but particularly gun and Exocet firing procedures. We replenished with *Pearleaf* during the forenoon. From midday, we started to
detect spoofing on some of our High Frequency communications circuits, with voices using the ship's call sign. In some cases, the voice was
heavily accented; at other times, it was clearly a recording of our own
transmissions being played back to us. This activity indicates a reasonable level of sophistication among the Arg operators.

We were due to get airborne today at 0945 during the RAS (L) with
Pearleaf, but we had a hydraulic defect. While the boys fixed the cab, we
continued HDS [Helicopter Delivery Services] with *Plymouth*'s Wasp.

There was a sensation at lunch today. The Padre was reading about

* Shakespeare, *As You Like It*.

Wedgwood Benn's latest pronouncements on the conflict and suddenly leapt up and exclaimed, 'That man is a prick!' This resulted in serious hilarity among the other officers and a £1 clerical contribution to the Guide Dogs.

We got airborne at 1400, to complete the transfers and load-lifting tasks. We then practised targeting and reporting for the Exocet drills and conducted a surface search ahead of the force until 1710.

A Nimrod detected a 707 to the north-west of us at 230 miles which it identified visually (no weapons to shoot it down of course), and it was heading towards us. Sea Slug started to get excited, but the 707 turned away a long way out. They seem to have got the message.

We got airborne again at 1500 and flew a surface search pattern ahead of the force and finished after some load-lifting between the ships at about 1715.

We came back to read signals indicating that there had been a sharp action involving *Glasgow* and *Brilliant* on the gun-line off Stanley and that *Glasgow* had been hit by a bomb that passed right though her hull without exploding. This is a rerun of the Type 42/Type 22 combo that *Coventry* and *Broadsword* tried the other day. It seems that the ships splashed three A4s out of four between them on a first raid, but failed to deal with a second formation of four, one of which struck *Glasgow* with this bomb that did not explode. *Glasgow*'s auxiliary machinery and a Tyne intake have been badly damaged and she is retiring hurt towards the east.

Glasgow's situation reports indicate that she might have been lucky not to have sustained more catastrophic damage. Coming after *Sheffield*'s failure to deal with the Exocet, another Type 42 seems unable to cope close inshore. You also have to wonder about the 42/22 combo. I suspect that they are not picking the aircraft up soon enough to vector the CAP or to alert and fire Sea Dart, with nothing to back it up if the aircraft gets through and Sea Wolf sulks. I am sure that I heard there is a software problem with Sea Wolf that makes it go tits-up when you least expect or need it. *Ark Royal* and her Gannets* – where are you now?

The QE2 sailed from Southampton today, with another brigade's worth of troops, and could be with us in 14 days if she keeps up 28 knots all the way (unlikely). I expect the Args can work that out as well.

* The previous conventional carrier which served in the Royal Navy until 1979 and her early-warning aircraft.

We lost a Sea King today – everyone was OK.

The Commander has come up with a novel wheeze for keeping the boys amused. He has been known for some time as Hagar the Horrible and now he sports a Viking helmet (a hard hat and horns), made for him by the gunner's party, as he proceeds around the ship.

He has also decided to open the Argentinian wine stocks we captured at South Georgia for general use in the Wardroom – apparently, it is not at all bad. Officers have to write chits for *Argie Red* or *Argie White* and each glass costs 50p, with the proceeds going to Guide Dogs for the Blind.

Thursday, 13 May

We were airborne from 0600 to sweep 100 nm ahead of the force for surface contacts and were back by 0830. At 1330, we flew again for sonar checks and another ASW and surface search patrol.

The ship thoroughly rehearsed its Damage Control routines during an NBCDX today and we completed our weapon preparations. We were used as a dummy target to ensure the alignment and accuracy of the radars, visual sights and 4.5 inch gun, Sea Cat and Sea Slug. This involved flying set profiles, running in from various ranges and different directions and at various heights down to 20 feet.

The *Scum* pointed out today that the average Leading Hand in *Antrim* would have been away from Portsmouth for eight weeks (1244 hours) and that he would have accrued £1,008 in pay. He would have consumed 40 eggs (£2.40), 20 feet 2 inches of sausages, 1 lb 6 oz of bacon and 20 tins of beans. He could have drunk 120 cans of beer (£33.60).

At home, it is reckoned that he could have 'got his leg over' 32 times and experienced 24 (at least) 'Not, tonight, darling, I have a headache' moments. He could have watched 16 episodes of *Crossroads* and/or *Coronation Street* and had the dog take him for a walk 56 times.

The *Scum* then asks: 'SO WHERE WOULD YOU RATHER BE?!'

The authority running the merchant ships taken up from trade (STUFT) sent a signal: 'Tesco are offering free thermal underwear to lady crewpersons and embarked nurses. Ships with women are to send total numbers in three sizes: small, medium and large.' The MCO had added a comment on the signal – 'HOT STUFT!'

The ship is full of Rubik cubes and some of the lads can solve the puzzle in minutes. They pass the time having competitions with each other, but, because they have anti-flash on, the manual dexterity tends to suffer.

I am sure that the Args are intercepting some of our voice circuits. There was a derisory attempt at spoofing yesterday on an HF voice circuit (AAWC [Anti-Air Warfare Coordination]), by a heavily accented Hispanic voice: '*Broadsword* [with the W pronounced] dees eez *Exerteer*, report chyor pozeezion, ovair', followed by: 'Dew chyou now kwair *Inveenzeeble* eez?' It was straight out of *Monty Python* and there were instant cries of 'No one expects the Spanish Inquisition!' around the Ops Room. We did not want to give away our position or call sign, and it took a while for someone to call GINGERBREAD (the brevity codeword for spoofing) and everyone to switch to another circuit. Not before some wag on the circuit had interjected: 'You're from Buenos Aires; you know nothing!' in mocking reference to Manuel in *Fawlty Towers*.

We had a serious case of spoofing on the AAWC circuit this morning. A raid from the west was called and counted down on AAWC, with clearly recognizable voices on the circuit – I think that I heard Ian Forbes in *Glamorgan*, with his unwaveringly calm, measured and authoritative tone, and other clearly identifiable British voices, including fighter controllers. The CAP was scrambled to intercept, but found nothing and had to go back to the carriers to refuel. Then, suddenly, in came a raid and it was quite clear that we had been on the end of a pre-recorded sequence of a previous day's activity that had been played back to us. It is assessed that the source might have been in West Falkland. We cannot afford to underestimate them!

Friday, 14 May

The weather has been very rough today, but clear – amid confused seas – and the LSLs have had to reduce speed to avoid damage. We met up with *Fort Toronto* in the early afternoon and she joined the force. She pumped over fuel to *Pearleaf* well into the night.

The afternoon was taken up with another Damage Control exercise, foreshadowed, unintentionally, five minutes before, by a fire in a classified waste bag on the Bridge. Initially, this was thought to be the kettle in the Bridge tea-boat and, initially, everyone ignored it. Then one of the radio operators pointed out that you did not usually get choking grey to black smoke from the kettle!

During the exercise, we did the usual hose runs, section base checks and shoring practice, while the engineers walked through the provision of back-up machinery and electrical solutions, including running emergency power lines, in the event of damage. On the basis of the *Sheffield* experience, the Commander and Declan reckon that we would have a serious shortage of breathing apparatus in the event of action damage. All the indications are that we would be immediately incapacitated by smoke, despite all the plans to control ventilation and limit the spread.

The Commander is uncompromising on the subjects of securing for sea and action, the importance of pragmatic routines and the maintenance of cleanliness. Despite the temptation to relax, he is unequivocal. 'You cannot go to war in a pigsty' is his frequent refrain. There is no doubt that he is right. Quite apart from the ship-shape-and-Bristol-fashion aspect, the maintenance of familiar routines keeps the boys' minds on the task in hand and dark thoughts away.

The Pusser has put us all on short rations on the basis that we do not know when or if we will be able to replenish again. That means 'wheaties' (cereals) and toast, with Marmite or preserves for breakfast, soup and a filled roll for lunch and 'pot mess', a stew-based derivative with potatoes (when we have them) for dinner. There has consequently been a run on 'nutty' from the canteen and it looks like we will deplete that source pretty rapidly.

The lunchtime soup situation has reached a farcical point. For about three weeks, we were getting either asparagus or celery soup – we seem to have the world's supply – and it was becoming tedious. Then the stewards started putting 'soup du jour' on the menu; when you asked what the soup du jour was, they answered asparagus or celery, which it was. Today, imagine my delight when I saw 'tomato soup' on the menu. 'I'll have the tomato soup, please,' I said. 'Actually, sir,' came the reply, 'it's celery. We were just trying to help keep morale up.'

Also, the stewards have jokingly (I think) taken to asking us to settle our mess bills before we go flying now, in case we don't come home. They obviously think that it is a great in-joke, but it is wearing rather thin, even though you could get superstitious about them not doing it after all this time.

Saturday, 15 May

The whole day was spent holding in position waiting for the *Fearless* Group. The weather, wind and sea-state, which have been extreme, have again caused the SIR Class landing ships and *Fort Toronto* some problems. We have endured sleepless nights and had very challenging flying conditions.

406 started with the familiar dawn surface search sortie from 0600 for two and a half hours, with no hostiles to report, but a reasonable picture gained of the various ships around us out to 100 nm.

It appears that the Arg Navy has not moved beyond the 12-mile limit since we told them that we would sink them if they ventured outside. It's very frustrating when one spends most days waiting to be bombed or zapped by missiles from the Arg Navy Air Arm or Air Force and one cannot have a crack at their ships.

Most of our time is spent waiting for all our ships to gather, interrupted by bursts of activity in response to particular threats, real or imagined. The atmosphere concentrates the mind very well indeed.

In the late afternoon, we went to collect mail – this makes us very popular with the ship's company. We have run out of chocolate though. We were on reduced rations anyway and, with the food high in carbohydrates and decidedly stodgy, not even the chance of losing weight, except through exercise.

The ship tried to replenish with *Plumleaf*, but, in the sea-state, her hose lines became hopelessly entangled and we had to have another go (successfully) this afternoon. While alongside, *Plumleaf* played 'Don't Cry for Me, Argentina' on her loudspeakers.

Last night, the SAS conducted a spectacular raid on Pebble Island, where there is a small Arg air base and destroyed 11 aircraft: Pucaras and Turbo-Mentors. *Hermes* and *Glamorgan* had dashed to the west in the night and had landed 45 D Squadron SAS troops by helicopter. They also blew a hole in the runway, while *Glamorgan* provided gunfire support.

We have just heard that the Arg troops and sailors who defended South Georgia so 'bravely' and 'resolutely' have returned to Argentina to a heroes' welcome. They were terrified and could hardly wait to surrender!

I am reading Thomas Hardy's *The Woodlanders* at the moment, which makes me reflect how precious England, its countryside and, of course, our home in Dorset are. The narrative and the place names are really evocative and I am probably being totally over-sentimental about it all.

I have written a long letter to A. I explained to her that she need not worry about anything she sees on the TV. With the time that it takes to get video back to the UK, nothing she sees is going to have anything to do with me.

In her last letter, A said that she had been to see the doctor. I detect that she was getting anxious about things. The doctor was obviously a good Christian and, instead of pills, prescribed her a healthy dose of Psalm 91: 'A thousand shall fall at thy side, and ten thousand at thy right hand; but it shall not come nigh thee.'

Part of my letters home now are devoted to maintaining morale and looking forward, even though that is something which is not encouraged onboard, at least in the Wardroom.

I have been trying to cheer up A by saying that we ought to start a family when I get back. I do not want to tempt fate, but it is probably about time anyway. There is nothing like the whiff of grapeshot to incentivize the genes and encourage getting on with producing the next generation.

Sunday, 16 May

The *Fearless* Group was delayed by the weather and we had to wait until 1700 before she and her group finally arrived. Both groups integrated and we are all now heading west, as if we mean business. We are now part of the *Fearless* 'Armada', as the Commander put it on CCTV tonight.

We received the hard-copy operation order for the landings. The mission is quite explicit: 'to land at Port San Carlos/Ajax Bay complex and establish a beachhead from which to launch offensive operations'. That finally confirms where we are going. The landing envisages a simultaneous assault by 40 and 45 Commandos and supporting arms in LCUs [Landing Craft Utility] to secure San Carlos and the Ajax Bay area. Then 2 Para and 3 Para are to be landed in LCUs to secure Port San Carlos settlement and a defensive position on Sussex Mountain. Phase 3 has a helicopter move ashore of artillery and air defence assets to cover the beachhead. 42 Commando are the afloat reserve at 30 minutes' notice. The operation seems to have a lot of moving parts and is complicated. I think it was Churchill who said that 'an operation like this has to fit together like a jewelled bracelet'.

I woke this morning to find that there was no water in the showers. It had been switched off. We are starting to have problems with water consumption and rationing has been introduced because an evaporator (one of two) is defective and cannot be fixed. We need to reduce our consumption below 50 tons a day apparently. In future, I will find out when the Senior Engineer is going to have a shower and plan my run-in accordingly – he will always know when the water is on!

During the late forenoon, Stewart and I conducted the usual surface search and sweep, mainly to find *British Esk*, because the Captain had heard that the *Sheffield* survivors were onboard and he wanted to invite Captain Salt to come across for an hour and tell us about his experiences. We picked him up, having deposited some mail, and he sat in Fitz's seat as we transited back to *Antrim*.

He was clearly still shocked by his experiences, but had a resilient, philosophical (or resigned) look about him. When I looked at him, when we were not talking, he looked like a man in grief. I was put in mind of the story of Henry I, who never smiled again after his only son was drowned in the White Ship in 1120. I tried to make conversation, but he was preoccupied with his own thoughts, possibly with regard to what he was going to tell us. It struck me that there is a real psychological gap between those who have been sunk – before they get back into action again – and those who have not. It's a case of 'he jests at scars that never felt a wound',* I suppose.

Once onboard, Captain Salt described, in a measured and unemotional way, how his ship came to be hit by the Exocet. What surprised me during his account was his admission that the ship, as the up-threat radar picket on the afternoon after we plugged the Arg cruiser, was not at Action Stations and that he was not in the Operations Room. He said that smoke from the explosion spread incredibly rapidly and that fires broke out amidships and within the superstructure at once. Apparently, the firemain and electrical power were lost immediately and the Rover gas turbine fire pump refused to start (there's a surprise!).

All this meant that the fires were well under way by the time other

* Shakespeare, *Romeo and Juliet*.

ships arrived to help. Another interesting feature was that people used their gas masks to get through the smoke, not that there is any air available; it just keeps the smoke out of your lungs and eyes. FOST [Flag Officer Sea Training] staff experts tell you never to put your gas masks on in smoke because it gives you false confidence and you could suffocate, but Captain Salt said that wearing them saved 12 lives, while only killing one person. People asked questions about what indications *Sheffield* had of the attack and why the firemain had failed and the water pressure dropped so quickly. I might have got it wrong, but I am sure that Captain Salt said that the firemain had not been isolated before the missile came inboard. From my limited experience, that would appear to be unusual and, if true, would have contributed to the problems.

It also appears that *Sheffield* did not detect the incoming missile and failed to fire chaff because her ESM was blocked by transmissions on her satellite communications.

After an hour or so, we returned Captain Salt to *British Esk* along with some outgoing mail at lunchtime. You cannot help feeling sorry and concerned for him. He has to live with that one catastrophic event – and how it could have/should have turned out differently – for the rest of his life.

Back in the present, this evening, for two hours, we replenished stores, food and ammunition from RFA *Stromness*, using the forward rig and the Flight Deck. We came back to discover a huge amount of mail being sorted on the deck in the Wardroom. It was like Santa's grotto. The Padre had several back copies of the *Church Times*, as well as a congealed mass of what had formerly been chocolates from his wife. We received lots of newspapers and girlie magazines from well-wishers – some of it pretty graphic! The latter were sold off at 10p a throw in the NAAFI and the Commander put a gentle version under the Padre's pillow.

We also heard that a pair of SHars had located two Arg supply ships, one at Fox Bay and another in Falkland Sound, and bombed and strafed them. There is a lesson for us there – do not get caught close inshore in the open without adequate warning and some anti-air cover. Interestingly, one of the SHars caught a round in his tail – lesson: lead in the air is good.

I need to record a section of Commander E's message to the ME Department last night. It speaks for itself and is priceless!

'Now that Active Service has been declared, our NAAFI staff who opted to enlist in the RN for the duration of active service now become naval ratings. All other civilians in the RFAs and STUFTs are now subject to the Naval Discipline Act, but it is only in cases where operational efficiency of the Fleet is concerned that the new powers will be invoked. *That means that the gay stewards on the RFAs can remain gay unless it affects the operational efficiency of the Fleet!'*

Well, that's all right then!

Ian, Stewart and I have been talking about the threat to us from Arg aircraft. Ian believes that he can out-manoeuvre a jet by getting inside – and staying inside – its turning circle and not slowing down. Stewart just nods. I say – what if there is more than one of them? Ian says that we will cross that bridge when we come to it. Apparently, we just do not need to get bounced, that's all. That's all! We are less confident about the Pucaras, which seem best suited to taking out ground targets and helicopters. They are firmly on our to-do list. We have the GPMG, but we do not need Fitz to shoot our rotors off!

Monday, 17 May

For a couple of days now, we have been under distant surveillance from 707 aircraft. They do not dare to close the force, but are clearly gaining some radar information about the size and approximate disposition of our forces, if not the precise composition. It happened again today. I wonder why we do not send the SHars off to splash it, but I suppose that they would only run away faster than the SHars with their limited fuel capacity could intercept them.

The weather over the Islands has been pretty bad today, so there has not been any appreciable enemy air activity. There were a couple of reports of Etendard radar in search mode, but nothing more.

The *Fearless* 'armada' is now heading towards the Falklands and we are making sure that we have everything in the right place, in the right order in the right ships. That will mean a heavy programme of load-lifting and transfers of stores and personnel in a pretty tight timeframe.

We flew the Captain and the Operations Officer across to *Fearless* early this afternoon for briefings and an early indication of what the landings are likely to look like, before we departed for an extended range surface search ahead of the force. We also deployed some Chaff Hotel, displaced well away from the force in various places, as decoys, to confuse the Arg surveillance aircraft.

On completion, at 1700, we refuelled in *Fearless*. There is a golden rule in the Fleet Air Arm that there are four things that you do not turn down, in case you might regret it later – food, fuel, a pee and sex – so we took a suck of fuel, nothing else being on offer, while we could, and, embarking the Captain and Operations Officer, went on our way.

When we returned, the maintainers noticed that we had oil staining and streaks around the engine compartment. They checked the magnetic plugs, which are probes fitted to the engines; they are designed to attract and collect small fragments of stray metal and debris in the engine.

'How are they?' we asked.

'Like Christmas trees,' came the answer from Fritz Heritier.

'So it's an engine change,' said Ian.

'It's an engine change,' said the SMR. 'We weren't planning on going anywhere for the next couple of days!'

There were clear indications that the engine was about to fail or break up. With the damage confirmed by a ground run on deck later in the evening, we would need a complete engine change before we could fly again. Fortunately, the spares outfit for a Wessex 3 embarked in a destroyer included a complete engine, stowed in a large protective box in the hangar.

Good old Humphrey! Instead of failing catastrophically at a time when we were over the sea, miles away or involved on some hazardous sortie, the engine had let us know quietly and gently that it had just had enough. That engine of course is the one that stood by us so manfully and did all the hard work up on the glacier.

Apart from the aircraft, the boys are concerned about the mail situation. We received mail yesterday and it seemed from the content that none has arrived home from us for some time. We last sent mail off with *Tidespring* to Ascension; this would have arrived in the UK on 12 or 13 May, so there has been no time for loved ones to reply and for the letters to reach us. It's logical, but still needs explaining to the lads.

I am being really scrupulous about what I write in letters home, just in case the mail is lost during transit, and recovered, or intercepted and opened at some stage. It is generally believed that censors are randomly opening mail and ensuring that no one is cheating. The gap between the despatch and receipt of mail means that any useful dialogue is largely impossible. It is like shooting into the dark, without knowing what circumstances will be like by the time that a letter arrives.

As a result, most of what I write is platitudinous and bland, alongside the rather formulaic reassurances about love and marriage and attempts to sustain morale at home.

Good news on the Exocet front – it seems that we have a Lynx specially equipped with ECM [Electronic Counter-Measures] equipment that can jam the Exocet seeker head. I am not sure how it works, but, as the missile has two modes – radar and home-on-jam – the idea must be that you jam the head so that it locks onto the helicopter rather than the ship. Part of the deal must be that you climb pretty fast at the last minute so that the missile flies underneath!

We also received the design details for an Exocet radar deflector. The Chippies and the Flight maintainers have knocked it up and this polyhedral thing has been fitted to the port weapon carrier. It is pretty urgent, so we put up with the excessive vibration on the carrier and the bracing struts. We would not want it to fall off in flight though. The device produced a tanker-sized echo on 992 at 15–20 miles and appeared to be effective although very direction-sensitive. We have been practising, especially the bit about climbing in good time.

In addition, we got hold of a portable HWR 2 radar detector, which is supposed to give us warning of hostile radars, but we never detected any. We could really do with the Lynx Orange Crop ESM, so that we could detect and classify threat radars and determine bearings with some degree of accuracy.

We have been discussing some novel ideas in the Mess:

Using the 4.5 guns to throw up a wall of water against incoming missiles, in the hope that they might be deflected off course or break their lock. This does mean that with the appropriate depression the shells have to pass about six inches above the ship's side!

I have been badgering the MEs about the possibility of making smoke. It worked really well inshore in both World Wars and when screening convoys. I think that we should give it a go.

We thought that we could make some improvised bombs out of beer kegs, just in case we came across an Arg ship unawares, or even over the land. The Greenies looked decidedly sceptical.

Finally, Williams and Glyn's Bank have pointed out to the Ministry of Defence that the Args still owe it £6m for the purchase of the Type 42 destroyers ARA *Hercules* and ARA *Santissima Trinidad*, with the clear implication (or imprecation) that, if at all possible, we should avoid sinking them.

Tuesday, 18 May

Today saw an early replenishment with *Pearleaf*, before we went to Air Raid Warning RED at mid-morning in response to a spurious detection.

While they conducted the engine change throughout the day, the boys simultaneously manned the Flight Deck for intensive load-lifting and transfers, working Wessex Vs, right through to 2000. The transfers were between the *Invincible*, *Hermes* and *Fearless* groups, which met up in the night. The bulk of the transfers for us involved taking onboard the SBS and their kit from *Fearless*, in anticipation of some advanced force operations which we will do before the main landings.

Ian, Stewart and I regularly go down to give the boys some encouragement and to show that their work is appreciated, but, frankly, they do not need it. They know what they have to do and almost take a perverse pride in delivering against the odds. In situations like this, you simply get in their way. There are times, it seems, when attempts at leadership are not required and can be counter-productive. I will take a few beers down later, when the SMR reckons that they have progressed sufficiently.

We have been looking at the formidable air defences that the Args have built up around Stanley. We reckon that they have upwards of 50 air defence gun systems and about seven missile launch sites. That is making low-level attacks by the SHars pretty dangerous. Meanwhile, the ships are being engaged by what we think are 155 mm artillery – about 15 miles range, but not that accurate. We assess that the Args are flying Hercules in and out every night and pulling their dummy craters across the runway every day. The Admiral's staff is ignoring our assessment.

One of the things that struck me was that the numbers of people going to church on Sundays has risen steadily as our latitude south has increased. Usually, church on Sunday is attended by the Captain, the Commander, a collection of in-zone shufflers hoping to increase their chances of promotion, the regular low church C of E types like me, and the hard-core God-bothering evangelists and oddly enough a lot of Supply branch ratings. The Junior Rates' Dining Hall was packed and it was a compelling scene with worship going on amid all sorts of war gear stowed against the bulkheads, in boxes and crates, with some small-arms ammunition in ammo boxes. Some of the lads were actually sitting on the khaki boxes and other paraphernalia.

Now that it looks like we are truly going to see some action, the faith levels seem to be on the rise and the Padre cannot quite understand what is going on. Even our visitors are trying to get some divine credit in the bank. This week, the Padre invited everyone to renounce sin and the Devil and one of them said, right out loud: 'I'm not sure that this is a good time to be making enemies, Padre!' Didn't Voltaire say that on his deathbed? They must be recruiting a more erudite type at Hereford nowadays!

I have noticed that people tend to avoid talking about the future, beyond the demands of the campaign, or what they are going to do when they get back. It's a superstition thing, because people think that it will give Death ideas. The only one who does not have a problem in this regard is Martin Littleboy, who goes on endlessly about the new Volvo he wants to buy when he gets home and the other night even brought some brochures into the Wardroom. Has he had them onboard the whole time? That is strange.

However, if I am to return to the people I love, to the people that I cherish and respect, I must be able to return with a clear conscience and the knowledge that I did my very best in everything during this conflict. I would not want to live the rest of my life knowing deep down that somehow I had fallen short, had done something of which I would be ashamed or failed in my duty.

'Duty is the great business of a sea officer; all private considerations must give way to it, however painful it may be.' Nelson and someone else said that the joy of a proper return home can only be grasped by unsullied, undefiled hands.

Tonight, we are all in a holding box 300 miles to the ENE of the Falklands, still consolidating the stores and personnel in various ships and waiting for the time to cross the Exclusion Zone.

Wednesday, 19 May

The boys had to work the Flight Deck through to 0140 this morning. I stayed up with them, as a show of solidarity, and took the beers down at about 0100, even though we were still conducting flying operations. The engine change continued through the night.

We finally saw *Hermes* for the first time just before lunch. She passed by light: 'Good to see you. Congratulations on your performance in

South Georgia.' With that, we remained close in on *Hermes* and the other big ships for continuous flying operations for the rest of the day and into the night, moving personnel and stores around.

There has been a massive transfer of troops from *Canberra* all day today, because it has now been decided that we do not want to have three Commandos or battalions in the same ship. 40 Commando are in *Fearless*, 45 Commando in *Stromness*, 2 Para in *Norland* and 3 Para in *Intrepid*. 42 Commando is lucky to have *Canberra* to itself.

The sight of the Battle Group and the amphibious assault force together was awe-inspiring and fascinating, with ships, aircraft and landing craft filling the horizon all around. Everything was in constant motion on a flat, calm sea and the whole scene exuded raw fighting power. The thought that I was part of this tremendous enterprise made the hairs on the back of my neck stand up. We have managed to send everything 8,000 miles, bring it together and are now poised to conduct a landing in combat and on a hostile shore.

A half-remembered quotation from Milton occurred to me:

'Methinks I see in my mind a noble and puissant nation rousing herself like a strong man after sleep, and shaking her invincible locks.' Looking around, my intuition compelled me to believe that we would be successful.

Life is pretty busy and pressured. It's hard to get a good night's sleep, with the weather, but the operational situation is not yet as difficult as I thought that it would be. No doubt that will change over the next couple of days, especially after D-day on Friday.

I wrote a short letter to A. I explained that the newspapers had got the South Georgia story all wrong and said that, by the time that she received the letter, she would know where we were and what we were doing.

I wonder if the politicians have the resolve to launch us against the Islands. The left-wingers – known onboard as the 'left-whingers' – like Foot, Wedgwood Benn and Dalyell – seem so incredibly squeamish about the prospect of action. Do they not realize that the easiest way to end this war is for the Args to lose it! So far, the application of force has been progressive and measured. We now need to get on with convincing the Arg forces that the Falkland Islands will cost them too much if they stick around – soon the serious killing will start. I think it was Jacky Fisher who said that 'Moderation in war is imbecility.' We have reached that point now and we have to be ruthless. We could have done so much more already, especially with regard to sinking more of their ships, but as they have been thoroughly frightened off by the sinking of the *Belgrano*, they might not put in an appearance. I would be amazed if they do not sally forth in response to the landings though. I think that a Nimrod is going to be on task to detect them if they do. Let's hope that the SSNs are in the mood.

In terms of conscience, I have no doubt that this is a just war. It does not get any better than this – we are up against a vicious dictatorship, supported by a military Junta that has systematically tortured and murdered its own people. They are a bunch of strutting poseurs, very much in the style of the fascist dictatorships in their preening, self-regarding arrogance and bravado. To top it all, by invading Islands that do not belong to them, they have given us the perfect excuse to give them a lesson not only in gunboat diplomacy, but also a lesson in what it means to have the (jack)boot on the other foot. I bet they also did not count on us being bothered to come all this way to get the Islands back, seeing as in their eyes we would be a clapped-out country on the wrong side of history, as witnessed by our having a woman Prime Minister.

On the other hand, we could get a good kicking, if all their assets turn up and they have the game of their lives. I can't help recalling what happened to the Russian Baltic fleet. It flogged all the way round from the Baltic to the Pacific in 1905, only to be given a complete hiding by the Japs at Tsushima.

While we are waiting for the cab to be serviceable, the thing on my mind today is how critical tomorrow is going to be. Amphibious landings are remarkably complex and notoriously prone to a range of unexpected happenings. On the basis of D-Day, Anzio and all the US landings in the Pacific, the timings are bound to go wrong and people will lose their way in the dark. The Args' best chance is to hit us while we are between sea and land, to stop us getting sufficient combat power ashore to defeat any counter-attacks and to build up all our guns, ammunition and logistics to support the subsequent drive across the island. If he can throw us back into the sea or sink enough of our amphibious ships and transports, he wins, because the winter will be upon us before we can regroup with another brigade's worth of men and kit.

However, Nelson said, 'the boldest moves are the best ones' and this is our Inchon moment. I think that MacArthur, like Beatty, was a complete bullshit-artist, but he got Inchon right. The enemy did not expect it. I seem to remember someone at South Georgia saying, 'They won't expect us to come from this direction!' I wonder.

Critically, we have a naval heritage and the Args do not (sorry, guys, the Spanish don't count and, anyway, do you want to call in aid the Armada?). We ourselves might be dwarfs sitting on giant's shoulders, but our tradition of war-fighting at sea must be worth something here, not just the expectation of success, but the tremendous psychological boost and confidence that the legacy of Drake, Blake, Nelson, Cunningham and an endless succession of fighting admirals gives us in terms of offensive spirit and motivation. Equally, it makes the shame even greater if we screw up – we would truly have to 'hold our manhoods cheap'. No, the Royal Navy does not 'do' defeat and people take the idea of it very badly. Having said that, as long as we go down with all guns blazing and against the odds, like with the *Revenge*, it would just about be tolerated. Against Argentina, I don't think so.

Our historic record must also affect the Args in a negative way, surely; they must be feeling the psychological pressure in that respect, although their air force probably does not care. In fact, I think that they have only ever had one war – in the 19th century, against Bolivia. We must not be complacent though; they will probably fight hard because they have no other choice. If we start winning on land, we will effectively be between them and home – for Stanley, read Stalingrad-on-Sea!

There is a serious problem with an Arg company that might be on Fanning Head, a high point of land framing the northern edge of the entrance to San Carlos and to the north-west of Port San Carlos. It is thought from electronic intercepts that a unit, comprising 50–80 men, is there with a recoilless rifle, mortars and other heavy weapons, which would threaten our ships. *Antrim* Flight has been tasked to insert the SAS or SBS into Fanning Head on the night of the landings, to neutralize the Arg company, along with *Antrim*'s 4.5 guns, ahead of the amphibious approach and landings.

Most of the Lynx flights seem to be tasked with flying surface search and ESM barrier patrols with their Orange Crop radar and missile detection equipment and other routine tasks like HDS. Burning holes in the sky cannot be that exciting, but the extra coverage and height do allow a great many more detections of incoming enemy ships, aircraft and especially missile control (Exocet!) radars.

On top of another ditched ASW Sea King today, I have just heard that we have lost a Sea King 4 conducting transfers between *Hermes* and *Intrepid*. There have been casualties, but we have had no details yet, either about the cause of the crash or the numbers.

As I write, we are preparing for replenishment with *Tidepool*. We are both fully darkened and will need to be careful on a particularly dark night. I do not think I have ever seen a night as inky black as this, without even a suggestion of a horizon.

Thursday, 20 May

Throughout the night, we transferred lubrication oil drums onto the Flight Deck from *Tidepool* and returned the empties. One of our main engineering pumps is not operating properly and it is just drinking oil.

At breakfast, John Saunders described how a darkened RFA nearly rammed us in the stern while it was still dark during his Morning Watch stint as OOW. We were in station on *Stromness* and the unknown ship came to about one and a half cables, suddenly realizing there was something else in the way, before sheering off. Both ships were fully darkened, without radars (to reduce detection opportunities for the Args), and I think that John Saunders' action as Officer of the Watch in switching on the navigation lights prevented a major collision.

The aircraft engine was finally fitted and Stewart started it up, with the helicopter restrained by a special assembly. The boys were like walking zombies by this stage and we took things slowly. You could tell how tired they were because they could not get any oil into the engine. The reason was that the tank and engine were already full!

For the past two days, the boys have worked like Trojans to change the engine. Everyone helped, either directly in removing the old engine or preparing the new one for installation, by unpacking and checking it or by fetching stores from within the ship. The other trades then took the opportunity to complete routine servicing on other components and kept those fitting the new engine topped up with tea and coffee and food, which no one had time to eat or drink in the dining halls. It was a difficult job, because the aircraft had to be parked half in and half out of the hangar, not only to use the test and lifting gear, but also to keep the Flight Deck clear for other operations. I reckon that some of the lads worked for over 36 hours at a stretch, still with the prospect of intensive flying after it was all over. Some managed to have cat naps, but the senior rates worked through. That's why we are going to win this war, because we have people like them and the Args don't!

We have been down to encourage and be with the boys from time to time and at odd moments during the night, but were conscious that they knew what they were doing and we would only be in the way. It occurs to me that officers need to be aware that their constant, hovering presence isn't always necessary to success and that good people who are given real responsibility will respond appropriately and well, especially under pressure. They do have to be good people in the first place, though! I recall the standard, unofficial 'Wardroom Fire Party', whose members always seem to be on hand looking to exert some leadership whenever there is an emergency or incident alongside. Of course, they merely get in the way of the duty watch, who are trained and rehearsed in getting the job done, despite the well-meaning, but distracting, proximity and influence of the officers.

In the Sea King 4 that we lost last night, it has been reported that there were 27 troops, three crew and lots of kit. That is an incredible load for a Sea King 4 and I am amazed that it managed to get airborne at all. It seems that only the pilots and seven others survived. I am not surprised. Not only would it have been a struggle for all those men to get out, but not all of them would have had seats and it would have been chaotic as the aircraft hit the surface and submerged. In addition, it was incredibly dark last night and the way in which helicopters were hovering in queues behind ships – some with under-slung loads – it would have been easy to get disorientated. Also, if the passengers were not wearing immersion suits, they would not have survived five minutes in the sea.

The final operation order for the landings arrived in the night and the ship is making its final preparations. *Antrim* is the force AAW coordinator for the defence of the AOA [Amphibious Objective Area].

We have been told to assess the strength of the Arg forces on Fanning Head using a thermal imaging device in a Wessex V, before the assault ships and landing craft steam through the small gap. The 'neutralization' will be done with the SBS and naval gunfire support from *Antrim*, with spotting from a Naval Gunfire Forward Observation team. 406 will insert the first wave, which will establish a 'Bardic T' (a portable arrangement of lights – in a T shape – that indicates where a helicopter should approach land) and will control the Wessex V on radar for subsequent insertions.

First thing this morning, before we fully closed up for Action Stations, I encouraged the Padre to offer Communion to those who wanted or needed to receive it. It was to my mind the sort of thing that you should do before battle. So a small group of us attended a short service in the Exocet power space – with Daddy S, Stewart, L Std Leckey and about half a dozen others.

'O Lord God, when thou givest to thy servants to endeavour any great matter, grant us also to know that it is not the beginning but the continuing of the same until it be thoroughly finished which yieldeth the true glory: through him, who for the finishing of thy work, laid down his life: our Redeemer, Jesus Christ. Amen.'*

The Padre looked worried throughout, but led some prayers appropriate to the circumstances. His hand was shaking when he offered the chalice and Stewart leaned across and said, gently and quietly: 'He'll look after us, Padre.' The Padre looked as if he still had some mediating to do on this issue, but the service completed with everyone seemingly strengthened in spirit and resolute.

Afterwards, the Padre asked me what was on my mind. I replied: 'Save and deliver us from the hands of our enemies, abate their pride, assuage their malice and confound their devices.' He looked at me as if I was from another planet. 'Be of good cheer, Padre,' I added.

We returned to our duties, went to Action Stations and started our transit across the Exclusion Zone at 1100.

As I write, we are now crossing the Total Exclusion Zone. We have with us *Ardent, Argonaut, Plymouth, Yarmouth, Broadsword* and *Brilliant* to escort *Fearless, Intrepid,* the five SIR Class landing ships, *Canberra, Norland, Europic Ferry* and *Stromness* to carry the troops, and *Fort Austin,* with her helicopters.

You would not believe the weather – absolutely thick fog and stormy seas. We are escorting the landing force – the amphibious and transport ships – in a huge formation and are initially heading towards Stanley, on a zig-zag course in case there are any submarines about. It could not be better for our transit, as the Args would have had a real problem getting their aircraft airborne and finding us, let alone attacking us.

* 'Drake's Prayer'.

We have just had Action Messing for feeding the ship's company – 10% are allowed away from their Action Stations at any one time and it takes about 45 minutes to get everyone through.

I have just found out that the Sea King 4 that ditched last night was carrying men of D Squadron SAS, the guys with whom we worked in South Georgia. That means that some of the men would have survived two crashes with us on Fortuna Glacier, only to perish in this third accident. Is it fate?

The cause of the accident has been ascribed to a bird strike – an albatross—on the compressor intakes. I am not sure that I believe that. I have not seen any birds flying at night and, given the conditions, wonder whether the pilot was disorientated by the extreme darkness and flew into the sea.

Although we went to Air Raid Warning YELLOW at 1520, with a whiff of Etendards and Exocets in the air, nothing materialized.

Ian and I took the aircraft for a Check Test Flight, to make sure that the new engine was operating properly at 1615 and, once we were happy with the indicators, conducted load-lifting and transfers with *Intrepid*, before returning to find that the Wessex V had embarked. The Wessex V, flown by Mike Crabtree, was folded and stowed in the starboard side-lane forward of the Flight Deck – Humphrey was in his customary position to port. Mike's second pilot, Paul Heathcote, was almost straight out of training – what a baptism of fire! I thought, I wonder if his mum knows where he is. We discussed the complex routine for getting the SBS ashore and the risks.

Very shortly, we will veer off to the north of the Islands to make for Falkland Sound and San Carlos. We are still a bit worried about submarines and mines as we close the Islands, but are individually and collectively concentrating on getting ready for this evening's entertainment and tomorrow's anticipated excitement once we have landed. It is edgy stuff, but I would not want to be anywhere else right now. I have to admit to an intense thrill. This is serious man's business and it feels great. We just have to be better than them – today, tomorrow and every day – and things will be fine. Complacency and unjustified feelings of superiority – those are the things that we have to look out for – and of course the perverse, random exercise of chance and the unexpected. That's THE LESSON from history.

Most of the junior officers are sceptical about our missiles; I suspect that the senior guys are as well, but they are not saying anything. Sea

Slug (the clue is in the name) is great against slow-moving, high-flying aircraft in open water when you have plenty of time to acquire and engage, but you almost always need the active cooperation of the target to achieve a successful engagement. Sea Cat is not great either, and when we have done missile firings, they have always missed or gone rogue. This has come up in conversation a lot and the Greenies say that you have to remember that the missiles were designed to deal with first- and second-generation jets. Yeah, well, the Args have first- and second-generation jets, so how does that work? I have asked the boys on the Flight to modify a revolving chair on which to mount the GPMG, so that we can get some lead in the air.

I went to the Wardroom for an early supper, where the Doc, Godfrey 'Fangs' Rhimes and his acolytes were starting to lay out their wares, just in case. That is, of course, the origin of the term 'ward room', its use as a casualty reception and treatment area.

We, as a Task Force, have had a signal from CINCFLEET – 'Everything I have seen in the last six weeks has confirmed my complete confidence in your skill and determination to carry this matter through until it is thoroughly finished.' It's not exactly up there with 'England expects every man to do his duty', is it? You would have thought that somebody could have conjured up something inspirational and memorable ahead of the biggest amphibious assault since the Korean War.

We have now had a signal from the Admiral, probably prompted, three hours later, by the CINCFLEET signal: 'The eyes and ears of the world are upon us. Be steady in resolve, strong in battle and merciful in victory.' It really is tosh and I wish we could do better than this – Shakespeare could encapsulate in one line more sense about the nature of battle than all the wooden signals that I have seen to date. Use *Henry V*, for heaven's sake! Nelson did!

> In peace there's nothing so becomes a man
> As modest stillness and humility:
> But when the blast of war blows in our ears,
> Then imitate the action of the tiger;
> Stiffen the sinews, summon up the blood,
> Disguise fair nature with hard-favour'd rage.

For tonight's SBS insertion, we were introduced to Captain Rod Bell and his impressive moustache. He had been brought up in Costa Rica and so spoke perfect Spanish. The bit that I thought was decidedly quaint involved – wait for it! – kitting up a Royal Marine who was quite clearly just doing his job and not a keen volunteer. He had been told to carry a loudhailer system and a pair of speakers hung round his neck like a milk-maid. The idea was that the Argentinians will be invited politely in perfect Spanish to surrender, under threat of instant death descending from the sky. If they do not do the decent thing, the 4.5s will open up and the SBS will kill the rest as they thin out from the impact.

I remember thinking that we were already past the point of pleasantries and that we should just get on with it.

In tasking us, I am not sure that people realize how difficult it is to do this sort of insertion at night. The planning for this sortie has been problematic and has stretched me, both practically and emotionally. I have had to construct a Heath Robinson pantograph (I nicked all the rulers I could find) to produce an overlay scaled up from the map and chart to give me a chance of controlling the Wessex V onto the landing site. The map is decidedly short of topographical features, especially contours, and ways of establishing our position as we run in.

Also, any failure of control by me – the radar is poor over land and the charts inaccurate – and we will stoof in. That will be the end of that (and this account). Even if we get there, we still have to land in the dark, without any external references. Another little worry is that I will be controlling the Wessex V at the same time, for the first and subsequent runs. Any miscalculation or loss of concentration by me and I'll kill them all. The ability to control them safely is a bit more marginal than we have let on to them. I am sure that they would think that it is far too risky if they knew the truth. I spoke to Ian about it, saying, 'I am going to have to be the best Observer in the Navy to pull this off', but, touchingly, he seems to have an inordinate faith in my abilities. We'll see. The accuracy of navigation and control might just be beyond my experience and training and the limitations of the radar. Just so that you know . . .

Once, or as long as, I get us in the right position in the dark, the plan is to establish a stable hover at about 200 or 300 feet above the landing zone on the radar altimeter and engage the Flight Control System, just like we did at South Georgia. We will then wind the height down on the control box until we hit the ground. It's the only way we can do it in the dark. Let's hope that we do not descend onto a slope or a pile of dead sheep.

If that's not difficult enough, we also have the added incentive of a possible hostile reception. I have told Fitz that if we are engaged on the ground in the dark, he is not to use tracer on the GPMG, because it gives the position of the helo away and we will get hosed down with everything they have. He has two boxes' worth, one of ball and the other with tracer.

I remember seeing a film (*Body Heat*, I think) just before we came away and, having written an excerpt down as a future reminder, I have it to hand in the back of my log book. The character said something like:

'I got a serious question for you: What the fuck are you doing? This is not shit for you to be messin' with. Are you ready to hear something? I want you to see if this sounds familiar: any time you try a decent crime, you got 50 ways you're gonna fuck up. If you think of 25 of them, then you're a genius . . . and you ain't no genius.'

It's a different situation, but the lesson holds good, I think.

As I write now, we are just steaming across the top of East Falkland, ready to enter Falkland Sound. We have briefed the sortie. I can't sleep or doze and am going over the sortie details – and how the hell I am supposed to do it – in my mind again and again.

Friday, 21 May

We flew off just as the ship was to the north-east of the entrance to Falkland Sound at about 2215, while the Wessex V was ranged and launched. The ship subsequently entered the Sound as the second ship just after midnight. *Ardent* was ahead of *Antrim*, no doubt pleased to be leading, but the word was that she was in the lead to check – again – for the presence of mines and was considered expendable! As the Commander said, every ship can be a minesweeper ONCE! Actually, it was the possibility of a submarine being in the area that worried us the most. With all this broadband noise and sheer volume of sound in the water from the wide variety of ship types, the racket must have been deafening. The whales and other marine mammals must have been confused too.

Once launched, I controlled the Wessex V high over Fanning Head and around the San Carlos area so that it could use its thermal-imaging equipment. The area was indeed occupied by troops of approximately company strength (80). We decided that we would run in to the first LZ

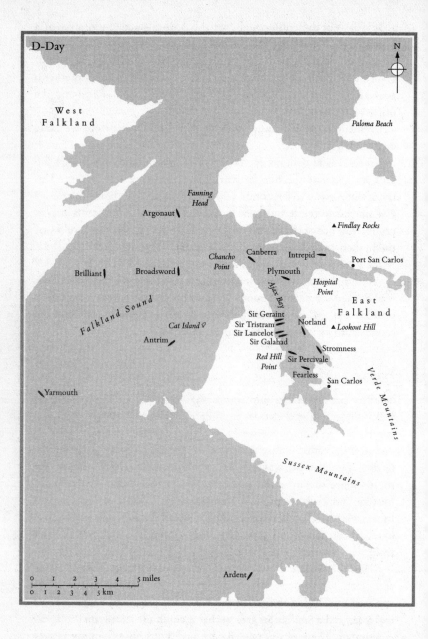

D-Day

N

West
Falkland

Paloma Beach

Fanning
Head

Argonaut

▲ Findlay Rocks

Chancho
Point

Canberra

Intrepid

Port San Carlos

Brilliant

Broadsword

Plymouth

Ajax Bay

Hospital
Point

East
Falkland

Falkland Sound

Cat Island

Sir Geraint
Sir Tristram
Sir Lancelot
Sir Galahad

Norland

▲ Lookout Hill

Antrim

Stromness

Red Hill
Point

Sir Percivale

Fearless

San Carlos

Verde Mountains

Yarmouth

Sussex Mountains

0 1 2 3 4 5 miles
0 1 2 3 4 5 km

Ardent

about one mile to the east of the enemy positions and returned to *Antrim* to refuel and pick up the four men who would establish the LZ.

Ardent continued down to Grantham Sound as *Antrim* turned aside to conduct the Fanning Head insertion and Naval Gunfire Support. *Ardent* went to bombard Arg positions around Darwin and Goose Green, as a distraction – to make them think that this was where we were landing – and to do as much damage as possible. She was a bit out on a limb and on her own.

We took Rod Bell, his pet Marine with the speakers, some of the SF guys and the Bardic T with us. The thought of being in the forefront of the landing was exciting, but I was apprehensive about what we would encounter ashore, especially if we stumbled across an Arg company or patrol. I navigated the aircraft to my selected start position west of Hospital Point and began conning Ian precisely along the route, to a point where I thought it safe to attempt the descent path in the dark. Any error to the left or right would put us into the side of a hill or mountain. The radar, of course, gave me no indication of overland features at all or obstructions ahead (because of the blind arc) and I had to rely on the accuracy of my fixing on the overlay and on a stopwatch. The pilots told me that they were flying through swathes of low cloud or fog – great! Initially, it looked as if we would not be able to land with radar and instruments alone, owing to the weather conditions and uncertain contours. However, as some low stratus cleared, I asked Ian to attempt a dummy run at 600 feet, using Paloma beach as a defined departure point.

Stewart meanwhile was peering through the so-called 'night vision' device, a small tube, which, because of the aircraft vibration and the mist, simply emitted a vague green glow. It was useless. Fitz was just looking at me with a resigned expression on his face from his position by the GPMG. The passengers, huddled in the back on the floor, just looked determined and quiet, but were barely recognizable in their camouflage clothing and war paint.

While the Wessex V went back to load, we gave it a go, without actually being able to make out the contours or the type of surface as we approached. During the descent, the Wessex V had launched and was under my radar control as it closed Fanning Head.

I started the control patter: 'Right 350 – three miles to run – height 800 feet – now left 345 – 2.8 miles – check height – still 800 feet' and so on. A little later: 'Coasting in – climb 1,000 feet (to clear an invisible ridge) – anything visual ("No!") – one mile to run – reduce 60 knots – can you make out any features ("No!").' At this point, I was working like a one-armed paper-hanger and expecting any minute to clatter into the side of Fanning Head. Is it skill or luck?

'OK – half a mile to run.'

'Showing 200 feet below us on the Rad Alt, now 150, now 100,' said Stewart.

I conned them to the landing zone and we came to the hover. In went the FCS and we started the descent – 180 – 150 – 120 – 90 (a bit of turbulence) – 60 (wobble) – 30 – (lurch).

'Fuck this,' said Ian. 'This is dangerous. I am going to put the landing lamp on and do it by eye.'

'We are a bit close to the Args,' I said. 'We don't want an anti-tank round inboard.' 'But, if it's misty, we might get away with it,' I offered helpfully.

'Let's see,' said Ian, switching on the landing lamp. I expected us to attract some attention. Nothing happened.

'You want to come left a bit, Boss, there's a fence or something below us,' said Stewart. 'The fog is pretty thick here, Flobs. We can't see a thing around us.'

Ian put the aircraft down, and after a bit of a bounce around on the rough terrain, off went the landing lamp. We had landed and were safe. I said to Ian and the others: 'Do you realize that we are probably the first unit of the assault force to land?'

Ian simply said, 'Was there a prize for that, then?'

'Yes,' I said, 'and because we did it so well, we get to do it again!'

Fitz pushed our passengers and kit out briskly. We took off, climbed vertically to a safe height and headed off back over the sea to *Antrim*. The Wessex V had already taken off with his stick of troops and was holding astern of *Antrim*, while we landed on and collected another stick. We relaunched and I took the Wessex V under control for his landing ashore.

We then went for our second approach, this time to a landing site closer to the enemy. This one was really difficult – and very marginal for safety. I was controlling the Wessex V on approach to the landing site at the same time as our own, with control instructions given to Ian and Mike, alternately, to the same level of tolerance and chances of error, with the nagging fear that I could get all of us killed. Ian was as cool as ever, while I was working my nuts off in the back. Mike Crabtree's voice in response to my control patter suggested that he trusted my instructions implicitly, as if it were a normal air traffic control talk down to an airfield. It is good if that is how he felt! He will never know how tight it was and how I clung to every radio call from them as evidence that they were still flying and OK.

While Mike was on the ground or reloading at the ship, I held off Findlay Rocks and watched the progress of the landings on the radar. *Fearless* and *Intrepid* were staying outside in Falkland Sound to launch their landing craft, which would have to drive all the way up San Carlos to their assigned landing positions without any close support, apart from *Plymouth*, for about two hours. There was no indication of any interest ashore, so the Args were either being very restrained until our troops closed within range or, simply, were asleep.

I controlled the Wessex V back to *Antrim* and he was too heavy to take off with his second stick. The lads told me that the Wessex V, unfamiliar with our smaller deck and heavy with the next detail of Marines, struggled to get airborne and flopped awkwardly back onto the Flight Deck. His tail wheel was over the side and resting on a fragile lamp bracket and trapped in the Flight Deck nets. His starboard wheel was at the deck edge in imminent danger of slipping over the side in the sea conditions. The Flight Deck team all moved quickly and bravely to push the tail pylon free and, luckily, whether he sensed the danger or not, the pilot pulled power and managed to climb away safely. If they had gone over the side it would surely have been curtains for all onboard in those conditions.

Happily, he recovered onto the deck. The ship provided a better relative wind and he staggered into the air. I took him into a waiting position, while we landed on to refuel. By this time, the Bardic T had been established ashore and, despite the mist, which was thinning, the visual indicators in the final phase of the subsequent approaches were easier.

We were soon airborne again and I controlled him into the drop zone and back to the ship, to collect the third stick.

While I was controlling the Junglie for the third time, an ASW Sea

King turned up and started dipping right in the area where we were in our holding pattern and bang on the glide path that I had established for the Junglie. He was really getting in the way and, as he was on the ASW Primary circuit, I asked the HC to call him up and tell him to bugger off. The problem was that he was like us operating without lights and transponder and every now and then I would lose him on the radar. I was concentrating hard on controlling the Wessex V and keeping him and us safe, but it was nagging away at me.

I controlled Mike in and returned him to the ship for the fourth stick at midnight and the fifth at 0025. Resisting the complacent thought that I was actually getting quite good at this – or getting away with it – I guided him into the landing zone for the final time and we both returned to the ship at 0045 (0245Z). All the time, I had in my mind the touching faith that the Wessex V pilots had in my ability to control them and keep them safe. I also thought about the Sea King crash of a couple of days ago, which resulted in the deaths of all those SAS guys. That could not happen again – I did not want that on my conscience.

By the time we had returned, the fog had lifted to reveal a beautifully clear night, with a multitude of bright, twinkling stars and a very pronounced Milky Way. The curtain had come up for the start of the performance, just like at South Georgia.

We folded and stowed 406 in the port side-lane and waited until Mike and his aircraft were back on deck at 0110 (0310Z) before we secured everyone for some rest. We had arranged some cabins for the Wessex V aircrew to rack out for a while. I went to the Ops Room to report on the sortie and explain where we had dropped the troops, to find that, because the Captain and the PWO (A), Pat Brown, were turned in asleep, the Commander and John Archer, both anti-submarine experts, were about to conduct the shore bombardment, with the Navigator!

I reckon that I earned my flying pay tonight. It was the most difficult thing that I have ever had to do as an Observer and I was concerned throughout that my control was not accurate enough, what with the lack of overland definition on the radar and poor mapping, to keep Mike Crabtree and his cab safe. That bloody Sea King wandering around did not help. I was really worried every time that I guided Mike's aircraft in that I would kill him and his troops. I am very tired, but, probably because of the nervous tension and anxiety caused by the strain of controlling the Wessex V safely, I need to wind down before I can sleep. I cannot read. It's enough to make you take up drinking.

I have just written up the events of this evening and intend to get into my rack now.

'What we do now echoes in eternity.'*

I must have fallen asleep, only to emerge into semi-consciousness as the first ranging shots of the bombardment were fired by the 4.5s. It must have been about 0250 and I felt as if I had been drugged. I then dozed through the main bombardment of Fanning Head, in response to spotting from the SBS guys whom we had landed. I was aware, as if in a dream, of the acrid, penetrating smell of expended cordite and the insistent crack of the 4.5s. About an hour later, I was again vaguely aware of guns firing, then a gap and then another sequence of salvoes. I thought or dreamt that I could hear the distant, shriller trajectory of other munitions – perhaps the Arg troops ashore were firing back or just firing blind.

I woke about 0715, as if it was an ordinary day and then remembered where I was and what had happened the previous night. Momentarily thinking, 'Did that really happen or was it a dream?' I lay there recollecting the night's events and realized that everything sounded really normal – and unnaturally quiet and still. The familiar sound of the ventilation and the soft hum of some anonymous generator were all I could hear. The ship was not surging around, but moving smoothly and gently though the water and – oh yes! – afloat and alive. Still in my goon suit, I washed and got my navigation bag, personal weapon and aircrew life-preserver together.

What am I thinking right now? I am struck by the fact that we have not been attacked by an Arg submarine. The underwater noise made by the approaching Amphibious Group must have been like Clapham Junction at the height of the rush hour. He could not fail to have heard all that noise in the water, especially *Fearless* and *Intrepid* and the merchant ships, as well as the active sonars of the warships.

Before I went down to the Wardroom for some breakfast, I had a few moments and recalled Jacob Astley's prayer before the Battle of Edgehill in 1642:

Oh Lord, thou knowest how busy I must be this day.
If I forget thee, do not thou forget me.

* Marcus Aurelius.

I then went up to the Bridge. We were between the main islands in Falkland Sound, off the entrance to San Carlos, on a racetrack between there and Cat Island to the south, with *Argonaut* patrolling off Fanning Head. The day was bright and clear, with hardly a breeze ruffling the water. It felt strange to be close to land, with its sharply defined features, covered in brownish-green vegetation, after so much time in the emptiness of the South Atlantic – 'the wild and wasteful ocean'. The Navigator and the Officer of the Watch were pretty upbeat about the night's events, especially because the whole Task Group had crossed the Exclusion Zone without incident. Everyone was concerned about what a great day it was for flying – from Argentina.

A lot of people are nervous and apprehensive, but everyone is showing typical gallows humour as we wait for what today might bring. The Args are going to be really narked when they find out that we have landed and will need to launch everything they have got while we are still trying to get our troops and all the kit ashore. There has been no sign of their submarine yet. Perhaps he is off East Falkland. After all, they would hardly have expected us to land the Royal Marines and the rest of the troops in San Carlos. I believe that the Args think that if we want to capture Stanley before the winter sets in, we would have to go straight in and kick the door down at Stanley. All their defences seem to be based on that assessment. I know that *Ardent* is supporting a diversionary attack on Goose Green, with the SAS, and *Glamorgan* and a few others are simulating an attack in the vicinity of Stanley, so perhaps the submarine does not know in which direction to go.

Antrim is the AAWC ship for the landing area today. That's a heavy responsibility for our operations team. A discussion last night exposed our worries about how many SHars we actually have to deal with the threat. Surely, the Args will launch everything against us that they can get airborne. With the carriers well out to the east, I reckon from the signals that a pair of SHars will be launching every half an hour, to service CAP stations off Pebble Island and to the south of San Carlos in the Sound. That means that we will not get continuous coverage and the Args will have plenty of opportunities to get through without seeing a SHar, especially if they receive traffic information from their radars at Pebble Island and at Stanley. The Args might even send over fighter cover today to take on – or take out – the SHars while the attack aircraft work their way in. I would!

Also, the area the escorts have to defend is far too great for overlapping or contiguous coverage. Then there is the difficulty of detecting Arg aircraft over land while we are inshore in time for our missile systems to acquire and engage. Finally, the escorts are being simultaneously employed in the anti-submarine role and the gun-equipped ships as fire support for the land forces.

I now need to go down to the Flight Deck, in case we and the helo are needed for ASW or to support the landings. I also need to see if the GPMG mount works. Let's pause for now.

Wow! What a day it has been!

I wandered down to the hangar to talk to the boys and, after they asked, told them about the insertion sorties last night. Everyone was a bit tense, with the older blokes worried ('It's a pension trap, sir'), the junior rates not knowing what to expect. Fitz was already up and about and the cab was sitting in the port side-lane, with a torpedo and a depth charge on the carriers. The Wessex V was spread on deck.

My GPMG mount was ready and I had a look at its ability to traverse left and right – not bad for a revolving chair – but it was incapable of elevating. I would have to go for targets that came at us low and engage at about 500 yards. I had the ammunition loaded for one in three tracer, because I thought that the deterrent effect would be just as useful as the crash and burn explosive rounds.

I went to the port side of the Flight Deck, to set up my GPMG and with a mug of tea. I looked up at an absolutely clear blue sky, not a cloud to be seen. There was a SHar at about 12,000 feet, lazily flying in figures of eight, which was reassuring, but with no sign of a CAP partner. I thought that he must have an amazing view of the landings and all the way to Stanley. Conversely, the Args must have been able to see him on their Westinghouse air surveillance radar, unless the SAS have managed to deal with it.

At 0850, we went to full Action Stations, Ian and Stewart arrived, and we briefed ourselves for any flying that we might have to do. Although we were tasked with ASW, we intended to remain flexible. The Wessex V then flew off to its next tasking. At 0945, we heard that some Arg helicopters had been destroyed by RAF Harriers on the ground somewhere.

At 1000, we went to Air Raid Warning RED and heard that two

Pucaras had made an attack on *Ardent*, to the south. We did not see the Pucaras.

At about 1005, I was chatting to the Secretary, who was the FDO [Flight Deck Officer], and was looking over at Fanning Head. I saw spouts of water heading towards *Argonaut*. Looking back at the source, I saw my first Arg plane – heading low, it was an Aermacchi, bold as you like, strafing *Argonaut*, with rockets or cannons. It then disappeared up San Carlos Water. We immediately got on the intercom to the Bridge to report the raid, and – silence! Could we get a response? No. So we started transmitting blind and eventually we got a reply which seemed as if it was responding to a routine call.

Then everyone jumped out of their skins as the chaff rockets fired off – why? There did not seem to be an Exocet or missile threat to us where we were. There were several confusing pipes on Main Broadcast reporting enemy aircraft closing, when suddenly we could see jet aircraft flying in from the west, and low.

I selected an aircraft less than a mile away on the port side, which was attacking *Broadsword*, and I happily fired away at him on the GPMG. AEM Craven was gamely firing at something with an SLR and I thought, that's the spirit, just the way to maintain morale and take your mind off things! Then, there was a noise like a high-volume blowtorch – one of our Sea Cats engaged, but missed. The ship was in a hard turn to starboard and was not helping my aim, when I heard a tremendous 'whoosh' behind me, and then a 'boom', and looked up straight into the rapidly receding jet exhaust, on after-burn, of what I recognized as a Dagger, climbing and cork-screwing vertically away. Bombs were falling around us, on either side of the ship and, with the subsequent shock waves and jarring motion, it felt like the hull was being struck underwater by sledge hammers.

I instinctively fell onto my back, lifting the GPMG off the seat and firing upwards as far as I could, but it was too late – the bugger had jumped us. No warning from the Ops Room!

As the Dagger climbed skywards, I thought, he's an Air Force pilot; no Navy pilot would do that – he would stay low, to avoid the flak and missiles.

I looked around – apart from everyone lying in various prone positions, there did not seem to be anything amiss.

I glanced at Stewart, who looked shaken and a bit gloomy.

'Are you all right, Stewart?'

'I tell you,' he said, 'I'd swear that bomb was coming straight for me. I saw it as clear as you like; it was like a giant finger pointing down at me.'

'I know that you are special, Stewart, but I am not sure that the Args have got the necessary intelligence or sensors to target you personally.'

'Yeah, you're right.'

'And we're still here,' I said.

The Main Broadcast pipe by Commander E indicated that we had taken some damage along the side of the ship, possibly from 30 mm cannon, although I had not seen any fired at us. We had a reported fire in 2P2 passageway and a flood and splinter holes along the length of 2 Deck.

Bob Tarrant, in a very cheery, excited voice, called down from the Emergency Conning Position, to tell us that he had seen two bombs explode close by on the starboard side.

'Did you see the one with the parachute?' he asked. 'It was caught on a whip aerial and dropped over the side.'

We hadn't as it happened, but we had definitely felt the shock of the bombs exploding alongside and the stern of the ship moving bodily sideways in response. The plumes of water had deposited themselves all over us on the port side of the Flight Deck – and onto the cab.

About 10 minutes later, another raid was reported closing. We went to Air Raid Warning RED again and SHars were tasked to intercept. We heard nothing further about the incoming raid after that.

I was standing on the port side of the Flight Deck, trying to maintain my balance as the ship was turning, under full helm and with what I thought was maximum power, towards the south. It was an impressive surge and the turn was pretty violent. AEM Craven was still banging away at something with his rifle. Suddenly, the ship shook powerfully and a Sea Slug rumbled off the launcher and blasted skywards to starboard. I thought that I saw it hit something, but it was only the booster rockets falling away. We had fired the missile in the GASH mode, as a bird-scarer. Then, another! The Flight Deck was covered in efflux and the orange and white, bitter cloud made us almost choke and our eyes were stinging. I felt a double shock wave and, as I cleared my eyes and recovered my wits, I was looking out for aircraft to have a go at with the GPMG.

However, my eye was drawn to the figure of our Chinese Number One, standing very unsteadily and with his clothes in shreds and covered in carbon and efflux. He had chosen to emerge from the laundry under the quarterdeck, just as the missile blasted off. It was odd, but he looked just like the cat in Tom and Jerry cartoons, when he has been frazzled by fire. I worried that he might have been badly burned and moved towards him a couple of steps, when he shouted out loud, 'This gotta be worth fucking British Empire Medal!' before he dropped onto the deck, from shock and fatigue.*

With just a hint of a sixth sense beforehand, I was acutely and suddenly aware of people around me hitting the deck and the sound of what seemed at the time to be someone running a metal bar very fast along a set of iron railings. I sensed most of the Flight personnel running towards – and into – the hangar and Ian pushing the SMR into the fuel-pumping space. I remember asking myself why he might be doing that. Then, someone shouted, 'Aircraft – get down!' I realized, a bit late, that the noise I was hearing was that of cannon fire – lots of it.

'Whoosh! Whoooosh!' – followed immediately by two ear-splitting, reverberating roars, as two or three Daggers (I think) roared over at low level from the stern and starboard quarter – we had been bounced again. They were so low that you could feel the pressure wave in the air as they passed, dropping bombs as they climbed away.

I vaguely recollect Ian and the SMR emerging from the aviation fuel space, into which they had both tumbled after a competition between them over who actually would get there first that would put the Olympic sprint final in the shade. They came out looking a bit ashamed – like a couple of teenagers caught snogging behind the bike sheds. Ian had taken a couple of shrapnel wounds in his left shoulder and left little finger, as he had tried to shut the metal door behind him, while the SMR just had the downstream effects of Ian, in his haste, falling on top of him. I reflected that the AVCAT fuel space was the last place that you would want to hide.

I could now hear someone crying out loudly: 'Me nuts, me nuts, they've got me nuts.'

* He was shocked, but largely unhurt, despite being covered in missile efflux. He received the British Empire Medal for his steadfastness and devotion to duty during the conflict.

It was Fitz, lying prone on the Flight Deck in his goon suit. I went over to him.

'Fitz, what's the problem? Where are you hurt?' I asked, although I could see that the legs of his goon suit had been shredded up to his thighs and blood was oozing from some of the slashes.

'They've done my nuts . . .'

'Look,' I said, 'the area round your bits is intact and I do not see any damage, but I am no expert. Listen to your voice, you are still talking OK. If your nuts were injured, you would have a high voice,' I said hopefully.

This seemed to reassure him. 'And,' I added, 'I believe that if your nuts go west, then your teeth hurt intensely. Any problems there?'

'No,' he said, in a disbelieving sort of way. 'But it is making my eyes water!'

'Let's get the first aid teams and the Doc onto you.'

He gripped me hard by the arm and said, 'Don't leave me here, Flobs, I am still bleeding.'

'Fitz, you are going to be fine, seriously.' I put my flying jacket under his head. 'Someone else needs some help too.'

While I was dealing with Fitz's concerns, I could see out the corner of my eye that the SMR was attending to another prostrate figure, with his hands clasped on his face, near the aircraft. I went over to them and saw that the casualty was Chief Bullingham. He had been working on the aircraft on the Flight Deck – some minor electrical servicing. I imagined that the Arg pilot had been aiming for the helo, in order to make the aviation fuel in it explode.

As I went over to him, I noticed how much debris was lying on the deck, and asked the SMR to get some medical help. He went over to the intercom. I knelt down alongside Chief Bullingham and reached for my basic first aid kit, antiseptic and dressings. He had been hit in the legs and arms, but what confronted me was the state of his head, which was covered in blood and fragments of metal and plastic, in and around his hard hat and goggles.

'I can't see, I can't see a thing,' said Chief Bullingham, trying to paw away at his face.

His left eye had been hit by something and his face was a congealed mess on that side. However, I thought that his right eye, although out-wardly seemingly untouched, looked rather unnatural in its movement. It struck me that he might have been blinded.

'Chief, I think that you are suffering from shock . . . concussed . . . or something,' I blathered, trying to say the right thing, and began to clear some of the gunge from the right side of his face. I did not want to touch the left side in case I damaged it further.

'The Doc will sort you out, as soon as he gets here. Try not to move and keep your hands away from your face. It's important.'

I thought, I can't believe that this is happening. Please let him be OK! Please let him be OK! I felt helpless. There was no negotiation with this; we just had to deal with it.

While I looked at his injuries, two things occurred to me. Firstly, he had double-thickness goggles and a reinforced, double-thickness flight helmet that we 'liberated' from the USS *Comte de Grasse* when *Antrim* was in company with her last year. This helmet, which was peppered with debris and shrapnel, and the goggles had almost certainly saved his life. I also reflected that I was not affected by the sight and feel of real blood and associated messiness. I was usually very squeamish when it came to watching graphic medical documentaries and films of operations.

Ian was sitting on a bollard, nursing his injuries. He was his usual phlegmatic self about it and quietly waited for treatment. I asked him how he was. 'It stings a bit!' he said. He would hang around, until they had time for him in the Sick Bay.

Meanwhile, some first aid ratings arrived to deal with the wounded, followed by the Doctor himself, who quickly disappeared to deal with other casualties, who were on the GDP among the Royal Marines and the radio operators on the signal deck. It seems that the CSM had been seriously injured. The S & S first aiders took one look at Chief Bullingham and decided that his injuries were above their pay grade and competence. In the end, the SMR organized for Chief Bullingham to be taken on a stretcher down to the Wardroom. PO Kurn and a couple of the Flight junior rates carrying him imitated the sound of an ambulance siren as they disappeared down the waist.

I looked around at the boys on the Flight, who were all pretty calm. The junior rates were terrific – they just shrugged their shoulders and had set about clearing up around Chief Bullingham and Fitz, who was now finally convinced that he might not have lost his bits. I think that these had been saved by the timely intervention of a thick gusset in his goon suit that had prevented penetration by the shrapnel. It had given him a serious belt in the nuts though.

That's something that we need to remember for the future. The teaching has been that the medics always come to the incident, but that is clearly flawed. With more than a few casualties, we need to take the wounded to them, and, anyway, the medics could get killed or injured themselves running around in situations like these. I have also noticed how long it takes to get people out of their initial state of shock. Once they are out of it, everything seems fine, as the novelty wears off and it begins to become habit or routine.

It was clear that something had happened aft and on the port side. We could see that smoke was pouring out of the port after end of the Flight Deck. A major breach in the fire main was reported in the vicinity of the after heads, together with a flood in 2P passageway, as well as a lot of splinter holes. Meanwhile, the 978 (navigation) and 992 (search and target indication) radars had also taken hits and were unserviceable. The Captain then ordered the ship to get closer to *Broadsword* at the head of San Carlos Water while we sorted ourselves out. We only had visual target indication for Sea Cat and 4.5 guns from the sights on the Gun Direction Platform.

Then someone remarked that the aircraft was pissing fuel all over the Flight Deck, which we reported to the Ops Room and HQ1. We considered ditching the helo over the side, in case there was another raid and 406 became a huge aviation fuel bomb. In fact, we were surprised that it had not exploded when hit. I told the senior rates to get some foam ready to lay down on the Flight Deck, just as someone on the Main Broadcast piped: 'Fuel spillage, fuel spillage on the Flight Deck' and stokers and others arrived to implement the actions that were necessary to contain the hazard. A foam blanket was laid on the Flight Deck. From the damage, we reasoned that 406 probably did not get a direct hit, but multiple shrapnel damage, all along the tail pylon, the port side and through the fuel tanks below the floor. Once the situation stabilized, and in between raids, the boys siphoned and drained as much fuel out as they could and put the aircraft back into the hangar. The cab's been so good to us – I would have been really sad if we had lost him, after all we have been through together. Let's hope we get him back.

When we looked around, we could see a bulge in the Flight Deck about four feet long and about two feet wide. Our first thought was that this was blistering caused by a large fire down below; this is what we reported to HQ1. I told the Flight Deck team to start boundary cooling the deck. Before they started, the Commander E invited some-one to feel the bulge to see if it was hot. I went over to the unsightly bump and looked at it. It wasn't hot enough for steam to come off, so I put my gloved hand onto the bump. No problem, so I took my glove off and to my surprise found the metal temperature to be normal.

We started looking around to see what might have caused the bump. Before going aft, we checked with the Sea Slug team that they were not about to fire off a missile and I went down the starboard ladder to the quarterdeck. I was about five steps down when I looked across at the launcher, more out of self-preservation than anything else, because if a missile had come out of the flash doors onto the launcher, I knew that I had seconds before the thing went burning off into the ether.

That's odd, I thought, almost mechanically. There's a jagged hole in the port flash door. Christ! What did that?

I ran back up to the Flight Deck and reported what I had seen to the Ops Room team. Pretty soon, a patrol established that we had a 1,000 lb bomb in the after heads under the Flight Deck, as well as a fire in the nearby pyrotechnic locker.

I went up to the Wardroom to see Chief Bullingham and Fitz. I was really worried that I might be squeamish about what I would see. In fact, I was shocked to see how many casualties that we had had, the result of a couple of aircraft strafing us as they closed for bombing runs. The upper deck weapons crews had taken a pasting, including the CSM.

I was pretty sure that Chief Bullingham might have lost his sight. When I went into the Wardroom, he was lying there with his head swathed in bandages and I said, 'Bad luck, Chief, I hope that things will be OK.' I did not know what to say really, looking at him, and felt pretty sick in my stomach about it. The Padre then arrived and was visibly shocked, trying to do his best for the injured. I had a word with Fitz, who quite clearly hadn't lost his bits and was reasonably cheerful about his prospects, although he reflected on the fact that he would not know for sure about full functionality until he had: a) had a hard on and b) got his end away. Thanks for that, Fitz. Glad to know that you are on the mend.

I went back to Chief Bullingham to find the Padre in tears. He was sniffing loudly and was clearly distressed, Chief Bullingham felt his way with his hand all the way up the Padre's arm and grabbed his chin like Yorick's skull and said, 'Don't worry, Padre, it'll be all right.' Has the world turned upside down?

At 1245, we managed to get our radars back again, as well as one of the Sea Cat systems, but we decided to take shelter in San Carlos Water. On the way, a Sea King arrived to take CSM Kendall (injured on the GDP in the kidneys and stomach), Chief Bullingham and Fitz to *Canberra*. We entered a packed anchorage at 1350. By now, the flooding aft was under control.

After the strafing incident, everyone on the upper deck not manning a formal weapon station was told to go down and remain in the Giant's Causeway [Main Drag]. I did not really want to go, as we would be sitting on top of the main magazine in the centre of the ship and you could not see a thing. There were about 80 people sitting in the Main Drag; I was with Stewart and Carlos. We tried to keep everyone's spirits up by chatting about how many Arg aircraft had been knocked down and how well the ship was doing.

All through, we had to rely on the Main Broadcast pipes from the Commander or Commander E in HQ1, which tried to paint the scene of sporadic raids by the Args and other events as coherently as possible. We all began playing the mental group game of how long did it take an Arg jet to close once the Main Broadcast announced a detection at a particular range. The range was then counted down not by words, but by people's various expressions of discomfort and alarm. I noticed that certain body positions and facial expressions, associated with intensifying levels of involuntary movement, were also exactly calibrated to decreasing ranges.

If the raid came nowhere near us, the Main Broadcast said nothing, so no one knew when any particular danger was over. People were just waiting – and waiting – for the impact. One young Able Rate asked Stewart what was going to happen and I noticed that the lad was looking frightened, seeking reassurance and a sign of hope.

'We'll be fine, just you see,' said Stewart and somehow the way he said it in his soft Scottish accent made it all the more convincing.

People are tired and overwrought, I thought, we need a game to take their minds off things.

'Right, let's call down the range together next time, every two miles to two miles and then every half mile,' I said, not knowing whether it was a good idea.

The next raid was called at 23 miles. I started my stopwatch and said, 'When I nod, we call "20" together and then "18" and so on. Got it?'

All I got was some desultory nods and suspicious looks. Working out the speed of incoming aircraft at 600 knots = 10 miles a minute, I nodded and said loudly: '20' almost immediately.

A few joined in, more at '18', until by '12' most people around us had joined in the count-down. We went all the way – nervously – to 'o' and nothing had happened. There was visible relief all round, but, just to make sure, I called 'Minus 2' 12 seconds later. There were a few laughs. And then 'Minus 4 – all clear, I reckon.' About 10 seconds later, the Commander came on the Main Broadcast to say that the raid had either turned around or had gone somewhere else. I looked around with an expression that was intended to say, 'I told you.'

Stewart quietly said under his breath to me: 'It sounds like a count-down to a Cape Canaveral launch – does that mean we get blasted into orbit at the end?'

Good point!

Ten minutes later, we heard about another raid inbound, so I said, 'Come on then, let's do it again – this time with feeling!'

So off we went and continued until the aircraft actually arrived in San Carlos, inconveniently a little ahead of time, and the Main Broadcast boomed, 'Alarm Aircraft, A4 Skyhawk, port side. Engaging. Brace, brace, brace!'

We all braced ourselves, the guns were firing, but there was no indication of anything hitting the ship. A minute or so later, we heard: 'All clear. One aircraft splashed; another heading for home.'

Next up, a formation of 12 aircraft from the east was reported on Main Broadcast as closing from the east. Groans all round. I thought about it and said, 'That cannot be the Args, from that direction.' The word goes round that it is the RAF riding to the rescue – people cheer. Fat chance, I thought to myself, where would they launch from? Anyway, said one wag, 'It's a Friday, the RAF won't be working on one of their weekend days.' Ha ha ha!

However, in the end, the constant strain of just sitting around waiting for something to happen to ME made me feel uncomfortable and restless. I was used to being in a position where I could see what was going on and I decided that being on the upper deck was a better option, even if it meant dodging 30 mm cannon shells. I could also retrieve my GPMG and take some pot shots at passing jets. It is not nice being between decks with nothing to do – it allows your imagination to take charge and you have time to worry. That was the first time, actually, that I had felt a bit apprehensive and uncertain about things. It's better to see what's coming at you rather than waiting for the flash, bang, wallop – of course, you get the 'flash' and the 'wallop' before the 'bang'. That is, as long as you make it to the bang part!

So I went back to the Flight Deck to have another go with the GPMG.

Just as I returned to the Flight Deck, I was approached by a couple of stokers, both concealed in action dress and anti-flash, one of whom said, 'What's happened, sir?'

'We've got a British-made 1,000 lb bomb in the after heads!' I replied, anxious to get on with things, and hurried past.

'Sir,' said a strong Brummie accent, 'why are the Harriers dropping stuff on us?'

'It was a Mirage,' I said, quickly – too quickly.

'No, sir, it really happened. I definitely heard it go over us,' said the Brummie.

I haven't got time for this, I thought, not knowing whether he was taking the mickey or not. I repented afterwards as, on reflection, I thought he might just have been in shock, but, frankly, I had other things to do.

I really could not traverse the GPMG that well on the swivel chair, so I concentrated on firing off rounds in the general direction of any aircraft that came near, hoping that the tracer would put the pilot off.

The Padre wandered down to the Flight Deck and asked if there was anything he could do.

The SMR simply said, 'Padre, you need to have a word with your Boss about all this. He seems to have given himself a make-and-mend.'*

The SMR and I had a flippant discussion about precisely which day God rested and remarked that, as today was a Friday, he had obviously gone on a long weekend. Ha! Ha! Ha!

The Padre looked appalled, either because of the implied blasphemy or because he suddenly felt himself in the presence of maniacs. He wandered away again.

A little while later, I was trying to line up the GPMG on an incoming but passing aircraft when I heard the unmistakeable ratt-a-tatt-tatt of bullets tap-dancing their way across the Flight Deck to the left of me and behind. I just rolled away to my right and curled up until it stopped.

* The naval expression for a half-day at work.

When the excitement died down, I looked at the marks on the deck with Chief McKee and LAEM [Leading Air Engineering Mechanic] Gigg. They were not at all like the cannon shell impact damage and we reckoned that they were 7.62 rounds. Almost in unison, we looked up at the ship on our port quarter that we had just passed during our hard manoeuvring and the truth immediately dawned on us – we had just been raked with GPMG fire by one of our own RFAs. That was not the kind of ammunition resupply that we were expecting! Thanks for that! We laughed – why not?

After I ran out of ammo, I went up to the Bridge. It was pretty exciting in San Carlos Water at this point, with Arg Skyhawks trying to have a determined go at the ships in the anchorage and the SHars being held well clear in case they were engaged by us. We were now well inside San Carlos, with *Canberra* just to port, looking large and vulnerable. The idea was that she should be in shallow water, so that if she sank, she would settle on the bottom and we could still use her and her stores. I was surprised that the Args had not attacked her yet.

I stayed on the lower Bridge, which had the advantage of visibility and the ability to hear what was happening on the upper Bridge and in the Ops Room. I put on a headset and listened to the battle. I noticed Lt Col Eve out on the port Bridge wing, as calm as you like, taking snapshots of the action, as if he were on a summer cruise through the Scottish Isles.

My hat goes off to the Navigator because we were manoeuvring at high speed in response to air attacks with very little water under the keel and in among all sorts of rocks and other ships.

Less impressive was the fact that the 4.5 gun was firing all over the place, as if it was out of control. It was obvious that it was slaved to the visual sights on the GDP where the operator was slewing his sight all over the place and the gun was following wherever he pointed the sight. It's amazing that we did not hit any of our own ships. At one stage, the guns were depressed so low that it felt as if we had blown the deck-edge off, with the percussion from the shells reverberating throughout the ship.

All the while, large numbers of Sea Kings and Wessex with underslung loads were flying back and forth and I could see huge dumps of materiel and stores growing on the shoreline. Every time that we had a raid, the helos would either drop their loads ashore or pickle them off into the sea and find somewhere to hide – sometimes with their loads – in the folds of the hills or low in the lee of the ridges.

I went back to the Flight Deck and found some more ammunition.

At 1532, four aircraft were reported astern which went for *Argonaut*. She was hit by bombs that did not explode and seemed to be out of control, heading for the rocks off Fanning Head. Our port Sea Cat locked on and nothing happened (it turned out that the operator failed to change his switch from SAFE to LIVE!).

At 1540, three aircraft closed San Carlos and departed without hitting anything.

After the raid, the ship headed out towards the Sound. *Argonaut* signalled that she was in need of a tow to keep her safe and the Buffer and the seamen started to rig the towing gear on the quarterdeck. This stopped about five minutes later when *Argonaut* announced that she had anchored instead.

Suddenly, at about 1550, there was the cry of 'ALARM AIRCRAFT!' as two A4s appeared and strafed *Brilliant* nearby, while we blocked the mouth of San Carlos Water. One of our Sea Cats engaged and missed, probably because the pilot of the target climbed vertically after his attack, and the launcher was on maximum elevation. He must have been an Air Force pilot, but, by a fluke, got away with it, even though you should normally stay low to avoid the flak. Lucky bloke!

By this time, *Ardent* had come back up the Sound and was about 2–3 miles away. She was bounced by a Skyhawk which released its bombs, but they did not hit – there were big explosions in the sea though! About 10 minutes later, I saw three A4 Skyhawks coming up the Sound from the south and attack *Ardent*. They did not seem interested in any other ship; my guess is that she was isolated and the pilots would have known that she only had Sea Cat rather than the fearsome Sea Wolf. One of our Sea Cats was launched against one of the A4s, but it missed. None came close enough for me to engage it with the GPMG. I watched as one flew up *Ardent*'s stern at about 100 feet and passed over the ship before climbing steeply away. I saw a couple of explosions, one of which looked like a perfectly formed mini-mushroom cloud. I thought that the hangar and Flight Deck had been hit. I thought of John Sephton and Brian Murphy and wondered how things were for them. John was a staff pilot when I was training on 737 Squadron; Brian Murphy was my Basic Observer Training course officer at Culdrose and had a really nice wife. I could not help thinking that the Type 21 superstructures were made of aluminium. They are known as 'cheap and cheerful' frigates – hmmm! We heard that she could still float and move, but not fight at this point. She was about two miles away and she looked to be on fire aft.

It was quite an intimidating sight and I have to confess to feeling a bit shaky at this point. For most of the day, it had seemed, in view of all the events and unfamiliar experiences, that I was watching a Hollywood film – I had a real sense that what was going on over there was not really happening and had nothing to do with us. I was curiously detached and it was as if everything was happening to other people and that I was immune to the scene in front of me and all the stuff flying around.

At that precise point, the illusion shattered and I instantly and powerfully felt vulnerable and isolated – it all became very immediate and personal. And what really shook me was the realization that the bombs were actually exploding. Up until that point, none of the bombs that had hit the ships had exploded. If they can do that just a couple of miles away, they might come over here and do the same to us! I looked around and saw that I was actually alone on the Flight Deck. I must admit that I felt a bit anxious, but suddenly I caught the image of Corporal Jones from *Dad's Army* in my mind – 'Don't panic, don't panic!' – and it was over, as soon as it had arisen. Yes, I thought, they don't like it up 'em and went back to my GPMG.

About five minutes later, *Ardent* reported that she was sinking and that they were considering abandoning her. This seemed strange to me at the time because she was upright and looked stable, even though she had a raging fire aft, with huge billowing clouds of black smoke, stretching high up into the sky. At this point, *Yarmouth* was alongside her and, in between sweeping around looking for hostile aircraft, I could make out through the binoculars that she and a Sea King were taking off survivors.

For the next hour, things were quiet and we tucked into the land, behind Chancho Point, ready to ambush aircraft entering San Carlos. With nightfall, the air raids ceased – as we thought they would – and we had time to reflect that, for a Friday, we had been working pretty late!

I looked at my watch. It was 1700 and I thought, there are people at Waterloo, possibly some who work in MOD, going about their normal business and catching trains home for the weekend right now. And here we are in the middle of it all!

It felt like we were making history though; I would not have wanted to be anywhere else right then. What would the World Service make of it all later?!

As I had surmised, the bomb had entered through the port flash door, went through the Sea Slug magazine and port pyrotechnic magazine and had dumped itself in the heads. It had shattered the porcelain in the heads and devastated the traps, but was virtually intact, despite the fact that it appeared to have punched its way through eight bulkheads, one way or the other. It was olive green, with a red band around it, and was tail-fused, although the fuse was damaged and wires were sticking out. Its identification plate indicated that it had been made in Derby in the UK (thank you, Derby!). It was considerate of the Args to have left in place the helpful advice 'Danger – handle with care'.

What I noticed particularly was the arming rotor on the rear of the bomb. The rotor was supposed to drive a fuse into the back of the bomb as it fell through the air and arm the thing before impact. It was clear that the rotor had not completed the requisite number of turns as it fell from the aircraft and had impacted inert. That had to mean that the aircraft were flying low to avoid our fire and had inadvertently failed to allow time for the bombs to arm. Best no one tells them, then!

In order to deal with the 'beast', as it became known, the ship had sent for a Bomb Disposal team, which arrived by Wessex V from *Sir Tristram* at about 1430. It was led by Fleet CPO (Diver) Mick Fellows, whom I knew from my dad's time in the RN, and he had LS (Diver) Sewell and AB (Diver) Pullen in tow. In the meantime, Chippy's team had cleared away the debris with POMEM Ellis and had immobilized the bomb with mattresses and soft wood wedges while the ship was thrashing around during the air attacks.

A plan emerged that involved cutting a hole in the Flight Deck, erecting some sheer legs as a crane and lifting the beast out. The DWEO, Nick Bracegirdle, Chippy and the Buffer comprised the team that was to supervise the proceedings from the ship's point of view and the rest of us were invited to keep well clear. The only edgy bit was the fact that the damaged pyrotechnics would have to be removed by hand and the cutting with an oxyacetylene torch would be up close and personal to Sea Slug missiles in the magazine!

Cutting the hole with the oxyacetylene torch took a long time, amid the violent manoeuvring of the ship and the inconvenient air attacks. At one stage, the noxious gases were so overpowering that the men involved had to wear breathing apparatus and masks, while others were cooling the bulkheads around the site to stop the Sea Slugs cooking off. In the end, the hole was cut, the fuse immobilized and the bare wires taped. The Sea Slug missiles in the magazine were fitted with deflection plates, to channel any subsequent explosion (as if!). A group of seamen erected the sheer legs above the hole and we were ready to lift. At this point, DWEO arrived with an urgent signal from Northwood: 'It says that we have to keep the bomb horizontal while we remove it,' he said. 'That's not possible.'

The erratic, exaggerated movement of the ship suggested that DWEO might be right.

'It's always impossible until you actually do it,' replied Mick Fellows. 'What else does it say?'

'They send . . . their best wishes,' said DWEO quietly, anticipating the reaction from everyone.

It was decided to leave the lifting gear in place and wait a more opportune time to coax the bomb out and over the side – after dark. So, the bomb was further wedged and mattressed in position and we hoped that it would not soon be joined – and encouraged – by one of its mates with a more explosive tendency.

The atmosphere in the Wardroom at our action supper was pretty sombre and quite a few people were visibly shocked and dead-beat. We had officers, senior rates and lots of other people, mostly visitors, crammed in together. I sat opposite Mick Fellows and asked him if he remembered my dad; he said that he did. He told me about the other clearance divers who were deployed; I knew some of them through my dad, including Brian Dutton, who had gone to *Argonaut*.

Suddenly there was a Main Broadcast pipe: 'Do you hear there? Jack Blair, Naval Tailors, now in attendance on the gangway.'

Everyone forced a smile at this echo of a pipe often made after a typical working day alongside in Portsmouth. Some wag was helping to boost morale.

No one said it, but nobody relished the thought of another day of intense attack like that. Nobody was really talking, certainly not having a drink, and there was some modern tune on the World Service or other transmission going on in the background which had some female singing about 'Britannia' and 'striking home'. I could not make out the words, but it sounded out of synch with what we were doing and a bit over the top. I looked around for the uckers bits, but could not find them. They had been secured for action, and so we did not have a game. Thought that it would improve morale if we were seen to carry on regardless, but people just seemed to want to get away to sleep or get ready for tomorrow.

Glamorgan sent us a signal: 'RPC Bog any time.* Bring own paper.'

We replied: 'Thank you. Will let you know but you are right – brown rice and bran not required. We now have lots of bog rolls, but a reduced number of bog stations.'

After dark, at about 1915, it was decided to remove the bomb. We were out in Falkland Sound again off Chancho Point. All personnel not on watch were moved forward. Stewart, Carlos, Ian and I went down to the Admiral's Day Cabin and lay on the floor, as instructed, for about an hour or so. We chatted about the day's events and how we had come through it. We reckoned that there had been around 50–60 air raids, but we had got a substantial landing force ashore, with just one injured soldier (and he had fallen into a landing craft). We thought the ship might do it better tomorrow: we needed many more rifles and machine guns on the upper deck and the Sea Cat aimers needed to be a bit more aggressive and sharper. We have loads of missiles.

'We took a bit of a hammering today,' said Carlos, rather resignedly.

I reached around for something to say.

'Lick 'em tomorrow, though!' I ventured, remembering Grant's words to Sherman during the battle of Shiloh, adding: 'We must have hacked quite a few of them today, so they will probably need to sort themselves out tomorrow, especially as their airfields are so widely separated. Maybe bad light or rain will stop play.'

'It's my birthday today!' said Carlos, almost apologetically.

We reflected with him, as the Deputy Supply Officer, that it was ironic that our rolls today contained corned beef that came from Argentina and that we had taken delivery of a British-made bomb.

We then heard on Main Broadcast that the 'beast' was lifted gently on the sheer legs and a chain hoist and – even more gently – placed on a torpedo trolley, manhandled across the Flight Deck and lowered over the side via the starboard hydraulic davit into the sea. Commander E came in to the Wardroom later and said that when the bomb was finally and gently lowered into the water, the winch rope snagged on a deck cleat in the dark and the bomb was bouncing and surfing along for a

* 'Request the pleasure of your company in our heads.'

short while across the surface of the water. An accomplished yachts-man, he moved fast to free it and the bomb sank below the waves. We continued on our way, concerned that the thing might go off when it hit the bottom. It didn't at the time. But it is still down there!

Ten minutes after the 'beast' departed, the ship – and everyone else – received a signal from CINCFLEET saying that, under no circumstances, should any unexploded bombs be moved!

How much luck is there left in our locker? It is noticeable that fears of being maimed rather than killed have been expressed the most today, even though people have been pretty resolute and philosophical. The mood was probably not helped by the news of Chief Bullingham's injuries rocketing around the ship on the bush telegraph.

In the middle of it all, at 2100, the Main Broadcast pipe was: 'Do you hear there? Nine o'clockers:* tonight's delight – salmon and caviar.'

Then a short pause, and: 'Correction to my last – pilchards!'

The lads were doing their bit for morale.

I cannot work out whether we were stationed out in the Sound as part of an interlocking, layered system of air defence or were deliber-ately set up to attract the Arg aircraft onto us rather than the amphibious and transport ships. I think that it must have been originally designed to be a defence in depth, which went wrong from our point of view, but right from the overall campaign perspective. I believe that the original idea was to try and counter both aircraft and submarines; that is why the escorts were dispersed in the Sound initially and, as a result, could not provide closer mutual support against the air attacks.

Once we realized that the submarine was not going to play, we all piled into San Carlos. There is no doubt that the ships are difficult for the attacking aircraft to get at in San Carlos and the landing site, with its surrounding hills and ridges, has been well chosen in that regard. The Arg pilots cannot see their potential targets until right up to the last seconds when they crest the ridge of Chancho Point to the west or enter through the entrance to the Sound. They do not want to bunt up too early or they will expose themselves to missile fire from the Sea Wolf ships, or even the Sea Cat. I cannot believe that any Arg pilot wants to spend the rest of his life saddled with the reputation that he was shot down by a Sea Cat!

* A late snack.

I am thinking that the Args had attacked the first things that they had seen in Falkland Sound and that they did not actually appreciate what was going on in San Carlos. I also wondered whether the planners back in the carrier and on the Admiral's staff appreciated how wide Falkland Sound is. That five- to eight-mile gap enabled their aircraft to approach over West Falkland or through the south of the Sound, where our radars could not detect them easily, and stay low over the Sound, where we had little chance of seeing them on radar before they arrived.

It's been a really eventful and exciting day and I am glad to be alive and unhurt. We have been told that we will leave San Carlos to get ourselves repaired. Everyone is decidedly relieved that we do not have to spend tomorrow in and around San Carlos. The other poor ships will have to tough it out again though. I cannot believe that they did not go for or get *Canberra*, stuck in the middle of San Carlos – big as you like and the whitest thing from here to Antarctica. I reckon that the Args thought that she was a hospital ship. That's why she was not attacked.

Still, if we have to go back in again, then that is how it will have to be. I am reminded of Cunningham's comment when the RN, most of whose ships had run out of ammunition, covered the withdrawal of the Army from Crete in the face of overwhelming Luftwaffe attack: something like 'it takes three years to build a ship, but 300 to build a tradition' – and Dunkirk. That's it. We don't – and won't – cut and run.

As the cab is knackered, I have volunteered to go on the Bridge watch-keeping list, in order to show willing and to ease the load on the guys who have been doing Defence Watches day in, day out. After all, I am a General List officer and, if I am honest or cynical (one or the other), it would give the right impression.

There has been a lot of signal traffic and talk again about the possibility of the 42/22 Combo, whereby a Type 42 destroyer, with a Type 22 frigate in the 'goalkeeping' role, operates off Pebble Island as a 'missile trap' for enemy aircraft attempting to close San Carlos. This would allow the Type 42 some sea room to make the most of her long-range radars and her Sea Dart, while giving her the close-in protection afforded by Sea Wolf in the Type 22, which the Args must now dread. It has already worked with the carriers and 22s together (although not yet in the face of a threat that closes the carriers), but I would imagine that the tactic needs some practice together to get it right if the two ships are not to foul each other's firing arcs or collide. I think that they are going to try this approach tomorrow. The Type 22 experiences inshore with *Coventry* and *Glasgow* so far indicate that the tactic is not entirely foolproof.

So double frustration. The Sea Slug is knackered and so is 406. The boys are currently assessing the damage, but we are doubtful whether we will fly her again. Bugger! It is like getting injured in the first game of the season and then being out for the rest of the season. Mind you, there were some pretty stunned faces in the Wardroom this evening and palpable relief all around the ship when the news came through that we were leaving San Carlos and heading out towards one of the holding areas (Tug and Repair Area), to get ourselves fixed. I was thinking that we might have usefully remained in Falkland Sound or San Carlos to act as a distraction or decoy for the incoming Arg aircraft.

The most uplifting experience I had today was when I hurried down to HQ1, to report what I had seen and found at the after end of the ship. Things were a bit tense, people were shouting, and buzzers, bells and lamps were in complete auto. Chaos and confusion threatened, but did not quite reign. Amid the pandemonium, a Leading Hand, whom I did not recognize in his anti-flash hood, but from his arm badge could see was a stoker, cried out loudly:

'STOP!'

Everybody turned to look and listen, even the senior officers present. He pointed in a decidedly animated fashion to the direction of the forward cross-passage and exclaimed, 'Zulus! Thousands of them!' and hurried off.

It was a brilliant piece of tension-busting humour (and spontaneous leadership) and I must find out who it was.

I was trying to think of a phrase that would sum up the visual impressions I have of today. I can do no better than quote Tennyson:

So all day long the noise of battle roll'd
Among the mountains by the winter sea.

Saturday, 22 May

We remained in Falkland Sound until 0300. At around 0200, we detected an Arg blockade-running aircraft radar. Nobody was tasked to shoot it down.

We then escorted *Canberra* and *Norland* out of San Carlos, as the Admiral's staff was concerned that they might be sunk in San Carlos. The severity of the attacks and the losses seems to have affected the thinking of the staff out in the Battle Group and some of their original assumptions seem to have gone awry.

As we headed north out of Falkland Sound and towards the Battle Group, we passed by *Glasgow*. She signalled by light: 'Welcome to the Unexploded Bomb Club.'

We sent back straightaway: 'Thank you, but I did not apply to join!'

Everyone was hoping that the weather would be too poor for flying jets from the mainland today or that the Args would have to regroup and lick their wounds. In the event, there was negligible enemy air activity. No one seems sure how many aircraft were splashed yesterday, but the intelligence people are obsessed with drop-tanks and whether the aircraft we saw had them mounted.

Throughout the night, but more energetically in the forenoon, we started to survey, assess and repair the damage that we had sustained on the previous day. By 1200, we were with the *Hermes* Group again and were designated as the close escort (decoy?) for *Invincible*. We conducted a series of helo transfers, including mail, and then replenished from *Regent* from 1500, taking on 450 rounds of 4.5 shells, assorted ammunition and chaff that we had expended, after which I did my first stint as Officer of the Watch on the Bridge. Keith Creates and Jon Saunders seemed grateful that I was supplementing the watch-bill and allowing them to get some sleep after the past couple of days. Even the Navigator failed to chime in with his normal jibe about the need for aviators to get at least eight hours sleep a day, with his observation that 'anything else at night is a bonus'.

During the watch, I had to maintain the air defence posture in a circle 5,000 yards around *Invincible*. While I was on the Bridge, I looked to see whether anyone had recorded the precise events of yesterday in the ship's log. Needless to say, it is largely incomplete and probably reflects the fact that the Bridge team had other things on their mind at the time. Even so, it compares pretty poorly with the measured, hand-written logs of men-of-war during battles in the age of sail. I suppose that things were a lot slower then and you could record events and data at your own pace.

Having *Canberra* and *Norland* away from San Carlos has created a problem according to the signal traffic. They cannot have unloaded all the kit that they had onboard while they were still in San Carlos. All the support and logistics for 40 and 42 Commando and 3 Para were in *Canberra* and the same for 2 Para in *Norland*. That means that they must still have most of the ammunition, stores and food in them. That will be a problem for the boys ashore and will stop them going too far from the beachhead. *Canberra* was also supposed to be the main casualty ship, ready to receive the injured, so I do not know what they are going to do about that.

I saw a news report or signal tonight that reported the Argentinians as saying that they would not be responsible for anything that happened to hospital ships that were in the combat zone. I reckon that they thought *Canberra* – with her white hull and superstructure – was a hospital ship and that is why the aircraft did not attack her yesterday. If that is true, that is decent of them and a stroke of luck for us, considering how much gear and how many people were onboard. I cannot think what a bomb exploding in her hull would have done to her.

People around the ship were glad today that we were out of San Carlos, but decidedly narked that we had been put out of action by the bomb. Most of the lads missed most of the action, but were aware from the Main Broadcast pipes that we had had a lively day. The Flight maintainers are in reasonably good spirits, despite what happened to Chief Bullingham and Fitz, and amazingly calm about it all. We are all worried about Terry B – the Doc reckoned that the impact of the 30 mm shell splinters and the concussion did for both his eyes. We are missing Fitz, who, by now, we think, will be chatting up a nurse somewhere. His wounds should heal and he will not be left with any permanent damage. According to the Doc, his genitalia are unscathed and, as far as he could tell, functionally intact. We are trying to get another aircrewman from one of the big ASW squadrons. Ian is sporting an oversize bandage on his injured hand.

Of course, we are not at all happy about the cab. It is absolutely riddled with cannon or rocket splinters and we wonder whether it will fly again, given that the fuel tanks have been punctured and the whole back end looks like a colander. However, most of the major components (engine, gearbox, sonar, radar, pilots' banana dispenser) escaped damage and we think that the integrity of the electrical looming is OK.

It is now clear what happened to the bomb when it came inboard. It entered from about Green 140 when the Sea Slug launcher was pointing to starboard at about Green 130. It ripped through the port flash door and pierced the port discard bay (missing an armed warhead on a waiting Sea Slug missile by about two feet). Going through bulkheads as if they were paper, it then visited a fan compartment and the port pyro locker, whose contents happily did not come out in sympathy, destroyed a calorifier and then ended up – no doubt because it was shitting itself! – in the after junior rates' heads. It smashed two traps, bounced against the underside of the Flight Deck (hence the appearance of the strange bump) and came to rest on the tiled deck.

Overall, though, we are doing quite well. We got a huge amount of kit ashore and all the troops, with no land force deaths, apart from a Gazelle crew.* We did expect to lose a few ships and apparently it is an accepted risk in all amphibious operations. Our losses are minimal compared to the evacuation of Crete in the 2WW and other examples from history. The submarine did not turn up and the Sound was not mined.

I can only think that the Args judged us according to their own thinking and planned their defence in accordance with what they would do – indeed did do – as the attackers. They expected us to walk in through the front door over by Stanley and that is how their defences are organized. I am not sure whether they really believe that this is the main landing or a feint. There is a lesson here – never judge what the enemy might do on the basis of what you would do.

The one brilliant bit of planning has been the choice of landing site. If you are an Arg pilot, San Carlos is very difficult to approach at anything like an attack profile until you have cleared the ridge to the west of the anchorage. As you pop up, you expose yourself to missile fire from the short-range AA fire. If you try and enter through the mouth of San Carlos, the Sea Wolf ship should get you. Once we get the Rapiers ashore and working, we should be able to get on top of it. Mind you, I am a bit surprised that a couple of the sites have been selected on or near the top of ridges – great as scarecrows, but most of their targets will be flying at altitudes below them. Surely that must mean a problem when you want to engage.

We are really suffering because of our inability to detect the Arg aircraft over land and at sufficient range to intercept them with the SHars, especially when the enemy aircraft are flying at low level. We are badly missing the AEW [Airborne Early Warning] capability that used to be

* Shot down by Argentinian ground troops near Port San Carlos.

provided by the Gannets in *Ark Royal*, as well as radars that can differentiate between the clutter produced by land returns and moving aircraft. The Type 22s, *Broadsword* and *Brilliant*, have radar 967/968, which seems to have much better discrimination close inshore and pick the aircraft up much more readily, especially over land. Also, the Args can still see all our SHar operations on their radar at Stanley, so they could route the inbound raids around our CAP stations, or bring them in while the SHars were off station refuelling. We need to take it out. Where are the SAS when you need them?!

I have just done the report on how people were injured on the Flight Deck and am looking down at Chief Bullingham's helmet. It still has a small USS *Comte de Grasse* tag on it and I recall that when the US Flight Commander came to visit us at sea – and to sample a couple of rounds of beer while he was at it – he left his own flight helmet in the hangar. Gross tactical error! On the back, he had the usual garish American logo and the words 'The Count' emblazoned in large letters, to reflect his afloat, embarked persona. By the time he re-embarked – merrier, but no wiser – in his helo, to be taken back to his own ship by his Junior Joe pilots, our Flight team had generously and thoughtfully removed the 'o' on his helmet logo and closed up the letters to advertise a totally different, more exotic persona. Happy days!

We had a tense command meeting this morning, where some of us said that we really had not provided enough lead in the air yesterday. The Captain got angry and asked what more could have been done. Duncan Ford bravely said that there was little point in having any rifles or machine guns loafing in the magazines in action. As a result, we have quickly established a proper system for providing more firepower on the signal deck at Action Stations – called the SQUAT (Signal Deck Qualified Under Attack Team). The Buffer is in charge of a motley group of gun-toting lads who can be spared from across the departments. They are armed with two GPMGs, three LMGs and four rifles and have been trained to load the 3 inch rockets, as they will be stationed up near the launchers.

I want to record an incident from yesterday because it epitomizes the spirit and sense of humour of this Flight. During the air raids, while AEM Craven was taking pot-shots with a rifle, I saw the SMR standing on the Flight Deck with two handfuls of nuts, bolts and other metal debris, as an Arg jet turned in for an attack.

'Get down SMR! He's inbound!' Stewart cried.

The SMR just stood there and, as the aircraft screeched overhead, he threw, one after the other, both handfuls high into the air.

'What the fuck are you up to, SMR?' I asked, reasonably, I thought.

'They are flying so low that I thought that I would do my bit and try to FOD* his engines with all that stuff!' replied the SMR.

The *Daily Oak* has just revealed that Spurs drew 1-1 with QPR in the FA Cup Final – surreal!

Tonight, we will replenish fuel from *Tidepool*, starting at 2330.

Sunday, 23 May

Last night's replenishment with *Tidepool* went on until 0140 and we returned to our position 5,000 yards around *Invincible*. Just as I was receiving the handover for my stint as Officer of the Watch for the Morning Watch (0400–0800), we had a submarine scare. *Ambuscade* reported a torpedo detection on her sonar about 10 miles to the south of *Antrim* and everyone took torpedo counter-measures. *Alacrity* and two Sea Kings joined her to investigate the datum and the source, but found nothing. It transpires that *Ambuscade* had detected her own 182 noise-maker while she was in a hard turn and called it as a torpedo!

We were conducting various transfers aft on the Flight Deck through-out the day. Importantly, a MARTSU team arrived at 1130 to survey 406, with a view to possible repair. They left at 1800 for *Atlantic Conveyor*, having surveyed the aircraft and recommended that the 406 was in fact repairable. We might actually get to fly 406 again – that would be great news.

A Constructor Commander also arrived to have a look at our ship's damage and make a few suggestions. With regard to the bomb damage, someone (probably Carlos Edwards) put a cartoon up on the Wardroom notice board which showed a representation of the devastated after heads with the caption, supposedly emanating from the Main Broad-cast, 'Do you hear there? The ship was generally well prepared and presented for Captain's Rounds today, with the exception of the port after heads, which were a complete shambles and will get a re-scrub.'

We had a day of unconfirmed reports of air raids and Etendard radars which did not amount to anything. We went to Action Stations at about

---

* Foreign Object Damage, or debris likely to foul aircraft engines and systems.

1700, firing off and wasting lots of chaff C and chaff D in response to what turned out to be a spurious Exocet attack. In fact, it has been a quiet day in the air during which the Battle Group and the ship have contrived to wind themselves up with false alarms. We have made it into a fairly tense and edgy day.

I spent some time talking to my division, mostly the junior rates, who wanted to know what was likely to happen. We all agreed that the best way to get home was to get on with winning the war. There is a popular desire among the ship's company to locate and splash the aircraft taking the Arg football team to the World Cup.

I did the Last Dog on the Bridge and agreed with Declan that I would do the last two hours of his First Watch as he had some Damage Control work to do.

Tomorrow, it seems that we are at last going to try something which has been discussed for a long time onboard now – the 'missile trap' comprising a Type 42 and a Type 22 operating together, for mutual support. *Coventry* and *Broadsword* are going to the north of the Sound to try and pluck Arg aircraft down before they reach San Carlos. It is thought that they might stand a better chance in open water.

The problem, as we have found, is that the raids, flying low, are masked by the terrain of West Falkland, with massive amounts of clutter and shadow zones. Without a modern moving target indicator function, it is impossible for a system, like Sea Dart, along with 965 and 992 radars, to alert in time if the aircraft just pop up over the coast and head straight for the ship.

The Type 22 is optimized for close-in action and its radar is not that bad over the land. The Sea Wolf, as we have seen, is terrific, so much so that everyone is calling it a HITtile, not a MISSile! *Brilliant* and *Broadsword* have already practised and been used as 'goalkeepers' with the carriers.

That's why the 42/22 combo has been devised, so that the ships can provide mutual support and make up for each other's deficiencies. But I reckon that it is something that you need to practise together and I wonder whether two new ships working together will handle it.

There is also another snag: Sea Wolf is designed to protect the ship carrying it – it is extremely short-range (just over three miles) and is not great at providing defence to other ships unless they are really close to the firing ship.

We heard that a Sea King 4 made an emergency landing in Chile ahead of the landings at San Carlos and the crew has been taken in by the authorities near Punta Arenas – it's 'Wiggy' Bennett, Richard Hutchings and their aircrewman. The story apparently is that they were on patrol over the sea, got into difficulties and had to make for land. I do not think so. For a start, I am not sure what routine task would have necessitated them being that far west, on their own, and, secondly, it was quite obviously a one-way mission. The assessment on the ship is that this was a Special Forces insertion and that the SAS are probably there to deal with the Arg aircraft on the ground, either to sabotage them or report on their movements. The timing, just before the landings, is probably relevant.

You have to wonder whose side the BBC is on. Tonight, we heard on the World Service that the reason why so many of our ships have survived direct hits (including us, of course) is because the Arg aircraft are flying too low during their attack profile and the bombs do not have time to arm. How unbelievably stupid and irresponsible that is! Surely, someone at the BBC has to recognize that this is not just a game, about which the taxpayer-funded BBC can have the luxury of being neutral. Luckily, they did not tell the whole world that the Arg 500 lb bombs seem to be working all right, as poor old *Ardent* found out!

The ME Department has done a clever thing today. The cannon shells in our port side did substantial damage to our electrical cables and, after a thorough survey, our MEs have got power running again by improvising. When we were in Gibraltar, they thought that one of the shore power cables might come in handy for a rainy day, so it was promptly lifted and hidden onboard. It has now been pressed into service as a temporary high-power cable running down the port side.

Monday, 24 May

I was still Officer of the Watch on the Bridge during the First last night as we continued to protect and be protected by the Carrier Group. It was pitch dark outside with no lights showing on any of the ships. The Captain and the Navigator were on the lower Bridge, and I started the handover to Keith Creates at about 2320 as he adjusted to night vision conditions. Once we had run through all the necessary briefing and finally cross-checked the positions of the various ships in company, I said, 'OK, heading 220, speed 14 knots. You have the ship.'

Before Keith could accept the responsibility for the ship, suddenly, without warning and making us all jump, there was a huge explosion that lit up the whole horizon and I distinctly remember seeing the ghostly silhouettes of ships appearing and then instantly disappearing as the ball of flame flared dramatically and then rapidly subsided. It immediately wrecked my night vision, even though we did not hear a sound. My heart sank. I thought, we've been bounced, probably by a submarine.

'Port 35,' I ordered, thinking that one of our group had been torpedoed. I did not want us to be the next target. I reacted instinctively to turn us away from the supposed threat, knowing that we did not have a consort to port.

'What the hell was that?' asked the Captain, running onto the Bridge.

'Sir, I think that one of the RFAs might have been torpedoed. There was an O-boat* on that bearing beyond *Hermes*.'

'PWO – Officer of the Watch, very large explosion bearing 330. Have we lost anyone?'

'Standby,' came the reply from the Ops Room.

'Come on, let's get on with it,' demanded the Captain.

'Aye, aye, sir.'

'Midships,' I ordered as I approached the new course that would put the threat on our quarter and ensure that our 182 noisemaker was not between us and the threat.

'Starboard 15,' I ordered and, as we steadied, 'steer 090.'

I asked the PWO to allow a quick burst of 978 radar so that we could check on how many ships were in company. We quickly transmitted and everyone was present and correct, even if shaken, and well and truly stirred. What had happened?

The answer quickly came through by tactical signal that *Hermes* had launched a SHar loaded with bombs that had either exploded on take-off or had crashed into the sea ahead of the ship. It turned out that it was Gordie Batt, an old friend of Ian, whose Command Examinations notes Ian had borrowed for the Spring Train deployment. 'Poor bloke, I reckon that he won't need those back now' was Ian's rueful comment on hearing the news. No one is yet sure how it happened. He might simply have not climbed away with enough power as he took off very heavy

---

* Meaning either RFA *Olna* or RFA *Olmeda*.

and in the dark could not see that he wasn't climbing. It used to happen in the old carriers and you see film of US carrier aircraft dipping slightly as they clear the front of the Flight Deck. Sad – and another precious SHar pilot has been lost. What must his family be thinking right now? As I write, they will just have heard, I would think.

After my watch, I had read a signal from *Broadsword* describing how *Antelope* had been hit and badly damaged by a couple of bombs that had not exploded. Join the club! There was also a totally reasonable analysis by *Broadsword*'s Captain of why the frigates and destroyers should not be exposed in this way in a constrained environment that so obviously put them at a severe disadvantage and in such unnecessary peril. It was pretty forthright and commendably logical stuff, claiming that the escorts would 'be picked off, one by one'. He recommended that we leave the air defence of the landing area to the SHars and Rapier and let the ships fight in the open sea, where they were likely to have more success. I did not see a reply and do wonder whether the Admiral and his staff out here quite realize what conditions are like inshore – or indeed on the Falklands. After all, they have not even set eyes on the Islands yet. It does sound like Captain Canning wants to have another go at the 42/22 combo.

Our biggest problem is that we have to remain close inshore to protect the Army and the Marines ashore, which is extremely disadvantageous to ship missile systems and we cannot detect aircraft until they are almost on top of us. Out in the open ocean, we can almost pluck them down at will, but the area around Falkland Sound is almost ideal for the Mirages and A4s, once they get past the SHars, which cannot be everywhere at once. There is also intelligence to suggest that, as fast as we are hacking their aircraft, Peru is supplying them with extra aircraft and spares, as well as maintainers. We need to sort them out afterwards!

I woke early this morning and lay on my pit thinking about how exposed our ships were close inshore and what we could do about it if we had to return to San Carlos. How many more can we afford to lose? I went down to the Ops Room first thing to brief for the Forenoon Watch and heard that one of *Antelope*'s bombs had gone off last night while it was being defused and that she was on fire and abandoned. She can only have been in San Carlos for about five hours before she was hit. The Arg pilots seem to like going for Type 21s. Perhaps it is because they are not concerned about Sea Cat, which they themselves have in the form of Tiger Cat ashore. We received a signal saying that bombs should not be removed from ships until more was known about them – so why did they do it?

I do not understand why the Argentinians persist with bombs when they could really screw us up with cannon fire and rockets. We have always known that our unarmoured sides can be penetrated quite easily and the aircraft have to expose themselves to much more flak if they close to bomb the ships. Perhaps it is a virility thing – you are a poof/*maricón* if you do not bomb! I was also thinking how bad it would be for us if they had air-launched torpedoes. They would be devastating in the confined waters of San Carlos or any other anchorage.

Come to think of it, it is strange that we do not use barrage balloons nowadays; they would be perfect for defence of places like San Carlos against low-fliers. Attach some bits of metal to the mooring lines and they might decoy missiles as well. It's funny how each generation forgets or ignores the lessons of previous conflicts and fails to notice that traditional solutions still apply. What else is there? The value of lead in the air against aircraft and the need for 4.5 guns on Type 22s might be good for starters.

After my forenoon on the Bridge, we replenished with *Olmeda* at midday.

My next call was to the hangar to see the boys and our cab. It seems that Humphrey might just fly again, which is remarkable considering the amount of shrapnel and other metallic debris that hit him on 21 May. I counted over 100 holes, including several penetrations of the fuel tanks and wiring looms. The boys are in good shape, with work on the cab focusing their thoughts and keeping their feet firmly on the ground.

I was standing on the Flight Deck at about 1430 talking to McGreal and Craven about how many Arg aircraft had been splashed when, without warning, the chaff rockets, with their ear-splitting, distinctive roar, fired off and the ship started manoeuvring violently. McGreal and Craven ducked into the hangar while I stayed on deck. Action Stations were piped, followed rapidly by Air Raid Warning RED. The Commander announced on Main Broadcast that EW [Electronic Warfare] had indicated that a raid was building to the west and that all ships had fired chaff in anticipation of an Exocet strike. Suddenly, I felt uniquely vulnerable and a bit lonely standing on my own on the Flight Deck and started to scan the indistinct horizon for low-flying missiles, as the ship weaved and bucked in a heavy sea. I knew that the warfare team had this clever plan to point the quarter or bow at the missile and I had a strange notion that it might be my bad luck to be in the wrong place at the wrong time. The thought soon passed and I reflected, from recent experience, that it was better to be able to see what was going on and that at least I would know what hit me.

It was all over pretty quickly as the raid went for the landing area and AOA in San Carlos. The CAP shot down three Mirages over by Pebble Island, it is reported. There are also indications on the World Service that the Paras might be about to attack Goose Green. I am not sure that it is a good idea to let the Args know about what we are planning to do.

Between 2100 and 2240, we conducted a heavy jackstay replenishment with *Regent*, to top up with various stores, yet more lubrication oil and more 3 inch chaff rockets. We have used a lot. We also needed hydraulic fluid to replace the hundreds of gallons we lost when the bomb fractured the pipes.

During the RAS, an unknown ship approached our quarter in the dark and did not respond to challenge and reply, or tactical comms. The night vision device made out a tanker at three miles, which turned out to be *British Tay*, whom we thought we would meet in Area TRALA.

John Nott was reported as saying on the World Service that the Args are on the run and that it would only take another 3–5 days to complete the operation. He also said that he thought that 'experts rather exaggerate the strength of the Argentinian Air Force'. Not from where I am sitting! Why hasn't he been sacked yet?

In fact, Mr Nott, tomorrow is Argentina's national day. No one else on board had pinged it, but I pointed out that their carrier was named *Veinticinco de Mayo* – *25th of May* – for a good reason. They simply must be preparing for a major push, if the weather is favourable and they have enough aircraft left and serviceable to undertake the mission load. How many AM-39 Exocets do we think that they have left? We are not sure, but reckon that it must be under six. They will be pretty pissed off about how it's going so far and the weather is not helping us it seems.

No sign of their other subs yet, although everyone says that one is in bits and another is in deep refit. That still leaves one though – perhaps I'll get another one to add to the *Santa Fé* – how many do you need before you become a sub-killing ace?! How many did Captain Walker get in the 2WW? A lot more than Argentina have, I'd say.

I have been thinking about the Junta today, because the Commander asked me what I thought would happen after the war. I said that, if we managed to pull this off, it could mean the end of that vicious regime in Argentina – people disappearing, tortured, murdered and everything. That would be a good result of the war, quite apart from getting the Islands back. Even people like Wedgie Benn might appreciate us.

I received two letters from A today, mostly regarding domestic issues and crises. A seems to find having the dog at home a bit of a challenge. She also gave me a hard time about an unopened letter from her to me when I was serving in *Bulwark* last year that she found in the garage. I am not sure that she has a handle on the money situation as I have absolutely no idea about what is going in and out of our account and she does not seem able to tell me. A war down here is an extreme way to save, but we must be building up a healthy balance by now.

Coventry and *Broadsword* have been operating the missile trap north of Pebble Island and *Coventry* splashed a couple of aircraft with Sea Dart today. The tactic seems to be working, as the Args are being intercepted at their most vulnerable point, just after a long sea transit and as they are settling for the final identification of San Carlos and their run-in. *Coventry* is worried that he is too close in on the land and wants to be further out, though. He is concerned that he is exposed to aircraft coming off the land without the time for Sea Dart to track and engage. The Admiral has told him – I paraphrase – to get back in his box and get on with it. Pat Brown and Duncan Ford are pretty buoyant about the missile trap tactic. With the Arg national day tomorrow, I hope that they are right.

The word is that one of our people has thrown a wobbly down in the Tiller Flat. I am not surprised, given the fact that he was down there on his own, with the armoured hatch clipped fully on, and with only the occasional junior rate roundsman to keep him occasional company. An Army guy in the Irish Rangers told me when we went to Berlin that the Army try and keep people in sight of each other in tanks and things and that they always have at least two soldiers in a foxhole, to keep up morale. Thoughtful!

Tuesday, 25 May

I am writing at lunchtime. This morning, I woke up to find that we were in the TARA [Tug and Repair Area] and about to rendezvous with an oil rig support ship named *Stena Seaspread*, which we had briefly passed on the second way down from Ascension.

We were alongside her, but not attached, at around 0900. The FMG [Fleet Maintenance Group] teams came onboard to help assess and repair our damage.

This morning, I replied to A's letters of yesterday. Amid the admin and morale-boosting stuff, I wrote:

'Life down here is, of course, still pretty tense, especially after losing *Antelope* yesterday. However, we seem to be hacking the Argentinians down in some numbers at last. Maybe soon, they will get the message. What is annoying is that loads of nations (Irish, Peruvians etc.) are casting us in the role of aggressors. Crumbs! Or should I say ¡*Ay caramba!*? If we were, we would have duffed their mainland bases by now – it's a real shame that it is politically unacceptable to do that. It would save a lot of trouble for us, although I wonder how we would physically do it. From what I hear on the World Service, the armchair tacticians do not realize what it is like to have bombs bouncing around you. I think that there is the prospect of us being back around the middle of July if all goes according to plan. Hopefully, the arrival of thousands more troops in the QE2 will convince the Argies to give up, although their air power is still a considerable problem.'

Today is Argentina's national day, after which their carrier is named. I was rather hoping that we would sink her – sinking her today would have really made their nationalistic eyes water. However, I think that all their warships are skulking in port or within their territorial limits and we will not or cannot get at them, because we said that we wouldn't. I reason that, if they are staying out of the way, they are not interfering with us and what we are trying to do. What does 'Heart of Oak' say?

We ne'er see our foes but we wish them to stay,
They never see us but they wish us away;
If they run, why we follow and run them ashore,
And if they won't fight us, what can we do more?

There is still no sign of their submarine though. I reckon that the CO has realized that running into us might be a pension trap and is keeping his head down. I talked to John Archer about it and he reckons that he has 'packed up and gone home'.

I do hope that the operational planners have taken the emotional significance of today into account. We do not know how many Exocets they have left, but it cannot be many. They will not waste them on escorts and will be out looking for the carriers. They really need a big hit at this point, for morale and propaganda purposes. They might also think that losing a capital ship will bring us to the negotiating table.

My worry is that we could be attacked without any overt surveillance by aircraft because the Args can work out roughly where the carriers are simply by tracking the SHars to and from their CAP stations with that Westinghouse TPS-43 area radar. We should have dealt with it by now! The best tactic for them would be to stage a diversionary raid, possibly one that turns back, see where the CAP comes from and returns to and then direct the Etendards, possibly off their tankers, to launch an Exocet strike.

While lying close to her, I had a quick look at *Stena Seaspread* earlier, which seems to have been modified to be the sort of afloat maintenance support ship that we used to have in the 1950s and '60s (like the old HMS *Triumph*, but a lot smaller of course). She is the oddest-looking ship you are likely to see, with a big superstructure forward, topped by a helo deck. In real life, she is a diving and oil rig support vessel in the North Sea. Our new friendship got off to a bad start when her Captain (Williams) became stuck in our Captain's lift (between the Ops Room and the Bridge). It jammed on the way up and it took our engineers 40 minutes to get him out! He had the odd grease stain, but took it pretty well.

She has about 160 engineers and other repair and maintenance personnel onboard, mostly lifted from the various Fleet Maintenance Units in the dockyards, along with workshops filled with hastily fitted rigs and machine tools that must have been requisitioned. Built to commercial standards, her facilities are like a hotel inside, with lots of accommodation, as well as additional Portacabins, storerooms and containers; she has stacks of food and stores and simply masses of steel sheeting and other shipwright stuff. Really well-equipped for diving and underwater repair, she has also been fitted out for aircraft support. Consequently, our boys have the confident expectation of being able to put Humphrey back together again. Great if they can – without the cab, I feel like a knight without a horse.

Just now, about midday, we received a signal from the Admiral ordering us to proceed to South Georgia to pick up CLFFI [Commander

Land Forces Falkland Islands] – Major General Moore – and 100 of his staff from the QE2 off South Georgia on 27 May and bring them back to the Battle Group.

In the afternoon, I went down to the Ops Room to listen to what might be happening on the Anti-Air Warfare control circuit. *Coventry* had splashed two aircraft in the morning and another had been downed at San Carlos. Then there was a lot of confusing and confused chatter on the circuit. What seems to have happened is that in the afternoon, just as two SHars were intercepting, *Coventry* and *Broadsword* were attacked by two pairs of A4s, the first of which wrecked *Broadsword*'s Lynx with an unexploded bomb. The second pair managed to put three bombs which did explode into *Coventry*. There seemed to have been a problem with Sea Wolf and the two ships appear to have got in each other's way. Also, I am sure that I heard *Coventry* call off the SHars just as they were about to engage the Skyhawks. In fact, I reckon that I heard one of the pilots say, 'You must be fucking joking! We've got them.'

Within half an hour, it seems that *Coventry* capsized pretty quickly and sank within an hour of the attack. A Task Force signal announced an hour later that *Coventry* was on her beam ends and about to sink. *Broadsword* had sustained minor damage and lost both her Lynx. *Uganda* was on her way, as well as eight Sea Kings and two Wessex. With night coming on, that is not good.

We do not know the casualties yet, but things do not sound promising, especially as the incident occurred just before dark. Al Rich, the Flight Commander, was one of my instructors on 737, and I know the pilot, Bertie Ledingham from Northern Ireland.

What I cannot understand is why the two SHars that were pursuing the incoming raid were called off – they could not believe it as they were about to attack. I suppose it must have been because they were in danger of entering the missile engagement zone of the ships. If this is the case, I am surprised because *Coventry* has had a few problems with her Sea Dart system recently and, from the point of view of the attacking pilots, the last thing that you are thinking about if you have a SHar about to light up your tail is the accuracy of your bombing run.

It did not get any better. Just after dusk, we started picking up details of an Exocet attack on the Battle Group. It was suggested that arrestor gear had been shipped to the Falklands and that the attacking Super-Es might have gone back to Stanley. *Glamorgan* was tasked to bombard the airfield, in case.

It was then signalled that *Atlantic Conveyor* had been hit by one or two Exocet missiles, launched at 28 miles, and was on fire. Her crew was abandoning ship and the tug *Salvageman* was on the way.

You have to ask why she was sent into the fray in daylight – on 25 May – with no close escort. We have been calling her our third aircraft carrier and yet she was steaming alone. This suggests sloppy thinking, a lack of appreciation of what life is like outside the Carrier Group bubble of complacency.

What did Kipling say? 'We have fed our sea for a thousand years, and she calls, still unfed.' What a day!

At the Captain's briefing this evening, the warfare team were talking gloomily about the rate of losses and how many more ships we can lose before the campaign becomes unsupportable. We are simply running out of escorts. Not only are we losing ships, but a good few, like us, are damaged, while others, like *Argonaut*, are totally out of the game.

Ian and I pointed out that the Args must be suffering severely from attrition as well and their serviceability cannot be that good. Our view is that they will concentrate on big pushes in future against identified high-value units and defined objectives; they won't come in penny-packets. They will also be aware that Rapier is – I think – finally up and running.

If I have a worry, it's because the Admiral's approach appears to resemble a game of chess, with the priority being to protect the king and queen (the carriers), at the expense, if necessary, of the other pieces. I'd say that the major amphibious ships and transports are the rooks and bishops, which might be dispensable once the landings have been successfully completed, with the destroyers and frigates in the role of knights and pawns, expendable for operational and tactical advantage – and to ensure that we do not get checkmated.

I have managed to borrow a cassette player from Stewart and am now able to play some music of my own choice from cassettes that I have borrowed from the midshipmen. I have also asked A to send some compilations of our favourite music. However, I am not sure whether she is spending much time at home in Dorset at present; she seems to be mostly at home with her parents in Worplesdon. That is only natural, I suppose, but it does mean that our letters are taking even longer to connect.

We have just, at 2110, detached from *Stena Seaspread* and are heading for South Georgia at 22 knots.

Ambuscade signalled tonight that she had experienced a near miss with the Exocets this afternoon and that her chaff D deflected the missile, possibly onto *Atlantic Conveyor*.

Wednesday, 26 May

Antrim is en route to South Georgia at 18 knots, in loose company with *Canberra* and *Norland*, which will pick up 5 Brigade from the QE2.

We heard this morning that the casualties from *Coventry* might not have been as bad as was feared last night. *Broadsword* had 154 survivors onboard and *Uganda* 30 injured, while *Brilliant* has 24 from *Atlantic Conveyor*. Some of her contents might be salvageable, so *Irishman* the tug is standing by to assist her. We think that we have lost 19 in *Coventry*, including her First Lieutenant, and 12 in *Atlantic Conveyor*, including the Master, Captain North. 'The sea's a tomb that's proper for the brave.'*

Casualties are mercifully low, compared to what we feared and what we have seen in past wars. However, it seems to me that casualties are only an issue for the press and the public if objectives are not being achieved and the campaign is not seen to be in the process of being won. The experience from the Vietnam War is that even low levels of casualties become a political problem if there is stalemate or a war is being lost.

I can scarcely believe how much we have lost in *Atlantic Conveyor*. The conversation in the Mess last night was pretty sombre. Why did they risk moving her into the Islands while it was still light and on Argentina's National Day?! Why didn't she have a close escort to protect her? I can only think that the staff wanted to have the maximum number of hours unloading in the dark as possible, before the Args found out she was there.

Apart from the casualties, we have lost four Chinooks (one got away we think), seven Lynx/Wessex Vs as well as all the makings of an airstrip which was to be set up ashore to refuel and service SHars and helos. That is a major setback as the plan was to use the helos to transport the Paras and Royal Marines – and their ammo etc. – across the island to get at the Args. Ian reckons that there would have been extensive workshop,

* John Dryden.

fuel, engineering and MARTSU facilities onboard as well, together with tents and other stuff.

It seems that yesterday's air attacks had two main components. After discovering the 42/22 combo to the north of Pebble Island, mainly because they were losing aircraft to it, the Args needed to deal with the threat. That's why the raids happened the way they did; it did take the heat off San Carlos though, although it's a high price to pay. Once again, I think our SHars going back and forth to our carriers must have betrayed their position to the Args watching on the Westinghouse TPS-43 radar that they have at Stanley. We should have taken it out long before now; it's giving the Args a complete picture of what is going on and allowing them, by routing their C-130s etc. around our SHars, to time their nocturnal air resupply runs into Stanley.

We started today with ground runs on the Flight Deck, to ensure that all 406's wounds were healed. A few electrical problems persisted, but the fuel tanks and lines seem to be fine. The holes in the airframe have been patched up with what look like sticking plaster, but there is no major structural damage to the main components or control surfaces. The damaged rotor blades have been replaced.

We sorely missed Chief Bullingham's experience and expertise on the electrical side, despite the best efforts of PO Williams. By 1325, we were ready for a Check Test Flight, which, although we metaphorically kept our fingers crossed while airborne, was, after a rigorous check of all the systems, successful, apart from a few minor adjustments and repairs. As the Commander said on CCTV tonight, Humphrey had 'demonstrated its Phoenix-like ability to rise again'.

Meanwhile, repairs to damage sustained by the ship in action continued, with most effort expended on finding out exactly what effect the cannon attacks had. Unfortunately, much of the damage seems to have occurred in places that are behind components or are inaccessible without cutting through bulkheads. This is taking time and manpower to resolve. The other main area is the restoration of the undamaged starboard Sea Slug system and the isolation of the damaged port side, so that we can at least fire one side in anger again. Mike Bonney and his team of maintainers are doing a great job, especially when you consider that the magazine was flooded by the sprays on 21 May. They have had various volunteers in there helping to mop up, including Godfrey Rhimes (the tooth-wright) and, amazingly, the Padre.

We received a chocolate signal from CINCFLEET – 'Please pass my congratulations to all those involved in unloading and supply operation in the San Carlos Bomb Alley. This bravery and persistence in the face of intense air attack has been widely admired and without them the bridgehead could not have been achieved.' I wondered if this was an attempt to sustain morale after the events of the past five days and a hint to the Admiral that he should have sent something.

Yesterday's Arg air attacks have caused the Carrier Group to move further out from the Islands and the CAPs are having to spend longer transiting to and from their stations defending the troops ashore and vessels in and around San Carlos.

There are several jokes doing the rounds of the ships about *Invincible* and *Hermes* being awarded the Burma Star as a campaign medal for the Falklands because they are so far to the east. Those ships that spend their time under daily air attack inshore are particularly vociferous about this issue. They believe that the Admiral and his staff really have no idea what conditions are like inshore.

However, I reckon that the Admiral is right to seek to keep his major, war-winning assets as safe as possible. The Args are after them all the time because they realize that the loss of one of them would have a major impact on our ability to provide air cover over the Islands, quite apart from the psychological and political impact. We have all reckoned that, if it came to it, we could afford to lose one carrier, but it would be a struggle afterwards, with *Illustrious* still not ready and no chance of *Bulwark* returning to service. There was talk of the US lending us an amphibious flat top, but it would be difficult to rush her into service in time. The loss of all the aircraft in a carrier – two whole squadrons (of SHars and Sea Kings) – would also make things very difficult. It does not bear thinking about. The Admiral is absolutely right in keeping the carriers as far out of the reach of the Arg threat as possible and we must accept that the escorts (including *Antrim*) are expendable by comparison. After all, that is what escorts are for!

Not wanting to tempt fate, but I need to do my command exams when I get back, so that I can capitalize on all this experience as soon as possible. I will put in for a PWO job next. Having done warfare at this pace and intensity, I cannot believe that the course or the job would be that different or difficult, even, as they say, for an aviator. If not, hopefully, they will give me command of a Lynx Flight next; that would combine a bit of independence with the opportunity to get into a different role. The way it flies, it looks like a sports car compared to the Wessex 3.

I have just heard that *Glamorgan* has fired a Sea Slug in the GASH mode against Stanley airfield. They intend to fire a few more tomorrow night.

Thursday, 27 May

We continued to accompany *Canberra* and *Norland* across to South Georgia and arrived at about 1130, having met and replenished with *Blue Rover*.

This morning's approach to South Georgia was hampered by increasing numbers of icebergs and floes and it is clear that winter is setting in rapidly. It has changed considerably since the last time that we were here and, as well as a large field to the south, there were some sizeable chunks of ice close to us, looking around for a victim. We replenished from *Blue Rover* over lunchtime and transferred mail to her.

Canberra had *Ardent*'s survivors onboard, *Norland Antelope*'s and RFA *Stromness* was following with *Coventry*'s survivors. They both entered the bay, while we patrolled outside and awaited the arrival of the QE2. We arrived at Cumberland Bay to find the four requisitioned trawlers, *Farnella*, *Junella*, *Cordella* and *Pict*, in residence and transferring stores to and fro.

We expected to meet the QE2 at 1200, but she signalled, no doubt mindful of previous encounters between totemic passenger liners and icebergs, that she would be delayed until 1500. I had the Afternoon Watch on the Bridge. We were approaching the mouth of the bay and, although we were tracking QE2 by radar, the scene was dramatic as the huge, impressive ship just loomed out of a bank of sea fog, funnel and superstructure first, about four miles away, just north of Cumberland Bay at about 1430. The whole scene, centred on the most famous, most iconic liner in the world sailing in the depths of the Southern Ocean and off such a strange shore, made you want to pinch yourself to make sure that you were not dreaming.

As she closed the bay, the helicopters started load-lifting between her and *Canberra* and *Norland* immediately. Maj. Gen. Moore, his staff and others (76 in all) transferred to *Antrim*, while the rest of the Brigade was moved, with its weapons and kit, by QE2's large boats, to *Canberra* and *Norland*.

Out of curiosity and a desire to know whom we might be fighting with, I decided to pop across to QE2. I hitched a lift with *Pict*, commanded by my old 826 buddy, Dave Garwood. Dave had been the squadron's QHI [Qualified Helicopter Instructor] and, much to his chagrin and the detriment of his ambitions, his nickname was 'Gashbag'. It was singularly inappropriate, because 'Gashbag' was one of the smoothest, most charming officers around and no woman was safe from his beguiling line in chat and his boyish good looks. At cocktail parties, he had the world record for 'trapping' women, especially in the US where they fell for the patter – and his reinforced English accent – every time. Usually Gashbag would hunt in a fighting pair, with a newly qualified pilot as his wingman, on the strict understanding that the wingman was there to deal with the less appealing of the two targets. As far as the rest of the squadron was concerned, that made calling him 'Gashbag', in public and in private, all the more appealing.

But 'Gashbag' was now a Lieutenant Commander and in charge of a converted trawler. When he came alongside *Antrim*, he was hailed by Ian: 'Hey, Gashbag, have you caught anything with that thing?'

I chipped in with 'Don't you mean trapped anything?'

Gashbag said nothing and looked a bit serious. 'Could we just have a chat down aft?' he asked, walking down to the deserted stern of his trawler. We made our way down the waist opposite him.

'Look,' he said, 'now that I am a two and a half * and a CO, I need you to call me David.'

Ian thought for an instant and said, loudly: 'OK, Gashbag.'

We both laughed, and in the end so did Gashbag, who accepted that pompous did not really suit him, especially in the winter wonderland of South Georgia.

Gashbag then came onboard for a drink in the Wardroom. All three of us had a cheery exchange of news and views and I went back for the trip to QE2. It was about 1600.

She was far bigger than I imagined and it was a struggle to find my way around. I wanted to familiarize myself – after the South Georgia experience last time – with the type of people with whom I might be dealing. The ship was full of soldiers doing all sorts of things and you

* A Lieutenant Commander, with two thick and one thin stripes on his uniform.

could tell that the Scots Guards were firmly led, as they moved around with purpose and vigour, with each carrying a mountain of kit. The Gurkhas were – well, just as you would imagine – demonstrably professional, quietly menacing and clearly up for it.

Because of my Welsh heritage and a distinct national pride, I purposely wanted to go and meet some of the Welsh Guards. I asked an NCO in the Scots Guards and he pointed me in the direction of one of the bars, where, as I approached, I saw several young officers – typical 'Ruperts' – enjoying their last evening onboard.

On getting nearer, I heard one Rupert say, 'Here's another one in fancy dress.'

'What are you?' said Rupert 2.

I had noticed from their rank tabs that they were both Second Lieutenants.

'Gentlemen, I said, 'I am Chris Parry, from HMS *Antrim* . . .'

'What do you do in your boat?'

My back was already up and I struggled to keep my cool. And, I thought, not a Welsh accent yet – actually scarcely an English one that you could identify.

'I am the ship's helicopter Observer.'

'So, you're a pilot?'

'No, I am the helicopter sensors and weapons man.'

They thought for a while about this. Then Rupert 1 said, 'A couple of things, Corp; firstly, I do not how you do these things in the Navy, but in the Army you address officers as "sir" and secondly this bar is for officers, not NCOs, especially not dressed like that.'

I lost it – 'Listen, you fucking idiots, I am not a Corporal, I'm a Lieutenant Royal Navy, which is the same as a Captain in the Army. While you have been drinking and sunning your way down here, better people than you have been fighting and dying for over a month. Go and fetch your Adjutant – I don't want to talk to you.'

Rupert 1 gave an arrogant, dismissive shrug, while Rupert 2 scurried away. Despite the frenetic activity, I looked around in my immediate vicinity, at a scene that resembled a gentlemen's cruise to the Southern Ocean. Rupert 2 did not return and the Adjutant never appeared. I thought, I have better things to do, and turned away.

I fired a Parthian shot to Rupert 1, 'You guys need to get your act together – you'll be in action with the Args within a couple of days.'

'Oh no,' he said, 'we are here to do garrison duty. We are not going to be fighting.'

'Then I think that you have a communication problem in your regiment,' I concluded as I went away, thinking about the curse of Welsh regiments over the years – Welsh soldiers and English officers.

By 1700, we were on our way back to the main Task Group at 24 knots, amid poor visibility and the ever-present threat of icebergs.

Tonight, we watched a film in the Wardroom – *Battle of Midway* (appropriately!). The soldiers could not believe how cool and matter-of-fact we were about it all. I showed a genuinely interested and very agreeable Major from the Scots Guards around the ship during the Dogs.

The troops ashore seem to be doing very well under the SHar and missile umbrella and we hope for great things from them soon. The sooner we take Stanley and its airfield, the better, so that we can forward base our aircraft there, instead of having to flog all the way in from the carriers. We would have had a portable airstrip at San Carlos by now, but it was lost in *Atlantic Conveyor*.

We certainly do not want another 1,000 lb beauty in our rear end, especially after *Antelope*'s visitor decided to blow up while it was being defused. What is really galling is that these bombs were bought from the Brits! I think that we even tried to sell them SHars for their carrier while the Type 42 deal was going through.

There was a raid by A4 Skyhawks on San Carlos today, but they went for the troops ashore. Rapier is now supposed to be up and running. Meanwhile, the damage caused by the bombs and Exocets has highlighted a great many of the problems with our ships, which the RN has blissfully ignored for the past 20 years and failed to impress on successive governments. I just hope that they learn and apply the lessons which will come out of this war and put new ideas into action soon.

The way in which reports of losses are announced by the government is irritating people at the moment, no doubt complicated by the distances involved. The trouble is that the initial news reports are so vague – 'In the course of her duties, a British destroyer has been . . .' (at this point thousands of families and loved ones have their hearts in their mouths) – before the ship's name is revealed. I sometimes wonder whether the MOD news service is designed to help the military campaign or protect the politicians. I suppose it should do both.

It is strange to think that the political survival of both the Arg and our own governments depends on the outcome of this war. Down here, it is difficult to avoid the impression, amid all the signs of normality and life as routine back home, that it is the Royal Navy and a few friends who are at war with Argentina, not the country as a whole. That attitude may reflect our isolation down here, but it seems that the British press is treating the war very much like a sporting contest, a spectacle that can be distantly enjoyed and vicariously experienced by the vast majority of the population without actually getting involved beyond contributing the requisite entry fee of blood (ours) and treasure (theirs, and some of ours as taxpayers). I am sure that most people are right behind us and patriotic, but would it be too much to say that there is a hint of voyeurism about it all back home?

Talking of sport, Spurs won the FA Cup Final Replay 1-0 according to the World Service.

Friday, 28 May

In the night, we came up to 27 knots to make the rendezvous with *Fearless*, despite heavy sea conditions. In the afternoon, we had a Damage Control exercise which certainly impressed our visitors with its realism, at least those not involved in briefings with the General in the revived Command Operations Room in the Admiral's Day Cabin.

Meanwhile, the soldiers were finding their sea legs:

Army Major: 'What's that bloody squeaking noise? I can't sleep.'

'It's the sonar.'

Another Major: 'Why do those green manholes have "ESCAPE" printed on them?'

The Greenies have managed to get the starboard half of the Sea Slug back working again. Mike Bonney has done really well with his team.

In 406, we completed a final Check Test Flight to ensure that the aircraft was fully recovered, including an extensive test of the Flight Control and sonar systems.

At 2210, we had signal traffic indicating that Port Darwin and Goose Green had been captured by 2 Para – overall casualties are unknown, but the Commanding Officer has been killed.

At 2345, we finally met up with *Fearless* and took up a position to defend her at 5,000 yards.

She sent a signal by light: 'Great to have you nearby once more. Hope your bones are mending well. Not so many sticks and stones to be seen since you left us. It has been a memorable week.'

We replied: 'Sorry to have left you so soon in Bomb Alley. Congratulations on your achievements. My sore tail has been treated and my sting semi-restored.'

The new 825 Squadron arrived in San Carlos today onboard *Atlantic Causeway*. They have 10 aircraft, with three more due to arrive, once they came from QE2. It has been formed from the staff pilots, aircrewmen and maintainers from 706, the Sea King conversion squadron. The aircraft have had their sonars and radars stripped out, so that they are better able to undertake the lift and shift of troops, ammunition and stores. That is just as well considering all the Chinooks that were lost in *Atlantic Conveyor*.

The squadron contains several of my former colleagues from 826 Squadron, including Phil Sheldon and Steve Isacke, and is commanded by Hugh Clark, the ex-Senior Pilot of 814. That will be interesting because, when we were embarked in *Bulwark* with 814 during 1979, there was constant professional rivalry, practical jokes and oneupmanship with 814. Hugh Clark did not always see the funny side of some of our pranks and teasing – and it showed!

Amongst the mail recently was a poignant reminder of the great support that we are getting back home. A package arrived with all sorts of chocolate, shampoo and other personal necessities from a primary school near Sunderland, along with letters (and pictures) from the children expressing their eagerness for us to deal with the Argentinians and saying that they were thinking of us.

It's clear that the kids come from ordinary, workaday homes and their sincerity and faith are really touching. Good on the parents, too. One letter said that they had been following *Sheffield*, but now that she had been sunk, they had selected us as their favourite. The young lad expressed the hope that we needed to be more careful as they were not keen to see their (I quote) 'second favourite ship' go down. We will take turns at writing back individual letters to the kids and I hope that we will get to visit them at the school afterwards and thank them.

A Skyhawk pilot who was injured in an ejection and taken onboard *Fearless* has been telling us about how things are from the Arg point of view. He said that half his colleagues had not returned and that they were being told to go back to different air bases, so that the senior command could pretend that they had been redeployed. They had been led to believe that the air defences in San Carlos were negligible.

Saturday, 29 May

We have started celebrity time-checks. The one this morning was by Commander S:

> Being adrift can be very dicey
> As the Jaunty* won't deal with you nicely
> So you must know the time
> And at the end of this rhyme
> It will be quarter to eight precisely.

We maintained station on *Fearless* and at 1130 started to transfer the General and his staff across to *Fearless*, using Wessex Vs. We were tasked with 406 to act as an airborne Search and Rescue helicopter in case anyone ditched in the sea, in conditions which, with winds of 25–30 knots and a long swell, were pretty marginal in peacetime for this sort of tasking. We also transported 20 Sea Cat missiles to *Fearless*.

As part of this, we transferred two Arg prisoners from *Fearless*, one a youngster and the other a hard, suspicious 35-something, who looked like a professional NCO. Both looked weary, bedraggled and completely pissed off with things. We decided that they should sit cross-legged, facing aft, in the space between the sonar instrumentation and the starboard side, just aft of the cargo door, in the back. With rotors already running, I went to make sure that they had lifejackets on – they did – and have a look at them. I then beckoned the ground crew to help them onboard. They did not want to get onboard and strongly resisted being helped up the step. I tried to encourage them by motioning with my arms, but they looked genuinely terrified at the prospect.

Now I know that the Wessex 3 has only got one engine, but it did seem a bit strange! I thought that perhaps they had never been in – or seen – a helo before. I tried with some Spanish, amid the roar of the engine and rotor: '*¿Qué pasa?*' The NCO vigorously shook his head and kept his arms rigidly by his side. The youngster looked panic-stricken.

In the end, the boys on the Flight Deck bundled them onboard and I

---

* Naval slang for the Master at Arms.

went back to my seat, to get ready for take-off. The prisoners sat in the darkness, but I could see the panic on their faces and they would not sit still. I told PO Kurn and a Leading Seaman Gunner ('It's all right, sir, I've got a black belt in origami'), whom we had taken with us as escorts, that if the prisoners moved they should get a 9 mm out and motioned to the two passengers that we were about to take off. This produced yet more agitation and I shouted across to them '¡tranquilíza!', which was my guess for 'Relax!' At this point, we were taking off and I just left them to it, while glancing across to make sure that they were not going to cause any trouble. I told the lads not to take any chances and do what was necessary if they jumped up. I was telling Ian and Stewart what was happening, too.

During the transit, I handed the NCO who was nearest a note with '¿Qué es su problema?' on it. He just started banging on in Spanish at a rate I could not understand in the noise and waving his arms around. In the end, I gave him a biro and a piece of paper – anything to keep him quiet. As I leaned across, I could see that the youngster was sobbing. He wrote something in the semi-darkness and passed it to me. It read, in Spanish, as I recall: 'sé que nos van a tirar por la borda', which I took to mean 'I know that you are going to throw us into the sea.' I was just amazed – and momentarily chilled – by the words and told the others about it. Why did they think that we might do that?

I leaned across and made sure that both Argentinians could see me and, trying to force a convincing smile, motioned up and down with my hands that they should not worry and passed a quick note back, not sure that it was right: '¿No se preocupen!' The NCO did not look totally convinced. I gave the paper back to him in case he wanted to write any more.

When we got to the other end, the relief on their faces was obvious, but they shuffled off without a word or a look in our direction. And the NCO nicked my biro!

By 1410, the transfer was over and the ship resumed station on *Fearless*.

The news came through that 1500 Args at Goose Green had surrendered.

We then set a course to rendezvous with *Hermes*. About 1550, all hell broke loose as a possible Exocet attack was called, in response to a warning from either Special Forces or an SSN close inshore that a Super-Etendard raid had taken off. Nothing materialized – better safe than sorry. San Carlos was attacked by four Daggers, one of which was splashed.

At 1820, we replenished from *Tidespring* (Hello again!), before meeting *Hermes* at 1950. We then did three and a half hours of load-lifting and passenger transfers, as well as passing mail to *Hermes* and *Invincible* – it was very busy. We also received a new aircrewman, Stapleton. Thank goodness – I had been doing all the work up to that point. We were complete by 2310.

Most concerns ashore relate to how useless some of the Para and Marine kit is, especially the boots, and the fact that, in the extreme conditions, they are starting to suffer from trench foot and severe diarrhoea. This is just like the First World War, only the poor guys have to move and fight as well. I cannot help feeling that I made the right career choice!

We finally had proof today that the censor is operating. Stewart had one of his letters completely rewritten and forwarded in a new envelope. We know that some of our sailors have been indiscreet because of articles that have appeared in the press, especially in relation to South Georgia. The father of one sailor sounded off in a pub and the press immediately picked up on it. We know who it is and he has been debriefed, without coffee and the opportunity to sit down, but not charged with an offence.

We were due to go in and do some bombardment on positions around Stanley tonight, but the weather – a Force 9, with winds up to 50 knots and very big seas – caused a cancellation.

Sunday, 30 May

Antrim is sailing around, doing various chores and defensive duties, while trying to stay clear of incoming trouble. Celebrity time-check was the Padre: ' "To everything there is a season, and a time to every purpose under the heavens" and in 10 seconds the time will be . . .' Not bad, Padre!

Ian, the new LACMN and I flew to *Hermes* at 0840, to transfer some stores and return with a passenger. Just after, the ship detached north from the Main Group to recover stores and spares that would be dropped by one of our C-130s later in the day at 1700. Along with two of *Antrim*'s sea boats, which would assist with hooking them on, Stewart and I were airborne to recover the 26 loads. The ship came in too close and the port shaft was fouled by one of the parachutes. We sent divers down and the shaft was free in 30 minutes. Good work!

We heard later that the C-130 was in the air for 24 hours and 25 minutes by the time that he returned to Ascension.

I think that we had a major, coordinated attack on the Carrier Group this afternoon. We are still trying to work it all out, but the raid seems to have included both Etendards and A4s. The reporting signal suggests that two Exocets were fired by two Etendards and that *Exeter* splashed two A4s. No ship seems to have been hit by a missile or by bombs and *Avenger* is claiming to have shot down an Exocet with her 4.5 gun (that would be an improbable first!). It could just be that we are starting to get our anti-ship missile defence right and the chaff decoyed the missiles. How many more AM-39 Exocets do the Args have left – surely the French can tell us?

We lost a GR3 to ground fire ashore, although the pilot seems to have ejected over the sea and was picked up unhurt (if damp). That will teach a Crab not to fly on a weekend!

Later we rendezvoused with *Glamorgan*, *Fort Austin* and *Canberra*, and, as I write, we are replenishing fuel and lubrication oil, from *Olmeda*, as well as stores from *Fort Austin* by helicopter (not 406) and mail from *Canberra*. We have also sent our two prisoners across to *Fort Austin*. We are due to finish the fuel RAS at 0115 and the stores one with *Fort Austin* at 0600.

The command brief tonight included a discussion of what is likely to happen next. 2 Para did really well in capturing Goose Green and 1500 Args; the enemy must be more concerned with our troops on the ground than the ships, although there is the ever-present threat of Exocets to keep us alert and interested. We must by now have accounted for a significant proportion of their combat aircraft and they must be running short of pilots and spares. It is possible that the constant pressure on Stanley will result in a sudden, early Arg collapse, but they are probably counting on us not being able to flog all the way across East Falkland.

Discussion within the warfare team has also been about how many AM-39 Exocets the Args have and whether they can get hold of any more. The SCO said that the French would not officially sell them any now. We thought that there cannot be that many missiles available on the open market either; they are sophisticated weapons and are bound to be mustered and tracked wherever they go. However, some regimes might want to do us harm and could conceal missile transfers to Argentina, possibly through countries acting as middlemen.

Certainly, the Junta is making noises as if it wants to find a way out. Galtieri is speaking about the 'unequal struggle against the UK and the US'. I wonder if the Navy will mount a coup against the Army-led Junta, to stop the Left taking over after the war. Probably not is the answer, as the Navy's prestige will be damaged severely by their championing of this war and its subsequent inability – except for their Navy's Air Arm – to prevent the recapture of the Islands. I reckon that the Navy are saving their ships and people for the political vacuum that will occur afterwards though.

The Wardroom is, once again, becoming a battleground between those who want to win the war and go home and those who want to advance their careers. There are times when I think that I want to leave the RN. I love my job, but I just do not have the tolerance of or appetite for the petty politics and the manoeuvrings that are required to get simple things done. The most irritating aspect is the way in which anything which looks new or innovative is treated with suspicion and cynicism.

The *Daily Oak* and World Service said that Spain became a member of NATO today. Around the uckers board, we thought that should mean that they will be on their best behaviour with regard to Gibraltar and in dealing with any Arg sympathizers or operations in their country.

Monday, 31 May

Alleluja! Something is being done at last about the Arg radars. The glory-seeking Crabs had a go at the Westinghouse radar at Stanley with a Shrike anti-radiation missile (must have fallen off the back of an American lorry, guv). The radar still seems to be operating though.

We have been detached to South Georgia again because there has been an attack on a British tanker, *British Wye*, heading south and the powers that be believe that the ships transiting to – and based at – South Georgia need protection. That will really piss off *Endurance*! Still, it takes us away from the prime danger zone; that will please the ship's company.

Just after lunch today, we met *British Test*, which started following us. The Captain sent a signal across: 'Are you just curious, or would you like to come with us to South Georgia? You are very welcome.' There was no reply and the tanker suddenly turned to the west.

The weather is pretty challenging – from the west and south-west and mostly between 30 and 40 knots. We are regularly being slammed from astern.

Tuesday, 1 June

Last night was very rough, with a violent swell and 50-knot winds. The sea was breaking over the Bridge, hitting the foremast and falling onto the signal deck above our cabins. We have been transiting back to South Georgia, to act as guard ship to ensure that the Args do not attack our ships there or those merchant vessels in transit. We reckon that only the Arg Canberras and the Hercules have the legs to get there. The electronics and radar aerials have been breaking down regularly today because of the bad weather, and paint has been flaking off the bulkheads as the ship's structure has been stressed and twisted continuously.

The boys on the Flight spent the day conducting routine maintenance on the aircraft. I took the time to show LACMN Stapleton around the ship and the relevant personnel and we also chatted about how we should work together as a team, both with the Flight and in the back of the aircraft. He has fitted in really well, has a very personable nature and is clearly very competent in the role. We are lucky to have him. He in turn is pleased to have a change of scenery and glad to be away from the relative anonymity of a large squadron embarked in a carrier.

It seems that another Crab attack with a Shrike destroyed one of the Skyguard AA battery radars at Stanley yesterday. An Arg C-130 was splashed by a SHar and the 707 has been out and about.

Another Crab lost an 801 SHar today because he flew within the missile (probably a Roland) envelope somewhere near Stanley. I do not think that he was doing anything other than patrolling. Everyone knows the envelope and what the Args have available, so that was pretty careless and cavalier, I'd say. The Senior Pilot of 820 Sqn and his crew found him alive in the sea just now, having risked their lives close in to East Falkland to pick him up. He's a lucky bloke and I hope that he remembers who his friends are in the years ahead, especially in MOD.

A lot of officers are wondering why the Admiral has not taken a trip into the Islands to see for himself what conditions are like inshore and ashore, now that the campaign needs additional momentum and the winter is coming on quickly. Also, some people have remarked that General Moore chose a strange way to travel to war – on the QE2 – and SCO said that the ship did not have the secure communications for him to be able to keep abreast of events on the Falklands for about 10 days from Ascension. No wonder he was briefing and reading like billy-o on the way back from South Georgia and spent a lot of time on the secure communications.

We have just entered a large iceberg field about 90 miles north of South Georgia and the weather is still bad. Apparently, we steamed almost 10,000 miles in May.

Wednesday, 2 June

It's all right and '*Oh what a lovely war!*' for some. We arrived back at South Georgia, which is almost becoming a second home for us, to find that *Endurance* had really made themselves at home, with their Flight Commander out shooting reindeer from the Wasp and bringing them back to enhance their diet. We have been in harm's way and have lost people while the guys from *Endurance* are treating the whole thing like a holiday, complete with country sports. I am sure that their Captain and the Pusser must be pleased, but, bloody hell! Don't they know that there is a war on! In *Antrim*, we are on soup and pot mess every day and they are dining on – venison!

Over in the Falklands, people are now worried that the Args have transported MM38 Exocets to the Islands to be mounted on trucks and fired at our ships inshore. Safety arcs and no-go zones have been designated. The missiles are reported as coming from the A69 Class corvettes.

We have taken Mount Kent, to the west of Port Stanley and the Paras are consolidating around Goose Green and Darwin, holding about 1400 prisoners and discovering a large quantity of Arg napalm in 90 or so containers. Some Arg commandos who parachuted into East Falkland were taken out near Teal Inlet. Maj. Gen. Moore is now ashore with his headquarters and Brigadier Thompson is planning and executing the main thrust on Stanley. I wonder how they are getting on – Thompson will not be happy to have the glory taken off him now that he has done the hard bit.

Also, the *Bahia Paraiso* is in Port Stanley, in her guise as a hospital ship. Everyone in the operations team and I would bet good money that the Args have used her, quite illegally, to take in ammunition and troops as well. *Argonaut* is being patched up by *Stena Seaspread*, before heading home.

At 1030, we came to anchor at Husvik harbour, before starting a major transfer of stores and mail around the ships and ashore. *Endurance*, *Resource*, *Typhoon*, *Saxonia*, *Pict*, *Junella*, *Farnella* and *Cordella* were already in harbour.

I have decided to persist with the beard, as I am getting rather superstitious about it all. For the same reason and for the moment, we four always fly together as a crew on operational sorties.

The Captain and the Ops Officer went by *Endurance* Wasp to *Endurance* for lunch – not venison, as it happened.

Thursday, 3 June

We were at anchor in Husvik overnight and the wind suddenly blew very hard indeed, a steady 30–40 knots, to the extent that *Resource* dragged her anchor and had to shift her anchor berth before sunrise. This was inconvenient because the converted trawlers were shifting vast amounts of stores from *Saxonia* to *Resource* throughout the night.

Even though the weather was poor, we started lifting and shifting stores, ammunition and other items around for M Company ashore from 1030.

Antrim was under way by 1400 and went to patrol a box to seaward of the entrance to Stromness Bay.

Stewart and Stapleton spent two hours in the late afternoon on various lifting and transfer chores, before returning to find that honours and awards had been announced for the original operation at South Georgia.

The Captain sent for me and told me that I had been mentioned in despatches, whatever that means. When I came out, I found out that he had been given a DSO, as had Ian, and Stewart and Fitz had been mentioned in despatches too. The Navigator was pretty caustic about aviators getting all the awards, 'as usual', but all the officers came to have a celebratory drink in the Wardroom.

I am glad for Ian – a DSO is a serious honour for a Lieutenant

Commander – both because he led us well throughout the operation and because, as he says, it represents an honour for the whole Flight. The hell, it does – it's a personal award – and that is how it will be seen. Stewart pointed out that we all shared the same risks and contributed to the result. Either way, we were only doing our jobs and what anyone else would have done in the circumstances. The really important thing for me is that I am still the only Observer in the RN to have successfully attacked a submarine since 1945. Somehow, it is something concrete to hold on to for all the bullshit and the hours spent on anti-submarine exercises. I also have a reply for all those wankers from civilian life who say that the Services are a waste of money, because we are practising for something that will never happen.

I was less pleased to learn that the Flight Commander of *Endurance* had been awarded a DSC, but rationalized it on the basis that our lords and masters were trying to spread the honours around. Still, it irritates me intensely when people who talk themselves up – and frankly push their version of events out first – get the goodies.

However, I did ask myself at one point this evening what you have to do beyond a fairly hairy glacier rescue and the disablement of an enemy submarine to get a decent gong, but reflected that the best medal you can wear is your life. Posthumous awards are given to compensate the living; they are hardly of any use to the dead.

I have just heard that one of our Vulcans has had to divert to Brazil after running out of fuel and that our troops are now within eight miles of Port Stanley.

Friday, 4 June

Overnight, we had an uneventful patrol in our allocated air defence box, but had to dodge lots of icebergs, the biggest of which was calculated to be about one third the size of South Georgia!

During the forenoon, *Pearleaf* appeared and we replenished fuel from her in appalling conditions, with driving snow and sub-zero temperatures. There was drifting snow on the upper deck and the temperatures are well into the minus category, with the wind chill an additional factor.

Once again, we split the flying duties. Ian and I did a one hour 40 minute slot from 1200, while Stewart and Stapleton did two hours from

1530. It was the usual combination of load-lifting and transfers of mail and stores, around the ships and ashore.

We received mail today. A had sent me two cards dated 20 and 21 May, which wondered what we were up to, saying 'the whole thing could be happening right now'! Well, yes! We, as a Wardroom, also received a humorous card from the Gateway Building Society, congratulating us on what we had achieved and wishing us well.

It's quite extraordinary how much rubbish we read in the papers which arrive here about two weeks after the events that they describe. Not only are the reporters to blame, but also the ships themselves, some of which are desperate to jump into the limelight, regardless of the truth. We heard by signal of some officer in *Glamorgan* who had said how life in her was so hard in comparison with other ships. It sounds very silly, but that sort of thing – show-boating and glory-grabbing – really winds the sailors up in a big way. They are parochial and ship-centred at the best of times, but the war has intensified that sentiment considerably.

The remoteness of the Falklands has kept prying eyes away from the conflict and hermetically sealed the events as far as the outside world is concerned. The inability of reporters to send video or other live despatches home is useful for us. I have told my parents and A that they need not worry about anything they see on the TV because by the time that they see it, it will already have occurred a long time before. If something happens to me, they will hear from official channels long before they see it on the screen.

Also, the fact that all press releases have to be carried by communications managed by the ships means that we can approve and authorize what is said in their reports. Of course, this is done for operational security reasons, but, knowing the instinctive suspicion of the Service of the media in general and the tendency of journalists to go for a story to make their names, the temptation must be to interfere with and obstruct the 'nice to know' stuff, and protect what is perceived to be 'need to know'. I would have thought that, as the journalists are embarked in the same ships and are largely sharing the same dangers, they would have a healthy appreciation of the perils of giving away too much. The key thing is that we can, to an extent, suppress reports of bad news, while we have them on hand to report success.

There is one problem, though. If we maintain our policy of silence and controlled release of information, it allows the Args the opportunity to say what they like and other news outlets to speculate and make things up, to our detriment.

The general mood at the warfare and command briefings today was that the Args would continue to snipe at us even after we have captured Stanley, so some sort of force will have to stay down here for a few years, after the bulk of the Task Force has returned home. That standing force would be composed of ships that has not come out yet. Certainly, it would ease our problem if the Arg fleet would come out and be demolished by our SSNs in the next couple of weeks, but I do not see that happening. If they cannot be induced to intervene to prevent the loss of the Falklands, they are not going to participate in a 'death ride' to destruction. In any case, when it is all over, the Navy grandees will want to have a solid base on which to base any bid for political power in the in-fighting and inter-Service recriminations that are sure to follow.

Intelligence suggested today that the Args have acquired SAN-7 surface-to-air missiles, and possibly Exocets, as well as MATRA air-to-air missiles from the Peruvians. Our Vulcan that diverted to Brazil yesterday has been released after being disarmed (Shrike missile, I think).

Our food is still fairly spartan and the celery soup is still performing to empty houses. I do not seem to be losing weight though, as the food we do get is high in calories, based on bread, rolls and sandwiches. I have not seen so much as a tomato, vegetable or mulligatawny soup since 17 March, 79 days ago.

We have just heard on the radio that the Args have claimed to have sunk *Invincible* for the third time. It really is incredible that they think that their people believe this sort of thing. We saw some news on video tape today, which had a scene from Argentina in which people were emotionally and theatrically giving up their jewellery to support the war effort. I would bet that the proceeds will be finding their way into some private Junta accounts in some shady corner of the world.

The *Daily Scum* reported an infestation of crabs in the South Atlantic, not an allusion to the increasing number of RAF down here, but the fact that the ship's intakes are being fouled by them close inshore. One specimen, reported as 'two feet long', was extracted from a strainer and had three stokers running for cover. There also seem to be some squid-like creatures, which were identified by MEA French. How did he know what they were? 'Well,' he said, 'they had eight testicles!'

Another important issue has emerged. We were kindly sent 50 pounds' worth of boiled sweets and 50 copies of *Penthouse* in the last mail by some well-wishers. The only problem is one of distribution and what constitutes fair shares for all. The Commander has put the Padre – as he has responsibility for monitoring morale – in charge of dealing with the issue.

We are due to be at sea overnight.

Saturday, 5 June

After another uneventful night for the ship, we came to anchor this forenoon at 1030 off King Edward Point, primarily so that we could take down machinery and systems for maintenance, but also so that we could take stores from *Saxonia*. The aircraft is also down for in-depth planned maintenance and some long-overdue component changes.

About a month ago, the NAAFI organized some *Antrim* 'Falkland Islands Spearhead Group' T-shirts. These have now arrived and are for sale. I have sent two off to A.

After the hectic action of the past two months, things are starting to drag. I hope that we will not have to spend the summer down here – that would be the pits. I have a feeling that it will not be too long before we are on our way home, though, for various reasons, the greatest of which is that I believe Port Stanley will fall very soon.

Meanwhile, the Paras and the Royal Marines are trying to race each other to Stanley, it seems. You just get the feeling in the tone and content of the signals – mainly in the logic and justification of what is being proposed to take the land campaign forward. It is above my level of responsibility, but I also notice a tension or rivalry between the way in which Brigadier Thompson (3 Commando Brigade) and Brigadier Wilson (5 Brigade) are conducting operations. It seems to have become a bit competitive and I wonder whether the command arrangements are entirely satisfactory. Similarly, 2 Para seems to get all the publicity, after Goose Green, and 3 Para just seems to get on with it. The Royal Marines, as you would expect, are moving forward remorselessly and doing the business, with huge packs and on foot.

2 Para now have a new Commanding Officer, a Lt Col Chaundler, who apparently parachuted into the action from 25,000 feet out of a Hercules. That's quite gutsy, I'd say.

The Brazilians are still hanging on to the Vulcan and Argentina is trying to obtain Exocets and Gabriel missiles from Iraq, Pakistan, Libya, France, Israel and Italy.

Meanwhile, the South Atlantic Fund has passed £1.5m, including £500,000 from the Cayman Islands. In *Antrim*, we have enough money for a guide dog and are now trying to sponsor another before we get back, if only for Chief Bullingham's sake.

People are beginning to notice that I receive more mail than anyone else in the Wardroom and the Commander has suggested that I should pay more on my Mess bill because of the distances involved and the space taken up on the supply ships.

I went ashore to have a look around Grytviken.

We are due to remain at anchor overnight.

Sunday, 6 June

Overnight, a solid ring of ice formed around the ship on the surface of the sea and we had a layer of snow on the upper deck.

> The ice was here, the ice was there,
> The ice was all around:
> It cracked and growled, and roared and howled,
> Like noises in a swound.

I am not sure what a 'swound' is though!

The clearance of snow from the upper deck is becoming a daily chore for the part of ship hands. In addition, this forenoon saw numerous snow-ball fights between the various parts of the ship. Initially, the boats party started on the ROs. They then combined to pelt the Flight, who then engaged the services of the quarterdeck hands to retaliate. The ROs then decided, using the advantage of height up on the signal deck and Gun Direction Platform, that it was a good idea to lob snowballs onto the focsle where the gunners were working part of ship. Bad idea! The gunners then took the battle to the enemy with some vigour, by assaulting the signal deck with large quantities of snowballs and employing a fire hose to spray the ROs and boats party. It was all good fun and the part of ship Petty Officers put an end to it at that point. Moral of the story – before you start something, think how it will end and – leave the gunners alone!

The ship sailed at 1000, just as we started a ground run on 406 to test the systems that had been replaced the previous day. Later in the afternoon, at 1600, we flew a surface search patrol to the north to plot the extent of the ice along the north coast and picked up one of our Chiefs (C Mech Tooley), who had been loaned to *Endurance*. We are still very much engaged in patrolling and escorting to make sure that the Args do not attack the merchant ships that are being used to ferry supplies through to East Falkland.

I wrote a number of letters today: one to A's parents, one to Ann and two to some primary school children in Portsmouth. We are actually rationed to four sheets of writing paper a day. The Commander has detailed all the officers off to write personally to the children. The letters from the children were charming; I dealt with one each from a boy and a girl. The boy said that he hoped that we 'were having a good time on our cruise and that we were not dead yet'. He added at the end: 'I heard my mum say that she really fancies sailors.' The girl said that she was really worried about us and asked us to make sure 'that the penguins did not get hurt'. Declan had to reply to a letter saying that the child's mum would be really happy to have an officer in the ship as a pen-friend! He is thinking about using a pen-name!

I also wrote to A containing the usual stuff about not being home until about 26 days (at least) after Stanley has fallen and expressing the hope that by the time the letter got home, we would actually be on our way. I must say that the gap between things happening and mail arriving in the UK is frustrating. It is difficult to give anyone our news and stories – not only because it involves classified information, but also because most things have usually been reported long before the letters arrive – so it is difficult to avoid platitudinous twaddle and to think up different ways of saying that you love and miss someone.

In almost all her letters, A is mentioning starting a family. This has been an issue for some time and she is very motivated in that direction. Her instincts are probably correct that the moment is now right. Although I do not want to tempt fate in thinking about the future, we will probably go for it and, after all this time down here, I am pretty keen to do my bit in that regard!

The ship went back to its patrol box overnight. We heard this evening that the likelihood is that when we return to the UK, we will have a month's Assisted Maintenance Period, followed by two weeks' trials and an immediate return to the South Atlantic. The Captain's decision was that we would not share that information with the ship's company just yet. I am sure that the buzz will get around the ship, even though the signal was coded for decryption by the SCO alone.

Monday, 7 June

Two tugs, *Yorkshireman* and *Salvageman*, arrived this forenoon along with RFA *Stromness*. We replenished fuel from *Pearleaf* and by 1300 were back in Cumberland Bay for a major Damage Control exercise. More lessons were applied and modifications made in the light of our recent experience. It is interesting that much of our previous training in this area has been proved as valid, but not all of it. We have also inadvertently discarded some age-old experience and lessons over the years. I am not sure how the Sea Training system is going to cope with people returning from the South Atlantic: 'I hear what you are saying, but it was not like that for real'!

At Sea Training, we practise our full Damage Control, including chemical defence, drills by closing the ship down completely. Throughout a major proportion of the ship, all external hatches and doors, with airtight seals, are tightly shut and an over-pressure induced in the ship to keep any potential chemical agents out. Entry and exit into what is known as the citadel would be through air locks and all exposed personnel on the upper deck – gun crews, Flight Deck personnel and other essential personnel – have to wear top-to-toe special protective NBCD suits and respirators. We also have a system that pumps seawater through nozzles to produce a spray that engulfs the whole ship in the event of chemical contamination or nuclear fallout.

The problem is that you have to go to Action Stations and go to Damage Control State 1, condition ZULU ALFA, the highest readiness state, and the whole process takes about three hours, with the upper-deck crews in NBCD suits and respirators for another two hours after that. It is all very necessary, but the boys tend to get bored, fed up and uncomfortable.

When I was in HMS *London*, we had one of these serials. I was the Missile/Gun Director Visual up on the Gun Direction Platform, supervising those dozen or so ratings who provided visual indication and allocation of targets to the gun and missile systems. At the time, a few years ago, training staff would employ a Fast Patrol Boat to speed around closed-down ships to test the airtight integrity of their citadels and the drills of the upper-deck personnel, by enveloping the target ship in a swathe of CS or other inconvenient gas. This aspect provided an incentive to get it right.

We did all our communications and systems checks within the first 20 minutes and 'stood to' in case we were subject to simulated attacks by aircraft and ships. I knew what my boys were thinking – only four hours and 40 minutes to go and two of those in respirators. So time for some leadership! We set up a quiz – with professional, general knowledge and topical questions – with competitive rounds every 15 minutes, while Chippy and team went around checking the door seals, nozzles and pipes which engineers find so endlessly fascinating.

Before long, the ship was pronounced ready and on went the respirators. Just two hours to go! After about 40 minutes, we saw the FPB coming in for its attack and everyone checked and adjusted their protective clothing. All our guns and missiles swung into action, but, of course, the FPB kept coming on because we were not actually firing anything. In the absence of live rounds, the gunners were supposed to go 'BANG, BANG, BANG' or 'RAT-A-TAT-TAT' (depending on the calibre) or, more modishly, 'DAGGA-DAGGA-DAGGA', although this was normally associated with the Fleet Air Arm or RAF – and thus considered, by the hard-nosed gunners, somewhat effete and possibly effeminate.

Anyway, on came the FPB and the destroyer manoeuvred hard under us, but we were still covered in gas. I intuitively checked the seal around my respirator, as the gas came on, and could not help making out through the gloop that AB ('Chuck') Norris was on his back, with his body arching and twitching violently. He's having a fit or a reaction to the gas, I thought, and went over to him, realizing that any first aid might expose him – or me – to the gas.

So I went to the intercom and shouted down to the command team in the Ops Room that we needed to suspend the serial. The trouble is that with a respirator on 'Stop the serial, stop the serial, we have a casualty' sounds, as I was subsequently told, very much like '*Shtong the squirrel, shtong the squirrel, ee aye acker salty.*' After several failed attempts to communicate, I pressed an alarm bell, the serial was interrupted and the ship sailed clear of the miasmic cloud.

'This had better not be a false alarm,' I heard the Captain muttering over the intercom.

Once the gas was clear, I returned to Norris who by this time was standing up and back at his station. I ordered the men to take their respirators off and asked Norris: 'Are you OK?'

'Fine, sir, how about you?' came the reply.

'What was happening with you on the deck just now? Were you ill?'

'No, sir.'

'Well, what about all the lying on your back and writhing?'

By this time, the Doc and the first aid team had arrived. This seemed to galvanize and encourage Norris.

'Sir, I'm OK. What happened was that I knew that we would be closed up for ages, so I had a load of Opal Fruits unwrapped inside my respirator. I had eaten all of them, but then I realized that I had a last one stuck down in the filter at the bottom of my mask. Lying on my back was the only way I could get it flicked into my mouth.'

That Opal Fruit cost me an extra duty weekend as Officer of the Day!

We are going back to sea overnight.

Tuesday, 8 June

We have had a quarter to half an inch of ice on all the upper decks today and the temperature has been well below 0 degrees C, amid freezing rain and hail.

The *Daily Oak* contained an *Observer* article that it claimed came from a letter home from a member of *Antrim*'s ship's company, describing the exploits of the 'Grey Ghost', as everyone now call us, 'because no one knows where the hell we are'. Other snippets are: 'It's a hard life on here, but, if it keeps us alive, that's all right by me' and (fortunately) 'morale is bloody good on board. Typical *Antrim* – water rationing with a tanker with 20,000 tons onboard next to us and blokes getting picked up for haircuts. They can't crack us.'

I am not sure about the water tanker bit, but the Commander has certainly been consistently rigorous in maintaining – and Commander S in enforcing – high standards. After all, as the Commander has continued to intone, 'You cannot go to war in a pig-sty.' I recall Adam

Smith said: 'Nothing is more useful than water, but it will purchase scarce anything; scarce anything can be had in exchange for it.'

We patrolled our air defence box today. *Wimpey Seahorse* arrived from Ascension with mail for us. She is here to establish mooring buoys at Leith, Stromness, Grytviken and Husvik, because there are so few suitable anchorage points in these harbours.

This evening, we heard that a Liberian tanker, the *Hercules*, had been bombed by an unidentified aircraft, 400 miles north of the Falkland Islands, and is listing. It is heading for the nearest port. That would be the Arg Hercules, ironically, given the name of the vessel, with his patent 'roll the bombs out the back' approach. They are sloppy!

I wrote to A explaining that there appeared to be a lull in the fighting while the land forces readied themselves for the final assault on Stanley. I said that I thought that as soon as the land forces attack Stanley 'it would be over in a day' and that the Args seemed terrified at the idea of the Gurkhas – 'kukris and all'.

What else did I say? 'It's somewhat quieter for us, although we're still rather wary of the two Arg submarines which are left and of which we have seen neither hide nor hair.'

It seems to me – and I wrote to A on these lines – that once Stanley has fallen, ships will start to go home for refit and leave, because the Admiral will have more ships then than he needs to cope with the maritime threat. Anyway, the ships are really running into the ground, what with the demands of combat and the continuously foul weather. Poor old *Alacrity* is pretty much clapped out and on her way home, despite Chris Craig's valiant attempts to stay and finish the job.

If the Args are going to continue the fight after Stanley has fallen, I suspect that they will find their airfields so much debris and their fleet at the bottom of the sea, especially if we extend the runway at Stanley to take Phantoms and other high-performance aircraft. Incidentally, *Norland* is returning 1,000 Arg prisoners from Goose Green back via Uruguay. Why are we giving back fighting men, who could be turned round to fight us again? There is an unconfirmed report that Argentina has bought 24 new Daggers, as well as Exocets at £600,000 each.

Just now, I heard that *Plymouth* in San Carlos and two SIR Class landing ships have been bombed, but we have no news of damage or casualties yet.

I went down to the Ops Room and it appears that *Plymouth* was in or around San Carlos and was bounced by a number of Mirages. She was struck by a couple of bombs, one of which went through her mortar well and detonated a depth charge. She has boiler, 4.5 gun and structural damage too.

The attack on the LSLs, *Sir Tristram* and *Sir Galahad*, sounds a lot more serious; they were in the vicinity of Fitzroy and the Welsh Guards were still onboard *Galahad* when she was hit by bombs that exploded. Why were they there on their own? There are casualties, but we do not know how many.

Wednesday, 9 June

We patrolled offshore all day and then went into Cumberland Bay for stores, mail and personnel transfer.

News is still coming in about the attack on *Sir Galahad* and *Sir Tristram* and there are indications that we have had heavy loss of life. For some reason, somebody thought that it would be a good idea to offload troops in broad daylight. All sorts of stories are emerging that, together, add up to a considerable cock-up. The Welsh Guards stayed onboard *Sir Galahad* for five hours in daylight in full view of the Args, on the hilltops a few miles away, before the aircraft attacks happened. I suspect that their (brigade or battalion) commander thought that, as there had not been any raids for a while, they would be safe to just hang around. Our experiences in San Carlos would have told him otherwise. The imperative on D-day was to get the troops and equipment off the ships as soon as possible. What makes this all so sickening is that not one soldier was killed and not one landing ship was hit when we were protecting them 21–23 May while we were in San Carlos, along with the other escorts. Where were the escorts for *Sir Galahad* and *Sir Tristram*? Why did we not have decent air defence set up before the ships arrived – Rapier?

The Args had to know that the ships were there. They went straight for Fitzroy and Bluff Cove – with no preliminary recce – and dropped their bombs on the first pass. That meant that they either had signal intelligence or an Arg army patrol or OP had tipped them off. In that case, the raid that hit *Plymouth* was probably a diversionary attack to distract – and attract – the CAP and the air defence ships in and around San Carlos.

Another seemingly contributory factor – and in the signals the Army were quite proud of this as an example of initiative – would appear to be that someone in the Army telephoned ahead – on the Falkland Islands telephone system – to the settlement at Bluff Cove or Fitzroy to ask if there were any Args there. On being told no, the officer said something like 'we'll be seeing you soon'. Why would you do that? The Args have spent several years repressing their own people and it is inconceivable that they would not have been monitoring the telephone system, if only to keep tabs on what the Islanders were saying to each other. It would have been all right to exploit that for deceptive purposes, but to hand them intelligence about our future plans like that is just plain stupid.

I remember speaking to officers in the Welsh Guards in QE2 at South Georgia, none of whom at the time seemed to know what they were going to be doing when they reached the Falklands. I also got the impression that they really did not appreciate how bad the conditions would be ashore – the survival challenges, the boggy, unforgiving landscape and the extreme distances involved. Some seemed to have enjoyed 'the cruise' down and seemed to have had little mental preparation for precisely what lay ahead.

One said, 'We are going to be garrison troops; we won't be going into the frontline straightaway.'

I said, 'I wouldn't count on it. We haven't won yet – nowhere near it. The Paras and Royal Marines have been hard at it for a while now and are already suffering from fatigue, the cold and the conditions.'

He said, 'You don't need to worry about it, old boy' – he actually said 'old boy'. 'We know what we are doing; you can leave the soldiering to us. You sailor chaps (!) just need to get us there safely and keep the aircraft off our backs.'

Well, yes!

Talking to the 5 Brigade staff officers onboard *Antrim*, who all seemed like decent men, there did not seem to have been much planning about how their Brigade was going to integrate with what was going on already. It all had an air of just pushing more infantry up to the frontline in the manner of the First World War in the hope that more troops would create overwhelming odds.

It appears that some cabs from 825 Squadron were nearby and did absolutely brilliantly, amid exploding ammunition and subsequent air raids, in rescuing survivors from both ships. I wonder who was involved? Almost certainly, it would have been some of my old chums from 826 Squadron, who mostly went to be instructors on 706, which became 825.

I received a very good introduction to life on a frontline squadron in 826. It was full of highly professional and experienced aviators and a particularly energetic bunch of spirited young pilots and observers. Well led by successive Commanding Officers, who believed that their people should work hard and play hard, and a Senior Pilot and Senior Observer who were entirely in sympathy, we had gregarious, outward-going personalities at every level and we competed with anyone and everyone, while we trained, exercised and played from one end of the NATO area to the other.

Typical of the spirit and vigour of the squadron is this episode from our time in *Bulwark* in 1980.

Bulwark was an old carrier that had been converted to take helicopters and Royal Marines. It normally contained 550 marines (a Commando), their vehicles and equipment, together with enough Wessex or Sea King 4s to lift them, as well as a resident anti-submarine squadron (826), with Sea King 2s.

It was always a ritual in 826 to congregate in the Wardroom ante-room, by the bar, on the evening that a newly embarked Royal Marines Commando arrived, ostensibly to welcome the officers onboard, encourage co-operation and foster friendly relations. In reality, it was an ownership issue – we were not going to let 'Roger Royal' take over our bar.

There were two electric fans, shaped like horizontal propellers, each with four blades, fitted to the deckhead [ceiling], one of which was by the bar, while its twin was mounted diagonally opposite on the far side of the ante-room about 20 feet away. The fan near the bar, for obvious reasons, was painted – just like the oars at Oxford – in our squadron colour of navy blue, together with a perky white seahorse with the trident on each of the blades. The other fan was not decorated; it simply spun around – fast.

The usual routine was for us to get the party under way and after about half an hour, once the junior Royals had had a few beers, we would select a few of our number to start the entertainment.

The first contestant would be lifted up in order to insert his head between the blades of the spinning 826 fan. The blades were slightly canted, so the edge of the blade did not make direct contact. On contact between his head and one of the blades, the fan would stop momentarily, and the injured and dazed aviator would fall onto the deck as the fan resumed its familiar motion. He would then roll around and groan, clutching his head as if in suppressed agony. The second contestant would repeat the routine, but would stop the fan and dismount apparently none the worse for wear. All the while, Royal would be watching this performance and, confident that aircrew were just a bunch of fairies, was gradually reaching the conclusion that anything they can do, we can do better. By the time that the third 826 candidate had been felled by his encounter with the blue fan, the Royals could not contain themselves any more. An enthusiastic crowd of junior Royals would mass under the other fan, firmly encouraged by their seniors not to be outdone by a bunch of bloody aircrew. Everyone a winner!

Up went the first Royal (Splat! Crunch!), only to be catapulted, dazed and discomfited onto the nearest Wardroom sofa. Then a second (Splat! Bounce! Bump!), then a third (Splat! Brave attempt to stay standing, then crumple!), who together made up a small heap of Royals, legs and arms akimbo, none of whom seemed to have realized, between minor concussion and the beer, quite what had hit them. At this point, another squadron officer put his head in the blue fan, stopped it, walking nonchalantly back to his beer with no obvious damage, and this only served to enrage and frustrate the Royals further. Up went another Lieutenant – splat! Scratch one more Royal! Ha, ha, ha!

At this point, we usually got the CO or Senior Pilot to say enough's enough; you're almost as tough as us, but, perhaps with a bit of practice, you might get better. This had the inevitable result as two more Junior Joe Royals were fed into the machine. Splat! Crump! Splat! Crump! They fell among the growing band of semi-conscious Marines, who had unmistakeable signs of their close encounters with the fan across their foreheads. As we did not reciprocate, apart from laughing until we cried, they decided to call it a day, silently fizzing away and vowing to get on equal terms as they continued to drink with us. The ship's officers enjoyed the spectacle as interested spectators, perhaps reflecting on the wise decision that had led each one of them not to be either an aviator or a Royal Marine. Round one to 826 – who owns this bar?

Now, of course, it should have been apparent to the meanest intelligence, but not to Royal, that there was an essential difference between our fan (we had home advantage after all) and their beast. One of the advantages of being in the Fleet Air Arm is that you have access to large numbers of talented, intelligent air engineering ratings, who are very resourceful and know how things work. The simple truth was that our boys had rigged the squadron fan so that the motor could be stopped by the slightest resistance, while the other had been powered up to its full capacity this side of serious injury and decapitation. In the land of the blind . . . !

Of course, it did not take even Royal too long to find out about this asymmetric advantage and they surreptitiously had the motors switched and challenged us to a re-match when we were next alongside. Unfortunately, they had returned some tools which they had borrowed to the shipwright's workshop, along with the precise instructions they had sought on how to swap over the various components. The stewards – Royal did not realize that some of them were squadron personnel – also told us about what had happened.

Re-enter our trusty maintainers to fit variable rate switches to both fans so that their speed could be adjusted by switches behind the bar. The job done, we had a couple of surreptitious check tests of the equipment, by clearing the Wardroom on the pretext of a top secret briefing on Soviet submarine signatures.

Once alongside and after the obligatory cocktail party, the challenge began. First of all, the Royals demanded that we swap fans. We said that our fan needed a special technique if people were not to get hurt. They assessed that we were bluffing and insisted we went first on their fan. With the fan adjusted, Stan Burgess easily stopped it and smiling walked back to his beer. This caused some confusion among the Royals, but their first man gamely marched over to the squadron fan, which promptly floored him as he attempted to stop it with his head. They then wanted to swap again ('Make up your minds, guys!), which we did ('Are you sure?'), with the same result. Not surprisingly, the entertainment level in the Wardroom was rising in proportion to the Royal Marines' inability to figure out how it was that we were walking away unscathed. They were not happy! One last round saw 'Spiv' Taylor do the honours for us, but he at least had the decency – and the cheek – to pretend that it had hurt. The next Royal was duly pole-axed and their CO decided that enough was enough – 'Let's play Mess rugby!' was his suggestion. That's a moral victory for us then!

We worked hard and played hard on 826 and, probably as a result, we were incredibly good at finding submarines of any nationality, UK, US or Soviet, which was, after all, our purpose in life. Our ship *Bulwark* knew that and just about tolerated our 'trophy nights' and other antics during Mess Dinners, which were terrific fun, but entirely corrosive of the usual order of things. But, operationally and as a cohesive, vibrant unit, we were very good and we had a lot of fun. Most of the aircrew and maintainers are spread around the various squadrons down here and heading south. That has to be a good thing and the Args better watch out!

Intelligence suggests that arms for Argentina have been intercepted in Luxemburg and that the Args are getting Mirage external fuel tanks from South Africa, in crates marked up as 'tractor spares' bound for Peru and Uruguay.

It is good that President Reagan is paying a state visit to Britain at the moment. It shows solidarity with us. He spoke to both Houses of Parliament and the Queen mentioned Argentina's 'naked aggression' in her speech at the State Banquet.

Thursday, 10 June

Overnight, the weather conditions offshore were severe, but the ship remained at sea for most of the day. All of us flew a delivery service around the various ships 1130–1230 and Ian and I did a one hour 45 loadlifting serial of 25 loads of food from *Stromness* to *Antrim* from 1640. We received some port and also – amazingly, at last – some chocolate and other nutty for sale in the NAAFI canteen.

We received details of the *Tristram/Galahad* attack today. It started with the World Service at 0400 and 0500 stating that the losses were worse than had been first thought. That sounded ominous. The scale of losses – of people – then appeared. It was horrendous, particularly among the Welsh Guards. In all, it looks as if we have lost about 50 men, almost all Guardsmen and about the same number of wounded.

From the signal traffic, it is difficult to determine exactly what happened. My detached view is that there seems to have been too many moving parts in trying to leap-frog the Scots Guards and Welsh Guards forward and the move was planned and executed on the hoof, on a whim and with insufficient coordination.

The problem, I suppose, is that our ships are too vulnerable close inshore during the day and they need half the night to steam to and from the Task Group, where they can sit under top cover from SHars and share the combined gun, missile and chaff resources of everyone else.

The BBC World Service is more or less continuous, when we have the right atmospherics, with updates every hour, always preceded by 'Lillibullero'. It is really inspiring to hear that stirring theme, from thousands of miles away, its volume rising and falling depending on the atmospheric interference, with its worldwide reach, its authoritative tone and faint sense of imperial longing. We are not too sure, though, of the extent to which the BBC is positively supporting the British campaign; the chat in the Wardroom is that the service, paid for by the taxpayer, is being even-handed and 'objective' to the point of allowing the Arg case to have a moral and political equivalence to our own. Leading democracy plays vile dictatorship – we should at least expect the crowd to be cheering for us!

We stayed at sea overnight in an Anti-Aircraft Warfare posture. We reckon that the Args have lost 81 aircraft to our eight SHars and Harriers.

The news tonight advertised the government's resolve to hold the Islands once we had captured them and reported that the rail unions were going to strike on 27 June. The National Union of Railwaymen's President said, 'The whole future of the industry is at stake. We are going down the plughole. This is a fight to decide.' I think that the survivors from the ships sunk out here will be really pleased to find that they cannot get home by rail when they arrive back in the UK!

Also, there were reports of the maltreatment of the Falkland Islanders by the Args – shot sheep, people confined, destruction of property and wanton looting. We are worried about the Islanders in the ever-decreasing Arg area of control around Stanley.

Friday, 11 June

Regent came in from the west this forenoon. We replenished from *Pearleaf*, during which Stewart and Stapleton took the Commander and Commander W to *Endurance* for a planning meeting ('the South Georgia Development Committee'). It was all about the facilities to be provided ashore for the garrison and what needed to be done about the *Santa Fé*, which is gradually decaying and sinking at its berth, full to the fin with water and packed with live torpedoes. All of us manned up so

33. Humphrey flown by Ian Stanley, with the author sitting at the cargo
door, during a load-lifting sortie.

34. Two Antarctic Teal
ducks during their twice-
daily swim in the officers'
bath, while en route
from South Georgia to
Ascension Island, and
then to a zoo in England.

35. Sea King
helicopters transferring
personnel, equipment
and stores between
ships of the Task Force
(including here HMS
Intrepid and *Hermes*) on
19 May 1982, ahead of
the main landings at
San Carlos Water.

36. A Wessex V (*right*) and Humphrey (*left*) onboard HMS *Antrim* on 20 May 1982, shortly before the SBS insertion and attack on Fanning Head, the first assault landings on the Falklands.

37. SS *Canberra* unloading in San Carlos Water on 21 May 1982, escorted by HMS *Plymouth*.

38. One of *Antrim*'s life rafts damaged by cannon fire from an Argentinian Mirage on 21 May.

39. A tight squeeze – manoeuvring the helicopter into the hangar.

40. A Sea Cat missile is fired from HMS *Antrim* against an incoming aircraft.

41. HMS *Ardent* is crippled by air attack on 21 May 1982, with HMS *Yarmouth* providing assistance alongside.

42. HMS *Fearless* under way in San Carlos Water on 21 May, with one of her landing craft (Utility) in the foreground.

43. The hole in the port Sea Slug missile flash door, behind the launcher, made by the Argentinian 1,000 lb bomb that did not detonate, on 21 May 1982.

44. The path taken by the unexploded bomb through the Sea Slug magazine bulkhead, with Lieutenant Kevin White.

45. HMS *Antrim* in San Carlos Water in the early afternoon of 21 May 1982. Action damage from aircraft cannon can be seen on the ship's side under the hangar and Flight Deck.

46. The scene on HMS *Antrim*'s Flight Deck shortly after an attack by an Argentinian Mirage on the morning of 21 May 1982. The folded helicopter has been strafed by cannon and fire-fighting foam has been laid to neutralize fuel pouring from the aircraft's fuel tanks. The two figures at the centre are Ian Stanley (*with back to camera*) and the author.

47. *Antrim*'s Flight Deck in the afternoon of 21 May 1982, during a lull in air attacks in San Carlos Water. Equipment is in place to remove the unexploded bomb through a hole cut in the deck; improvised sheer legs and lifting gear are clearly visible, as well as a cargo trolley. Stewart Cooper is the figure in anti-flash hood and flying overalls walking towards the camera.

48. Sea King helicopters load-lifting 5 Infantry Brigade equipment and stores from the QE2 at South Georgia, 27 May 1982.

49. Celebrations in *Antrim*'s Wardroom to mark honours and awards for the ship's Commanding Officer and the aircrew, from left to right: Stewart Cooper, Captain Brian Young, Ian Stanley and the author.

50. Humphrey returns to Fortuna Glacier on 18 June 1982 to recover abandoned SAS equipment and weapons from the two crashed Wessex Vs.

51. The site of the crash of Wessex V YA during the 18 June return trip by Humphrey in less turbulent conditions.

52. Humphrey lifting a replacement gyro unit onto the Bridge roof, June 1982.

53. Humphrey's Falklands Battle Honours, denoting one submarine 'kill', two medical evacuations, two special forces missions, twenty rescued SAS personnel and aircrew (Fortuna), three rescued SAS men from an inflatable boat and two men overboard from HMS *Conqueror*.

54. The 100-mile charity relay run around the upper deck on 4 July 1982.

55. HMS *Antrim*'s 'Folklands Evening' and Grand Falklands draw and BBQ on the Flight Deck on 6 July 1982.

56. The celebratory Mess Dinner in the Wardroom (*with the author in the centre*), heading north, 3 July 1982.

57. HMS *Antrim* passes NATO warships and HMS *Victory* on her return to Portsmouth on 17 July 1982.

59. Ian Stanley and Chris Parry show off the ceremonial battle ensign from ARA *Santa Fé*.

58. *Antrim* passing the Round Tower at the entrance to Portsmouth Harbour.

60. *Antrim* Flight aircrew – Ian Stanley, Stewart Cooper, the author and David Fitzgerald – at the Fleet Air Arm Museum in 2008, during the filming of the National Geographic TV documentary *Helicopter Wars*.

61. Humphrey at the Fleet Air Arm Museum, Royal Naval Air Station, Yeovilton.

that the pilots could have some instrument flying practice and we did surface search for an hour and a half.

The ship nosed into Cumberland Bay at 1315 and moved around a racetrack, while Ian and I helped position a 4.5 gun barrel in the turret.

Geestport arrived this evening, amid driving snowstorms and blizzards.

In the Falklands, a Sea King 4 from 845 Squadron fired two AS-12 missiles at General Menendez's HQ building this morning, but we have not heard about results. That will not be good for his morale!

One of the really frustrating things is that we have bombarded the airfield at Stanley with what I reckon must be a couple of hundred bombs and countless NGS rounds and we have still not managed to put it out of action. As far as I can judge, the Args are still flying in and out. Part of the reason must be that it is too dangerous to put our ships close enough in to interdict the traffic. Another must be that the Arg Westinghouse area radar enables them to see when our CAPs are out and about, and where they are, and the supply aircraft are routed around, in time and space. What I cannot understand either is why the Args did not extend the runway at Stanley to enable their A4s and Mirages to operate from there; they knew that we were coming and had plenty of time to fix it. That would have really given us a serious problem. Perhaps inter-Service issues and coordination prevented the issue even being discussed.

We are expecting a big push towards Stanley tonight, with *Glamorgan* going in to help with shore bombardment.

There was another typically wooden signal of encouragement today from the Admiral, to the land forces: 'On this, the eve of your main battle, we afloat share your hopes and determination for a swift and successful outcome. May your aim be true. See you in Port Stanley.' It's straight out of a 'penny dreadful'!

Stewart seems to be sleeping rather a lot at the moment and we discovered that he had a huge hoard of 'nutty' hidden in his cabin. Ian remarked that Stewart has more time off than Rip van Winkle's bunk light!

Saturday, 12 June

On AAWC, at about 0640, we heard a strangled cry that 'Call sign J had been overflown by a hostile 10 miles south of [indecipherable]'. It turned out that *Glamorgan* had been hit by a shore-based Exocet this morning, after supporting 45 Commando in its attack on Two Sisters.

This has resulted in ships being withdrawn from close inshore, although *Active*, *Arrow*, *Avenger* and *Yarmouth* are scheduled to go in and bombard Arg positions in support of the land assault and advance tonight.

Antrim has spent the day in Cumberland Bay. We have had a good, varied day's flying today. Firstly, we spent an hour and a half this forenoon helping change the barrels on the 4.5 gun. We collected the specialist lifting gear from *Regent* and returned the barrel we had removed yesterday. We also brought a new barrel back to the ship, to be prepared for installation.

In the afternoon, we went well offshore and completed a full simulated ASW 'Jumpex', which tested our procedures, techniques and equipment while operating the sonar and Flight Control System. It kept the pilots in date for routine operations and we practised simulated emergencies as well.

I do not understand why *Glamorgan* did not stay outside the known Exocet danger area, which had been marked clearly on our Ops Room office map, the GOP and all of our displays. Looking at the reported position of the engagement, it seems to me that she took a short cut across the south-western corner of the danger zone. She must have been in a hurry to get somewhere, but surely nothing justified hazarding the ship in the face of a known threat – and an Exocet at that. She was lucky to survive – if the missile had penetrated the Sea Slug magazine, it would have been all over. There is a suggestion that she was turning hard to port at the time and the missile hit the upper deck outside the hangar. Even so, she was lucky to survive and it says a lot for the traditional construction of this type of ship that she did. In fact, once she had the fire under control, she steamed away without assistance.

It did hit the hangar, though, and the fuel in 'Willie' exploded, completely destroying the helicopter and killing six of the Flight maintainers, as well as the aircrewman, Colin Vickers, and the Flight Deck Officer. Three others were seriously injured. The three aircrew officers had just made their way forward for breakfast and escaped the blast.

Although every loss is a tragedy, the death of Colin Vickers is a tremendous shock to me. He was the best aircrewman I had flown with up to now and had helped me a lot while I was going through flying training. Calm, professional and a thoroughly decent man, he was a terrific operator, with a fine sense of purpose and humour. When I heard that he was coming back to sea from 737 Squadron staff, I quickly phoned Draftee to see if he could allocate him to us in *Antrim*. He said that he had only that morning assigned Colin Vickers to *Glamorgan* and Fitz to *Antrim*. I did not know Fitz at the time. So, despite the fact that Fitz has been terrific and a really good companion and an excellent operator, whom I have come to admire, like and know really well during our time together, it's ironic how it has turned out. Life depends so much on such small margins of chance and timings – or is it destiny?

The land forces are preparing carefully for their final assaults on the hills around Stanley, where most of the Arg troops seem to be dug in. We now have and hold Mount Longdon, Two Sisters and Mount Harriet. Like everyone else, we are expecting a major coordinated attack by our forces – on Tumbledown, Mount William and Wireless Ridge, tonight or tomorrow night, and reckon that it will end the campaign, as these heights dominate Stanley. Once we have the airfield, the carriers will not be essential to the defence of the Islands.

We also heard the disappointing news that three Falkland Islands people – all in a house in Stanley – were killed during last night's NGS. The view is that the Args are hiding some of their artillery and mortars in among the houses. You would hope that this sort of tactic is against the Geneva Convention, but I suppose that they do not have much space left now to park their equipment. The more concentrated it is, the easier it will be to bombard them into submission.

It is clear to me that this war will be won by the side that hangs on the longest. It will be a close call, though. It depends on how many stores and reserves of ammunition that the Args have left – as well as willpower – and they are still flying stuff in every night, it seems. They must surely realize that we only have what we brought with us – and I assess, from the signals, that it is all a bit tight. As for the Args, that's the trouble with never going on the offensive – you always have things done to you, rather than sticking it to the other side. You would have thought that they might have at least tried to counter-attack in strength – San Carlos, Goose Green? I suppose it could be that their ground troops only ever envisaged moving around by helicopter in the terrain and that, without those, they thought it was pointless. So, we would appear to have moral and physical superiority over them, right now.

I have written to A to tell her our news and to say how proud I am of the way that she has coped. I also needed to deal with some admin issues at home, mainly to do with the bank and various bills. We certainly have saved a lot since I have been away and while A has been working. If it were not for my flying pay, we would struggle without A working. Ordinarily, despite the pay rise, we do not get paid that much for what we do in the RN, especially in comparison with people of my age and experience in civilian life. I am always surprised when I speak to Rob and my other chums from university about how much they earn as lawyers and accountants and in various other professions. Having said that, I always say to them that I cannot believe that they actually pay me to fly in the RN and that it is worth £50,000 a year in terms of job satisfaction alone on top of what they actually pay me. And I mean it!

Finally, I have just heard that the rescues of survivors at Bluff Cove were performed by the CO, Hugh Clark, Phil Sheldon and Steve Isacke (both ex-826), as well as John Boughton in a Wessex V. We were all embarked in *Bulwark* and deployed together in 1980. The last three are all terrific guys and I have very happy memories of them and our times at sea together. I shared a cabin with Phil Sheldon in *Bulwark*. I enjoyed his good company and companionship and we had a lot of laughs.

Sunday, 13 June

For most of the forenoon, the weather was clear and bright, with very light winds, so Stewart and I were able to complete the barrel change at 1230, return the lifting gear to *Regent* and transfer 17 loads from her to *Antrim*. Unfortunately, we had left Commander S and some yeast behind. By 1600, we were heading out to sea for the usual patrol overnight.

Over in the Falklands, we are expecting a big battle tonight and things have been quiet while the troops prepare. From the signals, it seems that Scots Guards will attack Tumbledown, which is supposed to be defended by the best Arg unit, the 5th Marine Regiment; the Gurkhas will assault Mount William and 2 Para Wireless Ridge.

The Args sent in a Skyhawk raid that went for our positions around Mount Kent and Mount Longdon. I do not think that we splashed any aircraft. Later, some Canberras came over and one of them was brought down. This evening, the RAF Harriers are due to use some laser-guided bombs for the first time.

Cardiff Flight were bounced today by a couple of Daggers as they were to the south of Falkland Sound and were attacked. From the reports, it seems that Chris Clayton managed to evade them by constantly turning inside their turning circles as they attempted to strafe him with cannon. I know the Observer, Pete Hulett, from before. They must have had a time of it because a really pompous signal came out from the Admiral's staff this evening demanding that any aircraft involved in an air-to-air incident was to report in the proper format – position, height, number of aircraft, heading, speed, time etc. That signal could only have been written by a non-aviator! As if you can always react calmly, while you are ducking and weaving like crazy to evade a couple of fighters. I recall that Pete wears glasses in the air and I wouldn't be surprised if he was trying to keep them on or scrabbling around looking for them at the time!

In the Wardroom tonight, the film was *The Four Seasons*, with Alan Alda.

Monday, 14 June

Well, it's probably all over.

Today started with the expectation that a bloody battle would start for possession of Stanley. We waited for news and got on with doing our bit as best we could away from the main action.

The main task of the day was to prove the 4.5 gun alignment and accuracy after the barrel changes, starting with balloon tracking. The ship decided to do a shoot against an iceberg, with 406 being used to observe and report the fall of shot. So we flew between 1400 and 1530. I selected a suitable iceberg for a target – named Leopoldo (after General Galtieri for the occasion) and the ship tracked it, before opening fire. The first two salvoes were beyond the target and to the left, but after some tweaks (technical adjustments) the fall of shot hit the target fair and square. Two confirming rounds also hit.

We then received the reports about the previous night's fighting. Mount Tumbledown and Wireless Ridge had been captured, both in direct assaults and because the Args were rapidly abandoning them. We started picking up good indications that the Args were surrendering from about 1300, but only received concrete evidence when we returned from flying.

A signal from COMAW [Commodore Amphibious Warfare] received at about 1730 confirmed the news:

'White flags reported flying over Stanley. Land fighting around Stanley ceased. Surrender negotiations being arranged with Arg Land Force Commander.

Situation is thus very delicate. Arg mainland reaction not known. Our guard must not be reduced, but we must not jeopardise results so far achieved.

No naval attack on Falkland Islands to take place without further orders. NGS ships proceed inshore but do not open fire on land targets unless specifically ordered.

Arg air threat overland remains and must be countered.

The threat at sea has not changed.'

Tonight we heard on the World Service that the Prime Minister had announced the sudden collapse of Arg resistance to a cheering Commons. Negotiations are under way to negotiate the surrender of Arg forces in the Falkland Islands. We want total, unconditional surrender and withdrawal, if lives are not to have been lost in vain. Apparently, Menendez has flown back to talk to his bosses on the Junta, but they are insisting 'that the honour of Argentine forces in the Islands' should not be compromised. That sounds ominous, but is probably just bluster.

The *Oak* says that people at home are overjoyed and proud to be British again. However, some things never change – the *Oak* included a particularly fetching *Sun* Page Three girl, with a very neat fighting top, called Helle, who is currently working in the Bahamas, but off for a holiday in Los Angeles – apparently! It's all right for some!

The overwhelming sense and mood reflect an attitude of 'job done, now let's go home'. Oddly, the sense of relief about the possibility of not being in danger any more does not seem to prevail, although most of the ship's company are clearly euphoric about seeing their first real wartime action and coming through unscathed. We probably made fewer mistakes than the Args did.

In the Wardroom, the dominant mood is relief that it is all over and satisfaction that our Armed Forces, especially the Royal Navy, did a good job. Everyone seems to think that it will put paid to the Defence cuts proposed last year and that the RN will do well out of any rearrangements. The ship's company just wants to know when we can go home.

Well, at last, the Args have surrendered. That was a nice surprise. It must be a bad day in Argentina as it seems that they lost 1-0 to Belgium in the World Cup qualifiers.

I feel another emotion or response though. The experience has been exciting; it has been immensely fulfilling and I will miss the thrill of operating on the edge, not knowing what each day will bring. I have also found out things about myself. I was able to confront danger and my own fears – and deal with them on my own terms.

We are still on full alert and on patrol to the north, off Jason Island, just in case.

Tuesday, 15 June

We spent today in blizzard conditions and the upper deck was out of bounds. Overnight, we received the formal notice of surrender of the Arg forces in the Falklands, from General Moore:

> In Port Stanley at 2100 Falkland Islands time tonight, the 14th June 1982, Major General Menendez surrendered to me all the Argentine armed forces in East and West Falkland, together with their impedimenta. Arrangements are in hand to assemble the men for return to Argentina, to gather their arms and equipment and to mark and make safe their munitions.
>
> The Falkland Islands are once again under the government desired by their inhabitants.
>
> God save the Queen.

I wrote a quick letter to A, which included:

'Well, it was great news to hear that Port Stanley has fallen – although the Argentinians were claiming a ceasefire, they threw down their weapons and surrendered. It is incredible that we have captured so many. Apparently, there are 11,000 in and around Port Stanley and 4,000 around the bazaars (2,000 in West Falkland, 1,000 at Fitzroy, 800 at Port Salvador). All along, we had been working on about 8,000 Argentinians all told. We have been patrolling our area and, as usual, it has been bitterly cold, with ice and snow on the upper deck. I cannot think what it must be like ashore in the Falklands, with the prisoners.

'It's a shame that the Argentinian A4s were able to attack our two landing ships last week, killing about 50 Welsh Guards – I seem to remember that the people who live next door to your parents have sons in the Welsh Guards.'

The prisoners are reported to be in a really bad way (no tents or shelter, with many suffering from exposure, frostbite, scabies and diarrhoea). In Stanley, they had three days' food supply and lots of small-arms ammunition, but very few artillery shells apparently. At present, it is a major disaster relief operation to get the Arg troops off the Islands before they freeze or starve to death. They had run out of supplies in most places, as they were not distributing the stuff they had, and our bombardment had destroyed their shelters and tents. The regime really is disgusting – leaving 15,000 men to their fate, without a serious attempt to relieve them. Still, I suppose that our SSNs had their ships all bottled up and their air force must be recovering from the body blows dealt to it (almost 100 aircraft down now?). So much, however, for fighting 'to the last drop of Argentinian blood' and for 'the honour of the Argentinian Army'! General Moore said, 'the world should know: this operation verges on disaster relief.'

The World Service reported that Argentina has stated that the POWs are our problem now! *Canberra* has been detailed off to take them to Santa Cruz Roads (really suggestive of the Spanish Main etc.!) in Argentina in two round trips, with *Norland* as a back-up.

What will be the reaction in Argentina? I expect that they will go hysterical, tear their hair out and launch the odd sporadic raid or attack to try and recoup some kudos. The capture of Stanley is certainly a turning point as we now have control of the airfield which will enable us to intercept Arg aircraft 200 miles to the west of the Falklands. Their fixed-wing pilots are no match for ours. It's not just a question of balls; it's down to training, experience and technical expertise. It would also mean that the carriers could go home, along with the escorts that have been supporting them. Hopefully, we will back at about the time when A is due to take her leave.

We spent the day patrolling at sea off Cumberland Bay in a total blizzard, at 6 knots. Another fight erupted on the Bridge wing and signal deck, when Commander E threw a snowball at the Officer of the Watch, Richard Hurley, who was trying to take a visual fix at the time. It drew in the ROs, the Navigator and the Commander, who had been on his way to say something to the Captain. This is senior-level stuff – and perhaps an indication of a release of tension after the news yesterday. However, for most of the day, the upper deck was out of bounds, with thick snow and ice covering the decks and superstructure.

For the first time, people are prepared to say what they will do when they get home. There are the usual desires to get back 'in date', become 'deck-qualified', 'achieve a fully calibrated, firing run', as soon as possible, although the Master Gunner reflected that he might put his suitcase down first. Ian suggested throwing a load of green Smarties out on the lawn, to occupy the kids for a while! I am not sure what those without wives or girlfriends (or both) waiting for them want to do when they get back. That's a sad thought . . .

However, we are worried that the Args might have the appetite for staging a spectacular raid or a desperate last gesture. The view at the command brief was that, on balance, they probably had too much on their minds right now. In the Wardroom, discussion among Declan, Alasdair, Carlos and myself during uckers centred on the possibility that rogue elements of individual Services might take the initiative and do something now that Galtieri and the Junta were discredited and their authority diminished.

It seems that *Endurance* has been tasked to go and evict the Argentinians from the South Sandwich Islands. We are not sure what the force package will be, but it obviously will not include *Antrim*, as the Captain is senior to Captain Barker. Also, she is used to operating in and around the ice and her hull is more resistant. At last, *Endurance* will actually get to do something operational, although I suspect that there won't be any resistance from the Args after the surrender on the Falklands. David Stanesby reckons that we will have to get on with the job because the Antarctic winter is almost upon us and the pack ice will be advancing rapidly northwards. Slowly but surely, the sea inshore is freezing over.

Stayed at sea for most of the day, but entered Cumberland Bay so that CO *Endurance* could come and chat (and he can chat!). We went to sea, overnight, just in case. By nightfall, the sea was rising, the barometer falling, and intense snow and hail showers were driving through. All the electrical connections on the upper deck were giving trouble and shorting out.

Wednesday, 16 June

The news overnight was that there had been riots in Buenos Aires, with people frustrated and annoyed about the 'ceasefire' and capitulation in the Falklands. There are demands for the replacement of the Junta and it may well be that the best thing to come out of the Falklands conflict will be the replacement of the regime.

We still do not have any official confirmation from Argentina about whether they consider that hostilities have ended. It seems that we are keeping a number of special-category prisoners – mostly senior officers – as a guarantee of Arg behaviour. Menendez has said, 'It's all over.' Right now, they do not seem too concerned about the vast bulk of the prisoners, who are out in the open around the airport at Stanley. Galtieri has 'refused to declare that there would be no further attacks' and 'saw victory sooner or later'. Dream on! The Junta has also said that it will not guarantee the safety of *Canberra*, if she takes the prisoners back.

Apparently, the Foreign and Interior Ministers have resigned and there are frequent civil disturbances in Argentina, some of which have been fomented by returning Falklands prisoners.

If the Args had done some decent thinking about the defence of the Falklands and the problems that we faced, they could have held out for a good deal longer and we would have had to withdraw in the face of the South Atlantic winter. As it is, the ships are pretty much on their last legs, with regard to deficiencies, spares and long-overdue maintenance, as well as the effects of being at sea for so long in decidedly challenging sea and meteorological conditions. Commander E and Commander W were looking glummer by the day as the campaign wore on, although they and their departments were amazingly resourceful when it came to keeping things going.

Antrim and *Regent* replenished from *Pearleaf* at the same time, with one each side, and Ian and Stapleton transferred loads between *Regent* and *Pearleaf*. *Antrim* went into Grytviken for boat transfers and returned to sea to maintain our AAW patrol off Cape Saunders.

Yarmouth and *Olmeda* are coming to join the *Endurance* banyan into the ice. It will not be too difficult from the military point of view, as the Arg military presence there (since 1976) is negligible, with scientists – and soldiers pretending to be scientists. They might have problems with the ice and the weather though. *Yarmouth* of course is the only escort that came down early not to have been damaged by enemy fire in some way so far.

We are now going to take over as the coordinating ship for South Georgia, while *Endurance* goes off to recover Thule, with *Olmeda* and *Yarmouth*.

The Captain had supper with us in the Wardroom this evening. We talked about the future prospects of the Falklands economy and concluded that fishing and tourism represented the best options, followed at some stage in the future by oil exploration and exploitation.

I was reflecting today that we have achieved several 'firsts' in this campaign:

- I fired the 'first shots' of the war when I depth-charged the *Santa Fé* at South Georgia.
- I was Observer of the first helicopter ever to engage a submarine.
- I was the first person to disable a submarine in action since the Second World War.
- When we landed 406 on Fanning Head on 21 May, we were the first unit ashore of the main landing forces that led to the recovery of the Islands.

Thursday, 17 June

Antrim was at sea all day. Stewart and I did two and a half hours of load-lifting and transfers with *Regent* and *Endurance*, as well as ferrying M Company patrols to various locations in Cumberland Bay and to Leith.

We were all then airborne for 45 minutes for HC training and emergency procedures.

The South Sandwich Islands recovery force comprises *Endurance* (with her Wasps and one of *Regent*'s Wessex Vs embarked), *Salvageman* (a tug, in case things go wrong in the ice), *Yarmouth* (for NGS), *Olmeda* (with a Sea King Mk 2) and M Company, to supplement *Endurance*'s Marines, as an assault force, along with some Blowpipes.

She and *Salvageman* left today. Whatever happens, you just know that the operation will be written up as the most heroic and professional event of the entire campaign, with a little red ship at the centre of everything.

At 1330, the ship went to Action Stations and we completed a Damage Control Exercise, which included Machinery Breakdown Drills and Flight Deck practice emergencies.

The news came through during dinner that Galtieri has been ousted and replaced by the (former?) Interior Minister (Which one? It seems to be like revolving doors!). In fact, I think his name is Alfredo St Jean. Galtieri appealed to his troops to support him and they did not fancy it, so the new head of the Army is General Cristino Nicolaides. We assess that it will settle down in Argentina now, at least for while, as they sort themselves out and decide whether the Military is so discredited and disgraced that they have to hand over to civilian politicians. At least, in Galtieri and his fellow Junta members, they now have scapegoats (probably justified) for the debacle in the Falklands.

We heard, too, that the Arg prisoners on the Falklands had gone on the rampage, when the rumour went around that they would not be shipped home. The Arg military police and officers had to restore order, but there was a lot of destruction of property and physical assaults on the Islanders. It is also clear that, during the conflict, they had stored munitions and hidden weapon systems in buildings designated as hospitals, with Red Cross signs. The Args were set to work to clear up the mess.

Nevertheless, right now, *Canberra* is sitting in Port Stanley with 5,000 prisoners onboard and a signal has been sent directly to the Commander of the Arg port of Comodoro Rivadavia: 'We are sending 5,000 Argentinian Prisoners of War in *Canberra* – request safe passage and unloading.' Perhaps they should have added, 'and safe departure'!

I have not heard from A since a letter of 21 May, so I do not know what is going on back at home.

Friday, 18 June

Today has been busy and the weather absolutely wonderful. A civilian tanker, *Scottish Eagle*, arrived in the forenoon, with some mail for us, and has taken up residence in Stromness Bay as a floating service station for ships to go alongside and refuel. We have fallen out from Defence Watches (six hours on, six hours off) and are now one in four (four hours on, 12 hours off watch). We finally stopped wearing our anti-flash hoods and gloves and ceased carrying our lifejackets and respirators.

Ian and LACMN Stapleton did three hours of transfers moving M Company around and collecting mail from *Scottish Eagle* (50 bags for us!). They also lifted the MRS 3 gyro onto the Bridge roof. It was quite a delicate operation and needed careful aircraft handling in among all the masts and aerials.

We had always had it in mind that, if the weather was good and the prospects were fine (!), we would attempt to return to Fortuna Glacier, in order to salvage as much of the equipment from the two cabs as possible. Knowing as we do now that you can get all four seasons in one afternoon here in South Georgia, we were careful to ensure that we at least started with a beautifully bright, clear and still day, with little wind and visibility as far as you could possibly want to see.

Consequently, Ian decided that – in view of the weather – we might return to Fortuna again. I changed into flying gear and jumped onboard, but Stewart did not want to come.

It felt strange going up there again; like venturing into somewhere you were not allowed to be – the staff room at school or a pub when you are under 18 – and we all felt that it might give the glacier another chance to have a go at us.

It took us a while to find the two cabs. The glacier was drawing them inexorably into its core and they were becoming part of the landscape of South Georgia. Someday, I expect that archaeologists will find their remains, just as one day we expect to find *Erebus* and *Terror* up to the north of Canada. YA was almost totally covered by a thick pall of snow whereas YF was iced into the glacier. We dug around and found the encrypted radios we were looking for, some claymore mines and some weapons, which we loaded onto 406. We also took some components – intercom boxes and small items – to give to Mike Tidd and Ian Georgeson as keepsakes. I kept an intercom box from YF and the cyclic control from YA.

The ship meanwhile attempted to replenish with *Pearleaf*, but had to break away because of a split hose. She managed to reconnect at 1220.

Olmeda, *Regent* and *Yarmouth* came into Cumberland East Bay from 1500 and started consolidating stores and embarking M Company personnel (desperate for some action!). Stewart and I did intensive load-lifting and transfers 1440–1710, ferrying loads and stores around the various ships, with the help of the Sea King from *Olmeda*. *Olmeda* and *Yarmouth* followed after *Endurance* at about 1800. We now have our own Royal Marines and about 30 others ashore as a garrison in the interim.

The weather has been truly brilliant today, with real warmth beating down, but as soon as the sun went down behind Brown Mountain, it became too cold to remain on the upper deck.

I received letters from Mum and Dad and from Alison. All the news reflected our time in San Carlos and various routine events at home.

At 1900, we anchored at Dartmouth Point, opposite Moraine Fjord. This evening, Sea Slug, the 4.5 gun and the Sea Cat stations and quarters personnel were stood down, although the Sea Cat missiles were kept on the launchers. The 20 mm guns and the chaff rockets were unloaded and the small arms were all returned to the store. It seems to be over. The Admiral is starting to think about returning ships to the UK, beginning with the damaged or clapped-out ones. As our damage has been largely rectified, we probably will not be among the early departures. A lot of other ships are on their way down and these will need reliefs in about five months' time, so they are going to have to think about sending us home soon.

I went up to the Bridge wing at about 2200. I looked across the vastness of Cumberland Bay, at the little church at Grytviken, bathed, for once, in the unnatural moonlight that reflected off the snow-clad mountains and, after a bit of effort, remembered:

A broken chancel with a broken cross,
That stood on a dark strait of barren land:
On one side lay the Ocean, and on one
Lay a great water (and the Moon was full).

I recalled that the adventure was coming to an end and that it was time to think about returning to the real world again. Life is never going to be the same.

Glamorgan, *Plymouth* and *Arrow* are off home, once they have had some repairs. *Invincible* has been operating to the north-east of the Islands, conducting maintenance and repairs, while the speculation is that *Hermes* will go home pretty soon.

Saturday, 19 June

'Elvis Presley' did the time-check.

We remained at anchor all day – 'the snow was deep and crisp and even' – while the Greenies did checks on the MRS 3 gyros. Ian and LACMN Stapleton did the load-lifting and stores rounds for two hours from 1030. Our Royal Marines spent the day with the remaining element of M Company, firing off all the captured Arg ammunition. I was hacked off about all the wanton destruction of buildings and other historic items, including some of the ships. Nobody gave a stuff about what I thought.

I did a lot of admin work this morning and went ashore to explore

Grytviken and its locale after lunch, once the Royal Marines had stopped devastating the place. I wandered round to see Shackleton's and Chief Artuso's graves in the cemetery and have a look at the crashed Arg Puma.

Several of the ship's company went fishing today and caught tons of fish, despite the close attentions of curious and territorially minded seals. There are no Fishery Protection issues here!

I once served on a small vessel involved in Fishery Protection off Northern Ireland. The local boys had come up with an interesting way of poaching salmon on the River Bann – overnight, they used small amounts of explosives to stun the fish which would conveniently arrive on the surface for collection.

I was put ashore with a Leading Seaman and an Able Seaman. They were armed with rifles and I had a handgun. It was in the middle of 'The Troubles' after all. We set up an ambush site where we thought the poachers were known to operate and, in long wellies, hid in the nearby vegetation. The night was cold and it was pretty boring, so I thought that I would exert some leadership by playing some games. I suggested a game that, for example, started with 'Manchester'. Manchester ends in 'R' so the next player had to produce a place beginning with the last letter – Rotherham. The next player would then supply a place beginning with the last letter of Rotherham – 'M' – Mansfield. Easy! Understand? Good!

I said, 'I'll start. London.'

The Leading Seaman responded with Manchester.

'Look,' I said, 'London ends with an 'N'. You would have to say Norwich.'

'Let's try again – Dorchester.'

'Norwich,' said the Leading Seaman.

At this point, I gave up. My leadership talents were wasted in these circumstances. The boredom deepened and the night just got colder.

I was not looking forward to the following night, but we went ashore with our rations and set up shop in the foliage. We concentrated on keeping warm and alert. Some hours passed until, at about 0230, a loud explosion nearby made us jump out of our skins. The sky rained river water, weed and other organic debris. We leapt out, the Able Seaman's rifle magazine dropped off and the rounds spilled on the ground. As the fines for lost rounds were punitive, he set about trying to locate the rounds in the mud on the river bank. The Leading Seaman and I sought to locate the source of the explosion. In the very dim light, we made out two figures, both of whom we immediately illuminated with our torches. I told them to stop and that we were armed. They ran. We gave chase and managed to collar the nearest (and slowest). We crash-tackled him to the floor and I sat on his chest, while the Leading Seaman put on the handcuffs.

Our captive was spitting and swearing, while trying to claim that he was just going about his business in the middle of nowhere at 0230 in the morning, with various artefacts and material normally associated with a low level of explosives in his pockets.

He then, without any prompting, exclaimed, 'You might have got me, but you won't get Paddy McGuinness!'

'Wow, thanks,' I thought. We radioed through to the Royal Ulster Constabulary and arranged for them to go round to Paddy's house. They arrived in time to greet a damp Paddy running down the street, with significant amounts of incriminating evidence about his person, as well as distinctive fragments of riverine detritus festooning his coat. The RUC picked him up. A good night's work!

The most remarkable features here at South Georgia are how clear the air is and how far you can see on a day when the visibility is good. From seaward, mountains like Mount Paget seem much closer than the 40 or 50 miles away they are in reality.

It is also astonishing how unconcerned the wildlife is at our presence. The birds virtually ignore us; you can actually go right up to them and they do not fly away. It seems as if they are not used to human beings, or the harm that some might do to them, and look at you as if to say, 'You're a pretty big penguin (admittedly, a lot bigger than an emperor), but you're a penguin all right.' The other birds that seem to think that we are penguins are the skuas, large, heavy creatures with lethal hooked beaks. On the basis that we are just over-large penguins, they fly straight at us at eye level and threaten to strike us somewhere on the face or head. This is clearly their way of taking out penguins and several of the lads have had near misses or nasty gashes on the forehead. We now carry sticks and always have a flag on a pole on top of our packs when we are walking ashore, away from the settlements.

Apart from the spectacular scenery and the force of nature experience, the really exhilarating thing about South Georgia is the feeling that you are in a place which hardly anyone else has visited and that you are sometimes treading on ground that nobody else is likely to have walked – ever. Also, there is an eerie, ghostly 'atmosphere' about the place.

The South Atlantic seems to retain the imprint of things that have happened here in the past. There is a sense of timelessness, reinforced by the remoteness, other-world atmosphere and almost monochrome greyness of the sky and the sea – and the ships – with the odd iceberg to punctuate the scene. It is a part of the world pregnant with barely recalled memories, of the great days of Empire and trade and intangible human imprints that seem to have been frozen in time. It's uncanny – there is a strange, brooding atmosphere about the South Atlantic. Possibly, it is partly to do with Byron's idea of the ocean being 'an image of eternity'.

The word is that Phantoms are to be based at Stanley for Air Defence and that Buccaneers may also come down, to threaten and, if necessary, bomb, air bases in mainland Argentina, if the Args do not cooperate.

It turns out that the Args were not so short of equipment and food as we had thought. Signals indicate that they had tons of ammunition of all types, as well as food, boots and clothing that was better than our own. It all seems to have piled up in Stanley and was never distributed around the various deployed positions. Also, we have had reports of Arg officers refusing to patrol with their men (result = the soldiers did not patrol, they just went out and took shelter somewhere, especially when the SAS are around); others shot their soldiers in the feet and legs to ensure they stayed in position and could not run away. Some shot their men outright.

Canberra has discharged her POWs into Puerto Madryn, escorted by an Arg Type 42 destroyer (probably glad to get to sea!). Meanwhile, in the UK, the rail unions are continuing to do their bit for the war effort, by encouraging the steelworkers and miners to join them in striking. British Rail has threatened to shut down the network for three months if the strike goes ahead!

Sunday, 20 June

The ship remained at anchor. At 1000, *Wimpey Seahorse* came alongside *Antrim*.

I went ashore to look at the wildlife. For my own education, I have been trying to identify the various penguins and seals around the place.

Elephant seals – which are between 16 and 18 feet long – seem to have only two modes of operation when on land – asleep and malodorous, and awake and very grumpy. I am sure that there is a third mode that involves making baby elephant seals (not a pleasant thought!), but it does not seem to be the season to be – well – jolly. They do appear to spend their entire day in a permanent state of irritation and it is best not to get too close. When surprised, they rear up and then flop down on anything unfortunate enough to be in the way. We have found that it is best to ensure that there is always an escape route and that it is advisable not to get between a bull and his harem, or any elephant seal and the sea. Despite their weight problems, they can move pretty fast over a short distance when they want to, as some of the boys have discovered. Their breath – all that digested and decaying fish, I reckon – can knock you down at 100 yards as well. The males have a huge, distinctive, highly mobile snout, which seems to assist and magnify the roaring.

When they threaten or attack, elephant seals rear up to their full height, emit a ferocious roar (with accompanying blast of knock-down breath) and inflate their necks to a formidable size. When fighting each other, which seems to happen often, males adopt this bellowing, erect posture and, in the manner of Sumo wrestlers, bash into each other, all the while ducking and weaving to find an opportunity for their power-ful jaws and massive teeth to inflict an injury. Just as with dog-fighting in the air, it pays to have a height advantage and often the seals can be seen squaring up to each other, just like Jack in a Portsmouth pub, reaching for the highest position with their heads, necks and extended shoulders in contact as if they were stuck together. It's just as well that they haven't discovered alcohol. Many of them have duelling scars and injuries, some of which are very deep and raw, although it could be that they got these in encounters with killer whales or other attackers.

Because of their bulk and relatively small fins, they seem to advance and attack in a series of short bursts and, as long as you have an escape route identified before going near them, you can normally outpace them. When they do move over distances, their blubber seems to mould around the shape of the things over which they are passing.

Normally, males lie down alongside their harem of females, for mutual protection, for proprietorial reasons and to conserve warmth. This has provided an opportunity for the *Antrim* 'dangerous sports society'. Some of the lads have taken to finding a colony of elephant seals, lined up side by side and asleep, and seeing how many they can clear, Evil Knievel style, with a running jump. The world record currently is either seven or eight although I understand that there is a stewards' inquiry about eight because one of the seals was thought not to be an elephant. It's important because the MAA thinks that money might be changing hands on the result.

The problem is that Jolly Jack does not always clear the elephant seals and people land awkwardly among them or on a ton or so of wobbly blubber. Not only have some injuries been sustained – the Doc says that they present as 'slipped on the ice, sir' – but there is the danger of death as a result of being crushed under the weight (and they weigh up to two tons).

As a result, the Commander has said that he is thinking of putting an Exclusion Zone around elephant seals because of the risks. How would you write the letter to the relatives explaining that their son/husband/ father would not be returning from war because he has mixed it with an elephant seal? How would you dress that up?

'AB Jack Tar died gallantly in the midst of insuperable odds . . . he died as he lived . . . striving to be the best . . . seriously tried to match the weight of expectation, but fell short etc.'

The island is also alive with fur seals, some of them – mature males I would think – up to seven feet long and probably weighing in at about 350 or 450 lb. Their fur is dark brown, but their undersides are cream or yellowy-white and the males all sport a mop of hair on their heads, although I have noticed quite a lot of variation in colour depending on size (and, I deduce, maturity). I think that the females are about four feet long and weigh proportionately less – they might be grey-coloured. Apart from the size and hairstyle, I am not about to get close enough to sex a fur seal, even if I knew how, as they are distinctly territorial and light on their feet. This is because they appear to be able to use their hind flippers more like legs than other seals do; in fact, these flippers seem more articulated and more suited to land 'warfare' than those of other breeds. They have a spectacular set of fearsome teeth and bark at or with each other.

They all smell decidedly musty and the males spend a lot of the day just lying around, sometimes on their backs when the sun is out, posturing and barking at – or with – each other. However, in the water, they are very efficient underwater swimming machines, with a speed and agility that shows that this is the environment to which they are best suited by evolution and inclination.

What I found interesting about watching the various seals is how human they appear in their characteristics – whether it is the young pups mock-fighting and playing or when they use their flippers in the manner of arms and hands to perform a variety of seemingly familiar gestures. I swear that I saw one move his flipper across his face to cover a yawn! When they are asleep, they seem to be in a continuous state of murmuring, snoring, farting and scratching – sounds familiar!

Tonight we had a repeat showing of *A White Powder Christmas* on CCTV – a compilation of various mistakes, verbal gaffes, howlers and swearing that did not make it into the normal programmes. It's been put together by the technicians at the BBC and is very funny, even the second time around. We also saw a slide show of all the photos taken by the officers that have been returned, developed, in the latest mail.

Monday, 21 June

The celebrity time-check this morning was 'Bruce Forsyth' – all cuddly toys and conveyor belt, and, of course, 'Good game! Good game!'

It is midwinter's day today.

We weighed anchor at 1000 and proceeded to sea, to test the new gyro. Balloon-tracking serials confirmed the accuracy and alignment and the 4.5s engaged a convenient iceberg. Another iceberg was pulverized as well. Their brothers and sisters were all around us, including one that was square with sides about four miles long and was about 100 feet above the water.

Stewart and Stapleton did a two-hour milk run 1100–1300. Later on, Ian and I did some 903 radar target-tracking runs in the wake of the gyro change and took Sub Lts Worrall and Brook flying 1400–1530.

Spurious pipes on Main Broadcast have started – this afternoon's was: 'R. O. Tate – Flight Deck.'

Godfrey the Dentist has been busy offering his services around the ships – he was with *Regent* today and saw a good number of people.

We were at sea overnight. A signal was received from *Endurance* at the South Sandwich Islands, saying that they had captured the place and had 50 prisoners. There was pack-ice and temperatures down to minus 10 degrees C (minus 30 degrees C with the wind chill). They added: '*Ice Station Zebra* has nothing on South Thule.'

I will probably never want anyone to read this next bit because I feel a bit guilty even thinking it. I am beginning to think that the Arg missiles and bombs had a special homing head that acquired its target by detecting bullshit. By bullshit, I mean complacency, arrogance and a failure to take the enemy seriously, with a strong dose of carelessness. *Sheffield* was the up-threat ship – on an afternoon on the day after we sank their second-biggest ship – and she wasn't at Action Stations, had not isolated her fire main or electrical systems, and her Captain and AAWO [Anti-Aircraft Warfare Officer] were away from their positions. She was even less prepared than for a FOST Thursday war! *Coventry* was probably a bit cocky after her really good day shooting down Skyhawks and decided that it would be a good idea to take the incoming raid with Sea Dart rather than let the SHars splash them. *Sir Tristram* and *Sir Galahad* were an accident waiting to happen, given all the confusion. There should be a new naval offence – carelessness, complacency and arrogance in the face of the enemy. It's not entirely about luck – luck, as we know, is when preparation meets opportunity or the unexpected.

Another signal – and the World Service at 2100 – announced that the Prince and Princess of Wales had been blessed with a baby son. This elicited a signal from the Admiral: 'For their Royal Highnesses, the Prince and Princess of Wales. With humble duty, the Flag Officer, Commanding Officers, Officers and ship's companies of the South Atlantic Task Force send their warmest congratulations on the birth of your son with every good wish for the future.'

Able Seaman Lawson, not known for his intelligence, fell in love/lust with a lady of somewhat elastic virtue, who was well – and frequently – known to several members of the ship's company. Despite all warnings, several children of doubtful provenance and clear evidence that she continued to like sailors a lot (and they her), he decided to marry her and attempt to make an honest woman of her.

Once married, Mrs Lawson made the most of her improved access to sailors and became very popular, especially when Able Seaman Lawson was required onboard for duty overnight or away at sea. The result was that Mrs Lawson became pregnant in the middle of a five-month deployment and it was blindingly obvious to everyone except Lawson that, with a nine-month gestation period, he could not possibly be the father. Nevertheless, Lawson pronounced himself to be delighted. Mrs Lawson was duly brought to labour and produced twins, while we were at sea, the news arriving by special telegram. Lawson was over the moon and gave up his beer ration to 'wet the babies' heads'.

Why? His Mess mates, in their wisdom and kindness, had told him that it took 18 months to make twins!

Time to record a few lessons, as they occur to me:

- We need to go from a standing start quickly when a crisis breaks – that means having the necessary infrastructure and retention of skills in dockyards and industry.
- Our ships, especially the gas turbine ships, needed a lot of fuel – that means a continued need for the Royal Fleet Auxiliary.
- Need for afloat specialist repair and rescue ships.
- The ability to access ships and aircraft 'from trade' is essential.

Tuesday, 22 June

Today is the third anniversary of my engagement to A, the same day that I received my 'wings' as an Observer. Stewart and I did two serials of SOOTAX – load-lift etc. – 1400–1435 and 1655–1755 (HDS), with *Regent* and *Wimpey Seahorse*.

The ship was alongside *Scottish Eagle*, fuelling, 1505–1730 in Cumberland Bay.

We had 'Splice the Mainbrace' at 1800 tonight (with those on watch catching up at 2000) – every member of the ship's company was allowed a tot (an eighth of a pint) of rum. This is unusual because the ratings are not permitted to drink spirits, only beer.

I wrote to A today, with 'news once again from the Western Front, where I can honestly say, it is all quiet once again. You can tell that an uneasy sort of peace has broken out!' The threat has receded at a greater rate than Alasdair Maclean's hairline!

Lots of serviceable equipment continues to be recovered in the Falklands, including vehicles, guns and helicopters. Argentina seems to have lost over a division's worth of kit, logistics and ammunition.

Meanwhile, we are still ploughing furrows in the sea, up and down, making sure that the Args do not launch random attacks. It seems to be a waste of time, as the Args are far too preoccupied at home for a Hercules to come trundling all the way out here, risking getting shot down – and for what?

The daily schedule over here is becoming rather routine: get up – eat – fly – eat – fly – watch a third-rate film – FOCCIF – command meeting – uckers – eat – write up diary and read – go to bed – get up . . . It's just a typical day at the office. The films are generally American ones made for TV and they are not great. FOCCIF has picked up again, but our supply of films has dried up and we are eagerly looking to swap our tired old stock with other ships. We have seen the various CCTV programmes over and over again, including some unofficial BBC tapes and bootleg videos. We are receiving some official videos, mostly documentaries and news compilations, as well as repeat comedy programmes – *Fawlty Towers*, *Dad's Army* and Benny Hill.

People are slowly adjusting back to the normalities and routines of peacetime. All the paperwork that was 'filed away' has now reared its ugly head and screams to be dealt with. In the Wardroom, people are less easy-going than they have been and some are noticeably grumpier. Mostly, I see instances among the more ambitious of claiming the credit for things, even though they were not involved, and a real desire to exploit participation in the war as a career opportunity. On the Flight, we are still getting on with each other well, even though our flying time is largely spent ferrying people and things around without much operational tasking.

Buzzes are rife around the ship, but no one is really sure what is to happen to us exactly. Pat Brown said that we probably did not appear on any list of Falklands ships because we are down at South Georgia and our future never gets discussed at Northwood. I am fairly confident that we will be back towards the middle to end of July.

The film tonight was *Escape to Athena*, an improbable romp with Roger Moore as a dodgy German officer/archaeologist/antiques dealer, Telly Savalas, David Niven and Stephanie Powers as a stripper.

Overnight, we are going to remain offshore. People are wondering whether the Admiral has forgotten that we are still down here. As the Commander said tonight, 'The ice is now drifting north at a rate of knots, but not *Antrim*.'

Lessons:

- Airborne Early Warning and better overland radar detection are needed to fight inshore.

- 'The proper way to fight the air is in the air'* – we need fixed-wing carriers.
- The sea-skimming missile threat has to be countered – all we have is Sea Wolf.
- SHar and AIM-9L Sidewinder and our aircrew selection and training – a decisive capability.
- Type 42 destroyers have been discredited and need to be upgraded, or replaced.

Wednesday, 23 June

We had very strong winds today. *Dumbarton Castle* arrived this forenoon.

First thing this morning, I was making my way along the main drag past the POs' Mess, when I ran into the Chippy and a couple of his lads, coming the other way.

'How are you, Chief? Which job have you been doing?' I asked.

'Unblocking the outflow pipe from the heads in the Admiral's Cabin Flat,' he answered.

'Rather you than me, Chief,' I said. 'Good for you – I really couldn't do your job, having to deal with all that shit and stuff.'

He gave me a long look and said, 'It might be shit to you, sir, but it's my bread and butter!'

Just as I was thinking, that told me!, he realized what he had said. We all laughed and went about our business.

Today was a day of chores and getting back up to speed with our aviation qualifications. I did a walk round the aircraft with Chief McKee and the SMR, in order to stay in date for Flight Servicing. I also brushed up on my Instrument Flight Rules – I will need to have my annual check when I return to the squadron.

406 conducted a full day of load-lifting and stores and personnel transfers. In a huge effort around all the ships, Ian, Stapleton and I flew 1100–1245, Stewart and I 1250–1450, and Ian and Stapleton 1800–1830 (a final mail drop to *Wimpey Seahorse* and *Dumbarton Castle*, before she left at 1800).

Antrim replenished with *Olmeda* at 1400.

* Admiral of the Fleet Viscount Cunningham, *A Sailor's Odyssey*.

At 2300, we challenged an unknown ship. It turned out to be *British Enterprise*, arriving with fuel and our mail.

I read a lot this evening.

I have just realized that life is a bit like being on *Desert Island Discs*! I have a Bible and a copy of Shakespeare and I already have my chosen book with me, Gibbon's *Decline and Fall*. I do not seem to have a luxury item though. It would have to be the Uckers board . . . but that is no good if you do not have anyone to play against. So let's have a telescope good enough to explore the stars.

And down here, it really should be *Desolate Island Discs*!

What music would I pick? The programme's pretty snooty when it comes to music, so it would have to be classical:

Ravel – *Pavane for a Dead Princess*
Tchaikovsky – *1812 Overture*
Smetana – *Ma Vlast* ('Vltava')
Holst – *Planets* ('Jupiter')
Elgar – *Enigma Variations* ('Nimrod' probably)
Any Welsh male voice choir – 'Cwm Rhondda'
Vaughan Williams – *Fantasia on Greensleves*
Palestrina – *Missa Assumpta est Maria*

But if it was pop music as well:
Meatloaf – 'Bat Out of Hell'
Melanie – 'Ruby Tuesday'
Tim Hardin – 'If I were a Carpenter'
Rod Stewart – 'Still Love You' or 'Sailing'
James Taylor – 'Carolina on My Mind'
Dire Straits – 'Sultans of Swing'
Bob Dylan – 'Lay Lady Lay'
Bruce Springsteen – 'Born to Run'

Lessons:

- You need to have realistic training and practice in peacetime if you want to be proficient and confident in war. That means training as close as possible to wartime conditions and sufficient live firing and experience of things that go bang – the classic 'smell of cordite'. You also have to be realistic and honest about the limitations of your kit. Everyone knew that Sea Cat and Sea Slug were not up to the job against the Soviets – yet no one among our Lords and Masters said or did anything.

- Soldiers and Royal Marines need to be physically and mentally tougher than the enemy. That means fitter and more resilient in the face of extreme conditions.
- Paras, Royal Marines and Special Forces have a greater impact because they have an elite ethos and exclusive attitude. It increases expectations about results though.

Thursday, 24 June

Today was our 100th day out of the UK, 88th since Gibraltar. We continued our defensive patrol to the north off the island, but by 1300 we anchored off Dartmouth Point. We were alongside *British Enterprise* in the afternoon; she had some mail and stores for us and then departed for the Falklands. Large numbers of 'gentlemen's magazines' – *Mayfair*, *Penthouse* – arrived too.

Stewart and I flew a two-hour load-lifting sortie around the ships and shore stations from 1100, which Ian and LACMN Stapleton completed between 1500 and 1530.

Endurance has come back from South Thule, with *Salvageman*. They seem to have done a good job in very cold, bleak conditions. The Args have been evicted and their installation 'slighted'. *Yarmouth* and *Olmeda*, with the prisoners, are on their way to – or have arrived at – the Falklands.

We remained at anchor overnight.

We heard that John Nott produced a White Paper on Defence yesterday that hardly seems to have changed since before the Falklands crisis, including the sentence: 'we should not rush to premature conclusions based on the dimly perceived lessons of the last few weeks.' That sounds like double-speak and Mr Nott should realize how 'dimly perceived' he himself is by anyone who has been down here.

I would have to say that the routine over the past week or so has been dull. Morale is pretty good onboard, but we have to be out and about a lot at the moment to keep people's minds fresh and their outlook positive.

The Commander said that he once served in a ship which had a weak, but well-connected and popular, commanding officer and a true martinet as a First Lieutenant. One Friday, alongside in Portland, the ship had taken severe criticism from Flag Officer Sea Training staff for the state of morale onboard and the First Lieutenant had gone on Main Broadcast to say to the ship's company, 'Do you hear there? FOST staff have reported that morale on the ship is appalling; it is to improve by 1600 or there will be no weekend leave.'

Lessons:

- We need to retain Gibraltar, Ascension, Cyprus and our other former colonies, if we want to intervene around the world.
- We need to do something about the relationship between the Press and the Forces. It has been terrible – misreporting, confusion, leaks of vital operational information (South Georgia and Goose Green) and Arg propaganda given too much credibility because we were staying tight-lipped. The Press must be given a story even if we cannot give them *the* story. (The Goebbels approach!)
- Large numbers of helicopters are required to conduct land and sea operations effectively – and the decks to accommodate them.
- The Army gets 'transported' to war; the Royal Marines are 'deployed' – ready to fight on arrival, although the Paras did well. An attitude thing? Or training, equipment and role?

Friday, 25 June

At 0400, *Yorkshireman* went to help *British Enterprise*, which had broken down, owing to a large object (ice?) being taken into her main circulating pump. This in turn damaged a piston and the cylinder block. The weather was good though and she is repairing herself with assistance from *Antrim* and *Endurance*. *Antrim* went to have a look at the Nordenskjold glacier close to, taking care to avoid the large bits that were continually breaking off.

Just before turning in this evening – in fact, we were still playing uckers – we received the news that we would be sailing for home. The Captain, sounding very pleased, got on the Main Broadcast out of hours to tell the ship's company, who no doubt would have been delighted to be roused from their sleep with the news.

Morale has shot up into the stratosphere, as one might reasonably expect.

It's difficult to explain how I feel. Of course, it will be wonderful to get back to the UK, to enjoy the normal things of life and to be with A again. We need to get on with our life together. But, it has been a terrific adventure and I will miss the raw excitement.

Lessons:

- We need to control the spread of smoke in ships that are hit.
- In high-temperature fires, water spray is useless – the oxygen and hydrogen separate, with the oxygen feeding the fire and the hydrogen exploding!
- More sets of breathing apparatus are required.
- We need all-over racing driver Action Working Dress – not made of synthetic (equals liable to melt) materials.

Saturday, 26 June

We weighed anchor, with ice all around us and went alongside *Scottish Eagle* to refuel between 0950 and 1150. We took 80 tons. Ian and LACMN Stapleton conducted the last load-lift and moved passengers around, including the working party that we had in *Wimpey Seahorse*. Our divers had been assisting with the salvage work on the *Santa Fé* and we brought them back as well. We had a brief worry about whether we should be flying them so soon after diving, so we kept low just in case.

At 1345, we sailed out of Cumberland Bay for the last time, to head up to the Carrier Battle Group. Most of the ice was well out to sea, although there were lots of 'bergy bits'. The snow-line was almost down to the water's edge.

At 2200, we rendezvoused with *Resource* and Ian, Stewart and I transferred passengers, mail and netted loads between 0000 and 0030!

After we received our order to sail for home yesterday, we had a signal from *Endurance* saying:

> Very many thanks for your support which has been much appreciated. It's alright for some B-A-S-T-A-R-D-S. The best of luck from the last of the Paraquets.

Cheeky buggers! – with their idea of us supporting them! I suppose that they have been away for eight months though.

Later on, we sent back a signal which I thought was rather restrained:

VMT [very many thanks] your signal. *Endurance* by name and *Endurance* by programme. Our guilt offset by the thought that we could be your relief. Good Luck.

From the Admiral came the signal:

Have received the following signal from Buckingham Palace:

Quote: Both of us send our warmest and most appreciative thanks to all those serving in the South Atlantic Task Force for their very kind signal on the birth of our son. We are delighted to think that our happy event should have enabled you to splice the mainbrace twice in a short space of time. We send our admiring best wishes for the gallant feats you have accomplished in the face of appalling conditions. Charles and Diana. Unquote.

I regret that the reference to splice the mainbrace refers to spurious newspaper reports not to fact. Only one mainbrace spliced.

This confusion was caused by the assumption in the press – no doubt stimulated by the thought that the mainbrace would be spliced after the victory in the Falklands – that there would be two issues of rum. There should have been!

I have started a *Mastermind* competition on the ship's CCTV with representatives from each Mess answering two minutes on general knowledge, to keep the lads amused and to keep my brain from going completely to rats. We had the first session tonight and the first contestants, with a couple of exceptions, proved very knowledgeable and the scores were impressive. We will continue until 10 July, when we will announce the winning Mess. I also plan to have a Grand Final – between some half-dozen of the best individuals, who will face two minutes of specialist subject, followed by two minutes of General Knowledge – at some stage after that. That way, I will not have too many specialist subjects to research amid the limited resources onboard.

Lessons:

- Nuclear submarines really coerce people, particularly in the wider world! They have strategic impact – as Pat Brown said, 'They frighten the fuzzies.'
- Old can be good and effective – Mk 8 torpedoes and Mk 11 depth charges (and barrage balloons and making smoke?).

I have just heard that the Crabs are operating Hercules aircraft into Stanley from Ascension, courtesy of in-flight refuelling. That's impressive.

Sunday, 27 June

We had a late-night sortie in 406 conducting the transfers to and from *Resource*, mostly stores and official mail, and the ship has been continuing towards the TEZ. Most people caught up on sleep ahead of Defence Watches. I went to church this morning – a reasonable number of people are still thankful for their deliverance.

We also did two time zone shifts – at 1630 and 1830 – to bring us into line with Falklands time. That made for a very long day, but left time for FOCCIF and five games of uckers. In fact, FOCCIF is going well every day, with people keen to be in good shape when they return home.

Having secured the ship for action at 1930, we went back into Defence Watches at 2000 as we entered the TEZ. The ship was secured for action. We wore our anti-flash, carried our survival suits and all the paraphernalia again and slept fully clothed. Our Damage Control section bases were manned and the weapons systems stood to just in case. No sucker punches for us!

As every day goes by, we are getting stronger and better established in and around the Falklands. The chances of an Arg strike are reducing all the time – fingers crossed.

I have also heard that I am likely to be leaving the Flight and doing a Lynx conversion, before returning to sea as a Flight Commander. I had wanted to be a PWO next, but it seems that we are so short of Observers at sea that I cannot be spared from flying duties. That's OK, because it will mean a good four months' conversion course at Portland and going home most nights. It will also be very rewarding flying a newer type of aircraft and to be in command of my own Flight in a destroyer or frigate. You also get to sit in the front of the aircraft!

Lessons:

- Realistic training and preparation are the secrets to success in war.
- 'The training ground is the battleground', Nelson. We were geared for war with the Warsaw Pact and not for the unexpected.

As one of 5 Brigade's staff officers said, 'We were prepared for war, but not this bloody war!'

- People will wobble under pressure and in combat, if they are not told what is going on, they are on their own and they are not occupied with something.
- The unexpected always happens – need for adaptation and improvisation. If it's not impossible, it's possible.
- The importance of maintaining a sense of humour – a distinctive British war-fighting characteristic.

Monday, 28 June

By 0630, we had met up with the Carrier Battle Group and were scheduled to conduct an Air Defence exercise with the SHars as the attacking aircraft, but the serial was cancelled because of bad weather. *Tidepool*'s Wessex V took and delivered a vast amount of mail, which had been flown down by air to Stanley airfield. I received separate letters from both Mum and Dad, congratulating me on my mention in despatches.

Between 1215 and 1305 – Ian, Stapleton and I flew the Captain and Commander S to *Hermes*, to say goodbye to the Admiral and have lunch. We stayed on the Flight Deck while the meetings took place and returned by 1410. It transpires that the Captain's godson, Miles Griffith, had been staying on a sheep farm in West Falkland before the conflict and had remained there during the war. He was now in Port Howard and the Captain had sought permission to take him back to Ascension – on Main Broadcast, he said: 'Actually, I do not care whether I get permission. I am the Captain and that is what I am going to do.' He is obviously demob happy!

So, at 1600, the ship headed for the Falklands, to enter the Sound from the south tomorrow and approach Port Howard.

We received a signal from CINCFLEET:

From Ascension to South Georgia and on to San Carlos, you were very much in the forefront of operations, the success of which finally resulted in British reoccupation of all the Islands. This together with your swift recovery from bomb damage allowing continued operations in the TEZ and off South Georgia won wide acclaim.

BZ and a happy return home.

I am sure that it was well meant, but it sounded formulaic and wooden to most people in the Wardroom.

Lessons:

- The person you have to impress with your professionalism and readiness is not the Captain, the Commander or some Admiral. You have to be ready to impress the enemy on the day he comes knocking and says, 'Are you good enough?' If you are not, he will kill you. Of course, he might kill you anyway, but you might as well go having given it your best shot. Eternity is a long time to reflect on why you did not do everything you could have done.
- In war, you learn a lot in a short time – about what is needed and about yourself.
- If something is being done in peacetime that is not going to work in war, it should be challenged. Too many shoddy compromises and unreasonable risks about our kit and weapon systems, taken by people who will never go to war, have resulted in ships being sunk and people getting killed and wounded. Plan for war, adapt for peace.
- There are no silver and bronze medals in war; it's the gold medal or nothing. You can't share that podium – Nelson stands alone on his column.

Tuesday, 29 June

Antrim saw – and was challenged by – *Cardiff* this morning, as she entered Falkland Sound from the south. We were airborne at 0800, picking up the Captain's godson from Port Howard, and returned at 0935. While we were away, the ship, as she passed, piped the site of *Ardent*'s sinking, which is now a war grave, and held a short service of remembrance.

At Port Howard we had a look around. *Cardiff* had been there to supervise the surrender on or around 14 June and her boys had a left a 'CARDIFF WOZ HERE' graffito. We had a clear view across the Sound to San Carlos. When we were in San Carlos, I wondered whether the Args could see what was going on from here and were reporting back to the mainland. A couple of empty Blowpipe missile launchers were lying around, one of which probably brought down the Crab in his GR3 over here – that was careless.

We were shocked to hear that John Hamilton, the SAS Captain with us at South Georgia, had been killed nearby. We went to the house where his signaller was held after his capture, in a cellar below where the Args were billeted. The Args who captured him seemed seriously to know what they were doing, as the place was fortified with sandbags and there were firing positions covering all the likely approaches. We asked how and where John Hamilton had been killed; it looks like the four-man team must have been detected and scattered about four miles away, with John and his man going one way and the other two escaping. We wanted to walk up the hill to where they said he was buried, but people said that there might still be mines out there.

I felt sad about him, stood on my own, said a few words and wondered what his family back home must be feeling. I realized that I knew absolutely nothing about him, or whether he was married, despite having had all that time together onboard and some 'interesting' shared experiences. He'd survived Fortuna Glacier, was almost certainly on the Pebble Island raid and now this had happened. I remember that he used to sit on the first aid box at the top of the Wardroom ladder, all kitted up and going through his routines ahead of any action, just like he was meditating or in a trance.

We came across a huge pile of abandoned Arg weapons on the road by the landing site, all very dirty and wet. They were mostly rifles and semi-automatic weapons, as well as some grenade launchers, pistols, sniper and recoilless rifles and countless boxes of ammunition. We took a sniper's rifle (a Garand), some pistols, a grenade launcher and a recoilless rifle back to the ship, so that they could go to a museum back home. We thought about taking some ammunition just in case the Args decided they wanted some more action and aggravation, but in the end decided that it would all need recording, storing in the magazine and . . . it was all too difficult, especially now that normal peacetime rules were clutching back in again. I would not want to upset the DWEO!

I also spoke to some of the newly liberated locals, who are very understated, but grateful. They told us that some of the best Arg troops were in West Falkland. They said that they had heard from their people in East Falkland that some of the Arg conscripts thought that they were actually defending mainland Argentina against us and had no idea that they were in the Falklands. They also said that their officers hardly ever patrolled with them, with the result that the soldiers simply went about a mile from their lodgings and radioed in that they were in all sorts of places. In fact, they just spent the day or night under cover and out of the weather. That was good news for us I would say, as it meant that they would have had little chance of detecting our preliminary operations.

They were also apparently terrified at the prospect of facing the Gurkhas. They were being told by their officers and NCOs about the sort of forces that we might bring down here and the subject of the Gurkhas came up. They seem to have picked up some interesting impressions. It seems that they believed that whenever the Gurkhas went into battle they had to shed blood with their kukris and, once unsheathed, they could not go back in until they had been bloodied, even with the Gurkha's own blood. Then, as we got closer, the word went round that the knives are used for beheading people. Finally, once we were on the ground, the word was that kukris were supposed to cut off the *cojones* – hence the farcical, but perhaps understandable surrender attitude adopted by some of the soldiers. We could not understand why, instead of putting their hands in the air and surrendering, some Argentinian soldiers were rolling up tightly into the foetus position. Now, we do! I get the impression that they would prefer to go back to Argentina without their heads rather than their *cojones*!

Once back onboard, we passed Fanning Head in daylight (how did we get away with it on the night of 20/21 May?) and, once we passed Cape Dolphin, we had typical South Atlantic weather to send us on our way home. By 1500, we had a Force 8, with wind speeds up to 50 knots. By 2000, we had a steady 60–65 knots from the south and the quarterdeck was being swamped, or pooped as the technical term has it. The seas were breaking over the gun turret and slamming into the Bridge. No one really cared – we were on our way home. The Captain's godson was very seasick and in quite a bad way until the Doc got to him.

I have put a meteorological chart on the back of my door and every day I intend to put the lat and long position on to mark our daily position. The daily progress won't be very much, but it's a graphic indication of where we are in the world and how close we are to home. I thought about shaving off my beard, but I am still superstitious about it. It has kept me safe so far and I do not want to tempt fate, now that we are probably past the combat phase.

We are now heading north, for home. I shall miss the raw beauty, the rugged landscapes and romantic remoteness of these Islands, as well as the sheer other-worldliness of feeling like you are on the edge of human existence. On a clear day, from the air, the unspoilt views of the Islands, set in a vast, glimmering ocean and stretching to the horizon in every direction, are spectacularly impressive. I would like to come back some day and explore their features in detail.

Wednesday, 30 June

I do not believe anyone had a good night's sleep last night. It was incredibly rough with a very violent sea and a continuous wind of 50–55 knots, with gusts to 65. As I write, at 2200, it is still at 30–35 knots, with the odd buffet to 45. We have been in company with *Blue Rover* since the early hours and looking to replenish when we can. Several members of the ship's company have cuts and bruises as a result of falling over while moving about the ship; one has a broken arm.

At 0800, the darken-ship screens and deadlights were removed for the first time since April and the covers went back on the Wardroom furniture. You could see real daylight through the Wardroom scuttles! Owing to the weather, breakfast was a shambles, with stewards manfully attempting to catch plates, cups and marmalade flying around, despite the non-slip table mats. The DWEO ended up wearing the contents of a jug of milk and Commander E won a bowl of cereal and a cup of tea.

The planned replenishment with *Blue Rover* did not happen because of the weather, even though *Antrim* is now down to 45% fuel. In any case, everyone was tired and, in many cases, seasick – even after all this time. It was not a day to attempt anything complicated or challenging. I mostly read and got on with routine work.

During the night, as I was awake a lot and it was the end of the month, I was reflecting on the campaign. We did pretty well, isolating the Islands, conducting an opposed landing 8,000 miles from the UK, without our allies and with patchy air control before the rapid onset of an Antarctic winter. I think that we had just enough SHars to have sufficient air control at the times that we needed it. The rest of the time it was touch and go and we lost ships. However, I was working out that for every Arg raid that attacked us, probably four turned back, ditching their bombs and drop tanks, whenever the SHars turned up to confront them. So, it is not just about what you do to them, it's what you prevent them from doing to you.

The Admiral came in for a lot of criticism for his abrupt manner, his brusque leadership style and the fact that he did not come ashore to see things for himself. However, none of that matters. He won the war – and he won it well. He has been absolutely vindicated in his insistence on keeping the carriers well out to the east and not risking them. Some of the senior Captains were putting him under real pressure, he knew the risks and he resisted. He always had his eye on the strategic aspects and was not unduly deflected by tactical considerations, although I think that he had too much faith in the Type 42/Type 22 combo close inshore. His instincts for this type of warfare were really good and we were lucky to have him. It takes a lot of moral courage and strength of purpose to hold out against that sort of pressure. You need to be right though and you need to deliver success!

I think that, in future, there will be a decided difference in the Royal Navy between those that fought in the Falklands and those that did not – a real us and them attitude ('And gentlemen in England now abed shall think themselves accurs'd they were not here, and hold their manhoods cheap whilst any speaks that fought with us' etc.). It has nothing to do with merit or potential; it is a matter of attitude, feelings of adequacy and complexes. There will be some who will really resent what others have experienced and it will play out in terms of prejudice, jealousies and side-lining of those with front-line experience. After all, most of our senior officers would not have seen as many days action in their whole careers as our junior ratings have down here.

It is also going to be interesting when people go back to Portland to do Operational Sea Training (OST), having experienced things for real. We have had to be resourceful and have broken all the rules when we have had to do so. I suppose that the rules give you a frame of reference from which to depart and let you know how far out of the box you are. I would say that they are the safe sea-shore that allows you to dive into the sea of initiative and something solid to paddle back to you when you get out of your depth. Initiative in the face of the unexpected is so important though.

I also hope that other countries might view the UK differently after this conflict. I do not think that anybody expected us to come all this way to sort things out. Let's hope that the Soviets have taken notice of what's been happening and have concluded that it might not be worth taking us on. The same goes for Spain, Guatemala and China and anyone else that might want to get their hands on our far-flung scraps of former Empire. I reckon that Exocet sales might get a boost, unfortunately.

Let's hope that the success of the campaign will be a welcome boost to the morale and confidence of the country. Socially and politically – and of course economically – we seem to have spent the last ten years or so in a perpetual state of gloom and despondency, giving an impression of studied uselessness in all those areas where once we were considered great.

Thursday, 1 July

The celebrity time-check was done by 'Ringo Starr', or rather an indeterminate 'Scouser'.

The ship spent the day on routine cruising passage with *Blue Rover*, with a very long swell on our port beam and strong winds from the south-west. Most of the ship's company were involved in departmental training or defect rectification.

We attempted to replenish at 0920, but, after about 20 minutes, the violence and confused movement of the sea caused the hose line to part. We broke away and found a more comfortable course running down sea between 1045 and 1200. Even so, the air temperature was up to 14 degrees C and we saw patches of blue in the sky. At midday, we were 45° 17′ S 044° 42′ W.

I was Officer of the Day today, completing without enthusiasm the usual muster of security keys, Confidential Books, crypto and the contents of the Officer of the Day's safe. I also had to investigate the cases of two ratings, both of whom had been adrift from musters it had been their duty to attend. They had overslept and I passed them on to the Commander to deal with at his table.

Heads and bathroom rounds were conducted by the Commander today. As Officer of the Day, I went along with him. All were assessed as Good; the after heads got a Very Satisfactory, which is amazing considering the bomb damage.

We flew between 1430 and 1555, so that the helicopter controllers could practise operational and controlled approaches and the pilots could fly under instrument conditions. I took the opportunity to show LACMN Stapleton how to use the radar and explained the other instruments on the Observer's side of the aircraft. He had never sat in that seat before, while the aircraft was airborne.

At 1630, we met up with the Cable and Wireless Ship *Iris*, which was carrying stores (another gyro unit for the MRS 3 director and some radio components) for us and a replacement for Chief Bullingham – Chief Russell – on her way to South Georgia. She was obviously a well-designed ship for cable-laying, but, with her broad beam and unorthodox superstructure, seemed an odd choice for operations in the South Atlantic. With her big hold, she will run stores back and forth between Ascension and the Falklands. We were not cleared to land on her newly fitted Flight Deck and we were going to have to conduct a winch transfer. The sea conditions were too rough even for that and we had to wait until 2350 before Ian, Stewart and I launched again for the transfer.

When we arrived over the deck in the dark, conditions were pretty marginal, with the ship bucking and rolling all over the place. We went in to pick up Chief Russell, with the deck rising and falling dramatically, with lots of spray and buffeting. As I lowered the winch from about 40 feet hover height, I could sense Ian having to fly the aircraft 'quite positively' as he would put it. As soon as Russell was in the strop, I quickly lifted him clear of the deck. Suddenly, the Flight Deck reared up and he was almost level with me in the cab and our starboard wheel was virtually touching the Flight Deck. I urged Ian to 'Go up, go up!', which he did, and I manhandled Russell into the cab.

Welcome to *Antrim* Flight, I thought. I said to Ian, 'That was a bit close.'

He said, 'Nah, all in a day's work. If you can't take a joke, you should not have joined!'

Chief Russell seemed oblivious to it all – unaware that a man could fly – as I strapped him into the spare seat. After that, it was back to the film set of *Wuthering Heights* over *Iris*; we picked up the stores without too much further drama and headed back to Mum.

Friday, 2 July

We flew between 1100 and 1225, practising instrument flying, anti-submarine drills in the dip and, again, operational approaches for the

HCs. Winds were still strong from the west (certainly not Masefield's 'warm wind, the west wind, full of birds' cries'). At the end of the serial, we collected *Blue Rover*'s CO for lunch.

As we walked up the starboard waist, we heard the Main Broadcast pipe by the Bosun's Mate: 'Relax from flying stations to enable piss-up in the Wardroom in celebration of Flight Commander's 4,000 hours', rapidly followed by the Navigator coming on, amid sounds of castigation, and saying, 'Correction to the last pipe . . . the Flight Commander has completed 4,000 flying hours and that is a cause for celebration.'

Well, it was true. We had laid on a little celebration for Ian's milestone achievement. Stewart had a soft drink and, with Stapleton, returned the CO of *Blue Rover* to his ship after a good lunch.

At midday, we were 40° 22′ S 040° 10′ W.

The port Sea Cat launcher, just outside the hangar, has a live missile on it. It is corroded and it has been decided to leave it where it is until the Greenies get some advice on what to do with it. Rather unconvincingly, Daily Orders stressed, 'IT IS NOT DANGEROUS', but wanted people to 'KEEP CLEAR'.

A major chore is that we are back to the six-monthly routine of mustering Confidential Books page by page, something that had been suspended while we had been in action. I did ten today, with Stewart.

The film in the Wardroom tonight was *Smokey and the Bandit* − a popular choice, even though it has been shown before, mainly because of the good-looking girl, the chase and Sheriff Buford T. Justice.

In the World Cup, Argentina have been beaten 3-1 by Brazil. They lost to Italy on 29 June, so they must be on the way out, with Italy yet to play Brazil. Everyone here is very happy!

Saturday, 3 July

We had a relaxed Saturday routine today and by midday we had reached 34° 52′ S 035° 21′ W. We still had a stiff 30-knot wind from the west and a pronounced swell. However, it was warm and sunny.

At 1000, we met up with *Southampton*, *Birmingham*, *Apollo* and *Bacchante* all heading south. We swapped pleasantries and *Southampton*'s Lynx did the milk round transferring stores, ammunition, mail and newspapers around the various ships.

At 1145, we had the Grand Final of the Beard-Growing Competition, which started way back in Gibraltar and is ending because people want to sunbathe. I am still superstitious and will retain mine. There were prizes for the Best (Chief Donovan), Worst (PO Cook Smith), Best Chinese (Mr Suen Ling Kan – the only qualifier) and Weirdie (to be judged tomorrow after people are allowed to shape/style them for a day). It had cost 50p to enter, with a £1 fine for those who shaved off early. We raised over £100 for the Guide Dogs. Under Queen's Regulations, anyone who wishes to keep his beard has to ask permission (not officers).

I have had my moments with the Guide Dogs charity in a previous appointment in HMS *London*. I was the charities officer and we had raised enough money to sponsor a dog through training and its keep in helping a blind person. The charity was keen to mark the event at their headquarters by unveiling pictures of the ship and the dog (called, appropriately, 'Cockney') together in a single frame, along with an inscription, which was to read: 'A Guide Dog for the Blind, sponsored by the Commanding Officer and ship's company of HMS *London*' and a date. The idea was that the Captain would go down and unveil the picture. I had the thing made up by the Chippy onboard and had intended to take it with me for the event, but the charity wanted to apply the inscription plate.

We arrived at the event and found the photograph already covered by the unveiling curtains. For once, I did not go and check, because I was taken away for a drink by a kind lady and the management did not want to disturb the arrangements. I had prepared some words for the Captain to say and invited him to conclude by reading what it said on the inscription verbatim.

There were a couple of speeches, before the Captain unveiled the picture. He then read what it said on the inscription: 'A Blind Dog for the Guides, sponsored by . . .' My heart sank, as did, temporarily, my career.

Holy Communion was at 1245, which I attended, along with decreased numbers of the ship's company now that we are heading north. It seems that the ship is progressively reverting to paganism as the latitude between us and home decreases.

In the afternoon, we had a programme of inter-Mess and inter-Department Flight Deck sports – football, volleyball and shinty, organized by the Clubswinger. Of course, the volleyball has to be tethered to the net to stop it going over the side, but it works pretty well and the footballs are made of cotton rag stuffing and masking tape bound around a number of times. Onboard shinty is the usual murderous, no-rules game of hockey combined with brute force/actual bodily harm, beloved of the Marines and sailors, especially when playing against the Wardroom or the Flight. It's all played with sticks and rope quoits as pucks, within certain bounds (no striking) and without excessive malice. We did pretty well actually and were only really stomped on by the Stokers. The bloodiest contest was between the Gunners and the Royal Marines – guess who won. Clue: it wasn't the Gunners.

In the evening, we had our first Mess Dinner since Gibraltar. We had a fairly riotous time, largely drinking booze that had been captured. The Commander reviewed the past few months and gave a speech that made everyone feel good. He also reflected that this was the last time that we would all be dining together, as several officers – including me – would be leaving within weeks of our return to Portsmouth. He also awarded prizes – the 'Ropey Trophy', to the Navigator and the DWEO for being so slimy when the women were onboard, the 'Damage Trophy', which he gave to me for being – so he said – so belligerent and aggressive. It was in the form of a brass hose-piece and, during the course of the evening, I managed to get hold of some thunderflashes and other materials that enabled me to use it as a cannon, firing lumps of wax from the candles. Belligerent – me?! We on the Flight presented the Commander with a trophy – for being an all-round good egg – made from the cyclic control rescued from one of the Wessex Vs that crashed on South Georgia.

We had some Mess games – nothing too rough – and then sang some sea songs together, with Martin (Eric Clapton, he ain't) Littleboy on the guitar. Ian, Stewart and I delivered a version of an old Fleet Air Arm ditty, which I had adapted, based on the form (A25) that you have to complete if you prang your aircraft:

The A25 Song
Out in our Wessex and pinging like mad,
Our Looker's dog-tired and the PO's all sad
A bloody great bang, some smoke and a cough
'Shit,' says the pilot, 'the engines gone off!'
Cracking show, I'm alive,
But I've still got to render my A25!

Flying from *Antrim* one night far away
The pilot is lost and he can't find his way
Up comes the Looker, 'This way to fly'
But Mother's not there and the fuel tanks are dry!
Cracking show, I'm alive,
But I've still got to render my A25!

Ten miles off Portland and one day off leave
A bloody great shudder and the cab starts to heave
It falls in the water and sinks in the murk
'Cause the rotor head's seized and the flot bags don't work.
Cracking show, I'm alive,
But I've still got to render my A25!

A chef ditching gash from the port waist one day,
Forgetting the Flight Deck, it's too far away
The aircraft approaches, it sucks in the muck
The engine runs down and the P2 cries 'Fuck!'
Cracking show, I'm alive,
But I've still got to render my A25!

The gentlemen of England are all up in arms
Concerning the hardware that falls on their farms
Two flot cans we've lost and a main cabin door
So fish-heads watch out – we may drop some more!
Cracking show, I'm alive,
But I've still got to render my A25!

Now we've been here for several long months,
There's constant air warnings, the HIFR* hose leaks
So roll on a week Sunday when we shall be gone
And you won't have to hear this ridiculous song.
Cracking show, I'm alive,
But I've still got to render my A25!

Incidentally, whenever anyone is killed in a flying accident in the

* Helicopter Inflight Refuelling.

Fleet Air Arm, the squadron involved tries, to reduce the chances of people getting the willies about flying, to get all the aircrew airborne as soon as possible and then repair to the bar. All the drinks are on the victims' Mess numbers, to celebrate their memory. As there is a charity that kindly pays off the outstanding Mess bills of FAA officers who are killed flying, we normally have a really good wake. I often wonder whether the kind benefactors ever stop to connect – in cause and effect terms – the enormous amount recently spent on booze and the adjacent flying accident.

Sunday, 4 July

Celebrity Call the Hands and time-check: Bill Haley – 'Rock around the Clock' (of course) – not very good.

In the forenoon, suitably late at 1030, we had a memorial service in the Junior Rates' Dining Hall (too blustery and rough on the upper deck) for all those lost and injured in the Falklands – about 200 turned up. I thought of all those I knew who had been lost – Colin Vickers, Brain Murphy and John Sephton and the rest, with a special thought for poor Chief Bullingham. I knew from Portland that Fitz was OK and I mused that, even as *we* prayed, *he* was probably in the 'missionary' position, getting what he used to call his 'wedding tackle' back up to its operational performance standard.

At midday, we were at 28° 46′ S 032° 17′ W.

At 1130, we started the 100-mile relay race around the upper deck, with the intention of breaking the official record. I did the 67th leg and, although I reckoned that I was pretty fit, it proved quite difficult keeping up the pace while running seven laps around the various obstructions on a pitching and yawing deck – and, early on, in a 30-knot wind. By the time that I ran, it was dark and we were behind the trajectory for the record, which was set ashore at 10 hours 2 minutes. I do not think that I got us ahead of the pace at all and realized that I had not done much running recently, despite FOCCIF. In the end, we finished at 2217 and achieved 10 hours and 47 minutes. MEM Hall ran the fastest lap.

I spent time this afternoon drafting the Flight section of the Report of Proceedings which is due to go off at Ascension, and attacking the outstanding routine paperwork, most of which was suspended during operations. Some of it will form part of the historic record and it is important to get it right. I already sense that, for political or career purposes, some rewriting of history is going on, both within the ship and beyond. I do not fully recognize some of the accounts of events with which I am personally familiar or was involved.

Meanwhile, the ME and WE departments have been compiling the vast maintenance programme and defect and damage rectification requirements list that will determine how long the ship stays in dockyard hands after we return to the UK. The Chief Staff Officer (Engineering) Commander and a senior engineering team from CINC-FLEET will come out to Ascension to look at the state of the ship, review the list and take it home. The boys on the Flight have done a similar job on the aircraft and the aviation facilities.

I spent some time researching Mastermind questions and we had a round tonight.

Monday, 5 July

On a beautifully calm day, it was hot and sunny. The ship's company are now into tropical rig. Ian and I were airborne 0900–0940, initially to complete an engine Check Test Flight with PO Kurn and to lift a new gyro up to the Bridge roof for installation into the MRS 3 director. The ship started preparations for a full power and full speed trial.

At midday, we reached 22° 51´ S 028° 40´ W. We replenished from *Blue Rover* in the early afternoon. We then thanked *Blue Rover* and she went on her way to her next task. I then stood the First Dog Watch on the Bridge.

Ian, Stewart and I have talked a great deal about honours and awards for the Flight personnel. If it were down to me, they would all get something as they have been, without exception, absolutely first class. I feel humbled by what they have done and cannot help feeling emotional about it all. To maintain 406 at such a high level of serviceability and available for every major requirement, together with several major engineering challenges – the sonar removal and rapid replacement, the engine change and the recovery from serious action damage – has been nothing short of remarkable. This intense maintenance load – and extensive Flight Deck operations with other aircraft – has all been achieved in the teeth of the worst operating and weather conditions that I have experienced, the constant threat of death and injury and a very high operational tempo. Nobody has wobbled, with morale remaining stoically and steadfastly high, and they have been mentally and physically tough. It would be difficult to single out any one over the others.

On that basis and on balance, we reckon that we are going to nominate the SMR for a BEM, both in his own right, for his highly effective leadership and all-round excellence, and as a reflection of the Flight's considerable achievements. Everyone else will have to get their rewards in their personal reports and recommendations for promotion.

It strikes me that a lot of people who have performed amazing feats of arms on this conflict are probably not going to be recognized with medals and awards. I have seen ordinary people achieve extraordinary things and not seek any reward or recognition. I expect that the gongs will be trotted out on the basis of being spread around, just as with the South Georgia awards, whereby those who shout the loudest get the most, regardless of the truth. I suspect that you are only as good as the person who writes you up. What did 'Dirty Harry' say? 'Medals are like haemorrhoids – sooner or later every asshole gets one!'

Actually, I do not know why I am writing this – it's a bit of a rant. The reality is that the best medal that you can wear is your life. If you come back from war in one piece physically and not mentally scarred, I'd say that that is something that you can cherish for the rest of your days.

There is a determined purge on long, scruffy hair. I am OK.

The other major drive is to stem the tide of porn that is on display around the ship. The Commander is worried about what the families will think on our arrival back in Portsmouth. Pictorial porn – carefully regulated in terms of what the lady in question is allowed to show off – has been on general release – well, pretty rampant – during the conflict and has played its considerable part in sustaining morale.

The spurious Main Broadcast piper was at it again today – 'POME*
Granite – Fresh Provisions Store.'

Tuesday, 6 July

Celebrity time-check: Dame Edna Everage – it sounded like Dick Van Dyke.

* Petty Officer Marine Engineering.

Today was our 100th day at sea since Gibraltar. Most of the day was taken up with departmental drills, calibration of weapon systems, and individual training and education. I helped teach NAMET English in the forenoon – and again in the afternoon. The sailors need better qualifications in Maths and English to progress through the ranks. We played games of 'Just a Minute', to increase powers of expression and introduce some fun and a competitive element. We just about hacked repetition and hesitation, but are still struggling over deviation (!). I also helped with asking candidates questions about aviation in the Operations Department professional examinations.

At midday, we were 16°38′ S 023° 10′ W.

The last week or so has been spent putting the Report of Proceedings together, so that it can be taken home from Ascension and despatched. Needless to say, there has been a certain amount of ex post facto rationalization and justification incorporated into the text, with everyone wanting to appear in the best possible light. The weapons – like Sea Cat – suddenly seem to have worked better than they did. In writing the Flight section, I tried to make it as historically accurate and objective as possible. If anything, I have understated things, just wanting to highlight a few important issues that really need resolution and improvement for subsequent operations and deployments.

The rest of the day was spent getting the Report of Proceedings draft though Ian and the Captain. I was also asked to have a look at the main Report and I was able to adjust some of the narrative closer to what actually happened.

This evening, we held the 'Folklands Evening' and Grand Falklands draw and BBQ on the Flight Deck. A stage was rigged on the forward end of the Flight Deck and various musicians, with instruments, and other imitators had their 15 or so minutes of fame. The Commander had allowed the junior rates three cans of beer each, but most of the lads were merry and in good spirits well before the start at 2030. Various artistes did their thing – including Dylan, Ralph McTell and Gordon Lightfoot stuff, along with 'Sloop John B' and the 'The Night They Drove Old Dixie Down'. Inevitably, we had several rounds of Shep Woolley's subversive counter-naval Establishment lyrics, including, inevitably, 'Ram it! I'm RDP!'

We then had *Antrim* community singing, with special song-sheets provided by LWTR Prescott and LWTR Taylor from the Ship's Office:

'All My Loving', 'Take Me Home Country Roads', 'Mull of Kintyre', a variant of 'Ram It, I'm RDP' on the Dining Hall Party theme ('Ram it, I'm DHP'), 'Sailing' and for the Advanced Leave Party (off at Ascension tomorrow) 'Leaving on a Jet Plane'. It was all very good-natured and the conversation and close engagement among all ranks during the BBQ (steak and chips) reflected the intensity of shared danger, experience and success over the previous few months. In fact, from the back of the Flight Deck, I took a long look at the human scene, unique in time and space, in its little bubble of light amid the enfolding darkness, in the middle of an immense ocean and under a star-studded sky. You could almost:

> Hold Infinity in the palm of your hand
> And Eternity in an hour.*

It was a moment caught in time. I looked at the individual faces of men who had achieved extraordinary things over the past few months. This scene, with its emotional charge and clannish resonance, could never be repeated. And it was hard not to feel sentimental – and maudlin – about it all.

In a previous ship, we had a Petty Officer who looked exactly like Roy Orbison, to the extent that he won a lookalike competition in the US. He took to going ashore dressed as Roy, replete with dark jacket, flared trousers and sunglasses. On one occasion when the ship was alongside in a South American port, I was Officer of the Day. The Captain invited several dignitaries, including government ministers, onboard for dinner. A lot of the ship's company were ashore, having a good time with wine, women and song, as we had been at sea for a while.

Towards the end of the evening, I made my way to the Captain's quarters in preparation for the guests' departure, ensuring that the upper deck was tidy and that the ceremonial was organized. When I arrived forward, the guests were leaving and I led them down the waist to the Flight Deck and the gangway. As I chatted in Spanish to them, I could see, out the corner of my eye, a taxi approaching along the jetty. Roy was in the back and he would arrive at the gangway at the same time as the Captain's guests.

On arrival at the Flight Deck, I tried to distract the guests by pointing

* William Blake.

out the helicopter, which was spread and ranged there. '*Esto es un heli-copter Wessex, con los torpedos . . .*' They were not paying the slightest attention to me, they were looking at Roy. More importantly, the Captain was giving me the sort of expression that could only be saying, 'Sort this out, or . . .!'

Before I could act, a strange scene unfolded at the bottom of the gangway, as the guests looked on in rapt attention. As he paid the taxi driver, Roy was the clearly the worse for wear and unsteady on his feet. He then slammed the taxi door and the taxi roared off. The only problem was that the wide flares of his trousers had become stuck in the door and were ripped off him as the taxi sped away. Roy spun round and landed on his bottom, looking confused at the turn of events. The Captain's guests were transfixed by the scene, which under the dim lights of the jetty looked almost theatrical. I felt that this was a career-limiting opportunity and stepped forward. Without thinking, I said to the Quartermaster, 'Leading Seaman Taylor, that Russian sailor seems to have come to the wrong ship. Just see him along the jetty, would you?'

'Sir, it's PO –' he started.

'Just see him along the jetty to his ship, the one that is two down from us,' I said, through my teeth, while motioning vigorously with my head in the direction of a large merchant ship astern of us and, simultaneously, for the sake of the guests, maintaining the appearance of normality.

The Quartermaster and Bosun's Mate hurried off the gangway to 'assist' Roy along the jetty. The guests made their farewells, remarking how considerate we Brits were, and departed in their official cars.

While this was going on, the Captain and I could see, behind their backs, the flaws in my plan. Roy knew, even in his drunken state, that he had come to the right ship – it was grey and had a helicopter on the back end. This had resulted in him resisting the attempts of the gangway team to 'help' him and a scuffle had broken out. Secondly, he was wearing a garish pair of Union Jack underpants! But we got away with it!

We now know that we should arrive at 1045 at Outer Spit Buoy off Portsmouth on 17 July and this evening, at 2330, we advanced clocks to ZULU time [Greenwich Mean Time].

It really feels like we are well up-track and homeward bound now – Ascension and the Equator are the next milestones.

Wednesday, 7 July

Just after 0800, the ship started a full-power trial and worked up to full speed. At 1005, Stewart and I were airborne for an hour, load-lifting. We also photographed the ship as she hammered along at 31 knots, while taking some members of the ship's company along for familiarization flights. The ship reverted to normal cruising at 1145.

At midday, we were at 10° 42´ S 017° 13´ W.

In the afternoon, the 20 mm were fired, so that the junior gunners could complete their task books. It all seemed very tame and procedural compared to what we have experienced.

A full programme of transfers and replenishment, including mail, has been issued for our stopover at Ascension tomorrow.

Main Broadcast joker is still at it: 'Seaman Stains – Bedding Store.'

At 2145, Ascension was sighted.

The *Daily Oak* contains news that there is a railway strike in the UK.

Thursday, 8 July

At 0105, we transferred our Advanced Leave Party, those who volunteered – or were selected – to go home early to Ascension Island by helicopters from Ascension. They will take some leave and be on hand as the duty team to look after the ship when we return on 17 July, so that the rest of us can go on leave. David Barraclough, Nick Bracegirdle and Martin Littleboy have gone, along with a small clutch of Greenies (Mike Bonney and Roger Insley) and ME officers and a representative sample across all departments. The transfer finished at 0240 and the ship went alongside the resident tanker, MV *Alvega*, and refuelled 0325–0445. The WE and ME officers were up all night discussing the maintenance requirements with the Portsmouth Dockyard team and the CINCFLEET staff. There was an 0300 steak dinner for everyone.

We stayed alongside until 0730 and then conducted helicopter transfers, which brought huge amounts of mail (some recent, but some that had gone down to the Falklands and back) and stores (for us and *Blue Rover*), along with, amazingly, fresh provisions, including bananas, the first that I had seen in 100 days. We raffled the six Wardroom-allocated ones for charity and raised £32. The mail included letters from A and

Mum and Dad, mostly about Ann's degree results, the Pope's visit to Liverpool and their relief that the conflict appeared to be over.

We continued on our way at 1040 and by 1200 we were 07° 39´ S 014° 36´ W.

One issue that I discussed with Ian today related to 406. We have received a signal from Portland saying that we will receive a new aircraft – XM 328 – on our return and that the likelihood is that Humphrey will become a hangar queen, cannibalized for spares and eventually scrapped. After all we have been through together, we cannot let this happen. Ian agrees and, as a result, I have drafted a signal, which we want the Captain to release, requesting that Humphrey is allowed to retire honourably and be sent to the Fleet Air Arm Museum on our return to Portland. I really could not bear to be around the main hangar at Portland in the months to come and watch 406 being cannibalized. I hope that some sentiment and Fleet Air Arm common sense prevail and that the usual bureaucratic indifference and inertia do not make it all too difficult.

The rest of the day was spent with routine administration and relaxation. I collated the Mastermind questions and we had another round tonight, which the Wardroom won, featuring a starring performance by the Commander. He won by one point, ahead of 3 Mess Chiefs, with the correct answer to the question 'What is the first station you come to when leaving London Waterloo on the Portsmouth train?'★ On the Commander's triumphant return to the Wardroom for dinner, the Padre complained that this had been an easy question – and was obviously a plant by me. The Commander retorted that any question is easy if you know the answer.

The film tonight was *The Riddle of the Sands* – very enjoyable and atmospheric. Everyone thinks that Jenny Agutter is very sexy in an English sort of way, but that you could not leave her behind while you went off to sea for long periods!

Friday, 9 July

Winston Churchill did Call the Hands and the time-check. I'd fight him on the beaches . . .!

★ Vauxhall.

At 0945, we Crossed the Equator and by midday were at 01° 10′ N 016° 13′ W. We are now in the North Atlantic.

We flew a lot today. In the forenoon, from 1000 to 1200, we did some FCS and ASW drills as a full crew and then Stewart and LACMN Stapleton took half a dozen of the ship's company for a familiarization, including the officers under training. One of the young officers fell for the oldest trick in the book of being winched out and then lowered almost to the sea. The aircraft then transitions gently forward and the unfortunate young man then understands how it is possible to walk on water, unless he wants to become shark bait, as the previously warned ship's company lines up on deck with their cameras at the ready.

The ship's company has spent the day either training, sunbathing or making sure that the ship is in good shape. The Commander is determined that we return to the UK looking smart; some officers think that we should go back looking as if we have been in a war and in the South Atlantic. On the upper deck, with the weekend coming up, there is some tension between those who are off watch and want to sunbathe and those who are getting on with things. Last night, on Daily Orders, a notice appeared:

> It is a well-known fact that sunbathers who engage in useful activity such as painting get a more even bronzy [tan] than those who lie around all day getting in everyone else's way. If you are pale and interested, apply to the Buffer now for free painting facilities. Do your bit to help make the ship look smart for the victorious entry into Pompey. This offer closes in 8 days time.

I stood the First Dog on the Bridge.

We have just come back from a night ASW and FCS session, to ensure that we all stay in date and current on role, and to make sure that our Fleet Form 3* returns are balanced before we return to Portland.

Apparently, we are also going to be visited by the Commander-in-Chief (Fleet), Admiral Fieldhouse, on the day before we return to Portsmouth. We are now also thinking about how we are going to deal with all the press interest, with the need to preserve security about some

* Training requirements on a monthly or periodic basis, to maintain operational capability.

of our operations and the activities of the SAS and SBS, who will not want their anonymity compromised.

We had another film tonight, *Zulu Dawn*, which was a historical indictment of the Army's way of doing things, some of which we have seen in the South Atlantic.

Saturday, 10 July

At midday, we were 10° 15´ N 017° 46´ W and, on a calm, sunny and clear day, the ship's company was basically relaxed, although there were knots of sunbathing painters – or painting sunbathers – on the upper deck. That is until a tropical downpour and a lively storm – out of nowhere – put an end to things at about 1130.

The Wardroom hosted a drinks session with the senior rates this afternoon, to say thank you for their professionalism, sacrifice and companionship during the conflict. I have got to know many of them really well, not just those on the Flight, but splendid personalities like the Buffer, CCY [Chief Communication Yeoman] Cosker, Chippy Gent and many others, especially among the POs, who have contributed so much.

After lunch, we had the usual bloodletting on the Flight Deck as we had another session of inter-Mess sports. We did quite well, no doubt because of the lubrication afforded at lunchtime. We won the volleyball and saw off three other messes in the shinty, before losing to the Royal Marines (who were all wearing boots). I scraped my right knee on the abrasive surface of the Flight Deck. It's certainly non-slip!

David Barraclough, who went home with the Advanced Leave Party, sent us a message via Admiralty Radio: 'Advanced Leave Party arrived safely. Prices up, petrol up, beer up – so am I.' *Glamorgan* arrived home today, to a welcome by thousands, with canvas covering her damaged hangar area.

Even though it would be great to be home, I would always have wanted to see this deployment through to the end – I think that it will be a truly life-affirming experience to sail back after this gap of time into Portsmouth on the end of a war. Somehow, I would feel that I had not done the whole thing or done it properly if I had flown home from Ascension. In any case, I think that it is healthy to unwind gradually from an experience like this and not be pitched back into things with a sudden jolt as if nothing unusual had happened. It is probably going to be a problem for all those people – like the survivors of ships that were sunk and the soldiers – who have been taken home as quickly as possible.

Mind you, it cannot be good psychologically for the guys in ships like *Invincible* which have been left down there. The guys will soon be bored by the routine and will miss the excitement of the war, with no immediate prospect of getting home. The problem could arise that they will bottle up all their experiences and sensations, because it would not be considered right or masculine to spin war stories. Add to that mix the temptation to hang around the bar for too long and on too many occasions. I am no psychologist, but that could lead to problems later. Just as with a car crash or an unpleasant or unfamiliar experience, you want – and need – to tell someone pretty quickly about what has happened to you, or it tends to fester and distract you. Once it is driven deep into your subconscious, who knows when it will come back to bite you. Perhaps that is why some old-timers from the War get a reputation for boring people with their recounting and repetition of endless war stories; they need to get something out of their system.

We know that the Main Broadcast joker did not leave at Ascension: 'Able Seaman Thalidomide – Small Arms Store.' That was beyond the pale and the Commander has put a price on his head.

There have been dire warnings from the UK about 'looted' Arg weaponry and equipment. Apparently, quite a lot has found its way back into the UK and the police are getting upset. Of course, we have a veritable arsenal of weapons in the Air Office, which I had intended to give to the Fleet Air Arm Museum. In conversation, I detected that the Commander was likely to take a pretty dim view of anyone in *Antrim* who had any Arg weapons and equipment. Of course, all the aircrew know about it, but I am beginning to get windy about it all. I will tell Stapleton to wait for it to get dark tomorrow and tell him to ditch all the weapons. It's a shame because there are some really nice rifles and mementoes.

We had a traditional Saturday night at sea – a good (steak) dinner together, followed by a *Mickey Duck* and a film – *The Fog*, a suspense thriller, which we could usefully have seen a couple of months ago! We played three games of uckers.

I am up late because I am doing the Middle Watch on the Bridge in a moment. I did have a couple of hours on my rack during the Dogs after the sports though.

Sunday, 11 July

I did the Middle Watch and the task was to identify and close *Blue Rover* in time for replenishment this morning. We had found her by the time that I turned over the watch and were in company when everyone was up and about. I felt fairly ragged round the edges, having only had about three hours' sleep.

Celebrity Call the Hands was by 'Jimmy Savile'. I do not know what is more irritating – the original or the imitator.

Ian and LACMN Stapleton did a transfer of mail and stores to *Blue Rover*, 0930–1015, and the ship replenished fuel 1005–1115, while the duty watch and various volunteers continued scraping and painting around the upper deck. I went to the church service and Holy Communion at 1030 in the Junior Rates' Dining Hall. It is our last Sunday at sea. I probably won't go to church next Sunday in Broadmayne.

At midday, we were at 17° 48′ N 017° 55′ W, with a steady breeze from the north. The ship's company were working part of ship on the upper deck and painting the masts, Sea Slug launcher and Exocet containers.

I spent the rest of the day preparing questions for the Mastermind rounds tonight, either from my own memory or from reference books that I have been able to find. I am resorting to my own *Pears Cyclopaedia* encyclopaedia for 1981–2, as well as a multi-volume encyclopedia from the ship's library, but I mostly have to write down questions as they occur to me. I am going to struggle when we get to the Final and the contestants will be able to choose a specialist subject.

Today was the day of the World Cup Final, with most of the ship rooting for Italy (rather than West Germany) and disappointed that England went out in the second round without actually losing a game (too many draws though, including one against West Germany). We found out from the World Service that Italy won 3-1. The Commander, who had been supporting Scotland (out after the first round and a thumping by Brazil), had been gamely plugging for England as well.

Canberra returned to Southampton, with the Royal Marines, to an amazing reception. There was a memorial service for the Welsh Guards in Llandaff Cathedral.

Monday, 12 July

Even though it was a Monday, we had a Saturday Sea Routine (half day) today as far as work was concerned. After lunch, most people were sunbathing or relaxing on the upper deck, despite a stiff north-easterly and a lot of sand in the air coming off the Sahara. Even so, with Captain's Rounds every day this week from tomorrow, a lot of cleaning and rectification was going on around the ship as well, together with training and education. I took two NAMET English classes today, one in the forenoon and one in the afternoon, and we concentrated on précis writing and the differences between various verb tenses. We also went through some past papers. I was also busy putting together questions for this evening's Mastermind event.

At 0930, Stewart and LACMN Stapleton took Chief McComb to *Blue Rover*, so that the 992 radar could be checked and calibrated. They then flew some profiles for the test and some circuits, practice emergencies and controlled approaches for the Bridge team and the helicopter controllers before going unserviceable with a faulty alternator. They did some ground runs and, once serviceable, resumed the trial and completed the serial by 1600.

At midday, we were 24° 42′ N 017° 10′ W.

We heard today that the Foreign Office has declared the war to be over and that all remaining prisoners are going to be returned. The UK will maintain the Exclusion Zone and a garrison of 2,500 troops on the Islands. The Queen's Own Highlanders are going out as replacements.

The other really good news today is that the staff officers at FONAC [Flag Officer Naval Air Command] have said that we can send Humphrey to the Fleet Air Arm Museum. On our return, a low loader will take it up to Yeovilton, once we have done all the paperwork and removed any specialist kit. It probably helped that the Captain is a distinguished senior pilot.

The stores people are frantically trying to relocate and account for various things that have gone missing during the conflict. There are frequent pleas on Daily Orders to return various bits of Service and personal gear, including 'one sheepskin coat – STD [Steward] Barrowcliff' and 'one lady's watch from the Chief Stoker's office – finder please return' (must be a wind-up! – get it?). I hope that we can write some things off – I lent my combat jacket to an SAS man and I never saw it (or him) again.

We had our final eliminator round of Mastermind tonight. The finalists on 15 July will be: Sub Lt Brook, POMEM Berry, RO Piper, Leading Caterer Marriott, LRO Morris, AB Curran and Can Man Bailey from the NAAFI.* I now have to get enough questions on each of their specialist subjects as well as some more general knowledge questions. We are going to pre-record on CCTV and show it later in the evening.

Tuesday, 13 July

I stood the Morning Watch after we had passed Tenerife and Gran Canaria during the Middle. There were several shipping situations that needed us to manoeuvre, mainly involving fishing vessels, but also a Spanish frigate (identified by intercept) that passed without exchanging identities.

At 1400, we replenished fuel from *Blue Rover*, as well as water, as the evaporators have been giving us trouble again. At 1500, we had to sprint west towards Madeira for a medical emergency and for us, on the Flight, an unexpected but brief trip to civilization. An MEM had a dislocated/ fractured elbow after falling down a ladder and we had to take both the patient and the Doctor into Funchal in Madeira, between 1700 and 2000. We were only on the ground long enough to hand the patient over to the civilian medical authorities, touch base with the consular staff and take a suck of fuel. We were a little bit worried that we might go unserviceable on the ground and not be able to make it back.

I had actually had my first run-ashore in *Antrim* in Funchal in February 1981. I had joined the week before, missing being my best chum's best man, and had conducted an ASW exercise with the Portuguese submarine *Barracuda* (not unlike the *Santa Fé*). It was now my last foreign visit (albeit very brief) as an officer in *Antrim*. It's strange how life goes around.

What was amazing was the incongruity of us arriving from a war zone into an environment that hardly knew or cared about where we had been or what we had done. We saw an inhabited and urban landscape, with its sophistication, busy people and modernity after all that time in the barrenness, bleak weather and vastness of the South Atlantic. There wasn't time for us to savour even a hint of the holiday spirit, just the bright lights indicating that thousands of people were going

* The civilian NAAFI Canteen Manager, who had been classed as a Chief Petty Officer while subject to the Naval Discipline Act during the conflict.

about their daily, routine business and others were on holiday having a good time. They have not seen what we have seen, or done what we have done. As we left the island behind, the immensity of the darkness, 'the womb of night', swallowed us up and took us back to our little world afloat in the vastness of the ocean.

Wednesday, 14 July

We sailed past Morocco and Portugal, in company with *Blue Rover*, and at midday we were at 37° 08′ N 011° 35′ W. We were into the Bay of Biscay – the weather was quite good, with a heavy swell to port.

Amid a lot of administrative work, such as writing up my division's personal reports and checking their career documentation, I spent most of the day researching the specialist subject and general knowledge questions for tomorrow's Mastermind Grand Final. It has been a challenge because of the paucity of source materials onboard. I have had to continue to rely on my own knowledge and the scattered scraps of relevant information in the ship's encyclopaedia and other available books.

The specialist subjects are (in order of difficulty of finding information):

• Fresh Water Fish and Fishing.
• British Birds.
• Greek History 800–399 BC.
• European Geography.
• Brazil.
• Football.
• Pop Music.

Thursday, 15 July

Early in the Morning Watch, we found *Blue Rover* and replenished fuel from her between 0845 and 0945, before she was detached for other duties. That is our last refuelling – we have done 42 while we have been away.

More painting of the upper deck and superstructure took place – including the Forth Road Bridge efforts on the Sea Slug launcher. It's going to be in marked contrast to the battle-worn and weather-beaten hull.

The coast of Spain was visible to the east at 0740. At midday, we were at 43° 43′ N 009° 09′ W.

I spent most of the day around the ship, completing the specialist subject questions for the Grand Final of the Mastermind competition.

We did FOCCIF (18 repetitions) during the Dogs.

We recorded the Mastermind Grand Final at 1830 and it was shown later on this evening. The competition has definitely attracted the imagination and interest of the ship's company and has thrown up a number of hitherto undiscovered mines of information. The finalists were: LCA Marriott, Sub Lt Brook, PO Piper, PO Berry, AB Curran, LRO Morris and Can Man Bailey. After the specialist subject round, the leader was Can Man Bailey, but he was overhauled by the winner, Sub Lt Brook, and PO Berry, after the General Knowledge round.

I went back to the Wardroom for supper and the 'final', deciding game of uckers. Declan and I won the game, but we fell for the 'best of three?' plea. We lost the second, but won the third by one throw of the dice, I reckon, because Alasdair and Carlos only needed to throw a 2 to win and we needed a 5. As the dice spun round, to reveal an emerging 4 and a 1 for us, they up-boarded before we could move our piece. By the end, the game had become something of a spectator sport for the rest of the Wardroom, as it has been throughout the deployment.

The Chiefs' Mess have heard about the South Atlantic Challenge – and the result – and want to play us tomorrow in the best of five games as we head Up Channel. Now the Chiefs fancy themselves at uckers – this is a serious ship credibility issue.

The film was the *Eiger Sanction* – a good thriller, although I spotted the bad guy early. We will round Ushant during the Middle Watch tonight.

A poem in the style of Kipling's 'The Dutch in the Medway' appeared on the Wardroom notice board today – from an original by Rear Admiral John Hervey. It is pure doggerel – but two verses seem to sum up the mood of all of us returning to the UK:

If wars were won by boasting
Or victory by a speech
Or safety found in voting sound
How long would be our reach!
But honour and dominion
Are not maintained so,

They're only got by sword and shot,
And this the ARGIES know.

NOTT wants to flog our carriers
And plans to axe our men.
As for the loyal opposition
It's in the hands of Wedgwood Benn.
But now the Argie aircraft
Have given our Fleet a blow,
There's going to be a reckoning
And this the COMMONS know!

At 2330, we went to ALFA time – British Summer Time. We are on the same time as the UK and we are just picking up fuzzy TV signals from our home country. It's a great feeling to be entering the Channel at last. I always thought that we would make it home.

Friday, 16 July

We passed 60 miles to the west of Ushant light at 0220. During the fore-noon, at 1030 we saw our homeland again – it was Mounts Bay. I deliberately went up onto the Bridge precisely at the moment that the coast of England appeared on the horizon. It was a clear, sunny day and it truly looked like a 'green and pleasant land', in marked contrast to the monochrome landscapes and seascapes to which we had become accus-tomed. There is an incredible emotional rush and strong sense of sentiment associated with returning from war and seeing your native country for the first time again. The context is different but:

Gwlad, gwlad, pleidiol wyf i'm gwlad.
Tra môr yn fur i'r bur hoff bau.*

The other thing that struck me was the large number of vessels that were not painted grey! There were yachts, fishing vessels, ferries and tankers of every colour, size and shape – something that we had not seen for some months, despite the presence of the ships taken up from trade. It was as if we had gone from black-and-white to colour!

* 'My country, my country, I am faithful to my country, while the sea is a wall to my pure, most loved land.'

We were off the Eddystone Lighthouse by midday. At 1300, we launched in 406 to take a medical case (suspected appendicitis – a pity, or a good thing, that the Mad Doctor was not available!) into Plymouth. He had been sedated in the Sick Bay for a while. After flying up the harbour and over the familiar naval city, we landed once more in England near the Wardroom at *Drake*. I purposely did not get out of the aircraft onto the ground. I wanted to save the moment.

As we made our way further up the Channel, the uckers game with the Chiefs had to be settled, so Declan and I sat down in the empty Captain's Day Cabin, forward of the Wardroom (the Captain has moved into the Admiral's quarters), to settle the issue with Chippy Gent and the Chief Stoker. The progress of the game was being relayed over the ship's CCTV. We were quickly two games down and it looked like humiliation beckoned. Then we clawed the third game back and, miraculously, the fourth. In the final game, we won by five pieces and romped home. We had beers all round and teased the Chiefs about lulling them into a false sense of security; the Chiefs said that they let us win (I don't think so!). The Commander came in and accused us of using dodgy Fleet Air Arm tactics (well, yes!) and we all subconsciously, I think, in our handshakes, acknowledged the unique sense of fellowship and professional friendship that we suspected would imperceptibly start to fade as soon as we got alongside.

In the late afternoon, a Wessex V from Portland arrived with 46 bags of mail and I received a kind letter from David Richards, the Headmaster of my school: 'A very short note from Portsmouth Grammar School simply to offer you our warmest congratulations on your recent mention in despatches.' Needless to say, among the ship's company, there was a lot more interest in the mail than in the imminent visit of the Commander-in-Chief!

Some of the ship's company are irritated that we were making a stately passage up the Channel and that we were going to anchor tonight, before entering harbour in the morning. They want us to get alongside as soon as possible. Mostly, it's the Pompey natives, who do not realize that the arrangements for our return were finalized a good week ago. The Dockyard needed to prepare facilities: friends and relatives who have to travel long distances have to know when to come.

At 1655, Ian and I flew into Portland to pick up CINCFLEET and his Flag Lieutenant from Portland and returned them to the ship at 1800. I had to get out of the aircraft to welcome Admiral Fieldhouse, so my first physical contact with England was, fittingly, at Portland.

We saw *Phoebe* at 1855 and she passed us a 'Welcome home. Well done. Glad you are back in one piece' signal by light.

We flashed back: 'Glad you are glad! VMT.'*

When CINCFLEET arrived onboard, he was met by the Commander and Captain, who walked the Admiral over to where Ian, Stewart and I were standing, waiting, as in a wedding line, to be introduced.

Ian shook hands with CINCFLEET and there was instant recognition and appreciation from Admiral Fieldhouse, together with some very complimentary words about the operations in South Georgia:

'The Prime Minister asked me to convey her personal thanks and appreciation to you.'

'Please say thank you to her,' said Ian, taken aback, I think.

'And this is our Flight Observer, Lieutenant Parry,' said the Captain.

I shook hands and looked him in the eye. The Flag Lieutenant, whom I knew from a previous visit to the ship, was chatting away in a social sort of way to the Commander behind him.

'So, what do you do onboard? Are you the Operations Officer,' the Commander-in-Chief asked.

It was my turn to be taken aback, seeing that I had just flown back from Portland with him in an anti-submarine helicopter.

'I am the Observer in the helo, sir; this is an anti-submarine Wessex — like a Sea King.'

He did not immediately relate to what I was saying. He can only think of pilots when he sees a helicopter! His eyes wavered; he didn't understand what I was talking about and he quickly moved on to Stewart.

I did not hear what he said to Stewart. I was thinking:

'Yes, Commander-in-Chief, we all flew as a crew at South Georgia and throughout the war. You know all about us from the ship's signals and reports. How do you think that we survived the glacier and got the bloody submarine?'

I understand that he is good man and appreciate that he had a lot on his mind, but, if you are going to come out to a returning ship to make it a special event, you need to have a grip on the detail. He must have

---

* Very many thanks.

been poorly briefed. As a leader, and someone stratospherically higher than me in the pecking order, he had made me feel distinctly unappreciated. Without real insight and understanding about people, this glad-handing is just coded insincerity.

CINCFLEET moved forward to chat to the Captain and have a session with the officers. He then had a quick tour of the ship, looking at various compartments and the action damage, and received a slide presentation on our deployment. He spoke to the senior rates and the lads around the ship and in their Mess decks. Finally, he went on Main Broadcast and told us how well we had all done and welcomed us home.

Ian and I took off at 2000 to take CINCFLEET to Lee-on-Solent and were back by 2020. At 2100, we came to anchor at Spithead 5, with seven shackles on deck. Here we are, back from war, like so many of our illustrious predecessors. We are part of that heritage now.

We embarked a piper from the Royal Irish Rangers, to accompany us into harbour tomorrow.

As one might have expected, our late dinner took place in a celebratory mood, with everyone looking forward to getting alongside and greeting our loved ones. We were all very relaxed and most were initially determined to finish off the Arg wine that we captured at Grytviken. The Captain came in, but seemed rather subdued and quiet.

In the end, no one stayed very long and people started to drift away, to clear their cabins and to get an early night. I went down to the hangar to see how the boys were doing, packing up all the equipment and baggage that will go back to Portland by road after lunch tomorrow. We reflected together on how well the Flight had done and how well the aircraft had held up thanks to their hard work, dedication and resourcefulness. We thought about our friends in *Glamorgan* Flight 'who have no grave but the sea'.

This is my last live diary entry for this amazing deployment and I feel that I am taking leave of an old familiar friend, someone with whom I have been conversing and sharing my life, hopes and fears, over the past few months. I do not think that I am a natural diarist, in the Pepys mould, and I do not intend to do this again, unless I am in another war.

Last thing, before I turned in, I went up to the signal deck. I looked out at the lights of the Isle of Wight and on the mainland on either side and knew that I was home. Under a clear sky, with a warm breeze from the west in my face, the Solent held me in a tender embrace.

Old men forget; yet all shall be forgot,
But he'll remember, with advantages,
What feats he did that day.

Saturday, 17 July

Call the Hands (no celebrity, at last) was at 0600 this morning. There
was not really any need to hurry people out of their bunks. People were
straight into their best blue uniforms and there was an atmosphere of
boyish expectation, excitement and light-hearted banter around the
ship. One thing that I did notice was that the strong sense of collective
spirit and tight bonding that had carried us through our adventure had
strangely weakened overnight and was evaporating. Certainly, everyone was committed to getting the ship alongside, but I detected in
people's eyes that their thoughts were now elsewhere, not just with
their families and friends, but with their usual preoccupations: the
rough and tumble of normal life and picking up the lives that had been
cocooned for four months.

After breakfast, the first formality was to clear Customs. The Customs
officers had come onboard by boat at 0800 and it did not take long – it was
not as if the ship was chock full of rabbits★ and other contraband obtained
on runs-ashore. As always, most of their time was spent ensuring there
were no irregularities with the tobacco and alcohol accounts.

On the upper deck, it was already a perfect summer's day, with a
clear blue sky and every topographical detail and local feature defined in
sharp relief by the bright sunlight ('hearts at peace, under an English
heaven'). I took time to acknowledge the familiar sights around me, all
giving the impression of solidity and permanence, while the ship swung
at her anchor in a moderate breeze. Not far away were Palmerston's formidable sea-forts either side of the main channel, the broad sweep of
Southsea sea front, the twin chimneys of the power station, poignantly,
the Royal Navy war memorial and – in the distance – Portsdown Hill,
which frames Portsmouth to the north. I could just make out my parents' house. We were home!

Already weekend yachtsmen and other craft were coming in close to
examine the latest warrior home from the wars. The Isle of Wight ferry

★ The naval expression for gifts and other items obtained on foreign runs-ashore.

hooted as she passed close by. The hovercraft from Southsea to Ryde roared past, taking a slight detour to take a look at us.

Then 30 members of the press arrived by boat. Ian, as Public Relations Officer, had organized a press conference in the Admiral's Day Cabin, where the Captain, the Commander and other worthies spoke of the ship and her exploits. I stayed down on the Flight Deck and chatted to the Flight maintainers as they prepared the ground equipment and other stores that were due to be craned off and transported down to Portland later in the day. The boys would travel down too, by road, and await the arrival of 406, flown by Ian and me, tomorrow. Stewart and LACMN Stapleton were going on leave straightaway once we got alongside.

The press wanted to do some interviews. Ian and I spoke to a couple of journalists, who really did not know what they wanted to ask and were just after a story – any story. Amid the routine 'what was it like?' questions, one of them asked what it had been like going without female company for all that time; another, what's the first thing you are going to do when you get home? I was tempted to say, 'Mow the lawn.' You just don't get it, do you? I thought.

One chap had a photographer and a good-looking young thing in tow – she was Miss Somewhere-or-other – and wanted me to pose for a photo with my arm round her. He was pretty narked and surprised when I said that I did not think it appropriate to be hugging someone – attractive as she was – when I had been away from my wife and in the South Atlantic for four months. She ended up having her photo taken with a couple of the lads who I could tell wondered what was wrong with me – thanks, guys! It just did not seem right somehow. I hope that the poor girl did not feel offended.

The real issue was to get on the starboard side of the flag deck for Procedure Alfa,* so that I could face the Portsmouth side on the way in to harbour. Gosport is OK, but every time that I have entered Portsmouth, I have always thrilled to the sight of the long passage up the channel close to Southsea beach and on to the Round Tower at the harbour entrance. I wanted to see places and features that were so familiar and dear to me, which I have known since my early childhood.

Today, the seafront on both the Southsea and the Gosport sides was packed with crowds of people, so many that the traffic had stopped. It

* Manning the ship's side, with the ship's company in their best uniforms.

seemed hardly possible that all these people had turned out to welcome us home and we wondered whether they were waiting for some other ship coming in behind us.

While we passed between Southsea Castle and Billy Manning's Funfair, four Gazelles of the RN's helicopter display team, 'The Sharks', flew down our port side in formation.

The Irish piper was so affected by the ship's motion – and as a result of his 'social duties' the night before – that he struggled to remain fixed in position on top of the turret. Resplendent in his traditional garb and much the worse for wear, he did really well, belting out the music, but, as I am no connoisseur of the bagpipes, I could barely distinguish one tune from another.

As we passed the Round Tower and entered the harbour, I could feel myself welling up and forced myself to swallow hard to avoid the tears. No way was I going to cry. No way. I bit hard on my lower lip.

NATO STANAVFORLANT* ships were alongside South Railway Jetty and the berths immediately to the north. Their sailors turned out to have a look at us and I wondered what would be going through their minds at the sight of a ship returning from war. I recalled that when we had operated with NATO forces the year before I had had quite a shock. After a particularly inept performance during a simulated missile engagement, where I was conducting the long-range targeting (accurately, as it happened), I drafted and had released a signal pointing out constructively how it could have gone better. At our next port of call, the Commander of the NATO force approached me at the cocktail party and thanked me for the comments, adding, 'Of course, you will learn, young man, that these Standing Naval Forces are not about enhancing capability, they are about enhancing cooperation and solidarity among NATO members.'

As we passed and piped *Victory*, I remembered thinking, we are part of that fighting tradition. Perhaps we are just dwarfs on giants' shoulders, but we have seen action now and stand a bit taller in future, able to say we have done our bit for the country.

As we approached our berth – North West Wall – poor old *Glamorgan* was berthed ahead of us and just around the corner. They had a couple of banners made up which said 'Welcome Home' and 'Well done,

* Standing Naval Force Atlantic, a force comprising ships from several NATO nations.

Wart' – good for them. I felt sad about the people they had lost and how awful it must have been for those families and friends who would have seen that *Glamorgan* was coming home, but knew that their loved ones were not onboard.

I could hear 'Heart of Oak' coming from somewhere – they had laid a band on for us. I defy anyone not to get emotional and proud when hearing that stirring tune, with all its historical – and tribal – associations in circumstances like that. It should be a theme tune for coming home from war. I made up my mind that if I ever commanded a ship that we would play that evocative tune every time that we entered and left harbour. A fighting service needs to remember its heritage and I would want my sailors to buy in to what I am feeling now.

Closer in, while tugs were fussing around the ship, I could see that the jetty was jam-packed with families and loved ones and it was difficult to pick out Mum and Dad, Ann, Jeanna and Tony, and Alison. Once the people onshore made out their loved ones, there were ripples (literally) of recognition and pockets of intense excitement, with lots of jumping up and down and manic waving. The heaving lines were thrown ashore and the ship was quickly secured alongside. I looked around at my fellow officers on the signal deck; they were all waving or holding down the tears.

Two gangways were very smartly put in place and after the Captain's wife came onboard, everyone else stormed over the gangway. The rush and weight of numbers were so great that the ship heeled over to starboard to a marked, even worrying, extent. By this time I had made my way down to the Flight Deck, to greet my loved ones and keep a wary eye open for the helicopter, which was in serious danger from the enthusiastic, the curious and the acquisitive. I was welcomed home with a mixture of joy and relief from Alison and got the longest hug I have ever had from my mum. The noise and the press were overwhelming and I managed to get everyone along the port waist to the Wardroom. It had been 123 days at sea since we left the UK and 111 days since we left Gibraltar. The ship's log simply read: 'Tremendous welcoming home.'

> He that outlives this day, and comes safe home,
> Will stand a tip-toe when this day is nam'd.

In the Wardroom, I introduced my family to the Captain, the Commander and all my friends and colleagues. We swapped stories and in-jokes and shared an early buffet lunch. Animated as the atmosphere was, the conversation was irrelevant and ephemeral; the simple fact, which dominated the scene and silently thrilled everyone, was that, after so many trials and dangers, we had come safe home. The strange thing was that, despite leave being piped early, my fellow officers seemed reluctant to go, conscious that something unique was about to be lost. Leave the ship – leave the magic circle – and the spell would be broken, for ever.

Very early, Alison told me that a surprise welcome home party had been organized for the following day back in Broadmayne by our neighbours and that I needed to be there. I felt torn. I could not possibly let down friends and people down in Dorset who had supported Alison all the way through. On the other hand, I really wanted to disembark with 406 for the last time on the following day and fly back to Portland with the rest of the crew. We had stuck together throughout and it did not seem right somehow. I also wanted to make sure that the dear old thing was actually heading for the museum as we had arranged rather than being cannibalized for spares and condemned.

The matter was taken out of my hands when Alison said to Ian, in front of the Captain, 'It's all right if Chris comes back with me tonight, rather than flying back tomorrow, isn't it?' Alison has a genuinely charming way of asking things which does not brook a refusal. As she asked, I was theatrically, but secretly, shaking my head behind her. Both Ian and the Captain could see me, but Ian said, 'It's not a problem; you take your man home.' That's a decision, then, I thought. Bugger!

I said to Ian afterwards: 'I really wanted to come back with you and the aircraft to Portland.'

He said, 'Take it from me, the smart move is to go home. It's a short hop down to Portland and it will be a sleepy Sunday on the airfield when we get back. We'll just put the cab to bed and go on leave ourselves. Relax!'

'Are you sure you can find your way without me?' I joked.

'Fuck off,' he said in his whimsical way.

So I obeyed the last order. I went and changed into civilian rig for the first time since Gibraltar on 28 March and departed the ship with my real family, leaving behind a treasured bundle of experiences, associations and memories that I knew could never return.

Coming home from sea to Portsmouth and sailing into the great natural harbour is a moving, impressive experience at the best of times. I never tire of the emotional pull of its remarkable topography, its extensive heritage (from the Romans onwards) and its character. This naval city, over the centuries, has seen hundreds of scenes like ours and, like no other, knows how to welcome its men home from war. It was quite the best day of my life.

We all went back home to Mum and Dad's to have lunch and chatted about how good it was to be back. They were all clearly delighted to see me fit and well, proud at what had been achieved, but I detected that they had been worried, especially my mum. She did not like my beard and expressed the thought that the experience away had changed me – for good or bad she did not say. My father was pleased that I had seen action, had had a reasonable 'war' and come safe home. Alison was relieved that she had her husband back in one piece; my sister, Ann, simply said, 'I knew that you would come home to us.'

I am writing this next section two days after getting back.

After lunch at my parents' house, A and I drove back to Broadmayne. I had no difficulty slipping back into the routine of family life, once I had gently reacquainted myself with my wife and my home. I thought that I would be initially restless, with little tolerance for enforced leisure or doing nothing in particular. Life was all so incredibly normal and it seemed as if I had not been away, although there were numerous plants and triffids in the garden that I did not recognize. I also did not recognize much of the music on the radio either. I was happy to be have been a 'warrior for the working day'.*

One thing that pleased me was that Isis our dog recognized me immediately as soon as we got home. I do not know what it is about dogs, but it must be that they have no sense of time. I would have been narked if she had not known who I was – after all, Odysseus' dog recognized him after all that time while he was away at Troy and on his Odyssey.

Mike McBryde had indeed organized a welcome home party for me on the day after my return and invited everyone from Spring Gardens along. It was great and I was humbled by people's generosity of spirit and genuine pleasure at seeing me safely home. I was a little bit embarrassed, as I felt that I was only doing my job and I was privileged to have

* Shakespeare, *Henry V*.

been among those who were in the South Atlantic. I said a few words thanking them for the welcome home and expressed how much A and I valued their steadfast and many kindnesses. Also, I wanted to tell them that all of us down south had drawn strength from the knowledge that people at home were so caring and enthusiastic in their support.

I should have followed my instincts and flown back to Portland with the cab though. The Squadron turned out in force to welcome us back and I was not there. Nor did I formally say a quiet and sincere thank you to our cab as it completed its last flight and gently passed into retirement. I will never forget the times that we have had together and how well you looked after me. I'll come and see you in your new home, I promise.

How do I feel? It's easy:

They that go down to the sea in ships and occupy their business in great
    waters,
These men see the works of the Lord and his wonders in the deep.

HMS *Antrim*

The ship

HMS *Antrim* was built at Fairfield Shipbuilding and Engineering, in Govan, Scotland, and was commissioned into the Royal Navy in 1970. She cost £16.8m at the time. Displacing 5,500 tons (6,200 tons full load) and powered by steam (two) and gas turbines (four), her twin shafts could drive the ship at speeds in excess of 30 knots. She was 505 feet (154 m) long, 54 feet (16.5 m) wide and 20.5 feet (6.3 m) in draught.

Antrim's normal ship's company comprised 33 officers and 438 men, a total of 471. With her extensive command facilities, her complement increased by 30 when an Admiral and his staff were embarked.

With extensive sensors and communications, *Antrim*'s primary role was as an Air Defence ship, providing command and control of anti-air operations for a Task Group or Task Force, as well as both area and point missile defence with her Sea Slug and Sea Cat missile systems. She also possessed a reasonably powerful anti-ship capability, with her four MM 38 Exocet missiles and twin 4.5 inch (115 mm) guns. For anti-submarine warfare, she had a medium-range sonar and a Wessex 3 helicopter, with a variable-depth sonar, depth charges and homing torpedoes.

For long-range air search, *Antrim* had a 965M radar aerial on her main mast. This provided medium- to high-level warning against aircraft out to 200 miles, but had gaps in the coverage, caused by the design of the huge 'bedstead' aerial, and near the sea's surface. For surveillance and target allocation out to about 60 miles – against ships, missiles and aircraft – the ship used the 992Q aerial on the foremast, in tandem with a 278M height-finding aerial behind the main mast. A Type 978 radar was fitted on the foremast, for navigation and helicopter control.

For weapon control, a director (MRS 3) on the Bridge roof provided radar control to the 4.5 inch guns; individual 904 directors abeam the after funnel controlled a GWS 22 Sea Cat missile system on each side, and the huge 901 radar, forward of the Flight Deck, controlled the Sea Slug missiles. The Sea Cats and the 4.5 guns could be targeted visually from a Gun Direction Platform between the foremast and the forward funnel.

Other sensors included electronic intercept and analysis equipment, used to detect and classify threat radars and missiles, as well as enemy communications.

Weapons

MM 38 Exocet

The ship-launched variant of the sea-skimming Exocet had a dual active radar seeker and anti-jam homing head and its effective range was 22–25 miles.

Sea Slug

A rugged, reliable, but largely obsolete weapon by 1982, Sea Slug had been in service with the Royal Navy since 1961. The horizontal magazine ran all the way along the centre of the ship, from the launcher on the quarterdeck to a position just under the Bridge. Up to 30 missiles were stowed and moved on a complicated rail system, likened to the 'best model train-set in the world', and were hydraulically loaded onto the launcher through two armoured flash doors.

The missile itself was guided by a beam transmitted by the large 901 radar forward of the Flight Deck. With a solid-fuel motor and four wrap-around booster rockets, it was a formidable sight as it left its launcher and the boosters detached. After separation, the main motor ignited to power the missile to the target at 1,370 mph (2,200 km/h). It was most effective against large, higher-flying targets, with a maximum range of 35,000 yards (32,000 m), but probably capable of engagements to about 45,000 yards, and a ceiling of 65,000 feet (20,000 m). It had a single-shot kill probability of 92 per cent, although only one target could be engaged at any one time.

There were three ways of engaging a target:

- LOSBR (Line of Sight, Beam Riding), in which the missile flew up a beam that tracked the target.

- CASWTD (Constant Angle of Sight, with Terminal Dive), with the missile climbing at a low angle and then diving onto a low-altitude target.
- MICAWBER (Missile in Constant Altitude, While Beam Riding), similar to CASWTD, but with a terminal low-level glide phase so that the missile could be used against ships. This mode suffered from problems associated with the surface of the water reflecting and scattering the guidance beam.

Sea Cat

Sea Cat was a short-range anti-aircraft missile mounted on two quadruple, manually loaded launchers. It was controlled by a radio command link under radar or visual guidance. Its range was about 3.5 miles (5 km).

4.5 inch (115 mm) guns

The 4.5 guns, mounted in a twin turret, fired high-explosive, radar decoy and illuminating star shells. Controlled by visual sights or the 903 radar, they were effective against ship, aircraft and land targets. They had a nominal range of 9.3 nautical miles (surface mode, maximum effective range) and 10.5 nautical miles (surface mode, maximum range). The rate of fire was up to 24 rounds per minute, with shells and cartridges mechanically supplied from below, and manually loaded in, the turret.

20 mm guns

The 20 mm guns were fitted to deal with small vessels at close range (out to 1,000 m). They were not generally considered effective against air targets.

The helicopter

The Wessex 3 was an all-weather, day/night helicopter, derived from the Wessex Mk 1. Its primary role was anti-submarine warfare. Its avionic and sea sensor systems resembled those in the Sea King Mk 2. In this role, it was equipped with a Type 195M variable-depth active and passive sonar, which was deployed through the floor of the rear cabin on a winch while the helicopter hovered above the sea, 'in the dip'. The advantage of the variable-depth sonar was that the transducer depth could be altered to detect and hold contact on submarines at various depths and in different acoustic conditions. The helicopter was helped in achieving and maintaining a stable hover position and height by an automatic computer-assisted Flight Control System, fed by a system of gyros and a radar altimeter. Its normal operating height in anti-submarine sorties was 150 feet, descending to 60 feet in the hover, with the sonar deployed.

Its normal crew was two pilots (in the front), an Observer and an aircrewman (in the rear cabin). The Captain of the aircraft, responsible for its safe and effective operation during particular serials, was the senior officer, either the pilot or the Observer, who was onboard the aircraft. The flying pilot sat in the right-hand front seat, with the pilot in the left-hand seat monitoring the instruments and assisting with emergencies and other 'housekeeping tasks'. Both would normally take turns at flying during sorties, but the right-hand-seat pilot would have control when taking off and landing at the ship.

In the rear cabin, behind the sonar housing, winch and transducer, were two side-by-side seats. The right-hand seat was occupied by the aircrewman, who manned the sonar instrumentation and the winch mechanism. The Observer, responsible for the navigation, communications and tactical employment of the aircraft, its sensors and weapons, sat in the left-hand seat, with a large radar and tactical display in front of him, tilted at an angle of 60 degrees. The radar displayed a trace that rotated once a second and was produced by inputs from the ARI 5955 radar housed in the distinctive hump (the radome) behind the gearbox on the spine of the aircraft. The tactical display allowed the Observer to see the radar trace, showing surface ship contacts, other helicopters and the outline of the land and other physical features, and sonar information, with other tactical information plotted on acetate overlays by the Observer with chinagraph pencil. The radar was also used for controlling other helicopters and for the detection and engagement of ship missile targets 'over the horizon' beyond the range of ship sensors or when the ship wished to be electronically silent.

The Wessex 3 was fitted with UHF radio for normal tactical operation, with an HF facility for long-range sorties beyond about 20 miles when at low altitude. The aircrew communicated internally through an intercom linked to throat microphones.

The aircraft could carry various weapons on two (port and starboard) carriers: Mk 44 and Mk 46 active and passive acoustic homing torpedoes, Mk II depth charges and illuminating flares. The torpedoes were dropped in the vicinity of a submarine and searched with their own onboard sonars either in 'circle' mode, or in 'snake-search', a narrow weave along a pre-selected gyro compass bearing. Both ran for about six minutes. The depth charges could be dropped against surfaced and shallow submarines and had a theoretical 'kill radius' of about 30–50 feet (9–15 metres), although significant damage was likely just beyond that range. The aircraft was also capable of carrying and launching a nuclear depth bomb.

Other additions included:

- A General Purpose Machine Gun (GPMG) could be mounted in the cabin door or at the starboard cabin window.
- Chaff Hotel – packets (skillets) of millions of small metallic strips could be dropped manually to simulate ship-sized echoes on radar, in order to confuse and distract the operator.
- A fuel tank that allowed an hour's extra endurance could be carried on the port weapon carrier.

The aircraft would be flown by a full crew at night, in marginal weather conditions and in complex evolutions, although one pilot was considered sufficient for all types of day flying. By day, a single pilot, Observer and Aircrewman could fly in the anti-submarine role. For routine passenger transfers and for load-lifting, for which a semi-automatic cargo release unit (SACRU) would be fitted to the underside of the helicopter, one pilot and one rear cabin operator were required. The helicopter also had a rescue hoist, above its rear cabin door, capable of lifting people or stores up to 600 lb and for search and rescue.

The Wessex 3's normal speed was 90 knots, but it was theoretically capable of 135 knots, cruising at heights from sea level up to about 6,000 feet. Its endurance without weapons or external fuel tank was about one hour and 40 minutes, although this would have to be balanced with the carriage of various weapon configurations and external loads.

Its known weakness was its single engine, which, in the years before

1982, had demonstrated a worrying tendency to fail, owing in part to the configuration of the compressor stage, and several crews had been killed in accidents. Unless the pilot was able to disengage the engine and enter into auto-rotation* within one and a half seconds of engine failure, it was rarely possible to land or ditch the helicopter under control or in a survivable condition, as the rotor speed would decay rapidly.

Whenever not required onboard, the County Class helicopter Flights were based at RNAS Portland in Dorset and parented by 737 Naval Air Squadron, which provided administrative, training and maintenance support, including a flight simulator. The squadron delivered advanced flying training for helicopter Observers, as well as conversion courses for those pilots, Observers and aircrewmen appointed to Wessex 3 destroyer Flights.

Command structure and leadership

Antrim was commanded by a senior Captain, always of the Seaman or Executive specialization, but he could be a surface ship operator, a submariner or an aviator. When an Admiral was embarked, he acted as the Flag Captain, ready to assist and advise the Admiral on the Task Force with his judgement and experience, if required – and if invited.

The second-in-command, or Executive Officer, was a Commander (again of the Seaman or Executive specialization – known as 'fish-heads' or 'the Master Race'), who was command-qualified and able to take command if necessary, particularly when the Captain was sleeping during intensive exercise and operational situations or indisposed. He was also responsible for ensuring that the ship's organization and management ran smoothly and efficiently in all circumstances. This included all aspects of the routine allocation of tasks, manpower use, discipline, cleanliness, Damage Control and operational effectiveness. Finally, he was the head of the Executive Department, which delivered the sharp-end functions, like warfare, aviation and medical capabilities, and, as

---

* The technique by which a helicopter, without engines, can descend using the air flowing through its rotors to maintain rotor speed, so that the pilot can slow the descent and, by flaring the aircraft, cushion the landing.

head of the Wardroom Mess, provided direction, guidance and advice to the officers.

He was *primus inter pares* in relation to the other Departmental Heads, who were also Commanders.

Commander E ran the Mechanical Engineering Department (known collectively as the 'clankies' or 'stokers'), responsible for the main engines, the propulsion, the production of water, the generation of electricity, fuel, and the integrity and preservation of the hull and internal pipes and fittings. His department also had a major role in repairing any damage, sustaining power and fire-fighting water supplies, and ensuring the watertight and gas-tight integrity of the ship.

Commander W, as head of the Weapons Engineering Department (the 'Greenies'*), ensured that the electronic components and services were maintained at the highest levels of serviceability and availability. His responsibility included every working part of weapon systems (such as the guns, the Exocets, the Sea Cat and the Sea Slug missiles), sensors (such as the radars, electronic support and intercept measures), communications, computers and the magazines (together with the various weapons contained within them).

Commander S was head of the Supply and Secretariat (known as 'Pussers'† or 'the White Mafia') organization within the ship. His responsibilities were associated with the logistical and life support aspects of the ship: feeding, clothing, paying and accommodating the ship's company. He also ensured that the correct spares and stores were in place, either to repair or to replace damaged, unserviceable or lost items. He sourced the items and components from stocks held onboard, within the wider Task Force or from the UK. Inevitably, he picked up the huge amount of paperwork associated with these processes, as well as supervising the external paperwork and exhaustive accounting mechanisms.

Each Department had a formal deputy, the Operations Officer for the Executive Department, the Deputy Marine Engineering Officer (known also as the Senior Engineer), the Deputy Weapons Engineering Officer (DWEO) and the Deputy Supply Officer (DSO), as well as a

---

* Because of the distinctive green colour that used to be worn between the gold rank stripes of the officers' uniforms.

† Derived from the Sailing Navy word 'Purser'.

range of section and specialist officers to perform specific functions and run various discrete parts of the respective empires.

Unique to the Royal Navy and formally dating back 250 years is the Divisional System, whereby each officer is responsible for the welfare, career development and personal reporting of some or all of the ratings working with him. This can be a 24-hour-a-day job that includes counselling (on all sorts of matters – debt, divorce and discipline), representation at Captain's table or in court and a general care for both work and home aspects of people's lives. It's actually a privilege, although the paperwork is a chore. My division in *Antrim* consisted of the Flight Senior Ratings (except the SMR, who was paired with the Flight Commander). In the past I had had up to 24 ratings in my division. However, that was probably too many. As the Master at Arms* in my first ship told me, 'Jesus Christ only had 12 in his division, sir, and one of those turned out to be a welfare case!'

---

* A Chief Petty Officer, head of the Regulating section, who is responsible for onboard disciplinary issues, standards of behaviour and appearance, enforcement of the Naval Discipline Act and the investigation of offences. Known colloquially as the 'Joss' or the 'Jaunty'.

List of officers

COMMANDING OFFICER
Captain Brian Young (CO)

EXECUTIVE OFFICER AND HEAD OF THE EXECUTIVE AND OPERATIONS DEPARTMENT
Commander Angus Sandford (COMMANDER/XO)

Executive and Operations Department
Operations Officer: Lieutenant Commander Martin Littleboy (OPSO)
Signals and Communications Officer: Lieutenant Commander Anthony Dymock (SCO)
Navigating Officer: Lieutenant Commander Chris Morrison (NO)
Advanced Warfare Officer (Above Water): Lieutenant Commander Duncan Ford (AWO (A))
Principal Warfare Officer (Underwater): Lieutenant Commander John Archer (PWO (U))
Principal Warfare Officer (Above Water): Lieutenant Pat Brown (PWO (A))
Meteorological Officer: Lieutenant Commander David Stanesby (METO)
Master Gunner: Sub-Lieutenant David Barraclough (MG)
Fighter Controller 1: Sub-Lieutenant Tony Pringle (FC1)
Fighter Controller 2: Sub-Lieutenant David Graham (FC2)
Officer of the Watch: Lieutenant John Saunders
Officer of the Watch: Lieutenant Keith Creates
Officer of the Watch: Sub-Lieutenant Richard Hurley
Officer of the Watch (and Damage Control Officer): Lieutenant Declan Ward (NBCDO)

Helicopter Flight
Lieutenant Commander Ian Stanley (FLT CDR)
Lieutenant Chris Parry (FLOBS)
Sub-Lieutenant Stewart Cooper (P2)

Medical Section
Surgeon Lieutenant Alasdair Maclean (MO)
Surgeon Lieutenant (Dental) Godfrey Rhimes (DENTO)

Chaplain

The Reverend Richard Sigrist (Padre)

HEAD OF THE WEAPONS ENGINEERING DEPARTMENT

Commander Chris Grace (COMMANDER W/WEO)

Deputy Head of Weapons Engineering Department

Lieutenant Commander Nick Bracegirdle (DWEO)

Section Officers

Lieutenant Kevin White

Lieutenant Lynn Alison

Sub-Lieutenant Mike Bonney

Lieutenant Roger Insley

HEAD OF THE MARINE ENGINEERING DEPARTMENT

Commander Mike Morgan (COMMANDER E/MEO)

Deputy Head of the Marine Engineering Department

Lieutenant Commander Neil Britten (DMEO/Senior Engineer)

Section Officers

Lieutenant Norman Cameron

Lieutenant Graham Hockley

Lieutenant Mark Willbourn

Sub-Lieutenant Steve Berry (Shipwright)

HEAD OF THE SUPPLY AND SECRETARIAT DEPARTMENT

Commander David Wakefield (COMMANDER S/SO)

Deputy Head of the Supply and Secretariat Department

Lieutenant Carlos Edwards (DSO)

Captain's Secretary

Sub-Lieutenant Jeremy Lindsay (SEC)

OFFICERS UNDER TRAINING

Sub-Lieutenant Mike Petheram

Sub-Lieutenant Andy Brook

Sub-Lieutenant Keith Worrall

Midshipman Bob Tarrant

Ranks and ratings: officers and men

Rank	Falklands War personalities
Admiral of the Fleet	First Sea Lord: Sir Henry Leach
Admiral	Commander-in-Chief Fleet: Sir John Fieldhouse
Vice-Admiral	Chief of Staff to CINCFLEET: David Hallifax
Rear Admiral	Task Force Commander: Sandy Woodward
Commodore	Commodore Amphibious Warfare: Mike Clapp
Captain	Commanding Officer HMS *Brilliant*: John Coward
Commander	Commanding Officer HMS *Alacrity*: Chris Craig
Lieutenant Commander	Neil Britten (Senior Engineer): HMS *Antrim*
Lieutenant	Kevin White (Weapons Engineering Section Officer) HMS *Antrim*
Sub-Lieutenant	Stewart Cooper (Second Pilot) HMS *Antrim*
Midshipman	Bob Tarrant (Under Training) HMS *Antrim*
Fleet Chief Petty Officer	Mick Fellows (Clearance Diver/Head of Explosive Ordnance Team)
Chief Petty Officer	Eric Graham (Chief Bosun's Mate)/Fritz Heritier (Flight Senior Maintenance Rating)
Petty Officer	David Fitzgerald (Aircrewman)
Leading Hand	Leading Writer Prescott
Able Rating	Air Engineering Mechanic (Electrical) 1 McGreal
Ordinary Rating	Seaman Shirley

All ratings were designated by their specialization and rank.
For example:

CWEA	Chief Weapons Engineering Artificer
CPOWEM	Chief Petty Officer Weapon Engineering Mechanic

CRS	Chief Radio Supervisor
CH OPS (M)	Chief Petty Officer Operations (Missileman)
POAEM	Petty Officer Air Engineering Mechanic
PO CK	Petty Officer Cook
POAEA (M)	Petty Officer Air Engineering Artificer (Mechanical)
LMEM	Leading Marine Engineering Mechanic
LRO	Leading Radio Operator
LSA	Leading Stores Accountant
Able Seaman (EW)	Able Seaman (Electronic Warfare)
MEM 1	Marine Engineering Mechanic 1st Class (Able Rating)
WTR 1	Writer 1st Class (Able Rating)
WEM (R) 2	Weapon Engineering Mechanic 2nd Class (Ordinary Rating)
SEA (R)	Seaman Radar (Ordinary Rating)
RO 2	Radio Operator 2nd Class (Ordinary Rating)

Officers' accommodation

The Admiral's Day Cabin and sleeping quarters are in the superstructure at main deck level behind the Exocets and under the Bridge. Astern of them are respectively the Captain's cabin and the Wardroom. The officers' cabins are mostly in the forward end of the superstructure, some at the same level as the Wardroom, but mostly on 01 deck, in two passageways, above the area occupied by the Wardroom and Captain's and Admiral's cabins. The port Wardroom passageway leads to the Bridge.

My cabin is up the ladder, outside the Wardroom, turn right (to starboard), walk forward and find the second cabin on the left (inboard) just past Stewart's cabin. It is 7 feet by 7 feet and has a bunk 5 feet off the deck, with drawers, a locker and a pull-down desk underneath. There is a basin, a foldaway seat, a small bookcase and a pull-down seat – and the hooks for my flying gear – and that is it. It is probably smaller than a prison cell, but at least I do not have to share. It is my own personal space where I can reflect, read, write and get on with things – most people on this ship do not have that luxury and have to live, cheek by jowl, with all their imperfections, emotions and fears on show. And another thing – I sleep above the waterline; most of the lads have their bunks deep in the ship.

The cabin door is always open with a curtain across the gap during waking and working hours. Officers need to be – and seen to be – accessible (and awake) and it is considered bad form to shut your door. I am sure that this convention is right. We aviators are subjected to the constant jibe that we are always getting our heads down. The usual joke among the fish-heads is that aviators have to get eight hours of sleep a day – and anything else at night is a bonus! There are issues associated with flight safety, of course, and in case we have to scramble for an emergency or fly at short notice for operational reasons.

Glossary

AAW	Anti-Air Warfare
AAWC	Anti-Air Warfare Coordination
AAWO	Anti-Air Warfare Coordination Officer
AD	Air Defence
ADC	Aide-de-Camp (a junior officer appointed as a military assistant to a General)
AEM	Air Engineering Mechanic
AEW	Airborne Early Warning
AGI	Auxiliary Gatherer of Intelligence (spy ship)
AIM-9L	Sidewinder air-to-air missile
AM-39	air-launched Exocet missile
AOA	Amphibious Objective Area
AS-12	Wire-Guided Air-to-Surface Missile
ASDIC	from Anti-Submarine Detection Investigation Committee: an early form of sonar in the First and Second World Wars
ash can	depth charge
ASW	Anti-Submarine Warfare
AVCAT	aviation fuel
banyan	party or picnic held ashore when deployed at sea
BAS	British Antarctic Survey
Booties	affectionate Royal Navy expression for the Royal Marines
BRNC	Britannia Royal Naval College
buffer	Chief Boatswain's Mate – the Chief Petty Officer responsible for traditional seamanship evolutions, boat running, rigging, wires and ropes, and replenishment operations, as well as the appearance of all upper-deck parts of the ship
BZ	the flag hoist BRAVO ZULU – 'manoeuvre well executed' or 'well done' – the opposite of NEGAT(IVE) BRAVO ZULU, 'not well done'
cab	colloquial expression for a helicopter

Can Man	head of NAAFI canteen staff onboard ships
CAP	Combat Air Patrol
Carl Gustav	a shoulder-launched anti-armoured vehicle weapon
CERTSUB	certain submarine
chaff	decoys, comprising radar reflecting dipoles, fired from guns (C) propelled by rockets (D) or dropped from helicopters (Hotel)
Chippy	ship's carpenter
Chukar	a pilotless drone used as a target
CINCFLEET	Commander-in-Chief Fleet
CLF	Commander Land Forces
CLFFI	Commander Land Forces Falkland Islands
CO	Commanding Officer
COBRA	codeword used on radio circuits to denote an anti-submarine torpedo operating in the snake-search mode (a narrow weave out to 6,000 yards)
COMAW	Commodore Amphibious Warfare
CPO	Chief Petty Officer
CPOMA	Chief Petty Officer Medical Assistant
Crabs	Pejorative term for members of the Royal Air Force
CRS	Chief Radio Supervisor
CSM	Colour Sergeant Major
Daddy S	Commander in charge of the Supply and Secretariat Department
dip, in the	a helicopter is in the dip when it is in the hover, with its sonar extended to the sea
Doppler (shift)	a distortion in sound frequencies which can be used to calculate the speed, range and relative velocity of, for example, a submarine as it passes a sonar. The received frequency is higher (compared to the emitted frequency) as a submarine approches, identical as it passes and lower as it goes away
DR	Dead Reckoning
DWEO	Deputy Weapons Engineering Officer
ECM	Electronic Counter-Measures (Jamming)
DSNONI	Deputy Senior Naval Officer Northern Ireland
EOD	Explosive Ordnance Disposal

ESM	Electronic Support Measures (Intercept)
ETA	Estimated Time of Arrival
FAA	Fleet Air Arm
FCS	Flight Control System
FDO	Flight Deck Officer
FLEET	the staff and organization of Commander-in-Chief Fleet
FLOBS	Flight Observer
FLT CDR	Flight Commander
FOCCIF	Flight Observer's Crash Course in Fitness
FOD	Foreign Object Damage
FOF I	Flag Officer First Flotilla
FONA	Flag Officer Naval Aviation
FONAC	Flag Officer Naval Air Command
FOST	Flag Officer Sea Training
FPB	Fast Patrol Boat
gash (bag)	Naval term for rubbish (and the appropriate container)
GDP	Gun Direction Platform
GOC	General Officer Commanding
goon suit	thick protective waterproof flying coverall, made of rubber and neoprene
GPMG	General Purpose Machine Gun
GOP	General Operations Plot (the combined display of tactical information in the Operations Room)
Greenies	members of the Weapon Engineering Branch (because the officers of the specialization used to have green between their gold uniform braid stripes)
HC	Helicopter Controller
hack	destroy or hit
HDS	Helicopter Delivery Services
HE	high explosive
HEAT	high-explosive anti-tank
HF	high frequency
HOD	Head of Department
HQI	the ship's centre for coordinating control and fire fighting

INMARSAT	International Maritime Satellite (communications system)
jackstay (transfer)	a system of blocks, pulleys and ropes used to transfer stores and loads between two ships, typically steaming in parallel about 80–120 yards apart
JOUT	Junior Officer Under Training
Junglie	amphibious Sea King or Wessex helicopter
LACMN	Leading Aircrewman
LCA	Leading Caterer
LMG	Light Machine Gun
LSL	Landing Ship Logistic (SIR Class landing ship)
LSTD	Leading Steward
LZ	landing zone
MA	Medical Assistant
MAA	Master at Arms: a Chief Petty Officer, head of the Regulating section, who is responsible for onboard disciplinary issues, standards of behaviour and appearance, enforcement of the Naval Discipline Act and the investigation of offences. Known colloquially as the 'Joss' or the 'Jaunty'
MARTSU	Mobile Aircraft Repair, Transport and Salvage Unit
MCO	Main Communications Office
MCR	Machinery Control Room
ME	Marine Engineering
MEM	Marine Engineering Mechanic
MEO	Marine Engineering Officer
METO	Meteorological Officer
MOD	Ministry of Defence
NAAFI	Navy, Army and Air Force Institute: a civilian stores company with sales staff (headed by a Can Man) onboard
NAMET	Naval Mathematics and English Test
NAS	Naval Air Squadron
NBCD	Nuclear, Biological, Chemical Defence (and Firefighting)

NBCDO	Nuclear, Biological, Chemical Defence (and Firefighting) Officer
NBCDX	Nuclear, Biological, Chemical Defence and Firefighting Exercise
NGFO	Naval Gunfire Officer
NGS	Naval Gunfire Support
nm	nautical mile (1,852 m, longer than a statute mile at 1,609 m)
Northwood	headquarters of Commander-in-Chief Fleet at Northwood, Middlesex
OOW	Officer of the Watch
nutty	naval term for any form of chocolate, candy or sweets
OPGEN	Operations General: a formatted signal detailing general information about operations and exercises
OPTASK	Operational Tasking: a formatted signal detailing the specific tasking that ships and aircraft are to perform, with weapon loads, mission timings and threat information
OTHT	over-the-horizon targeting
PO	Petty Officer
POACMN	Petty Officer Aircrewman
POMA	Petty Officer Medical Assistant
POMEM	Petty Officer Marine Engineering Mechanic
POSSUB	possible submarine
propagation	the behaviour of radio waves when they are transmitted and received, conditioned by atmospheric, meteorological or technical characteristics present at particular places and times
Pusser	the Supply and Secretariat Branch, one of its members or, more generally, an expression for the Royal Navy (as in 'Pusser's Rum')
PWO (A)	Principal Warfare Officer (Above Water)
PWO (U)	Principal Warfare Officer (Under Water)
QHI	Qualified Helicopter Instructor
racetrack	a holding pattern for aircraft that are waiting for opportunity tasking or for ships conducting routine surveillance or transfer tasks

racket	intercept of a radar or communications transmission
RADALT	Radar Altimeter
R&R	Rest and Recreation
RAS	Replenishment at Sea
RAS (A)	Replenishment at Sea (Ammunition)
RAS (L)	Replenishment at Sea (Fuel)
RAS (S)	Replenishment at Sea (Stores)
RDP	Run Down Period
Regulator	a member of the Regulating Branch, responsible for ship's discipline, routines and mail
RFA	Royal Fleet Auxiliary (civilian-manned, UK government-owned tankers, support ships, etc.)
RM	Royal Marines Commando
RO	Radio Operator
ROE	Rules of Engagement
RPO	Regulating Petty Officer: responsible, under the Master at Arms, for ship's discipline, the implementation of standards and the processing of offences against the Naval Discipline Act, as well as, more popularly, the receipt and despatch of mail
SAS	Special Air Service
SBS	Special Boat Squadron
SCO	Signals and Communications Officer
serials	specific missions or exercise periods
shackle	a measure by which ships' anchor cable lengths are designated, comprising 15 fathoms (or 90 feet/27.43 m)
SHar	Sea Harrier
SITREP	Situation Report
SLR	Self-Loading Rifle
SMR	Senior Maintenance Rating (on ship's helicopter Flight)
SNONI	Senior Naval Officer Northern Ireland
snort	use of a snorkel tube by a diesel-electric submarine to recharge its batteries while submerged at periscope depth

SOOTAX	the administrative transfer of personnel by helicopter (from Staff Officers' Operational Taxi)
SSN	nuclear hunter/killer submarine
stoof (in)	colloquial Fleet Air Arm expression and verb for crashing an aircraft
STUFT	ship taken up from trade
Sunset	the time at which a formal ceremony is conducted by Royal Navy ships at anchor or in harbour to haul down the White Ensign and Jack (Union Flag) – known also as 'putting the Queen to bed'
TEZ	Total Exclusion Zone
TRALA	Tug, Repair and Logistic Area (originally known as the TARA – Tug and Repair Area)
UHF	ultra-high frequency
VERTREP	Vertical Replenishment (by helicopter)
WE	Weapons Engineering
Z	when applied to time, ZULU is Greenwich Mean Time; it is also a Damage Control State associated with Action Stations and the highest state of readiness
ZAP	unofficial badge and label, usually stuck surreptitiously onto other people's aircraft

Watches and Routines at Sea

Watches

Middle	0001–0400
Morning	0400–0800
Forenoon	0800–1200
Afternoon	1200–1600
First Dog	1600–1800
Last Dog	1800–2000
First	2000–2359

Action Stations: the ship is at its highest material and manning state, ready for combat, with watertight doors and hatches closed and the arrangements for propulsion, power generation and Damage Control systems all optimized for the maximum flexibility and resilience. The most qualified and experienced personnel operate and man the weapons, sensors, systems and machinery, while others prepare to respond to emergencies, breakdowns, action damage and casualties.

When Action Stations is piped, the ship is secured for action, all personnel immediately stow any non-essential gear, don Action Working Dress, anti-flash hoods and gloves, and carry lifejackets, respirators and survival gear.

Defence Watches: the ship is divided into port and starboard watches, with half the ship's company on watch, able to operate and fight the ship for short periods (until Action Stations can be closed up), while the other half rests or conducts training. Watches are normally six hours on watch and six hours off.

Cruising Watches: the normal day-to-day watch system at sea, with personnel typically standing one watch in four, normally of four hours, but of two hours during each of the Dog Watches, which serve to vary the actual watches undertaken by sailors from day to day. When not on watch at sea, personnel usually conform to a normal working day from

Call the Hands to Secure (0700–1600) on their part of ship, or engineering responsibilities and training, and take their rest at night.

Damage Control States and Conditions

Damage Control States related to manning levels:

State 1	Action Stations
State 2	Defence Watches
State 3	Peacetime cruising, with normal watch-keepers closed up

Conditions related to the watertight integrity of the ship, with various hatches and doors marked X, Y or Z, which all had to be shut during certain activities and evolutions. The conditions were usually associated with:

Z – ZULU	Action Stations
Y – YANKEE	Defence watches
X – X-RAY	Normal cruising

However, for situations involving risk, as in replenishment, entering harbour and when operating in confined waters, Condition YANKEE would be assumed, even during cruising watches, and a team of specialists – Special Sea Dutymen – would close up, in case of emergency.

A typical pipe would be: 'Special Sea Dutymen close up. Assume NBCD State 3 Condition YANKEE.'

He just wanted a decent book to read ...

Not too much to ask, is it? It was in 1935 when Allen Lane, Managing Director of Bodley Head Publishers, stood on a platform at Exeter railway station looking for something good to read on his journey back to London. His choice was limited to popular magazines and poor-quality paperbacks – the same choice faced every day by the vast majority of readers, few of whom could afford hardbacks. Lane's disappointment and subsequent anger at the range of books generally available led him to found a company – and change the world.

'We believed in the existence in this country of a vast reading public for intelligent books at a low price, and staked everything on it'
Sir Allen Lane, 1902–1970, founder of Penguin Books

The quality paperback had arrived – and not just in bookshops. Lane was adamant that his Penguins should appear in chain stores and tobacconists, and should cost no more than a packet of cigarettes.

Reading habits (and cigarette prices) have changed since 1935, but Penguin still believes in publishing the best books for everybody to enjoy. We still believe that good design costs no more than bad design, and we still believe that quality books published passionately and responsibly make the world a better place.

So wherever you see the little bird – whether it's on a piece of prize-winning literary fiction or a celebrity autobiography, political tour de force or historical masterpiece, a serial-killer thriller, reference book, world classic or a piece of pure escapism – you can bet that it represents the very best that the genre has to offer.

Whatever you like to read – trust Penguin.